Literary Theory / Renaissance Texts

Literary Theory/

Renaissance Texts

.

EDITED BY

PATRICIA PARKER

DAVID QUINT

The Johns Hopkins University Press

BALTIMORE AND LONDON

The Johns Hopkins University Press, 701 West 40th Street,
Baltimore, Maryland 21211
The Johns Hopkins Press Ltd., London

The paper used in this publication meets the minimum requirements of American
National Standard for Information Sciences—Permanence of Paper for Printed
Library Materials, ANSI Z39.48-1984.

LIBRARY OF CONGRESS CATALOGING-IN-PUBLICATION DATA

Main entry under title:

Literary theory/Renaissance texts.

    1. European literature—Renaissance, 1450–1600—History and
criticism—Addresses, essays, lectures.   I. Parker, Patricia A., 1946–
II. Quint, David, 1950–   .
PN721.L58 1986   809'.031   85-23799
ISBN 0-8018-3294-2 (alk. paper)
ISBN 0-8018-3295-0 (pbk. : alk. paper)

CONTENTS

ACKNOWLEDGMENTS

SEVERAL ESSAYS in this volume are republished from earlier versions. John Freccero's "The Fig Tree and the Laurel: Petrarch's Poetics" first appeared in *Diacritics* 5 (1975): 34–40; Eugenio Donato's *"Per selve e boscherecci laberinti*: Desire and Narrative Structure in Ariosto's *Orlando furioso*" in *Barocco* 4 (1972): 17–34; Thomas M. Greene's "The End of Discourse in Machiavelli's *Prince*" in *Yale French Studies* 67 (1984): 57–71; René Girard's "Hamlet's Dull Revenge" in *Stanford Literature Review* 1 (1984): 159–200. Ullrich Langer's "Gunpowder as Transgressive Invention in Ronsard" has been translated from a French version that appeared in *Romanic Review* 73 (1982): 184–94. We thank the journals that have graciously consented to the present republication of their materials.

An earlier and different version of Timothy Reiss's "Montaigne and the Subject of Polity" appeared in French in *Montaigne*, ed. Steven Rendall, Jr. (Paris: Jean-Michel Place, 1983), pp. 127–52.

We wish to thank all our contributors for their hard work and patient forbearance in the drawn-out process of putting this volume together. We wish especially to thank Timothy Hampton who collaborated with us in the editing, translating, and preparation of the manuscript. We acknowledge with gratitude the courtesy and expertise of our editors, Eric Halpern and Mary Lou Kenney.

1. INTRODUCTION

■

DAVID QUINT

Some one says to me, "You don't express yourself as if you were Cicero." What of that? I am not Cicero. I express myself.[1]

I

WITH THESE fighting words Angelo Poliziano rejects the strict Ciceronianism advocated by Paolo Cortesi in favor of an eclectic Latin style imitated from a wide range of ancient writers. He also describes an ideal humanist practice of reading and writing that still informs the methodological and pedagogical assumptions of those who profess the humanities today. Renaissance humanism reinvented the *author*, defined by a unique individual style, and set the production of such authors as the utopian goal of its educational program. Even when this program did not result in a new man of letters, its method of reading with an eye toward stylistic formation could still involve the student in a process of self-discovery. Poliziano urges the reader of classical authors to combine their various voices into a new personal voice that is more than the sum of its parts. His method produces—and presupposes—the student's recognition of his own human individuality, an individuality that demands a distinctive mode of self-expression.

This emphasis on the individual will persist when Montaigne later revises the humanist project, arguing in his essay on education (1.26) that the student should read the ancients less for their style than for their ideas; the two were virtually indistinguishable for a Poliziano.

> For if he embraces Xenophon's and Plato's opinions by his own reasoning, they will no longer be theirs, they will be his. He who follows another follows nothing. He finds nothing; indeed he seeks nothing. *We are not under a king; let each man lay claim to his own self* [Seneca]. Let

him know that he knows, at least. He must imbibe their ways of thinking, not learn their precepts. And let him boldly forget, if he wants,
where he got them, but let him know how to make them his own.
Truth and reason are common to everyone, and no more belong to the
man who first spoke them than to the man who says them later. It is no
more according to Plato than according to me, since he and I understand and see it in the same way. The bees plunder the flowers here
and there, but afterward they make them honey, which is all theirs; it is
no longer thyme or marjoram. Even so with the pieces borrowed from
others; he will transform and blend them to make a work that is all his
own, to wit, his judgment. His education, work and study aim only at
forming this.[2]

The passage puts its own precepts into practice, for beyond the
direct quotation from Seneca's *Letter* 33, the often-quoted metaphor
of the bees and much of the gist and wording of Montaigne's argument derive from the same Seneca's *Letter* 84. Reading becomes a
form of appropriation whereby each Renaissance student can lay
claim to the legacy of classical culture. He must use his judgment in
selecting the ideas and forms of thought that he wishes to make his
own, and the educational process for Montaigne leads in a circular
way to the discovery and cultivation of that judgment, itself, to an
understanding of what and how one knows: Montaigne's "Que
sais-je?"

In these versions of humanist literary study, the modern measures himself against ancients who, Montaigne argues, do not enjoy
a privileged status simply by having come first; they are now viewed
with a historical perspective that humanism is often credited with
having invented. This new conception of the classical writers as
historical individuals rather than as so many contributors to a timeless wisdom of the ancients at once lessens their prestige and empowers their Renaissance readers. The practice of reading that Poliziano and Montaigne advocate is dynamic and critical, and far from
a simply passive reception of stylistic models and moral exemplars
from the classics. It is, as a corollary, generally opposed to an older
method of allegorical reading that "normalized" the ancient texts by
grounding their meaning in apparently stable systems of ethical or
revealed truths, a method that also played down the individual
differences of one ancient author from another, hence the preferred
method of a Renaissance "syncretism" that continued older medieval modes of thought. These differences emerged from the pains-
taking philological analyses of humanist scholars who aimed to
understand the classical writer by placing him within his given historical context. As the humanist saw how the ancients differed his-

torically, he perceived his own historical difference and individuality. It was, in fact, the recognition that his experience produced circumstances that the ancients had not and could not have known that limited their authority over the modern age and authorized the modern's appropriation of their style and thought to his own purposes and personality. He was presumably repeating the process of self-creation through reading, which the ancient author whom he read had himself undergone vis-à-vis still earlier writers. By seeing both the classical writer and himself as individuals shaping themselves in history a basis for dialogue could be found to exist.

Larger cultural factors underlay the humanist model of self-creation. Humanism developed within a society of early capitalism, particularly in Florence, a city of merchants and bankers. The injunction to make the classical authors into one's own personal intellectual property—to create a style that belongs to oneself alone—has clear parallels in a culture of bourgeois acquisition. At the end of the same passage cited above, Montaigne inserts an addition filled with economic metaphors.

> Let him hide all the help he has had, and show only what he has made of it. The pillagers, the borrowers, parade their buildings, their purchases, not what they get from others. You do not see the gratuities of a member of a Parlement, you see the alliances he has gained and honors for his children. No one makes public his receipts; everyone makes public his acquisitions.[3]

Montaigne's great-grandfather, a wealthy merchant, had bought the lands and title his noble descendants enjoyed; both his father and he himself were first members of the Bordeaux Parlement and later mayors of the city. In such stories of family success and social mobility, Montaigne finds analogies for the educational process by which the reader makes and displays the classics as his own. Von Martin noted in his pioneering study the similar social origins and mentalities that united the new humanist intellectual and the "novus homo," the capitalist entrepreneur: "The idea that an author or an artist could claim any property rights in 'his' works arose only with the new wish to be original, to be a 'uomo singolare' or 'unico.'"[4] The humanist pedagogical project of leading the student to discover and create his own identity is thus partly an aspect of a larger bourgeois individualism: in his freedom to choose among literary models and his power to incorporate them into a new and autonomous self, the humanist resembles the self-made man of capitalist venture.

In a later stage of bourgeois society, Burckhardt looked back in 1860 and viewed the emergence of the individual as the defining characteristic of the Italian Renaissance. Here was the link between Renaissance civilization and Burckhardt's own culture: in his individuality the fifteenth-century Italian was "the first-born among the sons of modern Europe." Burckhardt did not explore the economic or class origins of this individualism; it is the weak point of his definition of both the Renaissance and modernity, which, in spite, or perhaps because of this omission, remains a notable contribution to nineteenth-century bourgeois ideology. He preferred to describe the Renaissance individual as a political actor, able to impose his will and personality upon events.[5] This line of argument was, whether Burckhardt fully realized it or not, the continuation and confirmation of ideas already put forward by humanist educators. The liberal arts that they professed were those thought to be appropriate to a free man. The humanists' advocacy of the active life of civic engagement, their emphasis upon rhetoric as the instrument of deliberative persuasion, gave a public orientation to their pedagogy. Writing and speaking well allowed the student to enter into a larger literate community: into both the private company of his friends and family—and here the humanists placed particular emphasis on the art of letter-writing, which they revived from Cicero and Seneca—and the society of his fellow citizens, where his literary efforts might take the form of orations and poetry for public occasions, parliamentary speeches, and government reports. The cultivation of an individual style was designed, von Martin writes, "in order to have a personal influence on others,"[6] and, conversely, the public arena might be necessary for the realization of the individual's talents. In his tractate on education, Milton urges students to exercise the arts of war and to gain knowledge of their country: "These wayes would trie all their peculiar gifts of nature, and if there were any secret excellence among them, would fetch it out, and give it fair opportunities to advance it selfe by, which could not but mightily redound to the good of this nation, and bring into fashion again those old admired vertues and excellencies."[7] Some obstacles to these civic, political aspirations became evident when humanism moved away from its origins in the Italian city-republics and became part of the culture of the court; the humanists now trained their students as future princely servants: soldiers, magistrates, counselors, ambassadors. On the other hand, the eventual adoption of humanist education by the aristocratic ruling classes helped to keep alive its claims to political efficacy, even as outlets for meaningful action shrank in the new absolutist nation states. The latter-day humanist Vico, forced to acknowledge that eloquence had little function in a monarchy, nonetheless refused to renounce the civic virtues and purpose of a literary education. He pointed out that at least the lawcourts remained as a free forum where the individual could play a role in public affairs.[8]

The humanist educational program thus carried with it certain implicit assumptions about the individual, an individual endowed with the freedom and capacity both to create himself and to shape his social and political environment. The center of this program was the reading of classical texts by which the student was to come to a self-recognition that he could test either in his own writings or in his personal actions—and in the influence which these had on his society. In this scheme, where publication is a kind of public action and a means of civic persuasion, the literary text becomes the locus where both the writer and reader seek to impose their individual wills and personalities upon the other. Both have recognizable property rights over the text, and in an ideal practice of reading these rights are mutually respected. An accurate reading of the text demands that its author's terms be reconstructed in all their historical specificity and individuality: here the humanists' philological methods came into play. But the reader can then make the text his own. Somehow bridging the historical gap that philology now disclosed opening between them, he can speak to its author as one individual to another. Both activities, writing and reading, have their origins in the individual, for all practical purposes an independent agent.[9] The pedagogical and critical usefulness of this last idea is undeniable and is not easily dispensed with. While the essays in this volume may question such individualist assumptions, they are for the most part addressed to one or more works of an individual Renaissance author.

II

Although Burckhardt asserted that individualism was a common feature shared by both Renaissance and modern, nineteenth-century men, his view of the Renaissance individual was, in fact, already tinged with nostalgia. Confronted by the growing corporatism of modern industry and of the modern bureaucratic state, he looked back at an earlier, more heroic stage of capitalism and contemplated what appeared as the titanic individualism of the Italians with admiration not unmixed with moral disapproval. The idea of the individual remains a potent demagogic myth in present-day Western societies, but it evokes a world of grass-roots capitalism and small-time, independent entrepreneurs that is fast disappearing. In an age of mass communications, advertising, and state propaganda, it is difficult to speak of man shaping his own cultural identity or exercising an independent political will.

With this demise of the individual and with the spread of mass education away from a small governing elite, the humanist ped- agogical program has lost most of its rationale. The liberal arts, increasingly displaced by the natural and social sciences in the mod- ern curriculum, no longer seem obligatory for entrance into the political discourse and workings of a faceless, technocratic society. They have instead been transformed by romantic thought into a refuge *from* that society, a sanctuary where the humane values of earlier, better times can be preserved and reverenced. The student has been taught not so much to appropriate the classics, to carry on their tradition by making them part of his own individual writing and living experience, as to appreciate in them the wholeness and integrity of personality that he himself lacks. Describing a change in educational philosophy and practice that had already begun in the nineteenth century, Lionel Gossman comments: "The reader's rela- tion to books was thus no longer in the first instance that of a potential writer, a producer, an equal; it was that, at best, of an adept or worshipper, at worst, of a consumer."[10] Literature became a trea- sured object in the museum of culture.

The advanced literary theory and critical practice of the last 25 years continue and extend this logic of modern alienation from the reader to the individual author as well. The interest of this volume, where Renaissance texts are read in the light of contemporary crit- ical thought, consists in the juxtaposition of works in which human- ist concepts of the text, writer, and reader were first formulated with a literary theory that has called those concepts into question and announced their supersession. Drawing from social anthropology and linguistics, the enterprise of structuralism has sought to place the text within a larger cultural system that preconditions its utter- ances. Semiotic analysis has attempted to isolate one part of this system, to reconstruct the repertoire of modes of signification avail- able to the writer; these, in effect, determine the possibilities of a text that is no longer "his"—the result of a personal selection among a series of constituent stylistic and ideological choices—but rather the product of choices that are largely made for him both by the literary system itself and by the ways of knowing, the "epistemes" of the larger culture. These ideological systems are bound up with struc- tures of power and social coercion. The text may thus be inscribed by one or more, often interrelated, codes of repression: codes engendered by the authority of the state, by the power of institutions, by economic and class interests, and—running across class lines, though in different guises—by the exclusion of women from power in a male-dominated society. These cultural forces find their analogies and may become internalized in the drives of the Unconscious, which further condition the act of writing. The task of the reader or critic is to separate out the various cultural discourses that intersect in the literary text. This project is largely descriptive, and although it may claim to seek the unity of these discourses in a controlling vision or "mentality" that determines the text's culture as a whole, description and categorization can become a critical end in itself. As interest shifts from the meaning of the text to the principles governing its act of signification, that meaning both breaks apart and expands beyond the text's "proper" boundaries. The text no longer seems to speak with a single voice of its own, the voice of an individual author with whom the reader might seek a common human understanding. Literature thus lives out the alienation and fragmentation of modern corporate society: it becomes a system in which the text loses its individual identity and significance and coalesces into an endless process of textual production. The deconstructionist movement within poststructuralism has transformed this alienation into a principle of skeptical suspension: it sees the investment of the text with an authorial voice not only as a humanist illusion but as the basis for a metaphysics of presence that has governed Western thought. The unmasking of this cult of textual personality leaves all meaning subject to the unsettling play of linguistic and semiotic codes.[11]

Proposing alternatives to the humanist practice of reading, contemporary critical theory finds confirmation of its ideas in the Renaissance humanists' own texts. Fissures and contradictions now appear in the humanists' assertions of authorship and creative individuality; the texts of the past, which the Renaissance writer claims to master and appropriate, may haunt him instead. In a now classic article on Petrarch's *Canzoniere*, John Freccero has shown that this Father of Humanism was himself locked in an oedipal struggle both with his poetic father Dante and with his spiritual father Augustine. Petrarch's quest for literary autonomy produces a poetics and thematics of willful idolatry: the worship of the linguistic signs, themselves, by which the poet constitutes his lyric persona. His poems and the earthly love for Laura which they describe become ends in themselves—and his love may itself be little more than a desire for the laurel of literary identity and fame which the poetry confers. This poetic self-creation is self-consciously inauthentic; with his lyric example, Petrarch may disclose how other forms of literary self-expression are determined by the exigencies of textual production rather than by individual life-histories. In his idolatrous love for Laura, moreover, Petrarch explicitly acknowledges the transgressive nature of his quest for originality. A similar acknowledgment is made by that other great ego of Renaissance lyric poetry, Pierre de Ronsard, in a series of poems that find a dark analogy for poetic invention in the Renaissance invention of gunpowder. As Ullrich Langer points out, the discovery of the cannon was widely associated in Renaissance writing with diabolic forces and with the pride of Prometheus who stole the fire of the gods. But it was also, along with the inventions of the printing press and the compass, one of the technological advances by which the Renaissance claimed to have surpassed the ancients and to possess a creative power of its own. Ronsard's appropriation of the creative spirit of the classical poets, as he seeks to overcome his position as son and latecomer in their literary tradition, thus does not come about without overtones of violence and struggle; his poetic self-engendering necessarily creates anxiety about the poetic fathers he displaces.[12]

If psychoanalytic modes appear to shed light upon these assertions of authorial identity, Stephen Greenblatt reminds us that psychoanalysis, itself, is the product of certain institutional practices that began in the Renaissance. In his meditation on histrionic impersonation in the story of Martin Guerre and in the Elizabethan theater, Greenblatt suggests that the inalienable selfhood presupposed by Freudian theory—even when it describes alienated states of consciousness—is foreign to Renaissance categories of thought. The Renaissance individual gains his identity not from the psychic history his body may contain, but as a form of property the right to which is granted and guaranteed to him by the laws and authority of his larger community. The human being here is the product, rather than the producer, of a complex set of cultural and material relations: it takes form not as some hidden inner subjectivity that rises from within to public view but rather as a public mask determined by the state's compulsive efforts to control and set the bounds of social identity. Greenblatt's argument that the human subject that psychoanalysis seeks to understand is a relatively recent, modern invention is complemented and amplified by Timothy Reiss's analysis of the political and legal constitution of the "moi" in the Essays of Montaigne: both critics draw inspiration from the thought of Michel Foucault. Reiss salutarily admonishes us that Montaigne's concept of the human subject should not be confused with the later Cartesian subject brought into being by the exercise of a universal reason common to all men. The skeptical project of the *Essays* is rather to demonstrate the insufficiency and instability of human reason and judgment, to disclose the realm of private thought that exists within the individual as unformed and without fixed position and being. Only by allegiance and subjection to the state—and, in the particular circumstances of Montaigne's France torn by civil war, to the authority of the king—can the subject gain a stable, public identity: Reiss carefully locates Montaigne at a juncture in the history of political theory when universal principles were sought not in the individual reason but in law and juridical institutions. Reiss's powerful analysis allows us to see Montaigne's political conservatism in a clearer light, to suspect a dimension of repression (not unique in the age of the Counter-Reformation) in his apologetic skepticism, his criticism of Stoic self-sufficiency, and his celebrated approval of the common man—the man who does not claim an independent identity (e.g., high nobility, Protestant) that might threaten the stability of the social order. But what has become of the humanist self-discovery and self-creation advocated by *On Education?*

The social identity of Renaissance men depended in no small part upon discourses that excluded or suppressed the voices of women. The situation has not greatly changed since, and Mary Nyquist's essay suggests how Milton, the first of the masculinists, has been treated by a subsequent history of interpretation that is, if anything, more misogynist than the depiction of the Fall of Adam and Eve in *Paradise Lost*. Male critics from Addison and Pope to the present day have been overly eager to place Milton's epic within a tradition of classical poetry and to explain it in terms of a "normative" misogyny which that tradition has transmitted through literary history. Milton, Nyquist persuasively argues, knows and attacks this tradition, not because of its sexism—to which he might quite well subscribe—but because it is an impure, secondary literature of representation attendant upon the Fall, through whose figures and fictions he and the reader must work back to the original prelapsarian meaning that his poem aims to recover and reconstruct. Yet, however much Milton may try to appropriate literary history in order to transcend it, he is, in turn appropriated by that history, by its sexist ideologies and representational codes—and by its sexist literary critics. It is, Nyquist suggests, in the interest of feminist criticism to keep alive the dynamics of this intertextual struggle, both to preserve the possibility of criticizing the ruling discourses of patriarchal ideology and to caution against the notion that these discourses can be easily overcome or erased from our cultural history. Diana Wilson argues that this latter utopian aim is precisely the project of Cervantes' last work, the *Persiles*. The opening episode of this romance, which features an escape from a Barbaric isle where women are bought and sold, resonates throughout the novel, as do images of androgyny—men assuming the dress and roles of women and vice versa. The *Persiles* attempts to rethink the languages that designate gender in Cervantes's culture; departing from the world of *Don Quijote* that was ruled almost exclusively by male fantasies, it seeks a new mutuality and dialogue between male and female voices. Cervantes, Wilson suggests, is one of the first feminists.

René Girard is a great original. While he denounces the poststructuralist enterprise with the voice of a Biblical prophet, his own criticism is also a poststructuralism of sorts, an unmasking of cultural hierarchies and differences to expose their foundations in what he posits as the mimetic, reciprocal structure of human desire and violence: in this view human beings become more and more alike the more they seek to differentiate themselves. His essay on *Hamlet*, which is representative of his recent work on Shakespeare, returns to the celebrated critical question of the hero's delay in taking revenge. For Girard, this delay can stand as the model for strategic thinking in the modern, post-Renaissance world: a dissatisfaction with the blood feud and its chain of undistinguishable victims—or with an apocalyptic nuclear exchange in which winners and losers are equally undistinguishable—that wishes neither to give in to nor, heeding the Biblical injunction, to give up on the idea of revenge. Hamlet's final conformity to the code of revenge, achieved with histrionics that disclose the schizophrenic's excessive zeal for normality, reflects Shakespeare's own inability to escape from the tradition of the revenge play that he criticizes or, for that matter, from the dramatic form itself with its demands for catharsis, the vestigial remains of the drama's sacrificial origins. Here Girard's critique becomes quite similar to Nyquist's analysis of Milton: Shakespeare is the victim of his own literary history and of a critical tradition—less monolithic, perhaps, than Girard suggests—that continues to perceive the revenge play as the norm and misunderstands the nature of both the playwright's and his hero's deviance.

The literary text, then, may be invaded and inhabited from without by the multiple ideological discourses and literary codes of its writer's culture to such a point that its own distinguishing contours and boundaries begin to disappear. But these boundaries—which would determine the text's "proper" meaning, a meaning that might correspond, however imperfectly, to the intention of the individual author—may be equally undermined from within, by the rhetorical play of its language against the logical structures of meaning predicated by language itself. There is a strong temptation in poststructuralist theory to view certain problems and strategies of writing as ahistorical constants. When read from the perspective of this theory, Renaissance texts indeed appear, with greater and lesser consciousness on the part of their writers, to share and even dramatize many of the same concerns poststructuralism raises about tropological and linguistic structures that generate not too little but too much meaning. The text is condemned always to say more than the writer intends, an excess that unsettles any univocal or fixed meaning the reader may wish to draw from it. Terence Cave, who has brilliantly explored how the rhetorical abundance promoted by Erasmus and other humanists could find its dark counterpart in Renaissance texts in images of endless Babelic proliferation, emptying, and dispersal, here discusses the inexhaustibility of Rabelais's fiction. He argues that the Rabelaisian use of the rhetorical practice of *contaminatio*—the combining of several literary models and *topoi*—transforms these source materials into a series of mutual glosses, in which no single source can claim mastery over the others. The resulting spill-over of meaning cannot be contained by a narrative that typically discloses the utopian goal—fullness of meaning, fulfillment of desire—toward which it seems to move to be another locus of desire that generates further narrative; this exuberant desire is ultimately, if not exclusively, directed to the "pleasure of the text" itself, to writing as a form of libidinal release. For the late Eugenio Donato, the *Orlando Furioso* also constituted an infinitely expandable narrative of desire; virtually all its characters are in pursuit of one desired object or another. Ariosto's poem, Donato argued, posits no point of closure or Archimedean point outside its narrative from which the narrative could be unified by an organizing authorial consciousness; within the narrative, the poet-narrator instead implicates himself in the same play of desire. Normally thwarted and frustrated, the desire depicted by the *Furioso* leads easily into madness. By contrast, the comparative festivity in what Cave describes as the similarly structured narrative of the Rabelaisian books may depend upon their Evangelical spirit and their faith in an eschatological End that subtends all human narratives.

This promised end, Patricia Parker argues, pervades the horizon of ideas which most Renaissance texts inhabited and distinguishes their concerns about textual excess and proliferation from more anxious modern theories of textuality, notably from Jacques Derrida's concept of "différance." She surveys the rich variety of meanings and cultural associations that gather around the verb "dilate" (from the Latin "dilato," itself etymologically linked to "differo"). If the most common meaning of the verb in Renaissance usage is simply "to narrate," it also names the specific rhetorical technique of extending a discourse at length, the evangelical spread and imperial expansion of Christianity before the Last Judgment, and finally a process of delay that, in its juridical context, aims at the putting-off or suspension of judgment. This last meaning suggests most clearly the kinship of Renaissance "dilation" with Derrida's punning "différance": textual abundance and proliferation may raise the threat of an infinite deferral of any ultimate meaning or truth. How Renaissance writers attempt to exploit and contain this threatening textual energy is the subject of Parker's essay, which reveals a high level of self-reflexivity—the interpenetration of the thematic by the rhetorical structures of the text—in works of Shakespeare, Cervantes, and Jonson. Thomas M. Greene discusses how the *Prince*, which may apparently share a structural opposition between textual excess and apocalytic closure of much the sort that Parker describes, in fact introduces a deliberate discontinuity between the two. Machiavelli's text produces a welter of contradictory historical examples and qualifying afterthoughts that finally dissolves the boundaries of the conceptual space that the text has sought to clear for itself, a space whose analogue is the territory carved out by the usurping prince whom the text imagines. The inability of Machiavelli's discourse to achieve self-sufficiency and a self-consistent closure is marked by the call for a redeemer of Italy in the book's last chapter, an apocalyptic imposition that, for Greene, is to be taken seriously only as an acknowledgment that the *Prince* cannot escape the literariness from which it tried to detach itself in the name of analytic truth. But Greene reimports a humanist perspective upon this very admission of "failure" by the *Prince*, which is, he argues, the very source of its enduring productivity. The conceptual collapse of the text and its entrance into an undecidable realm of myth require successive generations of readers to lend their own imaginations and historical experiences to the puzzles it leaves unsolved. The refusal of a closure that is anything more than formal leaves Machiavelli's text open for a dialogue with history.

The troubling excess produced by theoretical analysis appears again as the subject of Derek Attridge's essay on Puttenham's *Arte of English Poesie*, and here, too, Derrida's thought and critical categories come into play. The excess of meaning in Puttenham's text takes the form of the *supplement:* that which is both excluded from its conceptual field and yet, as it turns out, necessary to complete that field. There is a structural similarity between the rhetorical activities of this supplement and the return of those forces whose repression makes political and psychic order possible. Beyond his elegant charting of how the founding categories of Art and Nature break down and exchange identities in Puttenham's text, Attridge pertinently reminds us that if the rhetorical structures that condition human habits of mind and cultural discourse inevitably reveal their instability, this instability may nonetheless be contained by other social and cultural mechanisms: in Puttenham's case by the power of the courtly elite who are the privileged owners, models, and final guarantors of the decorum his treatise attempts to teach the would-be poet. If the process of writing may lead to aporetic moments because, as Puttenham himself explains the term *aporia*, "oftentimes we will seeme to cast perils, and make doubt of things when by a plaine manner of speech wee might affirme or deny him," such moments do not put an end to textual and ideological production.

Louis Montrose analyzes Spenser's role in the making of Elizabethan ideology in an essay that touches on several of the theoretical issues raised by other essays in the volume. For Montrose, Queen Elizabeth, the woman ruler of a patriarchal male society, already exists for her poets as a text, the product of a series of gender-determined discursive codes of her culture that both she and the poets manipulated for their common interests. Spenser repeatedly appropriates this text, depicting himself as the creator of the Queen as well as her fawning creature. Arguing against Greenblatt's more deterministic and constraining model of self-fashioning and textual production, Montrose suggests ways in which Elizabethan writers imposed their own personalities upon the fictions of political ideology by which they were ruled. The Petrarchan conventions they employed to praise Elizabeth were, as Freccero's essay points out, the traditional means by which the male poetic imagination, by creating the female Other as the object of its own fantasies, could assert its autonomy. The reintroduction of the human subject (and this includes Elizabeth just as much as Spenser) into the process of writing—of choosing among and reshaping the available discourses of its culture—is linked by Montrose to recent developments in Marxian theory that describe power not as a single force neatly flowing downward through a socioeconomic hierarchy, but as a series of shifting arrangements and congruencies of interests among various social classes and groups: the individual, then in the Renaissance and now, has a stake in shaping his or her history. Richard Halpern's essay on Skelton, on the other hand, describes the poet's resistance or reluctance to join in the ideological ordering of the nascent Tudor nation-state. Using Marx's analysis of the transition

from feudalism to the modern social order with its concentration of
capital and centralization of power, Halpern finds a historical loca-
tion of the notoriously unclassifiable Skelton. The refusal of an organizing structure in *Philip Sparrow* in the name of a free-floating
and random pleasure that is both textual and sexual may be understood as a response and counter-movement to a whole cultural
transformation effected by a new and intrusive state power. Halpern concedes that such a response, in its inability to engage the
very question of power and mastery, is utopian and may be as
immature as the young woman narrator of the first part of the poem;
Skelton seems to acknowledge as much when he introduces a second part, narrated by his own persona, that attempts to appropriate
and contain what has gone before. At issue in Halpern's essay is the
larger critical problem of whether poststructuralist analysis, once it
has destructured all master discourses, can be effectively integrated
into Marxian theory. It calls into some question, by noting the possibilities of its co-optation, the critical orientation within poststructuralism toward a poetics of pleasure, the "jouissance" of textual
play.

Victoria Kahn's essay concludes the volume with an examination
of possible points of contact between the humanist educational project and the interest of present-day humanists in literary theory. The
Renaissance humanists were situated historically between two systematic modes of theory, between scholastic logic and the mathe-
matically based new science of the seventeenth century. Their emphasis on prudence and the practical application of knowledge was
distinct both from such theoretical systems *and* from any kind of
method—such as Ramism—that aimed at regularizing or standar-
dizing the products of knowledge, at transforming learning into an
easily reproducible *techne*. The deliberative rhetoric by which the
humanists sought knowledge, with its appeals to the various emo-
tions and its wealth of individual and often mutually contradictory
topoi and examples, was able to unsettle the certainties of logic; but,
Kahn cautions, it should not therefore be identified with the irony
that the late Paul de Man posited within all language and grammar:
the humanists contained this irony by an appeal to social consensus.
After wittily surveying various positions held by contemporary critics about the place of theory in the teaching of literature, Kahn
advocates an ongoing and open-ended dialogue between theoretical inquiry and the practice of reading and interpretation, a
dialogue that would neither exclude nor privilege one or the other.
Theory is here produced by the reflection of reading upon its own
procedures, and the articulations of theory are themselves subject to

readings that seek to analyze and identify their context of interests, drives, and desires. Theory as well as practice is located within a contingent, changing history; the aim of pedagogy is to make the student aware of how, as a reader, he or she is constantly being produced by that history.

III

Kahn's proposed realignment of literary theory with the practice of criticism—and with humanism's traditional heremeneutic goals of practical knowledge and self-knowledge—could describe the general practicality of the essays in this volume: their engagement with contemporary theory, their resistance to its most radical conclusions and consequences. The classical model of hermeneutics—an intersubjective dialogue between individual reader and writer—is hardly compatible with a poststructuralist theory that regards the individual subjectivity that was supposed to speak through the text as a text itself, the product of other texts and discursive codes that both proliferate and coalesce under analysis. As an authorial presence recedes from the text, so does the possibility of organizing its various discourses into a single meaning or self-reflexive truth. This destructuring of the hierarchy of discourses within the individual text has implications for the larger literary canon as well. A very real achievement of structuralist and poststructuralist thought has been to provide a *theoretical* basis for the displacement of the classical canon of humanist letters—the dream and goal of modernist movements since the French Revolution that have objected to the prescriptive authority and truth-value vested in the canon by political and religious establishments. Literature can be freed from a deadening official culture and ideology and allowed to speak a multitude of human discourses rather than with one (transcendent) voice; hitherto excluded victims of history may be given a hearing. But the further corollary of poststructuralism—and of the dismantling of the literary text into its various cultural codes, its literary and ideological systems, its rhetorical structures—is to blur the identity of literature itself as a separate cultural product. The issue is of some moment in a pluralistic modern culture where, with or without structuralist theory, the modernist dream has already come true: the traditional canon not only has lost its hegemony, but may no longer even enjoy common currency.

The present essays steer a middle course between the univocal text and triumphalist canon on the one hand and the dispersion of both text and canon on the other. These opposing and symmetrical positions *both* appear to depend upon an ideology, now supposedly superseded, that identifies the human with the individual. The choice seems to be all or nothing: the totalizing concept of the individual, who, in the person of author or reader, appropriates the text and imposes closure upon its meanings; or a corresponding "de-humanization" of the text, the reduction of its meaning to impersonal procedures of writing, at once aleatory and rigorously determined. For the most part, these essays avoid such a choice. They set practical limits upon a potentially infinite play of textuality in order to make historical discriminations, to argue for, and hence to privilege, patterns of meaning in the literary text, and to claim, at least implicitly, the human interest of this meaning—a meaning that is arguably more human because it is shifting and inconclusive, the reflection of unassimilable motives and intentions. What may also be implied, if unvoiced, in their criticism is the assumption that the open-endedness and semantic play that inhabit all cultural discourses are disclosed with a particular and even programmatic clarity in the literary text; and this assumption remotivates the idea of a humanist canon: one whose function would be to distinguish literature, as a discourse that foregrounds problems of writing and reading and suspends questions of ultimate meaning and truth, from other discourses that are more mechanical, more dogmatic, more ideologically manipulative. The transmission of a canon is of special interest for these critics, whose vocation as scholars and teachers of Renaissance literature may condition their resistance to the extreme modernist implications of poststructuralist theory. But the canonical text does not represent for them a normative wisdom of the past, and here, Kahn argues, they may share the urbane, ironic distance that the Renaissance humanists could themselves achieve vis-à-vis the classics; nor is that text the expression of an integrated individual personality, the object of romantic nostalgia. It is rather the place where writing diverts and reexamines human aspirations to wholeness and autonomy. To the extent that these essays negotiate a humanism that no longer depends upon the logic of individualism informing the humanist tradition, they measure their relationship of distance and continuity with the Renaissance texts they seek to understand.

Notes

1. *Prosatori latini del quattrocento*, ed. Eugenio Garin (Milan, 1952), 902.
2. *The Complete Essays of Montaigne*, trans. Donald M. Frame (Stanford, 1965), 111.

3. Ibid., 111–12.

4. Alfred von Martin, *Sociology of the Renaissance* (1932), trans. M. L. Luet-kens (1944; New York, 1963), 40. See also the suggestive essay of Robert Weimann, " 'Appropriation' and Modern History in Renaissance Prose Narrative," *New Literary History* 14 (1983), 459–96.

5. Jacob Burckhardt, *The Civilization of the Renaissance in Italy*, trans. S. G. C. Middlemore (1929; New York, 1958), 143–46. On Burckhardt's position in the history of thinking on the Renaissance, see Wallace Ferguson, *The Renaissance in Historical Thought* (Cambridge, Mass., 1948), 179–252.

6. Von Martin, *Sociology of the Renaissance*, 40.

7. *The Prose of John Milton*, ed. J. Max Patrick (Garden City, N.Y., 1967), 239.

8. Vico, *On the Study Methods of Our Time*, trans. Elio Gianturco (Indi-anapolis, 1965), 39.

9. This individualism is the basis for a whole tradition of hermeneutics that originated in Renaissance humanism and has continued into this century in the work of Heidegger and Gadamer. For the current structuralist challenge to this tradition, see Manfred Frank's aptly titled *Das individuelle Allgemeine* (Frankfurt, 1977), 44–86.

10. Gossman, "Literature and Education," *New Literary History* 13 (1982): 355.

11. Some prominent recent studies may be briefly mentioned here. Terence Cave, in *The Cornucopian Text: Problems of Writing in the French Renaissance* (Oxford, 1979), provides the most comprehensive critical revision to date of Renaissance literature from the perspective of poststructuralist theory. The humanist goal of rhetorical abundance, he argues, produced in Re-naissance writing both tropes of authorial plenitude and an anxiety about proliferating, self-emptying discourses. His critical position may be com-pared with that in other recent works that are similarly inspired by the thought of Jacques Derrida, Patricia Parker's examination of structures of deferral in Renaissance and later versions of romance, *Inescapable Romance* (Princeton, 1979), and Jonathan Goldberg's study of Spenser's sprawling poetic web, *Endlesse Worke: Spenser and the Structures of Discourse* (Bal-timore, 1981). Drawing on late medieval philosophical traditions, Ronald Levao demonstrates analogous Renaissance anxieties about the fictions that get out of their author's hands in *Renaissance Minds and their Fictions* (Berkeley and Los Angeles, 1985). In two important essays, Giuseppe Mazzotta has described how Boccaccio's *Decameron* portrays literature as a marginal discourse of play that discloses an unsettling playfulness within putatively "serious" cultural discourses; see "The *Decameron*: The Mar-ginality of Literature," *University of Toronto Quarterly* 42 (1972), 64–81, and "The *Decameron*: The Literal and the Allegorical," *Italian Quarterly* 18 (1975), 53–73. For a careful response to Cave, see Thomas M. Greene, "Erasmus's 'Festina lente': Vulnerabilities of the Humanist Text," in *Mim-esis, From Mirror to Method*, ed. John D. Lyons and Stephen G. Nichols, Jr. (Hanover, N.H., 1982), 132–48. Cave devotes considerable space in his book to Rabelais, whose multiple discursive styles have been a fertile ground for structuralist analyses: among these are the distinguished

work of François Rigolot, *Les Langages de Rabelais* (Geneva, 1972), *Le Texte de la Renaissance* (Geneva, 1982), and "Cratylisme et Pantagruélisme: Rabelais et le statut du signe," *Etudes Rabelaisiennes* 13 (1976): 115–32, and Michel Beaujour, *Le Jeu de Rabelais* (Paris, 1970). Mikhail Bakhtin's *Rabelais and His World*, trans. H. Iswolsky (Cambridge, Mass., 1968), which was written in 1940 but only appeared in 1965, has yet to be integrated fully into modern Rabelais studies; it has, however, provided a powerful and widely influential model for discussing how literature can destructure the reigning hierarchy of cultural discourses.

The converse process—how that hierarchy can impose itself upon acts of writing—has been studied by other critics. Timothy Reiss, in *The Discourse of Modernism* (Ithaca and London, 1982), has followed Michel Foucault and demonstrated how the seventeenth century saw the solidifying of a new practice of writing and knowledge that exercised a disciplinary function over culture. Stephen Greenblatt has also studied Foucault's thought and brought it to bear fruitfully upon modern ethnographic theory: his *Renaissance Self-Fashioning* (Chicago, 1980) offers a provocative theoretical statement about the relationship of writing to forces of cultural repression. Louis Adrian Montrose has examined similar preoccupations from a neo-Marxian and feminist perspective in his brilliant article on *A Midsummer Night's Dream*, "Shaping Fantasies: Figurations of Gender and Power in Elizabethan Culture," *Representations* 2 (1983): 61–94. In another recent essay, "Fabula and Historia: The Crisis of the Universal Consideration in *The Unfortunate Traveler*," *Representations* 8 (1985): 14–29, Robert Weimann offers a cogent discussion of the interrelationship between the emergence of the writer as a member of a new professional class and the rise of Elizabethan narrative fiction.

Greenblatt and Montrose include psychoanalytic strategies in their studies, and there has been a general movement to relocate psychoanalytic criticism alongside the historical study of class and gender hierarchies. Some notable works are Francesco Orlando's analysis of *Phèdre* in *Toward a Freudian Theory of Literature*, trans. Charmaine Lee (Baltimore, 1978), Richard McCoy, *Sir Philip Sidney: Rebellion in Arcadia* (New Brunswick, N.J., 1979), and the recent collection of essays edited by Murray M. Schwartz and Coppelia Kahn, *Representing Shakespeare* (Baltimore, 1980). Margaret W. Ferguson, in *Trials of Desire: Renaissance Defenses of Poetry* (New Haven, 1983), has brilliantly shown how codes of social and political repression can be discovered interacting with what Harold Bloom argues is the anxiety of influence that governs acts of poetic creation. John Guillory also applies Bloom's theory to the problems of Renaissance authorship in *Poetic Authority: Spenser, Milton, and Literary History* (New York, 1983). Other examinations of the idea of the author are offered by Richard Helgerson in *Self-Crowned Laureates: Spenser, Jonson, Milton and the Literary System* (Berkeley and Los Angeles, 1983), and Jonathan Crewe, *Unredeemed Rhetoric: Thomas Nashe and the Scandal of Authorship* (Baltimore, 1982).

12. The images of transgression that accrue around Renaissance authorship have also been explored by Margaret W. Ferguson in her fine essay, "Nashe's *The Unfortunate Traveller:* The 'Newes of the Maker' Game," *English Literary Renaissance* 11 (1981):165–82, and by Richard Helgerson, *The Elizabethan Prodigals* (Berkeley and Los Angeles, 1976).

2. THE FIG TREE AND THE LAUREL:

PETRARCH'S POETICS

■

JOHN FRECCERO

AFTER six centuries Petrarch's reputation as the first humanist remains unshaken. Cultural historians have generally accepted his own estimate of himself as the man who inaugurated a new era, leaving behind him what he called "the dark ages." His reputation as a poet is equally secure, at least in the literary histories; he is in many respects the most influential poet in the history of Western literature. Critics have failed, however, to define adequately the ways in which his poetry was as revolutionary as his humanistic writings. The poetics of the *Canzoniere* remain as elusive as the persona that emerges from its lyrics. The purpose of this essay is to offer a tentative definition and to suggest the ways in which Petrarch's greatest work deserves its reputation as the precursor of modern poetry.

Petrarch's poetic achievement, for all its grandeur, would appear to be decidedly conservative with respect to the Middle Ages. Far from repudiating the verse forms of his predecessors, he brought them to technical perfection and established them as models for future generations of poets. The poems of the *Canzoniere* seem to be crystallizations of previously invented verse forms: the sonnet, the sestina, the Dantesque canzone. In content, they are equally familiar, not to say banal, for they elaborate with spectacular variations a tired theme of courtly love: the idolatrous and unrequited passion for a beautiful and sometimes cruel lady. Apart from the extensive use of classical myth, there is little that is radically new in the thematics of the *Canzoniere*.

The extraordinary innovation in the *Canzoniere* is rather to be found in what the verses leave unsaid, in the blank spaces separating these lyric "fragments," as they were called, from each other. The persona created by the serial juxtaposition of dimensionless lyric moments is as illusory as the animation of a film strip, the product of the reader's imagination as much as of the poet's craft; yet, the resultant portrait of an eternally weeping lover remains Petrarch's most distinctive poetic achievement. Because it is a composite of lyric instants, the portrait has no temporality; only the most naive reader would take it for authentic autobiography. For the same reason, it is immune from the ravages of time, a mood given a fictive *durée* by the temporality of the reader, or a score to be performed by generations of readers from the Renaissance to the Romantics. It remained for centuries the model of poetic self-creation even for poets who, in matters of form, thought of themselves as anti-Petrarchan.

Literary self-creation in the Middle Ages could not fail to evoke the name of Saint Augustine, the founder of the genre. The *Confessions*, Petrarch's favorite book, is at the same time the model for much of Petrarch's description of the lover as sinner. Both stories are ostensibly attempts to recapture a former self in a retrospective literary structure, a narrative of conversion (*Canz.* 1.4: "quand' era in parte altr'uom da quel ch'i'sono"), but Petrarch makes no claim to reality or to moral witness. Instead, he uses Augustinian principles in order to create a totally autonomous portrait of the artist, devoid of any ontological claim. The moral struggle and the spiritual torment described in the *Canzoniere* are, as we shall see, part of a poetic strategy. When the spiritual struggle is demystified, its poetic mechanism is revealed: the petrified idolatrous lover is an immutable monument to Petrarch, his creator and namesake. In this sense, the laurel, the emblem both of the lover's enthrallment and of the poet's triumph, is the antitype of Augustine's fig tree, under which the saint's conversion took place. The fig tree was already a scriptural emblem of conversion before Augustine used the image in his *Confessions* to represent the manifestation of the pattern of universal history in his own life. Petrarch's laurel, on the other hand, has no such moral dimension of meaning. It stands for a poetry whose real subject matter is its own act and whose creation is its own author.

The two emblems, the fig tree and the laurel, may be said to stand respectively, as we shall see, for different modes of signification: the allegorical and the autoreflexive. The first is the mode characteristic of Christian typology, while the second, extended over the course of the entire narrative, is Petrarch's own. The fig tree and the laurel stand for the two poles of a verbal universe whose principles were shared by Augustine and the poet. Before defining the differences between them more precisely, we must turn to review some of those principles.

For Augustine, consciousness begins in desire. To discover the self is to discover it as in some sense lacking, absent to itself, and desire is the soul's reaching out to fill the void. This reaching out toward an as-yet-unspecified object is at the same time the birth of language, or at least of the paralanguage of gesticulation, literally a reaching out toward signification. The first chapters of the *Confessions* represent language and desire as indistinguishable, perhaps even coextensive. The child learns to speak in order to express its desire; at the same time, however, it learns what to desire from a world of objects that adults have named. Language is not only the vehicle of desire, it is also in some sense its creator, first through the agency of others, the mother and the nurse, and ultimately, sometimes insidiously, through the power of literary suggestion. From the first words of the child to the final utterance, the process remains essentially the same: far from being the sole interpreters of the words we use, we are at the same time interpreted by them. For Augustine, then, as for contemporary semiologists, man *is* his own language, for his desires and his words are inseparable.

If this is so, it follows that the end terms of both language and desire are one and the same. So it is, inevitably, in a theology of the Word. The ultimate end of desire is God, in whom the soul finds its satisfaction. The ultimate end of signification is a principle of intelligibility in terms of which all things may be understood. God the Word is at once the end of all desire and the ultimate meaning of all discourse. In the ninth book of the *Confessions*, just before the death of Monica, Augustine speaks of language in terms of desire and of desire in terms of language:

> If, for any man, the tumult of the flesh were silent: if the images of the earth, the waters and the air were silent: if the poles were silent; if the soul itself were silent and transcended itself by not thinking about itself . . . if they were silent and He spoke . . . by Himself, Whom we love in these things; were we to hear Him without them and if it continued like this, would it not be entering into the joy of the Lord? (9.10)

All creation is a discourse leading to Love, just as all desire is ultimately a desire for the Word. The theology of the Word binds together language and desire by ordering both to God, in whom they are grounded. From a naturalistic standpoint, it is impossible to say whether human discourse is a reflection of the word or whether the idea of God is simply a metaphoric application of linguistic theory. Whether we accept Augustine's theology in some form or translate it into what might be called a semiology of desire, we remain within a verbal universe, reaching out for a silent terminal point that lies outside the system.

The Word, the silence that subtends the system, grounds both desire and language. In its absence, however, both threaten to become an infinite regression, approaching ultimate satisfaction and ultimate significance as an unreachable limit. This is probably most clear in terms of Augustinian desire, which is insatiable in human terms. Each of the successive desires of life are in fact desires for selfhood, expressed metonymically in an ascending hierarchy of abstraction: nourishment for the child, sex for the adolescent, fame for the adult. In an Augustinian world, there is no escape from desire short of God: "Our heart [he says] is unquiet until it rest in Thee" (*Confessions*, 1.1).

As all desire is ultimately a desire for God, so all signs point ultimately to the Word. In a world without ultimate significance, there is no escape from the infinite referentiality of signs. Signs, like desire, continually point beyond themselves. In the *De Magistro*, for example, Augustine says that signs cannot convince an unbeliever, but can only point in the direction of reality. For the unbeliever to perceive the Truth, Christ must teach him from within. Short of the Word made flesh, there can be no bridge between words and things: "All other things may be expressed in some way; He alone is ineffable, Who spoke and all things were made. He spoke and we were made; but we are unable to speak of Him. His Word, by Whom we were spoken, is His Son. He was made weak, so that He might be spoken by us, despite our weakness" (10.33ff. See also M. Colish, *The Mirror of Language* [New Haven: Yale University Press, 1968], 57).

In our own day, we have learned about the infinite referentiality of signs, "unlimited semiosis," from Saussure and from Peirce, among others. Anterior to the written text is the spoken text, anterior to that is the acoustic image, in turn dependent upon a concept that is itself linguistically structured. Our attempt to make the leap from words to things seems doomed to a continual feedback that looks like infinite regression. C.S. Peirce speaks of the phenomenon in terms that are reminiscent of the *De Magistro*:

The object of representation can be nothing but a representation of which the first representation is the interpretant. But an endless series of representations, each representing the one behind it, may be conceived to have an absolute object at its limit. . . . Finally, the interpretant is nothing but another representation *to which the torch of truth is handed along* and as representation, it has its interpretant again. Lo, another infinite series.[1]

For Augustine, the central metaphor of Christianity provided the grounding for this infinite regression. Reality itself is linguistically structured. It is God's book, having him for both its author and its subject matter. Words point to things, but those things are themselves signs pointing to God, the ultimately signified. The metaphor of God's book halts the infinite series by ordering all signs to itself. In germ, this is the foundation of Christian allegory and of salvation history.

The fig tree, in Augustine's narrative, is a sign, just as it is in the gospels when Christ says to his disciples that they must look to the fig tree if they would read the signs of the apocalyptic time. The fig tree in the garden of Milan, in the eighth book of the *Confessions,* for all its historicity, is at the same time meant to represent the broader pattern of salvation history for all Christians. The moment represents the revelation of God's Word at a particular time and place, recapitulating the Christ event in an individual soul. Behind that fig tree stands a whole series of anterior images pointing backward to Genesis; Augustine's reader is meant to prolong the trajectory by applying it to his own life and extending it proleptically toward the ending of time.

In the Old Testament, the prophet Micah looks forward to the day when the promise will be fulfilled: "He shall sit every man under his vine and under his fig tree" (4.4). The hope of the Jews, their nationhood, is represented by the same tree that in Genesis suggested their estrangement from God. At the beginning of the Gospel of John, the words of the prophet are perhaps recalled when Nathanael is called out from under the fig tree by the Messiah: "Before Philip called thee, when thou wast under the fig tree, I saw thee" (1.48). So in the *Confessions,* Augustine's calling, in the voices of children who sing "tolle, lege," takes place under the tree of Micah and Nathanael, whatever its botanical species. The paradigm of salvation history is made manifest at the end of an historical evolution and provides another "testament" to the interpretation of a man by God's Word.

Because Augustine's narrative is patterned after the same model that he took to be the principle of intelligibility in all human reality, the question of its historicity is meaningless. It might be said that the redemption itself depends upon a literary understanding of God's relationship to the world: the manifestation, at the end of a syntagmatic chain, of a significance present from the beginning. Like the intentionality of a sentence that preexists in its utterance and emerges concretely, in retrospect, from that utterance, the uncreated Word produces its signifier and is in turn made manifest by it.

Like language, the Redemption is tautology, ending where it began. Exactly the same relationship exists between Augustine's narrative and the reality it presumably represents. Is the story that we read a faithful portrayal of a life interpreted by God, or is that conversion experience the illusory feedback of plot structure in a narrative of the self? Conversion demands that there be both a continuity and a discontinuity between the self that *is* and the self that *was*. Similarly, a narrative of the self demands that author and persona be distinguished until they are fused at the narrative's culminating moment. Just as it is impossible to say whether God's presence is the reality of the Bible or the illusory projection of it, so it is impossible to say whether the conversion experience is the cause or the creature of the narrative that we read. When language in some form, however metaphorical, is the ultimate reality, we must be content with words upon words.

It must not be imagined that this is a modern distortion of Augustine's conception of his enterprise. In the text of the *Confessions*, conversion is always a literary event, a gloss on an anterior text. He correctly interprets the voices of the children to be a command to pick up the Bible and read a passage at random because he remembered Ponticianus's story of the two men who read the life of Antony and were thereupon converted. Antony himself, he remembered, "happened to go into a church while the gospel was being read and had taken it as a counsel addressed to himself when he heard the words, 'Go home and sell all that belongs to you . . . and follow me.' By this divine pronouncement he had at once been converted to You" (8.12). So Augustine picks up the Bible and reads the passage that interprets him and is thereby converted. The following moment points to his newly acquired vocation, for he then passes the Bible to his friend Alypius, thereby suggesting that his own text is to be applied proleptically to the reader himself as a part of the continual unfolding of God's Word in time. Consequently, the "truth-value" of Augustine's narrative depends, not upon its hypothetical conformity to brute "fact," supposing such a thing to exist, nor upon the illusory projection of human representation, but upon the arbitrary privilege granted to God's Word as the ultimate significance of all discourse. The fig tree, under the shade of which all this takes place, stands for a tradition of textual anteriority that extends backward in time to the Logos and forward to the same Logos at time's ending, when both desire and words are finally fulfilled: "Justi et sancti fruuntur Verbo Dei sine lectione, sine litteris."[2]

We must turn now, for contrast, to a passage in the first book of Petrarch's *Secretum*, in which Francesco is scolded by his fictive interlocutor, Augustine, for a moral weakness with which they were both familiar: a certain paralysis of the will. Augustine reassures Francesco by describing his own conversion.

> Yet, for all that, I remained the man I had been before, when finally a profound meditation brought before my eyes all of my unhappiness. Thus, from the moment that I willed it fully and completely, I found the power to do it, and with a marvelous and joyful rapidity, I was transformed into another Augustine, whose story I believe you know from my *Confessions*.
>
> Francesco: I know it, of course: nor can I ever forget that life-giving fig tree, under whose shadow this miracle happened to you.
>
> Augustine: I should hope not, for neither myrtle nor ivy, nor even that laurel dear (so they say) to Phoebus, should be so welcome to you. Even if the entire chorus of poets should yearn for that laurel and you above all, who alone among all of your contemporaries were worthy to have its sought-after leaves as your crown, yet the remembrance of that fig tree should be dearer, if, after many tempests, you one day arrive in port, for it portends a sure hope of correction and pardon.[3]

The note of preciosity, here as elsewhere in the *Secretum*, derives from the fact that since both voices are Petrarch's the inconclusive conversation about moral paralysis constitutes an elegant dramatization of its own subject matter. Like the historical Augustine whom he so much admired, Petrarch was expert at drawing real literary strength from fictionalized moral flaws. Of much more interest, however, is the very un-Augustinian homage that Augustine pays to the poet laureate, thereby betraying the real point of the exchange. Francesco compliments Augustine for the *Confessions* and acknowledges the fig tree as an example for all men. The laurel, however, the symbol of poetic supremacy, is his alone. We must turn now to the implications of Petrarch's claim.

We have seen that the fig tree is an allegorical sign. It stands for a referential series of anterior texts grounded in the Logos. It is at once unique, as the letter must be, and yet referential, pointing to a truth beyond itself, a spiritual sense. While it is true that the being of the letter cannot be doubted, its meaning transcends it in importance. As all signs point ultimately to God, so it may be said that all books, for the Augustinian, are in some sense copies of God's Book. When Dante affirms that he is simply a scribe, copying down the words that love dictates to him, he is echoing this theory. On the other hand, for the laurel to be truly unique, it cannot *mean* anything: its referentiality must be neutralized if it is to remain the property of its creator. Petrarch makes of it the emblem of the mirror relationship

Laura-Lauro, which is to say, the poetic lady created by the poet, who in turn creates him as poet laureate. This circularity forecloses all referentiality and in its self-contained dynamism resembles the inner life of the Trinity as the Church fathers imagined it. One could scarcely suppose a greater autonomy. This poetic strategy corresponds, in the theological order, to the sin of idolatry.

In his *Religion of Israel* (trans. M. Greenberg [Chicago: University of Chicago Press, 1960]), Yehezkel Kaufmann has shown that the Jews' conception of idolatry was a kind of fetishism, the worship of reified signs devoid of significance. The gods of the gentiles were coextensive with their representations, as though they dwelt not on Olympus or in the skies, but within a golden calf, a stone, or a piece of wood. Signs point to an absence or a significance yet to come; they are in this sense allegorical. Idols, as the Jews understood them, like fetishes, were a desperate attempt to render *presence*, a reified sign, one might almost say a metaphor.[4] It is almost as if the gentiles, in the Jews' reading, sought to evade the temporality inherent in the human condition by reifying their signs and thereby eternalizing significance in the here and now. Stones are mute, but as a compensation they last forever.

This theological problematic has its exact counterpart in the linguistic realm, except that its terms are reversed: in order to create an autonomous universe of autoreflexive signs without reference to an anterior logos—the dream of almost every poet since Petrarch—it is necessary that the thematic of such poetry be equally autoreflexive and self-contained, which is to say, that it be idolatrous in the Augustinian sense. The idolatrous love for Laura, however self-abasing it may seem, has the effect of creating a thoroughly autonomous portrait of the poet who creates it; its circular referentiality, like that of the Trinity (Father, Son, and the Love that binds them), cannot be transcended at a higher order. The laurel lives forever, no matter what happened to Francesco. This is the human strategy, the demystification of Petrarch's deliberately idolatrous pose. If the gentiles, in the Jews' interpretation of them, sought to make their gods present by reifying their signs, then we might say that Petrarch sought to reify his signs, objectify his poetic work, by making his "god," the lady Laura, the object of his worship. Critics given to psychologizing have repeatedly tried to reconstruct Petrarch's spiritual torment from his verses; where language is the only reality, however, it would be more prudent to see the spiritual torment as the reflection, the thematic translation, of his autoreflexive poetics.

We may observe in passing that the semiological meaning of idolatry, that is, the reification of the sign in an attempt to create poetic presence, is consonant with Augustine's sign theory. In the first chapter of the *De Doctrina Christiana*, in the middle of a discussion of the referentiality of signs, he introduces his famous distinction concerning human desire (1.2): God alone is to be enjoyed [*frui*], all other things are to be used [*uti*]. Sin consists in enjoying that which should be used. The distinction seems somewhat out of place until we recall that all things are signs and that God is the terminal point on a referential chain. Once language is equated with desire, then it is clear that to deprive signs of their referentiality and to treat a poetic statement as autonomous, an end in itself, is the definition of idolatry.

Perhaps the most obvious example of Petrarch's attempt to short-circuit the referentiality of his signs is to be found in the sestina numbered 30 in the *Canzoniere:* "Giovene donna sotto un verde lauro." Augustine's conversion took place in a single moment, the *kairos*, in the shadow of the fig tree. Petrarch transforms the moment into a cyclical lifetime in the shadow of the laurel:

> seguiró l'ombra di quel dolce lauro
> per lo più ardente sole e per la neve,
> fin che l'ultimo dí chiuda quest'occhi.

The *lauro* here represents the lady, whose shadow the lover will follow all the days of his life, just as the lover in Dante's sestina, from which Petrarch's is derived, spends all of his time searching "dove suoi panni fanno ombra."[5] Because Petrarch's *lauro* is literally a tree, however, that symbolic search is a turning around in a circle, following the shadow cast by the tree through the hours of the day and the seasons of the year. The exterior quest has become an internal obsession; the image of the beloved (*idolo*) is quite literally an idol: "l'idolo mio scolpito in vivo lauro."

In his brilliant article on this sestina, Robert Durling has produced further evidence of the idolatrous quality of its content.[6] It is, he reminds us, an anniversary poem celebrating the poet's meeting with Laura. Since this occurred on Good Friday, a private liturgy of love is here substituted for the liturgy of the cross. Moreover, the laurel, with its branches of diamond, has become an idolatrous cross of glory. In other words, the most significant of Christianity's *signs* has become virtually a proper name. The pun, underscoring the opacity of the sign (*Laura/lauro*), makes any mediation impossible.

There is a further point to be made about this sestina, concerning its last lines:

> L'auro e i topacii al sol sopra la neve
> vincon le bionde chiome presso agli occhi
> che menan gli anni miei sì tosto a riva.

The comparison of Laura's face to gold and topaz on the snow, sparkling in the sun, is not only reified and coldly beautiful, it is radically fragmentary in a way that scarcely seems accidental. One of the consequences of treating a signifier as an absolute is that its integrity cannot be maintained. Without a principle of intelligibility, a collection of signs threatens to break down into its component parts. To put the matter in medieval terms, we may say that the Spirit is the "form" of the letter in the same way that the soul is the form of the body. In the absence of such a principle of anteriority, signs lose their connection to each other. So it is with Laura. Her virtues and her beauties are scattered like the objects of fetish worship: her eyes and hair are like gold and topaz on the snow, while the outline of her face is lost; her fingers are like ivory and roses or oriental pearls, her eyes are the pole stars, her arms are branches of diamond. Like the poetry that celebrates her, she gains immortality at the price of vitality and historicity. Each part of her has the significance of her entire person; it remains the task of the reader to string together her gemlike qualities into an idealized unity.

The same may be said of the unity of the *Canzoniere*. In order to remove from the poems all traces of temporality and contingency, poetic instants are strung together like pearls on an invisible strand. The lyrics themselves counterfeit a *durée* by their physical proximity and so create a symbolic time, free of the threat of closure. The arrangement of these *rime sparse*, whatever its rationale, may be thought of as an attempt to spatialize time and so to introduce a narrative element in a way that does not threaten to exceed the carefully delimited confines of the text. It is reminiscent to us of cinematographic art, a counterfeit of time wherein a series of images are spatially juxtaposed, awaiting a temporality that will give them life from the outside. Since Petrarch's day, the strategy has been used by innumerable authors of sonnet-sequences, so that it remains one of the most familiar devices of literary self-portraiture.

I have spoken repeatedly of Petrarch's *attempt* to exclude referentiality from his text. His success, of course, was only relative. Not only is referentiality intrinsic to all language, but also there towered behind him the figure of Dante, to whom all love poetry, especially in Italian, would forever after be referred, if only by contrast. Beatrice is in many senses the opposite of Laura. She was a mediatrix, continually pointing beyond herself to God. Throughout most of the *Paradiso*, for example, the pilgrim looks to her eyes only obliquely so that he sees what lies beyond her. Laura's eyes, by contrast, are "homicidal mirrors" in which her narcissistic lover finds spiritual death. When we translate that theme into poetic terms, we conclude that the lady celebrated by Petrarch is a brilliant surface, a pure signifier whose momentary exteriority to the poet serves as an Archimedean point from which he can create himself.

One of the Dantesque themes that most clearly suggests Beatrice's epistemological function as a sign is the theme of her veil, used extensively in the last cantos of the *Purgatorio*. Her unveiling of her face is peculiarly apt to illustrate the parallelism of language and desire in the Augustinian tradition, for the motif is at once erotic and semiotic: her feminine beauty *revealed* within the context of an intellectual and doctrinal *re-velation*. In the canto of the Medusa (*Inf.* 9.63: "Sotto il velame de li versi strani"), Dante had already referred to the significance of his poem with the same figure: his verses were a *veil* to his meaning. It seems likely that in analogous passages, most notably that of the Siren (*Purg.* 19.63), we are meant to perceive this metalinguistic dimension of meaning. Even in our own day the figure is still used to describe the process of representation. C. S. Peirce, in the passage cited above, makes suggestive use of it: "The meaning of a representation can be nothing but a representation. In fact, it is nothing but the representation itself conceived as stripped of irrelevant clothing. But this clothing can never be completely stripped off; it is only changed for something more diaphanous. So there is an infinite regression here" (*CP*, 1.117). the Freudian (or neo-Freudian) implications do not concern us here; the point is that from St. Paul to Dante the veil covering a radiant face was used as a figure for the relationship of the sign to its referent.[7] In the light of this tradition, it can hardly be fortuitous that Laura's veil, though also a covering, was at times her only reality.

This is the significance, I believe, of what seems otherwise to be simply a charming madrigal (*Rime* 52):

> Non al suo amante piú Dïana piacque
> quando per tal ventura tutta ignuda
> la vide in mezzo de le gelide acque,
>
> ch'a me la pastorella alpestra et cruda
> posta a bagnar un leggiadretto velo
> ch'a l'aura il vago et biondo capel chiuda;
>
> tal che mi fece, or quand' egli arde 'l cielo,
> tutto tremar d'un amoroso gielo.

[Diana did not so please her lover when, by a similar stroke of fortune, he beheld her completely naked amid the icy waters, as did the cruel alpine shepherdess please me, seated to wash a pretty little veil that protects her [Laura's] lovely blonde hair from the breeze: she made me, now when the summer sky is burning, tremble all over with an amorous chill.]

Laura's name, hidden in the pun of the sixth line, is her only presence in these verses, just as her veil is her only presence in the charming anecdote. Her veil, bathed in the water like the naked goddess seen by Acteon, functions as a fetish, an erotic signifier of a referent whose absence the lover refuses to acknowledge. So poetically, the reified verbal sign, wrenched free of its semantic context (*l'aura*/*Laura*), must be read as an affirmation of poetic presence, the *word* (and by extension the poem) as its own sole and sufficient meaning. For all of its lightheartedness, the poem illustrates the fundamental strategy of the *Canzoniere:* the *thematics* of idolatry transformed into the *poetics* of presence.

I do not mean to imply that the sin of idolatry exhausts the thematics of the *Canzoniere*. Many of the later poems suggest that the love for Laura was ennobling, at least in a literary or humanistic sense. My point is simply that idolatry, however repugnant to an Augustinian moralist, is at the linguistic level the essence of poetic autonomy. Because language and desire are indistinguishable in a literary text, we may say that by accusing his persona of an idolatrous passion Petrarch was affirming his own autonomy as a poetic creator. To psychologize about "spiritual torment" in the *Canzoniere* is to live the illusion that Petrarch was perhaps the first to create.

Many more studies of this length would be required to illustrate the full implications of this affirmation for the history of love poetry. In germ, it suggests that all the fictions of courtly love have their semiotic justifications: the love must be idolatrous for its poetic expression to be autonomous; the idolatry cannot be unconflicted, any more than a sign can be completely nonreferential if it is to communicate anything at all. Spiritual struggle stands for the dialectic of literary creation, somewhere between opaque carnality and transparent transcendency. Finally, it might be suggested that the illicit or even adulterous nature of the passion has its counterpart in the "anxiety of influence": communication demands that our signs be appropriated; poetic creation often requires that they be stolen. Petrarch's prodigious originality is that he was entirely self-conscious about the principles of which his predecessors were only dimly aware. By transforming the Augustinian analysis of sin into a new aesthetic, he made self-alienation in life the mark of self-creation in literature and so established a literary tradition that has yet to be exhausted.

The *Canzoniere* ends with a prayer to the Virgin for forgiveness.

Laura, he says, was a Medusa who turned him into a man of stone. Nevertheless, I have shown that the deadend nature of that passion is a sign of the poetry's monumentality. In the same poem, he addresses the Virgin as the antitype of his beloved, affirming that the Queen of Heaven is the only true mediatrix: *vera beatrice*. At one level, of course, his refusal to capitalize that familiar word suggests that Dante too had his problems with idolatry and reification. At another level, however, it identifies his own beloved with that of his literary ancestor. On that ambiguous note, both the passion and the poem are concluded and Petrarchism is born.

Notes

1. *Collected Papers* (Cambridge, Mass.: Belknap Press of Harvard University Press, 1960), 1:117.
2. *In Psalmos* 119, 6, quoted by M. Pontet, *L'Exégèse de S. Augustin prédicateur* (Paris: Aubier, 1946), 117.
3. *Secretum I.* I have translated from E. Carrara's edition of *Prose*, ed. G. Martellotti et al. (Milan: Ricciardi, 1955), 41 ff.
4. For a different, although analogous, interpretation of "idolatry" which omits the erotic dimension of meaning, see Owen Barfield, *Saving the Appearances: A Study in Idolatry* (London: Faber & Faber, 1957). I am grateful to my friend Giuseppe Mazzotta for bringing this book to my attention.
5. Dante, *Rime*, ed. G. Contini (Turin: Einaudi, 1965), 159.
6. "Petrarch's 'Giovene donna sotto un verde lauro,' " *MLN* 86 (1971): 1–20.
7. Second Corinthians, 3, where the veil hides the face of Moses, that is, where the "letter" covers the "spirit." For the veil, see also D. W. Robertson, *A Preface to Chaucer* (Princeton: Princeton University Press, 1962), *sub voce.*

3. "PER SELVE E BOSCHERECCI LABIRINTI": DESIRE AND NARRATIVE STRUCTURE IN ARIOSTO'S *ORLANDO FURIOSO*

■

EUGENIO DONATO

Artes è quel che vo' vu' dite
maquillage o trucco.
—C.E. GADDA

Les Dieux sont morts:
mais ils sont morts de rire.
—G. DELEUZE

ARIOSTO at the beginning of the *Orlando Furioso* stages Angelica's escape from Paris. Angelica is the object of both Orlando's and Rinaldo's desire: they both pursue her, but since she does not reciprocate their feelings, at the first opportunity she gets on the back of a horse and heads straight for the woods. This first incident is quite characteristic of both a predominant leitmotif that will run throughout the development of the narrative and the privileged topography within which the latter will deploy itself. Practically every incident in the vast construct of the *Orlando Furioso* consists of a tale of characters pursuing, with more or less success, the usually elusive object of their desire. The nature of the object matters little; it can be a woman, a helmet, a sword, a horse, or simply glory and renown.

The privileged locus of this quest is a space most often represented by woods through which knights and ladies roam freely but which has its own topology, which determines encounters between them and also governs the devious paths they follow in their movements. This particular space is not simply to be confused with any particular geography to which it might apply, for the laws that govern the crossing of woods apply as well to journeys through deserts, seas, and skies.

A geographical space is euclidean; that is to say, given any two points in it an individual can move in a straight line from one to the other, whereas the "selva oscura" (2.68), the "scuri boschi" (43.91), and the "selve oscure" (1.22) are mapped by a "torta via de l'intricata selva" (19.5), a "strano sentiero" (20.104), or "calli obliqui" (1.22) forming a "labirinto . . . di stretti calli" (18.192) or "boscherecci labirinti" (13.42) that force the travelers into "strani viaggi" (1.33). This space may include or border on various other spaces such as cities, enchanted castles, and traditional pastoral settings, each governed by laws and defined by properties that are different from those of the "selve oscure": knights may leave the woods to inhabit them for a while but they invariably, sooner or later, plunge time and again into their natural habitat. The Ariostian wooded labyrinths do not constitute a frightful space from which characters have to flee, but on the contrary the "selve oscure" are places of predilection to which they have regularly to return.

To illustrate succinctly this need for the characters to err in the woods let us briefly examine Rinaldo's arrival in Scotland. Rinaldo is in search of Angelica and, believing her to be in Paris, returns there only to be assigned by the besieged Charlemagne the task of going over to England to fetch help. This is much against Rinaldo's wishes as he would have preferred to continue his pursuit of Angelica. Anxious to accomplish his mission as quickly as possible he travels to Calais and sets sail the same day. A storm blows him off course and he eventually sets foot two cantos later on the coast of Scotland. Incidentally let us note that the function of storms in Ariosto is to map upon the seas a typology similar to that which governs the woods; because of them nobody is ever sure of arriving at the destination he has originally set out for, or, if he does, what devious paths he may have to take or what distractions he may encounter on the way.[1] Actually Rinaldo need not have landed in Scotland except for the fact that on those shores there are some very special woods consecrated by a long tradition.

> Sopra la Scozia ultimamente sorse,
> dove la selva Calidonia appare,
> che spesso fra gli antiqui ombrosi cerri
> s'ode sonar di bellicosi ferri.
>
> Vanno per quella i cavallieri erranti,
> incliti in arme, di tutta Bretagna

> e de' prossimi luoghi e de' distanti,
> di Francia, di Norvegia e de Lamagna.
> Chi non ha gran valor, non vada inanti,
> che dove cerca onor, morte guadagna.
> Gran cose in essa già fece Tristano,
> Lancilotto, Galasso, Artù e Galvano,
>
> et altri cavallieri e de la nuova
> e de la vecchia Tavola famosi:
> restano ancor di più d'una lor pruova
> li monumenti e li trofei pomposi.
>   (4.51–53)

[At last he landed in Scotland, where the Caledonian Wood appears, amid whose shady oaks are often heard the sound of warlike sounds. Knights errant, famed in arms, traversed that Wood, from all of Britain and from near and distant regions, from France, from Norway, and Germany. Let the man who does not possess great valor proceed no further, for where he seeks honor, he will earn his death. Great deeds were once performed here by Tristan, Lancelot, Galahad, Arthur, and Gawain, and by other famous knights of the new and old Round Table: there still remain monuments and imposing trophies commemorating more than one of their exploits.]

Needless to say, Rinaldo, who "di vedere e d'udire ebbe / sempre aventure un desiderio innato" ["had an innate desire always to see and hear of adventures"] (42.72), can hardly resist the temptation of losing himself in such a famed wood and, forgetting his original quest for Angelica and his pressing mission, heads for it in search of adventure. "Senza scudiero e senza compagnia / va il cavallier per quella selva immensa, / facendo or una et or un'altra via, / dove più aver strane aventure pensa" ["Without squire and escort, the knight travels through that immense wood, taking now one and now another path, where he most thinks to find strange adventures"] (4.54).

Having come across a monastery, Rinaldo has his hopes confirmed by the abbot and the monks. "Risposongli ch'errando in quelli boschi, / trovar potria strane aventure e molte" ["They replied to him that, by wandering through those woods, he could find many strange adventures"] (4.56). They promptly send him off to save the daughter of the King of Scotland.

At one level the complexity of Ariosto's narrative is nothing more than the result of having to tell of the devious and endless journeys of his characters who move in such a labyrinthine space already filled with a well-established literary tradition. Ariosto's literary enterprise, by the avowed task it sets itself, will have to be as mediated by tradition as his characters' actions are since the latter are nothing but the quest for their desire's objects. A narrative that describes mediated desires will inevitably move in a literary space. If literature mediates between the characters and the objects of their desire the characters in turn mediate between the narrative and its own literary quest. The "selve oscure" are thus the ideal place where desire and literature meet and become conjoined in an inextricable way.[2]

But let us return to Angelica who is presented at the beginning of the *Orlando Furioso* as a desirable object par excellence, for we soon discover that she is not only desired by Orlando and Rinaldo but also by Ferraù and Sacripante. There is no doubt from the start that we are going to find ourselves in a classical situation of intersubjective relationships dominated by mediated desires. Angelica herself, by not reciprocating and by being distant and disdainful, "dura e fredda più d'una colonna / . . . non le par ch'alcun sia di lei degno" ["harder and colder than a column . . . she thought no one worthy of her hand"] (1.49), represents the elusive, idolized, impenetrable object constituted by the mediated desire itself—as a great deal of contemporary criticism has taught us to recognize.[3] But then the motif itself is given in such an obvious way so as to immediately underscore its inevitable consequences. The dominant theme focuses more on the necessary rivalry between the various knights than upon the merits that would make Angelica intrinsically desirable. The main consequence of Angelica's chase is to pit Rinaldo, Orlando, Ferraù, and Sacripante against each other.

Our knights at the beginning are presented to us as being identical to each other. The lack of difference between them is in fact often explicitly stated: "Tra Gradasso e Ruggier credo che sia / di valor nulla o poca differenza" ["I believe that there is little or no difference in valor between Gradasso and Ruggiero"] (30.22). Differences of faith matter little and they have small regard for the communal enterprise in which their respective kings are engaged; what makes them what they are is their solitary quest:

> Oh gran bontà de' cavallieri antiqui!
> Eran rivali, eran di fé diversi,
> e si sentian degli aspri colpi iniqui
> per tutta la persona anco dolersi;
> e pur per selve oscure e calli obliqui
> insieme van senza sospetto aversi.
> (1.22)

[Oh the great goodness of the knights of yore! They were rivals, they were of different faiths, and each still felt the pain of the other's bitter and cruel sword blows aching through all his body; and yet they rode together through dark woods and turning paths without mutual mistrust.]

The eventual possession of Angelica would be a way of establishing a difference between them, but the converse would also be true: by fighting each other they would establish a difference beyond their identity and the possession of the coveted object would ensue. The interminable sequence of battles and jousts only confirms the continuous necessity of forever establishing such differences.

Angelica, in fact, remains desirable only for as long as she remains unreachable, since as long as she remains unreachable she can sustain rivalries. If she had been possessed all interest in her would vanish—or rather it would have to be supplanted by interest in a new object capable of generating new rivalries.

> Come segue la lepre il cacciatore
> al freddo, al caldo, alla montagna, al lito,
> né più l'estima poi che presa vede;
> e sol dietro a chi fugge affretta il piede:
>
> così fan questi giovani, che tanto
> che vi mostrate lor dure e proterve,
> v'amano e riveriscono con quanto
> studio de'far chi fedelmente serve;
> ma non sì tosto si potran dar vanto
> de la vittoria, che di donne, serve
> vi dorrete esser fatte; e da voi tolto
> vedrete il falso amore, e altrove volto.
>   (10.7–8)

[As a hunter pursues a hare through cold and heat, on mountain and shore, and ceases to prize it once he sees it caught, and only hastens after what flees away: so, ladies, do these young men, who, so long as you show yourselves proud and hardhearted towards them, love and revere you with all the zeal that a faithful servant should muster; but, no sooner can they boast of conquest than you will have to turn from being their ladies to become their slaves; and you will see their false love taken away from you and directed elsewhere.]

Sacripante's famous comparison between a virgin and a rose reiterates the same theme, subordinating the value placed upon an object to its capacity to keep alive a desire whose real quest is the establishing of a difference from one's rivals:

La verginella è simile alla rosa.
. . . .
Ma non sì tosto dal materno stelo
rimossa viene, e dal suo ceppo verde,
che quanto avea dagli uomini e dal cielo
favor, grazia e bellezza, tutto perde.
La vergine che 'l fior, di che più zelo
che de' begli occhi e de la vita aver de',
lascia altrui còrre, il pregio ch'avea inanti
perde nel cor di tutti gli altri amanti.
                        (1.42–43)

[A young virgin is like a rose. . . . But no sooner is it plucked from its maternal stem and from its green stalk than it loses all the favor, grace, and beauty it had received from men and heaven. The virgin who lets another gather her maidenly flower, for which she should care more zealously than for her fair eyes and for her own life, loses the worth that she hitherto has held in the hearts of all her other lovers.]

The logic of desire that governs Ariosto's *Orlando Furioso* is such that there cannot be a successful resolution of amorous relationships. The moment Angelica marries Medoro she becomes irrelevant to the poem and disappears, leaving behind her the mere tale of her loves, which is recuperated in the poem as literature, as a narrative that tells of the hopelessness of Orlando's quest and exasperates his desire to the point of driving him to madness. It is also significant that the happy resolution of the other major amorous relationship, namely that between Ruggiero and Bradamante, coincides with the end of the poem.

Desire is quite independent from the objects it seeks and is in no way determined by the value or desirability of the latter. In this respect no discussion of the problem of desire would be complete without at least a mention of the Fiordispina incident, in which the systematic inversion of the sexual roles shows how amorous relationships are subordinated to a problem of desire rather than the latter being an immediate consequence of a natural attraction. It could be argued of course that the presence of such androgynous figures as Marfisa (compared by Ariosto to Penthesilea) and Bradamante is enough to show that the characters' quests are independent from the particular sex of either the desired subject or object. The Fiordispina incident reasserts this proposition by carrying it to its extreme logical conclusion. Ruggiero saves a young knight who looks exactly like the Bradamante he loves. The young man turns out to be Ricciardetto, her twin brother, who tells Ruggiero how he landed in the quandary in which he found him.

One day Fiordispina, while hunting in the woods, comes across a pastoral setting where she finds Bradamante asleep and falls in love with her at first sight. The eventual discovery of Bradamante's sex can in no way diminish or dissolve her desire but, by taking away the possibility of its fixing itself on an object, renders it on the contrary infinite. "D'ogn'altro amore, o scelerato o santo, / il desiato fin sperar potrei; / saprei partir la rosa da le spine: / solo il mio desiderio è senza fine!" ["I could hope to achieve the desired end of any other love, whether criminal or holy; I would know how to part the rose from the thorns: only this desire of mine is without end!"] (25.34).

Fiordispina, in her lament about her homosexual desire, goes on to state how desire, far from being the result of natural attraction, often creates bonds that are unnatural and monstrous.

> In terra, in aria, in mar, sola son io
> che patisco da te [Amor] sì duro scempio;
> e questo hai fatto acciò che l'error mio
> sia ne l'imperio tuo l'ultimo esempio.
> La moglie del re Nino ebbe disio,
> il figlio amando, scelerato et empio,
> e Mirra il padre, e la Cretense il toro:
> ma gli è più folle il mio, ch'alcun dei loro.
>
> La femina nel maschio fe' disegno,
> speronne il fine, et ebbelo, come odo:
> Pasife ne la vacca entrò del legno,
> altre per altri mezzi e vario modo.
> (25.36–37)

[On earth, in the air, in the sea, I alone suffer this bitter fortune from you, Love; and you have done this so that my error may be the utmost example of the extent of your empire. The wife of King Ninus possessed a wicked and impious desire, loving her son, and Myrhha loved her father, and the Cretan Pasiphae a bull: but my desire is madder than any of theirs. The female made designs on male, hoped for a consummation, and achieved it, so I hear tell: Pasiphae entered into the wooden cow, others found a way by other means and various guises.]

Fiordispina will, of course, eventually find a way of obtaining satisfaction through Ricciardetto, who in appearance is identical to Bradamante but who can, because of his sex, be an adequate object for Fiordispina's desires. But even this is not to happen until Ricciardetto appears first before her as a transvestite to look like his sister.

In summary it is sexuality that is subordinated to desire and not desire that is subordinated to sexuality.

Since the object is thus subordinated to the desire that seeks it, there is no necessity for it to be a woman and, as we said before, a horse, sword, helmet, or insignia can be valorized and rendered desirable as long as more than one knight wishes its possession.

Gradasso's presence in France, for example, is only determined by his desire to have Orlando's sword and Rinaldo's horse:

> Avea quel re gran tempo desiato
> (credo ch'altrove voi l'abbiate letto)
> d'aver la buona Durindana a lato,
> e cavalcar quel corridor perfetto.
> E già con più di centomila armato
> era venuto in Francia a questo effetto;
> e con Rinaldo già sfidato s'era
> per quel cavallo alla battaglia fiera.
> (31.91)

[That King had for a long time desired (I believe that you've read about it elsewhere) to have the good sword Durendal by his side, and to ride that perfect steed. And already he had come once to France with an army of one hundred thousand to achieve these objectives; and he had already once challenged Rinaldo to a fierce duel for that horse.]

Almost anything then can be an effective pretext to bring about a relationship of rivalry between any two knights. This rivalry is itself resolved only by the establishment of a difference generated between them through the unleashing of violence controlled in the form of a ritualized combat.

Through the whole poem there probably does not exist a better illustration of this mechanism than that particular moment when Rodomonte, Ruggiero, Mandricardo, Sacripante, Gradasso, and Marfisa are all pitted simultaneously against each other. Mandricardo had taken away Doralice who had originally been promised to Rodomonte, so it is through a woman that they are to differentiate themselves. The bone of contention between Rodomonte and Ruggiero is a horse, Rodomonte having taken away Frontino, Ruggiero's horse, when it was being sent to the latter by Bradamante; and, since both Ruggiero and Mandricardo have the white eagle as their emblem, it is a mere symbol that sets them against each other. Since the pattern of their rivalry is hence rendered completely circular, not only are we faced with a sequence of combats to differentiate them, but the very order of these becomes in turn a matter of contention.

Since the objects that generate quarrels matter little and for any practical purpose are interchangeable, every quarrel is identical to any other and there is absolutely no possible way of establishing an order within the quarrels themselves except through the drawing of lots—that is to say, by establishing from the very beginning purely arbitrary differences where there is nothing but identity.[4]

The drawing of lots produces an order. Rodomonte is to fight Mandricardo; should the latter survive he would have to fight Ruggiero, who in turn would have to fight Rodomonte; and in the eventuality of Rodomonte being eliminated Mandricardo would have to fight Marfisa. As if this inextricably complex situation were not enough, two more characters enter the arena. Sacripante also claims Frontino, whereas Gradasso claims Mandricardo's sword, and hence a new order of battle emerges: Mandricardo against Rodomonte for a woman, Ruggiero against Rodomonte for a horse, Sacripante against Rodomonte for a horse, Gradasso against Mandricardo for a sword, Ruggiero against Mandricardo for an emblem, and last, but perhaps most important of all, Mandricardo against Marfisa for nothing.

If the various objects that the characters desire are interchangeable, they are hardly necessary at the limit. It is enough that any two rivals simply, through the exercise of violence, establish a difference among themselves—if we were to use a more Hegelian vocabulary we would say establish the mastery of one over the other. Referring to Ruggiero's and Rodomonte's confrontation, Ariosto had already warned us that "'l lor litigio è un zero" (30.29); Marfisa's confrontation with Mandricardo is one of pure prestige simply to see who is the better knight of the two.

Marfisa from this standpoint is an extreme character in as much as she desires nothing except to prove herself. To her the task of establishing her superiority and hence her difference from other knights becomes an end in itself: "e 'l dì e la notte armata sempre andava / di qua di là cercando in monte e in piano / con cavallieri erranti riscontrarsi, / et immortale e gloriosa farsi" ["and she went about, always armed, day and night, seeking here and there, on mountains and in the plain, to encounter knights-errant in battle, and to make herself immortal and glorious"] (18.99).

Here we see how the incessant quest for adventure is nothing but a quest for recognition through the establishment of one's superiority—that is to say, one's difference from the others. In this Marfisa, of course, is not alone. We have already seen Rinaldo's desire for adventure. Ricciardetto, his and Bradamante's brother, says: "ben vo pel mondo anch'io la parte mia, / strane aventure o qua or là cercando" ["I go for my part through the world, seeking strange adventures here and there"] (25.22); and, in a way, a circle here is closed, since it is the knights' desire that sends them in the "selve oscure"—but then it is only by erring in the "selve oscure" that they can submit to their desire's unfulfillable ends.[5]

The unending enterprise of the knights-errant produces its own aristocratic ideology with its own values of glory, honor, renown, and immortality; but even more important, it sets them apart from the kings, on the one hand, and from the common people on the other—both of whom incidentally live in big cities and do not roam in the woods. Kings fight with armies for common causes and even though the "cavallieri privati" owe them nominal obedience, their solitary destiny belongs in a different space, in pursuit of a different goal. Incidentally, let us note that the few descriptions of army battle scenes are dominated by the heroics of individual knights and that the war between Charlemagne and Agramante does not end in a big confrontation between their two armies, but in the individual confrontations of six knights on a deserted island.

If the knights cannot be equated with their kingly lords, they can be even less so with the rest of humanity, which they—and the narrator—despise.

The "vil plebe," "vulgo sciocco e ignaro," is only capable of obedience. "Ma 'l populo facea come i più fanno, / ch'ubbidiscon più a quei che più in odio hanno" ["But the people acted as most do, obeying most those whom they most hate"] (37.104); and, since they are incapable of risking their lives, they are not worthy of living: "vulgo e populazzo voglio dire, / degno, prima che nasca, di morire" ["the commons and rabble I mean to say, worthy of dying before they are born"] (16.23). Humanity is gregarious, knights are solitary.

> Marfisa . . . pigliò alla ventura il suo viaggio,
> dicendo che lodevole non era
> ch'andasser tanti cavallieri insieme:
> che gli storni e i colombi vanno in schiera,
> i daini e i cervi e ogn'animal che teme;
> ma l'audace falcon, l'aquila altiera,
> che ne l'aiuto altrui non metton speme,
> orsi, tigri, leon, soli ne vanno;
> che di più forza alcun timor non hanno.
>   (20.102–103)

[Marfisa . . . took up her journey towards adventure, saying that it was not praiseworthy that so many knights should travel together: for starlings and doves go in groups, as well as deer and stags and all animals that fear: but the daring falcon and the proud eagle that do not put hope in the help of others, bears, tigers, lions all go alone; for they have no fear of any force greater than their own.]

This animal taxonomy is eloquent enough for us to dispense with any commentary.[6]

If cities inhabited by kings, feudal lords, and their ordinary subjects are at the edge of the "selve oscure," the latter borders also on a more threatening type of space, namely that of enchanted castles. Knights can always leave cities and pursue their personal goals no matter how inopportune their departures might be; but once they enter an enchanted castle there is little they can do to leave it, not because enchantment bars their physical exit, but because enchanters know that the best way to keep the knights prisoner is to offer them the illusion that they are possessing an object they desire, or else to offer them the constant illusion that they are finally about to possess that which they have long craved for. Under these conditions the prisoners will stay voluntarily, and the only way they can be rescued is by the intervention of somebody from the outside.

The two most famous enchanted castles are of course Alcina's and Atlante's second enchanted palace. The two palaces are very different from each other. Alcina's palace represents—if I may be allowed to use a contemporary concept—the fetishistic pole of desire. Ruggiero is fascinated by her, desires her, possesses her, and is quite satisfied with his situation. Alcina to her lovers represents the most desirable object possible in as much as she unifies in herself that which in the world is dispersed through a multiplicity of objects; as Astolfo puts it:

> Io mi godea le delicate membra:
> pareami aver qui tutto il ben raccolto
> che fra i mortali in più parti si smembra,
> a chi più et a chi meno e a nessun molto;
> né di Francia né d'altro mi rimembra.
> (6.47)

[I enjoyed her delicate limbs: it seemed to me that there was gathered together there all the well-being which is divided and distributed in many parts among mortals, to some more, to some less, and to no one very much; and I did not remember either France or anything else.]

Her lovers get the satisfaction of being differentiated from the others by Alcina's recognition.

Io da lei altretanto era o più amato:
Alcina più non si curava d'altri;
ella ogn'altro suo amante avea lasciato,
ch'inanzi a me ben ce ne fur degli altri.
Me consiglier, me avea dì e notte a lato,
e me fe' quel che commandava agli altri:
a me credeva, a me si riportava;
né notte o dì con altri mai parlava.

(6.48)

[I was loved by her as much or more: Alcina cared no longer for anyone else: she had left aside all her other lovers, for before me there had indeed been others. She had me as her counsellor, day and night by her side, and she made me the one to give orders to others: she trusted in me, she relied on me, and never spoke night and day with others.]

This is not however as important as the fact that Astolfo—or any of her other lovers—never gets tired of her and that she can indefinitely sustain their desire, which is completely absorbed by her. Again to quote Astolfo's words: "Stavomi sempre a contemplar quel volto: / ogni pensiero, ogni mio bel disegno / in lei finia, né passava oltre il segno" ["I remained always gazing on her features: my every thought, my every fair design ended in her and never passed beyond the sign"] (6.47).

Alcina is, of course, nothing but mere appearance, not the ultimate object of desire but only its simulacrum. It matters little, however, that "[quel che] di beltà Alcina avea, tutto era estrano / estrano avea, e non suo, dal pié alla treccia" ["that beauty which Alcina had was all extraneous: from head to foot it was extraneous and not hers"] (7.70). To possess an object is to possess its outward appearance, but the possession of appearances is quite sufficient as is demonstrated by both her lovers and the artist himself, whose craft deals only with the fascination of appearance. Everything she has from head to toe may be "estrano"; nevertheless this "otherness" is made of the same stuff as the painter's craft: "Di persona era tanto ben formata / quanto me' finger san pittori industri" ["Her body was formed as beautifully as industrious painters know how to feign proportions"] (7.11). The poet himself cannot resist being fascinated by her and giving a detailed and suggestive description of her outward appearances.[7]

The poet's fascination with Alcina is appropriate, since she and her court are in turn quite taken with literature. Ariosto's narrative may tell of the vicissitudes of human desire, but this same desire is the cause of the telling of more tales concerning desire.

> A quella mensa citare, arpe e lire,
> e diversi altri dilettevol suoni
> faceano intorno l'aria tintinire
> d'armonia dolce e di concenti buoni.
> Non vi mancava chi, cantando, dire
> d'amor sapesse gaudii e passioni,
> o con invenzioni e poesie
> rappresentasse grate fantasie.
> (7.19)

[At that banquet zithers, harps, and lyres, and various other delightful instruments made the surrounding air tinkle with sweet music and good harmonies. There was not lacking one who knew how to tell in song of the joys and passions of love, or, with inventions and poetry, to represent pleasant fantasies.]

Our lovers themselves read the tales of other knights and their loves.

> Non è diletto alcun che di fuor reste;
> che tutti son ne l'amorosa stanza.
> E due e tre volte il dì mutano veste,
> fatte or ad una ora ad un'altra usanza.
> Spesso in conviti, e sempre stanno in feste,
> in giostre, in lotte, in scene, in bagno, in danza:
> or presso ai fonti, all'ombre de' poggietti,
> leggon d' antiqui gli amorosi detti.
> (7.31)

[No single pleasure is left out, for all are present there in the amorous chamber. And two or three times a day they change garments, fit now for one, now for another occasion. They banquet frequently, and are always attending festivals, jousts, wrestling-bouts, plays, bathing, and dances: now near fountains, in the shade of the hillside, they read the amorous writings of the ancients.]

Literature then is not really that different from the desire it describes in as much as desire is the source that generates literature in the first place. Ariosto's narrative cannot tell us the truth about desire since it is inextricably entwined with it. The tale of Ruggiero and Alcina is part of the tale that Ruggiero and Alcina tell each other and the simulacrum of her beauty is not different from the poet's artifact, which is there to fix in narrative discourse the desire of the reader to whom it is addressed.

Atlante's enchanted castle has some traits in common with Alcina's. Knights are drawn into it following a mere image, and once in

it are incapable of leaving it of their own volition because of the state
of their desire.

> A tutti par, l'incantator mirando,
> mirar quel che per sé brama ciascuno,
> donna, scudier, compagno, amico, quando
> il desiderio uman non è tutto uno.
>
> (13.50)

[Everyone seems, on seeing the enchanter, to see the thing which he
most desires for himself: a lady, a squire, a companion, a friend, inasmuch as human desire is not uniform.]

But then, of hardly any character in the poem can it be said that his
or her desire is "tutto uno." What the evangelist will say to Astolfo
when he gets to the earthly paradise, "né la causa del camino / né il
fin del tuo desir da te sia inteso" ["you understand neither the cause
of your journey, nor the end of your desire"] (34.55), is true of
everybody. Hence Atlante's palace is less the product of an extravagant imagination than a possibility open to everybody.[8]

Orlando, pursuing what he takes to be Angelica, enters Atlante's
palace:

> E mentre or quinci or quindi invano il passo
> movea, pien di travaglio e di pensieri,
> Ferraù, Brandimarte e il re Gradasso,
> re Sacripante et altri cavallieri
> vi ritrovò, ch'andavano alto e basso,
> né men facean di lui vani sentieri;
> e si ramaricavan del malvagio
> invisibil signor di quel palagio.
>
> Tutti cercando il van, tutti gli dànno
> colpa di furto alcun che lor fatt'abbia:
> del destrier che gli ha tolto, altri è in affanno;
> ch'abbia perduta altri la donna, arrabbia;
> altri d'altro l'accusa: e così stanno,
> che non si san partir di quella gabbia;
> e vi son molti, a questo inganno presi,
> stati le settimane intiere e i mesi.
>
> (12.11–12)

> Una voce medesma, una persona
> che paruta era Angelica ad Orlando,
> parve a Ruggier la donna di Dordona,
> che lo tenea di sé medesmo in bando.

Se con Gradasso o con alcun ragiona
di quei ch'andavano nel palazzo errando,
a tutti par che quella cosa sia,
che più ciascun per sé brama e desia.

(12.20)

[And while he paced now hither, now thither, full of travail and wor-
ries, he ran across Ferraù, Brandimarte, King Gradasso, King Sacripante, and other knights who were going about high and low on paths
no less fruitless than his own; and they complained of the villainous,
invisible lord of that palace. All went in search of him, all blamed him
for some theft he had made from them: one is pained because of the
horse he has stolen from him, another is angered because he has lost
his lady, another accuses him of something else: and so they remain,
because they do not know how to escape from that cage; and many,
captured by this deception, have remained there entire weeks and
months.

The same single voice, the same body which had appeared to be Angelica to Orlando, seemed to Ruggiero to be the lady of Dordogne and
kept him beside himself. If he speaks with Gradasso or another of
those who were wandering about the palace, it seems to all of them to
be that thing which each most yearns for and desires for himself.]

We can see that the particular originality of this place is the incessant
circular movement to which the characters are submitted in pursuing in vain the image of that which they take to be the object of their
desire.

The Alcina and Atlante enchanted palace incidents represent two
opposite extremes within desire's problematic. Alcina represents
desire's fixation upon a singular object and its incapacity to detach
itself from it; essentially it is a moment of stasis. Atlante's palace, on
the other hand, represents the interminable quest for an ever-
elusive object.

Both extreme alternatives in fact lead to dead ends. Alcina's inevitably leads to the stillness of characters transformed into animals,
trees or stones, whereas Atlante's ends with the characters moving
endlessly in a perpetual circular motion. Needless to add, the ideal
lies between these two limits and is constituted by a desire that,
erring endlessly through its labyrinthine space, can at times displace
its objects and at other times temporize in its quest. Yet at all times
desire itself must recognize that the object is only a subsidiary in its
endless quest of itself as desire.

Orlando in a fortuitous way meets, as the law of the wooded
labyrinth would have it, Mandricardo: since the latter is after the

former's sword, an inevitable battle follows—interrupted, however, by the Saracen's horse, which unbridled canters back into the woods. Orlando, after having waited for three days in the vicinity, heads for Charlemagne's camp, but not before having looked for his opponent. Given that no path in the woods runs in a straight line,

> Lo strano corso che tenne il cavallo
> del Saracin pel bosco senza via,
> fece ch'Orlando andò duo giorni in fallo,
> né lo trovò, né poté averne spia.
> Giunse ad un rivo che parea cristallo,
> ne le cui sponde un bel pratel fioria,
> di nativo color vago e dipinto,
> e di molti e belli arbori distinto.
>   (23.100)

[The strange route which the Saracen's horse made through the pathless wood caused Orlando to follow two days in vain; he neither found him, nor was able to get a trace of him. He reached a stream that looked like crystal, by whose banks a fair meadow was in flower, lovely and decked out in its natural colors and adorned by many lovely trees.]

In this pastoral setting we are confronted with a different type of space, one traditionally associated with the meeting of the object of one's desire. Ariosto, however, denies his heroes such a happy outcome; Orlando's stumbling across such a place will in fact lead to his madness. But before turning to that episode let us briefly try to characterize the properties of pastoral settings in the *Furioso*.

Angelica, after having crossed "selve spaventose e scure," after "strani viaggi," comes across "un boschetto adorno, / che lievemente la fresca aura muove. / Duo chiari rivi, mormorando intorno, / sempre l'erbe vi fan tenere e nuove" ["a fair little grove, through which a fresh breeze lightly moves. Two clear streams, murmuring about and around, produce forever new and tender grasses there"] (1.35). In fact this first staging of the traditional "locus amoenus" is extremely elaborate so as to leave no doubt in the reader's mind that we are in a different setting and not in just an extension of the woods. Sacripante joins Angelica and behaves according to the role that literary tradition demands:

> cominciò con suono afflitto e lasso
> a lamentarsi sì soavemente,
> ch'avrebbe di pietà spezzato un sasso,
> una tigre crudel fatta clemente.

Sospirando piangea, tal ch'un ruscello
parean le guancie, e 'l petto un Mongibello.
(1.40)

[he began with a grieving and woeful voice to lament so sweetly that he
would have caused a stone to split out of pity and made merciful a cruel
tiger. He wept sighing, so that his cheeks appeared to be a rivulet and
his chest an Etna.]

Of course, the object of Sacripante's desire is none other than Angelica. After such an elegant posture, Sacripante abandons the role
of a lamenting lover and decides to take advantage of his unexpected good fortune and attempt to possess Angelica, but the scene
is invaded by an unknown knight who comes from the woods,
defeats him, and then disappears into the woods again. Shortly
after, the scene is again invaded, this time by Rinaldo, whose arrival
only underscores the irony of the characters' coming time and time
again face to face with the object of their desire only to discover that
their feelings are not reciprocated and to be forced again to the
inevitable unending quest for the desired object. According to a
pattern that will often repeat itself, the knights fight while the object
they desire disappears in the woods, where they are obliged to
blindly pursue.

Among the many instances in which the traditional pastoral setting appears in the poem, I should like to mention just one more
example, which involves Angelica again and which in a way stands
half way between the preceding example and Orlando's accidental
stumbling across one that will lead to the episode of his madness.

Ruggiero, after leaving Logistilla, instead of searching for Bradamante indulges in another "viaggio strano," this one through the air
on the hippogryph, rather than through woods or over seas.

Ben che di Ruggier fosse ogni desire
di ritornare a Bradamante presto;
pur, gustato il piacer ch'avea di gire
cercando il mondo, non restò per questo,
ch'alli Pollacchi, agli Ungari venire
non volesse anco, alli Germani, e al resto
di quella boreale orrida terra;
e venne al fin ne l'ultima Inghilterra.
(10.72)

[Even though Ruggiero's every desire was to return quickly to Bradamante, this did not stop him, nonetheless, once he had tasted the

pleasure he received in exploring the world, from wishing also to visit
the Poles, the Hungarians, the Germans, and the remainder of that
dreadful northern region; and he came at last to furthermost England.]

As a result of this detour, he runs across Angelica, who is about to be
fed to the sea monster, saves her, takes her on his mount, and,
unable to resist her naked beauty, "si va volgendo, e mille baci /
figge nel petto e negli occhi vivaci" ["he turns backwards as he rides,
and plants a thousand kisses on her breast and her lively eyes"]
(10.112), forgetting his pledged faith to Bradamante.

> Di Bradamante più non gli soviene,
> che tanto aver solea fissa nel petto:
> e se gli ne sovien pur come prima,
> pazzo è se questa ancor non prezza e stima.
>
> (11.2)

[He no longer remembers Bradamante, whom he used to have so
greatly fixed in his heart: and if he does remember her as he formerly
used to do, he is crazy if he does not prize and esteem Angelica as
well.]

He tethers his mount in a traditional pastoral setting.

> Sul lito un bosco era di querce ombrose,
> dove ognor par che Filomena piagna,
> ch'in mezzo avea un pratel con una fonte,
> e quinci e quindi un solitario monte.
>
> (10.113)

[By the shore there was a woods of shady oaks where Philomel appears
still to be singing; in their middle was a meadow with a fountain and on
either side a solitary mountain.]

Ruggiero is attempting to make love to Angelica when she realizes
she has in her possession a ring that can make her invisible. She puts
it in her mouth and disappears from Ruggiero's sight, making her a
kind of counterpart to Alcina, since the latter is appearance without
reality, whereas in this incident Angelica is reality without appearance. As for Ruggiero,

> ogn'intorno riguardava,
> e s'aggirava a cerco come un matto;
>
> . . . intorno alla fontana

brancolando n'andava come cieco.
Oh, quante volte abbracciò l'aria vana,
sperando la donzella abbracciar seco!
(11.7–9)

[he looked all around and turned in a circle like a madman; . . . around
the fountain he went groping like a blind man. Oh how many times he
embraced the empty air, hoping to embrace the damsel with it.]

Ruggiero then, faced with this incorporeal presence, can only
stumble around like a madman, attempting to grasp the presence of
the object of his desire. The incident is of little consequence, since
Ruggiero's real quest is for Bradamante, and he is distracted from his
lascivious pursuit of Angelica by coming across what he takes to be
the real object of his desire, but which will turn out to be only
another elusive image. Ariosto's characters, then, in pastoral settings do come across what they desire—but only to have the object
of their quest disappear under their very eyes.

Let us now return to Orlando, who had accidentally stumbled
across another idyllic pastoral setting. As we may expect, he runs
into the presence of the object of his desire but with a twist; Angelica's presence (which is all pervasive) is given to him in the form
of a simulacrum. She is everywhere, but only in the form of graphic
signs. In fact, what Orlando encounters is Angelica transformed
into literature. The passage is complex enough to warrant a careful
reading. First Orlando recognizes Angelica's handwriting: "Volgen-
dosi ivi intorno, vide scritti / molti arbuscelli in su l'ombrosa
riva. / Tosto che fermi v'ebbe gli occhi e fitti, / fu certo esser di man
de la sua diva" ["Turning around there, he saw writing on many
bushes along the shady bank. As soon as he gazed firmly and fix-
edly upon them, he was certain that it was the handwriting of his
goddess"] (23.102).

This piece of writing at first exists as pure signifier—each letter
stands by itself: "Quante lettere son, tanti son chiodi / coi quali
Amore il cor gli punge e fiede" ["These letters are so many nails with
which Love pierces and wounds his heart"] (23.103). As a graphic
inscription, it refers to other graphic inscriptions it resembles. "Poi
dice [Orlando]—Conosco io pur queste note: / di tal'io n'ho tante
vedute e lette" ["Then Orlando says, 'I indeed know these words: I
have seen and read many such'"] (23.104).

Nevertheless, signs have to signify and point to the names of
Angelica and Medoro—but then proper names are themselves signifiers that only denote the code that uses them as signifiers.[9] Orlan-

do himself is aware of this, since for a moment he envisages the possibility that the code used might be different and the name Medoro might be applicable to him. "Finger questo Medoro ella si puote: / forse ch'a me questo cognome mette" ["She could be making up this Medoro: perhaps she puts in this name in place of mine"] (23.104). Eventually these signs, besides referring to themselves, come to narrate the loves of Medoro and Angelica—but even then the situation is fraught with ambiguity. When Orlando first comes across the inscription on the trees, Ariosto warns us that, "Questo era un di quei lochi già descritti, / ove sovente con Medoro veniva / da casa del pastore indi vicina / la bella donna del Catai regina" ["This was one of those places already described, where the lovely lady who was queen of Cathay often would come with Medoro from the nearby house of the shepherd"] (23.102). "Già descritti"— Orlando has in fact involuntarily entered into literature, and more specifically into the very narrative of the *Orlando Furioso*, from a character being transferred into a reader. The process is, in fact, repeated, since he has first to read the description of the loves of Angelica and Medoro and then to hear them narrated by the shepherd; both refer to stories that were told in the poem. If Orlando stumbled on the "già descritto," what he reads and hears is already in the "già detto": not only because the story had already been told, but also because the story itself does nothing but refer to literary commonplaces. The shepherd's narrative ends up being hardly anything more than a sequence of clichés:

> [Il pastor] incominciò senza rispetto a dire:
>
> > come esso a prieghi d'Angelica bella
> > portato avea Medoro alla sua villa,
> > ch'era ferito gravemente; e ch'ella
> > curò la piaga, e in pochi dì guarilla:
> > ma che nel cor d'una maggior di quella
> > lei ferì Amor; e di poca scintilla
> > l'accese tanto e sì cocente fuoco,
> > che n'ardea tutta, e non trovava loco.
> >   (23.118–119)

[The shepherd began heedlessly to tell how he, at the entreaties of the lovely Angelica, had brought Medoro, who was gravely wounded, to his house; and that she cured the wound and in a few days healed it: but Love struck her heart with a greater wound; and from a little spark He kindled in her so great and so hot a fire that she burned with it completely and found no peace.]

This dissolution of the narrative into the general discourse of literature can only have as a consequence the transformation of Orlando from the subject of the narrative to a stereotyped, traditional, lamenting lover worthy of the most extreme Neapolitan Petrarchist:

> giù dagli occhi rigando per le gote
> sparge un fiume di lacrime sul petto:
>
> Di sé si marviglia ch'abbia in testa
> una fontana d'acqua sì vivace,
> e come sospirar possa mai tanto;
> e spesso dice a sé così nel pianto:
>
> —Queste non son più lacrime, che fuore
> stillo dagli occhi con sì larga vena.
> Non suppliron le lacrime al dolore:
> finìr, ch'a mezzo era il dolore a pena.
> Dal fuoco spinto ora il vitale umore
> fugge per quella via ch'agli occhi mena;
> et è quel che si versa, e trarrà insieme
> e 'l dolore e la vita all'ore estreme.
>   (23.122,125,126)

[Down from his eyes streaming across his cheeks, he sheds a river of tears upon his breast:

He marvels at himself for having so gushing a fountain of water in his head, and at how he can ever sigh so greatly, and he often says to himself in his weeping: "These are no longer tears which I let drip from my eyes in such a broad stream. My tears were not equal to my grief: they ran out when that grief was barely half-assuaged. Now, impelled by the fire of love, my vital humor escapes by the path that leads through the eyes, and it is this humor which is being poured out and which will draw with it both my grief and my life in my last hours."]

What we have just witnessed is the same process that we came across in Alcina's palace, but now it is internalized within the narrative itself.

In the Alcina incident we had been shown the mutual dependency of desire and literature; in a more fundamental way, what we are witnessing here is the conjunction of literature and madness. We can now begin to appreciate perhaps Ariosto's systematic insistence on the similarity of his own position to Orlando's with regard to madness, and his insistence that his narrative itself has to be contaminated by it. Anything that can be said of the characters applies to the author as well, who is willing to take upon himself any ethical judgment that one might bestow upon his characters' errancies or upon his narrative enterprise.

> Che non può far d'un cor ch'abbia suggetto
> questo crudele e traditore Amore,
> poi ch'ad Orlando può levar del petto
> la tanta fé che debbe al suo signore?
> Già savio e pieno fu d'ogni rispetto,
> e de la santa Chiesa difensore:
> or per un vano amor, poco del zio,
> e di sé poco, e men cura di Dio.
>
> Ma l'escuso io pur troppo, e mi rallegro
> nel mio difetto aver compagno tale;
> ch'anch'io sono al mio ben languido et egro,
> sano e gagliardo a seguitare il male.
> (9.1–2)

[What cannot this cruel and treacherous Love do to a heart that it holds subject, if it could remove from Orlando's breast the great allegiance that he owed to his lord? Formerly he was wise and full of reverence, and a defender of the Holy Church: now, on account of a vain love, he cares little for his uncle, little for himself, still less for God. But I, alas, excuse him, and I rejoice to find such a companion in my own weakness, for I, too, am sick and fainthearted in pursuing my good, healthy and vigorous in pursuing my evil.]

There is a paradox here which we must face. Ariosto presents himself as the author of the *Orlando Furioso*. He is neither a "Scriba Dei," recounting a preexistent transcendental discourse, nor is he the impartial neutral third person distant narrator who professes to display a discourse of truth adequate to things. Nor does he present himself as having gone through but transcended the experience of desire. His is simply the stance of an ordinary narrator. In as much as one errs because of desire and madness, his own narrative is neither immune from them nor privileged with regard to them.

On the other hand, his narration, being a narrative and nothing more, does not point to anything except to itself as narrative, and in its deployment engulfs its own narrator and stages him like any other character.

At this point one might object that the staging of the narrator within the poem is essentially different from that of the characters since the latter come to the *Orlando Furioso* from a long literary tradition and are projected at the end of the poem into a possible further literary existence, whereas the narrator's self exists within the poem in the form of a *Romanzo dell'Io;* that is to say, his journey within the poem comes to an end. Such a reading entails, of course, several consequences. The poem acquires a linear unity that becomes quite different from the isomorphism we suggested with the general pattern of errancy that is a consequence of desire. This in turn will mark the distance from the staged narrative self to the "true" narrative voice, which speaks from outside the poem and therefore can embed in the latter a transcendental truth that might escape all the characters, including the narrative *I.* In fact, such a reading bends the *Orlando Furioso* to fit it within the morphology of a different type of discourse. Let us first remark that the harbor of the last canto, which is supposed to mark the end of the narrator's journey, is not significant per se, or rather within the *Orlando Furioso* there are many harbors, but none of them are points of arrival or points of rest, but simply incidental locations within the more global geography in which the characters move.[10] Furthermore, to wish to see in Ariosto's description of the end of his narrative journey the type of ending that exists within the novelistic tradition that stages the narrative self as essentially different from the other characters in the work—be it in Augustine, Dante or Proust—is a misreading of this very same tradition. The real point of arrival within the novelistic tradition is constituted by the projecting of the narrative *I* outside of literary discourse—as, for example, the endings of both the *Divina Commedia* and the *Recherche du Temps Perdu* emphatically illustrate—rather than embedding the narrative *I* within it. As a matter of fact, when the narrator stages himself in the poem and encloses its generative mechanism completely within the poem, the poem can go on forever—as the *Cinque Canti* will demonstrate.

It is, of course, evident that a narrative discourse can achieve this without ever necessarily stating it, that is to say without stating within itself its own genesis. Nevertheless, when in incidents such as those involving Alcina's palace and Orlando's madness, literature states itself as literature, when the narrative systematically deploys as its characters both the author and reader—as when in the *One Thousand and One Nights* Scheherezade tells the story of the *One Thousand and One Nights* in which there will be a character named Scheherezade *ad infinitum*—we have to accept the fact that we are in front of a pure narrative and face the consequences.

Before turning our attention to the narrative itself, let us make one last remark about Orlando and his madness. It is important to underscore the fact that Orlando's madness differs from desire only in degree and not in nature or in essence and, in the same way that desire was a general condition from which there was no possibility of remission, madness is also general. Orlando and the narrator are no different from the other characters: they are first among equals; their madness may differ quantitatively, but not qualitatively, from that of others. In fact Rinaldo is as mad as Orlando:

> Io ti dico d'Orlando e di Rinaldo;
> che l'uno al tutto furioso e folle,
> al sereno, alla pioggia, al freddo, al caldo,
> nudo va discorrendo il piano e 'l colle:
> l'altro, con senno non troppo piú saldo,
> d'appresso al gran bisogno ti si tolle;
> che non trovando Angelica in Parigi,
> si parte, e va cercandone vestigi.
>
> (27.8)

[I tell you, Charlemagne, of Orlando and Rinaldo, for the first, totally raving and mad, goes naked traversing plains and hills, under clear skies and rain, in cold and heat: the other, his wits not too much more sound, leaves you at your moment of great need; for not finding Angelica in Paris, he departs, and goes searching her tracks.]

Astolfo, having reached the moon, discovers how, without knowing it, he himself has lost his own intellect with the rest of humanity, and when the list is drawn of objects in which man has alienated his intellect, literature will of course be present.[11]

> Altri in amar lo perde, altri in onori,
> altri in cercar, scorrendo il mar, richezze;
> altri ne le speranze de' signori,
> altri dietro alle magiche sciocchezze;
> altri in gemme, altri in opre di pittori,
> et altri in altro che più d'altro aprezze.
> Di sofisti e d'astrologhi raccolto,
> e di poeti ancor ve n'era molto.
>
> (34.85)

[Some lose their sanity in love, some in honors, some crossing the sea in search of riches; some in lodging hopes of reward in their lords, some in magical foolishness; some in gems, some in works of painters, and some in other things that they prize above all else. There were the lost wits of sophists and of astrologers gathered there, and of many poets too.]

To the demand of a literature that requires of its author and readers "intelletti sani," Ariosto proposes a literature that responds with a laughing silence.

It has been argued, in particular by René Girard, that the very essence of our novelistic tradition is constituted by a discourse upon desire, and in our analysis we have often used Girard's categories. The fundamental form of the novel would be determined by the plight of a character who, victim of the illusions of a mediated desire, comes to recognize the nature of his illusory quest, realizing that his desire for what he had believed to be an object is in fact conditioned by an idolized mediator. Such a scheme implies a linear development in the form of the novel itself, which has to take into account both the journey of the character through the domain of desire and at the end his distancing himself from it to establish the epistemological privilege of the subject's claim to hold a discourse that is not the discourse of desire but a discourse about desire and about the truth of desire. Dante, Cervantes, and Proust confirm in an exemplary fashion the Girardian thesis.

Side by side with the particular narrative structures that deal with the truth of desire one must also envisage the requirement that our Western culture has imposed upon language—namely, that language should be the language of Truth, that is to say that it should be adequate to the world of things. Derrida's critical enterprise has shown us how such a requirement eventually comes to engender the theological concept of the book.[12] The book superimposes upon the infinite proliferation of language the formal necessity of an origin, an end, and a linear development in an attempt to represent by identification a reality outside of itself and to adequate it to the intentions of consciousness that stand outside language. When we look back at certain texts such as the *Divine Comedy* or the *Recherche du Temps Perdu*, we realize how the quest for a true discourse about desire and the quest for the book are in fact two inseparable problematics.

Ariosto's narrative does not fit into the canonic forms of a literature that claims the possibility of disclosing the truth of desire. Nor does it in any way fit Derrida's concept of the book or its concomitant type of discourse.

Let us first parenthetically remark that in every instance where a book is mentioned in the *Orlando Furioso*, it is either in a theological context or in the domain of negative theology of which necromancy partakes. We do not have in the *Orlando Furioso* the Bible and the Koran as books, but if we were to make a list of all the other ones we would have to include the book of the hermit who practices necromancy, the book that Melissa uses to conjure up the spirits that will show Bradamante her future, Atlante's book inherited by Astolfo, the book that Malagigi uses for his magical practices, and finally the book that Merlin uses for his magical constructions.[13] Not once to the best of my knowledge in Ariosto's vast narrative is the book as book associated with literature in general or his own enterprise in particular. This is hardly surprising, for if we now are to turn to the book as a concept we should readily see that Orlando's narrative denies every one of these principles, not simply by questioning their validity, but by constructing a mode of discourse that dissolves them and makes them irrelevant.

Ariosto's narrative is infinitely deployable. It contains neither its origin nor its end, but by referring within itself to the previous narratives of which it is a sequel and to the future of the characters it has invented, the poem makes its discourse infinitely expandable. Ariosto's infinitely expandable discourse is not linear, not because of the purely formal complexity it displays, but because it is a self-referential narration. It is a narrative that narrates itself being narrated. As a narrative it does not point towards an outside world, pretending to describe it or represent it.

The referential aspect of Ariosto's narrative is simply the indefinite realm of other narratives. Finally, Ariosto's narrative discounts any outside consciousness—be it that of an author or that of a reader—which might behold its "Truth," inasmuch as the narrative stages them both in the same domain as that of its imaginary characters and at times raises these pure literary artifacts to a status that should have been that of the consciousness that should have controlled its deployment.

If I may be allowed the formula, Ariosto's literary enterprise is to narrative what Mallarmé's is to poetical discourse.

Borges, in his *Manual de Zoologia Fantástica*, recalls the strange genealogy of Ariosto's hippogryph, which is "Non finzion d'incanto, come il resto, / ma vero e natural. . . ." (4. 19). Born in the fantastic imagination of Virgil from the crossing of a horse with a griffon, it had come to signify in the proverbial expression "jungentur jam grypes equi" the impossible. Ariosto adopts this creature whose literary reality denotes an ontological void, gives it a name, reinstates its pedigree, gives it a natural habitat, and keeps it with us till the end of the narrative to then let it vanish into the nether regions from whence it came. I suggest that this animal, which Borges calls a second degree monster of imagination, might be a fitting emblem for Ariosto's narrative enterprise.[14]

Notes

1. This similarity at times extends to the vocabulary Ariosto uses to describe the movements of characters through a storm. One example among many is this: "Tre dì e tre notti andammo errando ne le / minacciose onde per camino obliquo. / Uscimo al fin nel lito stanchi e molli, / tra freschi rivi, ombrosi e verdi colli" (17.27). (First number = canto; second = stanza)
2. One might be tempted at this point to develop the argument historically and attempt a reading of the equation desire = irrationality = woods in a neoplatonic textual tradition that begins with Chalcidius's commentary on the *Timaeus* and culminates in Landino's commentary on Dante's *Selva Oscura*. On this subject see Eugenio Garin, *Studi sul Platonismo Medievale* (Florence, 1958), in particular pages 58–62. The problem with such a reading would be with its inability to define properly the relationship of Ariosto's text to those of his predecessors, since most critical traditions using such readings have had to rely either upon an individual-centered theory of influence or a more general and vague "history of ideas." In our particular case both attitudes would lead to unnecessary hypothetical oversimplification. The real problem is not to locate Ariosto within a literary tradition that might go through Florentine neoplatonism nor to locate his narrative within a more diffuse intellectual context (as some recent readings of the *Orlando Furioso* have attempted to do) but to see within a theory of intertextuality yet to be elaborated how Ariosto's poem is explicitly an ironic *comment* on the very tradition that has identified the woods with irrationality and hence with misguided desire.
3. Especially the works of René Girard. See in particular *Mensonge Romantique et Vérité Romanesque* (Paris, 1964) and "De l'expérience romanesque au mythe oedipien," *Critique* 222 (November 1965).
4. The drawing of lots to establish original differences when there are none is all the more important since it sets *Fortuna* as the ultimate source from which differences, that is values, derive. It is impossible to assign to Ariosto's narrative a nonliterary (a nontextual) origin, absolute principle, or transcendental signification that orders its deployment. When divine providence is invoked, it is more often than not identified with *Fortuna*— see for example 30. 22—and the latter becomes an aleatory principle that excludes the existence of any one rational *order*.
5. This theme of an unsatisfiable quest for adventure to establish one's superior difference is of course quite common to a whole literary tradition; yet the way Chretien de Troyes stated it in his *Yvain* (vv. 358–63) is so exemplary as to warrant its quoting:

> —Je [Calogrenant], sui, ce voiz, uns chevaliers,
> Qui quiez ce, que trouver ne puis;
> Assez ai quis et rien ne truis
> —Et que vouldroies tu trouver?
> —Avantures por esprover
> Ma proesce et mon hardemant.

6. It is very difficult to understand, in view of Ariosto's utter contempt for
   everything that is not aristocratic, the theme so common in Ariosto criticism of his "humanism," and how some critics have presented his ideal
   as being nonaristocratic. I suspect that even the most cursory sociological
   analysis would reveal Ariosto upholding the conservative ideology of an
   aristocracy threatened by a rising bourgeoisie on the one hand and by the
   establishment of unified monarchic states on the other. As a matter of
   fact, for Ariosto the nonaristocratic is associated with money, "Questo
   vulgo . . . altro non riverisce che richezza" (44.50–51), and money in turn
   is seen—as, for example, in the story of Argia and Ansel in canto 43—as
   an irresistible agent of corruption.

7. See 7.11–15. The narrator's commitment to the world of appearances with
   regard to the world of Alcina is humorously stated in his refusal to question whether the walls of her city are made of gold or not:

> Lontan si vide una muraglia lunga
> che gira intorno, e gran paese serra;
> e par che la sua altezza al ciel s'aggiunga,
> e d'oro sia da l'alta cima a terra.
> Alcun dal mio parer qui si dilunga,
> e dice ch'elle'è alchimia; e forse ch'erra,
> et anco forse meglio di me intende:
> a me par oro, poi che sì risplende.
>
> (6.59)

We must also not forget that Alcina has a "true" counterpart; but what it is
extremely important to underscore is the poet's absolute incapacity to
describe Logistilla and his reducing the description of her realm to a
minute fraction of Alcina's. It must also be added that outward appearances that might incur an ethical blame because of what they hide
cannot become the subject of an ethical judgment inasmuch as appearances are constituted by art itself.

> Oh quante sono incantatrici oh quanti
> incantator tra noi, che non si sanno!
> che con lor arti uomini e donne amanti
> di sé, cangiando i visi lor, fatto hanno.
> Non con spirti constretti tali incanti,
> né con osservazion di stelle fanno;
> ma con simulazion, menzogne e frodi
> legano i cor d'indissolubili nodi.
>
> Chi l'annello d'Angelica, o più tosto
> chi avesse quel de la ragion, potria
> veder a tutti il viso che nascosto
> da finzione e d'arte non saria.
> Tal ci par bello e buono che, deposto
> il liscio, brutto e rio forse parria.
>
> (8.1–2)

8. In this respect it is interesting to note the different way in which Ariosto talks of Atlante's first enchanted castle as opposed to the second. The first one was merely a place to which he took the knights by force and kept them prisoners by satisfying all their needs and wishes—in other words, the palace of Alcina without Alcina, which of course makes the palace of very little interest. In fact Ariosto hardly mentions the first palace, whereas the second one, inasmuch as it is fully integrated in desire's problematic, gets quite a lengthy and privileged treatment.

9. See, in particular, Roman Jakobson, "Shifters, Verbal Categories and the Russian Verb," in *Russian Language Project* (Department of Slavic Languages and Literatures, Harvard University, 1957).

10. In this respect—as for the woods—Ariosto's harbors must not be interpreted in terms of a literary tradition as terminal points of arrival, but must be seen within their own context as a negative commentary on a literary tradition that constitutes the unity of its discourse by granting itself a *telos*.

11. And the *Orlando Furioso* in particular, since among literary texts are singled out the "versi ch'in laude dei signor si fanno" (34.77).

12. See, in particular, his *De La Grammatologie* (Paris, 1965). In a lecture entitled "Le livre ouvert," Derrida elaborated on his concept. I should like to quote extensively from his lecture both because of the importance of the critical concepts involved and because they permit us to see implicitly how Ariosto's narrative discourse is of a different order and how in fact a great deal of the dilemma of Ariostian critics stems from not having perceived this difference.

Un livre est une sorte de micro-cosme, une totalité, comportant un commencement et une fin.

Cette totalité doit avoir un auteur qui soit au commencement du livre, et par conséquent d'une certain maniére comme initiative, l'initial exterieur du livre.

Que le livre nous reconduise toujours au nom de son auteur signifie que, passant par une langue naturelle, il implique toujours la possibilité de la voix, c'est-à-dire de la présence de l'auteur, la présence à soi représentée d'un auteur. Le livre est toujours, se donne toujours pour la manifestation d'une parole.

. . . l'idée du livre implique la présence et le privilège du *logos* en ce qui présentement le profère, la parole. Un livre est toujours censé représenter l'unité et la totalité d'un discours parlé qu'on aurait seulement transcrit.

C'est pourquoi il est linéaire.

On se représente la parole comme linéaire parce que, temporelle, elle semble passer de point de présence en point de présence, irréversiblement, allant de son commencement à sa fin selon un ordre lui-même irreversible.

Ce n'est pas un hasard si le concept et la valeur d'imitation, de *mimesis*, ont commandé, de façon déclarée, immediate ou détournée, la représentation que l'Occident depuis Platon et Aristote s'est faite de l'art et de la littérature. Représentation de la représentation: on s'est représenté l'art et la littérature comme représentation.

En tant que double, image, imitation, répétition, le livre ainsi a défini donc son origine, qui est aussi son modèle hors de lui. Ce modèle, c'est ou bien ce qu'on appelle la réalité elle-même, la chose même, ou bien la réalité telle qu'elle est pensée, perçue, vécue, etc. par un sujet qui écrit et décrit. Le modèle, c'est donc ou bien la réalité présente ou bien la représentation de la réalité, la réalité présente ou la réalité représentée.

13. See, in particular, 2.15; 3.21, 60; 4.25; 15.13, 14, 79; 22.17, 23; 26.128; 30.4; 35.81; 42.34.
14. To this day the most understanding reading of the *Orlando Furioso* is provided by Borges's poem "Ariosto y los Arabes," in *El Hacedor* (Buenos Aires, 1960), 89–91. To quote just a few lines:

> Nadie puede escribir un libro. Para
> Que un libro sea verdaderamente,
> Se requieren la aurora y el poniente,
> Siglos, armas y el mar que une y separa.
>
> Así lo pensó Ariosto . . .
>
> Como los ilusorios esplendores
> Que al Indostan deja entrever el opio,
> Pasan por el Furioso los amores
> En un desorden de calidoscopio.
>
> Ni el amor ignoró ni la ironia
> Y soñó asi, de podoroso modo,
> El singular castillo en el que todo
> Es (como en esta vida) una falsía.
>
> Escoria de los sueños, indistinto
> Limo que el Nilo de los sueños deja,
> Con ellos fue tejida la madeja
> De ese resplandeciente laberinto.
>
> Europa entera se perdió . . .

In many ways this chapter is as much a reading of Borges's poem as it is of the *Orlando Furioso*, but since it was Borges himself who initiated us to the intricacies of Pierre Menard's version of the *Don Quixote*, this is hardly surprising.

4. THE END OF DISCOURSE IN
MACHIAVELLI'S *PRINCE*

■

THOMAS M. GREENE

I

MACHIAVELLI was a writer preoccupied with the gravity of endings, oppressed even with the pathos of human terminations, but
he was capable of discriminating between what might be called their
degrees of decorum.

> Egli è cosa verissima come tutte le cose del mondo hanno il termine
> della vita loro; ma quelle vanno tutto il corso che è loro ordinato dal
> cielo, generalmente, che non disordinano il corpo loro, ma tengonlo in
> modo ordinato.

> [There is nothing more true than that all the things of this world have a
> limit to their existence; but those only run the entire course ordained
> for them by Heaven that do not allow their body to become disor-
> ganized, but keep it unchanged in the manner ordained.][1]

This sentence moves, not uncharacteristically, from a universal fa-
tality to a sense of human obligation to perpetuate things (most
notably, political regimes and institutions) through their natural or
prescribed career. Things that attain their destined end expire decorously as things that are botched by human misjudgment, are neglected or aborted irresponsibly, do not. Few things in fact do attain
that decorum for Machiavelli; part of the oppression of human affairs lies in the interruptions, the truncations of natural curves, in
the human impotence or malignity that produces amputated history. It is the unique achievement of the Roman republic, as analyzed
in the *Discourses on Livy,* to have sustained its own natural course for
so many centuries, but the more common pattern is the uneven,
jarring, indecorous rhythm of *The Prince, The History of Florence,* the

capitolo "Di Fortuna." In *The Prince* endings tend to be violent, disastrous, and simultaneous with fresh beginnings that are themselves shallowly founded and insecurely extended. The kind of harmonious change that dovetails each new structural addition (chapter 2) appears in the context of the entire work as a rare exception.

The treatise indeed would have no reason for being were this not the case. It assumes and addresses the indecorum of contemporaneous Italy. It *assumes* the political muddle like a weight to be carried and disposed of, and in so doing it abjures the false decorum of belles lettres. The dedicatory epistle repudiates rhetoric; the clipped opening chapter repudiates the graces of humanist elegance; from the beginning, the book refuses to be literature, that most refined corrupter of communal discipline (*History*, 5.1). *The Prince* signals its willed estrangement from the cultural processes it claims to analyze. It will not enjoy the ritual comforts of the products of high culture, including the factitious ending, the dialogue that fabricates consensus, the generous unrealities and bland conclusions of fiction that passes for description. It will remain outside all that, so that any closure it succeeds in attaining will be the hard-won closure of the intelligence embedded in that actual history that frustrates natural endings. "Unlike writing, life never finishes," wrote Robert Lowell. Machiavelli's authorial stance as his book opens seems to reject that *textual* conclusiveness and promise only whatever *analytic* conclusiveness can be wrung from the perennially continuous. This honesty of method is the honesty that would leave the *Discourses* essentially unfinished and the last sentence of the *History* opening onto the ruin that continued to engulf Italy endlessly.

But the reader who begins *The Prince* is not discouraged from presuming that a decorous analytic closure lies within its author's power. What the reader first encounters are the curt distinctions of a new, embracing political science. All states are either republics of principalities. Principalities are either hereditary or acquired. If acquired, they are either entirely new or grafted. We appear to enter upon a total system, a Thomism of statecraft which within its modest length will find a place for all possible political conditions and define their constituent elements from a position outside and above them. Yet the chapters that follow are devoted to successive individual cases, and the reader receives rather the opposite impression: he or she is down on the ground of history, watching the author clear away limited areas of general truth, moving not inward from universal principles but outward from concrete events. This is the first shadow cast upon the presumption of analytic closure. The author's goal is to clear away a conceptual space uncluttered by prejudice or ethics or loyalty or myth, a space where the pure intelligence can operate freely to discover the laws of political behavior and precepts for political success. But this enterprise has no basis in axiomatic first truths; it is rigorously, bravely inductive.

The faculty engaged in clearing this space is elsewhere termed *discorso* by Machiavelli ("Proemio" to *Discourses*, 1.73), a term that might be glossed as the power of rational analysis. It begins with concrete experience and history, such as the debacle of Louis XII's Italian wars discussed in chapter 3, and its actual power can be measured in the tightness of the correspondence between example and generalization. The generalizations in chapter 3, "Composite Principalities," are based upon the negative examples of Louis's failures, but the failures have prescriptive value: they can be used to produce rules for success. Louis can be said to have made five errors, which historical analysis can isolate from his experience and others'. In the future a ruler who wishes to graft a new member upon an established state, as Louis did, can be taught how to proceed effectively. This is a small clearing of conceptual order, since it involves only one particular situation among many hypothetical situations confronting a prince. But in theory this clearing can be duplicated in the analyses of all other situations. When this has been accomplished, then a legitimate analytic closure would be reached.

In chapter 3, little is said of individual *virtù*, because *virtù* is an explosive, improvisatory, antisystematic capacity for which the emergent political science has no need nor indeed any place. It appears in the brief opening chapter as a kind of enabling talent that would permit the apprentice ruler to attain a position where scientific precept would be useful to him. But *virtù* only begins to emerge as a significant force in a chapter devoted to legendary legislator-founders, and then later, more dangerously, in Cesare Borgia's sanguinary epic. *Virtù* in these earlier chapters is not contained by analysis, but it does not threaten seriously to blunt analytic reason, or *discorso*. It might be said merely to complicate that close correspondence between precept and event which is essential to the writer's method. Thus governments set up overnight "are destroyed in the first bad spell . . . unless those who have suddenly become princes are of such *virtù* that overnight they can learn how to preserve what fortune has suddenly tossed into their laps" (54) [. . . se già quelli tali . . . che sì de repente sono diventati principi, non sono di tanta virtù, che quello che la fortuna ha messo loro in grembo e' sappino subito prepararsi a conservarlo (19)]. Already in this passage exceptions have to be made for genius, and in the very negative, concessive formulation the text admits an energy that gathers power from its semidismissal. Contrary to custom, contrary to precept, a wayward dynamism enters the text, is created by the text that seems to dismiss it. But it does not here threaten the very logic of the argument.

The conceptual space cleared by intellectual power is however progressively perceived as hemmed in by all the immense body of history that resists generalization. Every law is vulnerable to the exceptions, the qualifications and inconsistencies of political experience, just as the intellectual power is vulnerable to any internal inconsistencies or faulty logic. Because there are no transcendental principles, because the analytic movement always works from the specific case outward, *The Prince* reluctantly reveals its radically *conative* dimension; it is obliged to strive against the complexities that hedge its clearings. Its language betrays the traces of an academic *disputatio*: "If you advance this objection, then I reply thus. . . ." "*Disputerò* come questi principati si possino governare" (7) ["I shall debate how these principalities can be governed" (33)]; the verb adumbrates an adversarial relationship. To extend the circumscribed area of truth requires a felt effort, a courage, a risk, as well as a violence upon convention and morality. Given the resistances, it becomes hard to believe that the extensions outward will come to control all the delimiting space. One suspects that something will always remain to be appropriated. Closure at best, it seems, will fence in a finite territory against the uncharted space always lying outside.

II

Machiavelli's effort to clear a conceptual space resembles the prince's effort to clear a politico-geographic space on which to impose his will and his order. The metaphor commonly applied to the prince's activity, the imposition of form on matter, can equally be applied to the writer's activity. The writer employs a conceptual violence, a sacrifice of myth, of ethics, of "literature," and this violence is vulnerable to conventional judgment as is the physical violence of the ideally ruthless ruler. The writer of *The Prince*, like his creature, has to wrestle with Fortune, who can jumble *post hoc* analysis as she frustrates *ante hoc* calculation. Each space, the conceptual and concrete political, is threatened by an inherent principle of disorder that must be allowed for and to a degree can be combated. Thus the hero of the book, the timeless hero with a hundred faces who battles and plots and kills to impose his discipline on a recalcitrant polity, is doubled by the thinker who in defining him has risked a murderous sacrifice of pieties in order to discipline the wayward details of history.

The common effort in which writer and statesman meet is termed "imitation." Imitation for Machiavelli as for many other Renaissance preceptors is an extension of reading, and in his specific extension writing and action come together. This duality is first suggested in chapter 6 of *The Prince*, and perhaps it is no accident that in this opening paragraph the word *virtù*, employed three times, makes its first important appearance in the treatise, as though through the pedagogy of imitation that antisystematic energy could be contained.

> Non si maravigli alcuno se nel parlare che io farò de' principati al tutto nuovi e di principe e di stato, io addurrò grandissimi esempli; perché . . . debbe uno uomo prudente entrare sempre per vie battute da uomini grandi, e quelli che sono stati eccellentissimi imitare, acciò che, se la sua virtù non vi arriva, almeno ne renda qualche odore; e fare come gli arcieri prudenti, a' quali, parendo el loco dove disegnano ferire troppo lontano, e conoscendo fino a quanto va la virtù del loro arco, pongono la mira assai più alta che il loco destinato, non per aggiugnere con la loro freccia a tanta altezza, ma per potere, con lo aiuto di sì alta mira, pervenire al disegno loro. (16–17)

> [No one should be surprised if, in discussing states where both the prince and the constitution are new, I shall give the loftiest examples. . . . So a prudent man should always follow in the footsteps of great men and imitate those who have been outstanding. If his own *virtù* fails to compare with theirs, at least it has an air of greatness about it. He should behave like those archers who, if they are skilful, when the target seems too distant, know the capabilities (*virtù*) of their bow and aim a good deal higher than the objective, not in order to shoot so high but so that by aiming high they can reach the target.] (49)

The writer implies that the prudent prince should imitate *him* in his own scrutiny of the most illustrious (ancient) examples; the writer and the prince are properly ranged side by side as they both put to use the book of the past. A later restatement of this theme will underscore the inseparability of reading and action.

> Quanto allo esercizio della mente, debbe il principe leggere le istorie, e in quelle considerare le azioni delli uomini eccelenti; vedere come si sono governati nelle guerre; esaminare le cagioni delle vittorie e perdite loro, per potere queste fuggire e quelle imitare. (39)

> [As for intellectual training, the prince should read history, studying

the actions of eminent men to see how they conducted themselves during war and to discover the reasons for their victories or their defeats, so that he can avoid the latter and imitate the former.] (89–90)

The prince in other words should do what in fact Machiavelli is doing in the composition of this treatise. In the prince's conduct we can judge his skill as reader, the skill that renders this particular treatise unique. The wise prince will join Machiavelli in rejecting history as mere belles lettres; he will scorn humanist reading for the creative, dynamic reading of history that acts upon the concrete present.

The fullest discussion of imitation appears in the Proemio to Book 1 of the *Discourses*. The neglect of the past by modern rulers, Machiavelli charges, is due to the lack of real knowledge of history (*vera cognizione delle storie*), which is read only for the pleasure afforded by its variety rather than for the purpose of active imitation, wrongly judged to be not only difficult but impossible. Machiavelli will study Livy so that his readers will be able to derive from it that utility in which true knowledge of history must be found. The author writes to perform (*operare*) things desirable for the common good, and the content of his labor will be those achievements filled with *virtù*, those "virtuosissime operazioni" wrought (*operate*) by ancient kingdoms and republics. The *Discourses* constitute an imitative *operazione* designed to inspire ulterior imitative *operazioni* on the part of the active "virtuous" reader-ruler. Thus this Proemio draws a distinction implicit in *The Prince* between the humanist/dilettante, the merely verbal imitator, and the true reader/knower/active imitator. The result of this distinction is to lump Machiavelli together with his ideal hero and his ideal reader, active imitators all.

This is the positive version of what Machiavelli is doing in writing as he does, but even in these optimistic formulations one discerns shadows of doubt. There is clearly doubt in the simile of the archer quoted above, who aims above his target in order to reach it. This tacit admission that the summits of ancient achievement will always prove superior to the modern reveals the intrinsic flaw in Machiavelli's imitative project. The affirmation of the unchanging character of man, made in the same Proemio in Book 1 of the *Discourses*, has to be balanced against the contrast between ancient *virtù* and modern vice, which, he writes elsewhere, is "clearer than the sun" (Proemio to Book 2). Machiavelli's historicism and his doctrine of imitation have to be accommodated to these antithetical perceptions, each often repeated but never fully reconciled. If the ruler/imitator is inherently corrupted, then his "reading" will be continuously vitiated and the thought of the writer/imitator wasted. The rejection of textual, fictive, mythical conclusions for analytic, prescriptive, operative conclusions may entail a final result in botched and vicious parodies.

This likelihood is increased since modern decadence confronts both thinker and ruler with the common challenge of *extension*. There is a risk, we learn from the *Asino d'oro* (*Golden Ass*), in the extension of power beyond the walls of the city state. The appetite for extending dominion is there represented as self-destructive, whereas German cities, content with no more than a band of 6 miles surrounding them, live in security.

> A la nostra città non fe' paura
> Arrigo già con tutta la sua possa,
> Quando i confini avea presso alle mura;
> E or ch'ella ha sua potenza promossa
> Intorno, e diventata è grande e vasta,
> Teme ogni cosa, non che gente grossa.

[Formerly Henry VII with all his might aroused no fear in our city, when her boundaries were near the walls, but now that she has extended her power round about and become large and vast, she fears everything, not only the strong.][2]

Florence's spatial expansion is a cause of insecurity although, as the *Discourses* suggest, a city like Rome might feel a compulsion to expand in order to preserve internal equilibrium. A still more serious challenge lies in temporal extension. Because Fortune operates in time, time itself is dangerous. A legislator may found a healthy state but his laws and institutions may be subverted before they have time to root themselves. If a state attempts to reform itself (Florence in 1502 under the Soderini republic), it may be crushed before it has time to conclude (Florence in 1512 after the return of the Medici). But if Fortune favors the state with victory and prosperity, these may lead in time to softness and corruption (*History*, 5.1). The paradigmatic story of Borgia is the story of a clever antagonist of time, who staves off ruin for a while through a protracted series of expedients. Even Cosimo de' Medici, the most successful single figure of the *History*, sees his public and private affairs "going to ruin" at the end of his life (7.6). Real duration in Machiavelli represents a (perhaps unknowing) concession to myth, since the true founders of enduring states—Moses, Theseus, Romulus, Cyrus—were all to some degree legendary. The modern archer cannot shoot so high; he must aim for narrower expansions, indecorous endings, briefer extensions, aborted reigns, precarious continuities.

This vulnerability of political extension affects the security of the thinker's conceptual extension. The potential collapse of a political order involves the viability of the cognitive order, since the cognitive discourse first presented itself as counsel for successful action. As the implicit distance widens between model and realistic goal, as the demeaning decline of culture stands revealed, then the double *operazioni* of imitation appear less and less plausible. The extension of the conceptual clearing assumes a fund of relevant nonmythical examples to be drawn upon to meet each problem of praxis. But this fund in *The Prince* proves to be shallow. The situation of Machiavelli as innovative thinker can be compared most readily with that prince who is a newcomer in a *principatus novus*. Of such a prince's task it can be said that "nothing is more difficult to arrange, more doubtful of success, and more dangerous to carry through" (51). To achieve something like decorous closure under these circumstances may require the surrender of hope for a single extended clearing; it may require one to settle for random patches of relative order, clusters of insight connected arbitrarily. The closing chapters of *The Prince* will be decisive in determining whether in fact it does adumbrate a calculus capable of scientific coherence.

III

This determination proves to be negative: analysis leading to precept is progressively abandoned in the last third of the book. Scientific pretensions are quietly withdrawn as the semblance of conclusive law fades from the text. In this progressive capitulation, a few stages can be roughly distinguished. Quite early one can trace a disturbing gap between example and precept: in the failures of the exemplary figures Cesare Borgia and Oliverotto da Fermo, in the blurred distinction between Borgia and Agathocles, in the success of Scipio whose leniency should in principle have proved fatal, in the success of French armies employing those mercenaries that are allegedly the root cause of Italian military disgrace. As the analysis proceeds one can follow the increasing effort of the precept to disengage itself from the entangling texts of recorded history and remembered history. *This* text begins with gestures ostensibly grounding precepts in past experience and then goes on essentially to unground them, to demonstrate in spite of itself the difficult struggle of the precept to stem directly from experience.

This struggle is rendered still more arduous by the progressive recalcitrance of the precept to remain simple, pure, clear-cut. The famous chapter 17 ("Cruelty and compassion; and whether it is better to be loved than feared, or the reverse") has been noticed chiefly for its ethical brutality, but for our purposes it can serve to exemplify the intensifying discursive qualification. Brutal this chapter may be, but the harshness emerges from an undergrowth of distinctions, reversals, exceptions, and modifications. The text is finding it increasingly necessary to complicate generalizations, turning back on its own discourse to raise objections or modify rules. One can work through chapter 17 noting the complications in purely lexical terms, in the frequency of expressions like "nevertheless," "but," "however," "on the other hand" (*nondimanco, pertanto, ma, pure, dall'una parte, dall'altra*). Not every usage involves a qualification of the argument, but taken together they underscore the difficulty of reaching firm guidelines in the shifting morass of human affairs. The conceptual clearing becomes more visibly overgrown.

In the chapters that follow, the ability to elicit unqualified rules from history will grow feebler. The long chapter 19 ("The need to avoid contempt and hatred") presents a new stage in the deterioration of analysis, a stage that substitutes contradiction for qualification and that in effect offers an alternative to precept. Two cases of contradiction can suffice. First instance: Machiavelli's lifelong support of the standing militia in preference to mercenary armies, support that is expressed elsewhere in *The Prince* (chapter 12), is subverted in chapter 19 by his analysis of the Roman army's destructive role in the empire and his congratulation of modern rulers on their freedom from this threat. Second instance: The confusing discussion of conspiracies argues that "there have been many conspiracies but few of them have achieved their end" (103) ["si vede molte essere state le coniure e poche avere avuto buon fine" (47–48)]. A survey of the factors that cause their failures and that should deter a potential conspirator leads to the surprising assertion that "it is unthinkable that anyone should be so rash as to conspire" (104) ["è impossible che alcuno sia sì temerario che coniuri" (48)], an assertion that denies the facts and denies what immediately precedes it. The contradiction remains if both generalizations are restricted to those regimes that have won popular support. This is the case of the one example offered: The Canneschi family conspired against and assassinated Annibale Bentivogli, prince of Bologna. But the Bolognese so loved the dynasty that they killed the Canneschi, then found a bastard scion of the Bentivogli and allowed him to rule until the rightful heir had time to come of age. Thus, writes Machiavelli, "when a prince has the goodwill of the people he should not worry about conspiracies" (105) ["uno principe debbe tenere delle coniure poco conto, quando el popolo gli sia benivolo" (48)]. This will not comfort Annibale, who perhaps should have worried about conspiracies somewhat more than he did. In his case men *were* rash enough to conspire and they succeeded in doing him in.

The alternative that in effect replaces the crumbling analytic precept in chapter 19 has maintained a vigorous presence through most of the treatise but is only now explicitly permitted to dominate the argument. This is the undefined, perhaps undefinable gift of *virtù*, whose mysterious significance in this book can only be grasped by triangulating contexts, and whose contexts themselves are richly, perversely various. What we learn from this chapter is that politics cannot be mastered as a science but must be intuited as an art beyond the reach of rules. Politics becomes an arena for flair, instinct, and genius, which no treatise can circumscribe and whose description can never be closed because it cannot, properly speaking, be begun. Why did the emperor Severus, a "new prince," keep his throne, when all the other emperors of his era who, like him, had recourse to undue cruelty were killed?

> In Severo fu tanta virtù che, mantenendosi e soldati amici, ancora che i populi fussino da lui gravati, possé sempre regnare felicemente; perché quelle sua virtù lo facevano nel conspetto de' soldati e de' populi sì mirabile che questi rimanevano *quodam modo* attoniti e stupidi, e quelli altri reverenti e satisfatti. (50)

> [Severus was a man of such *virtù* that, keeping the soldiers friendly, even though the people were oppressed by him, he reigned successfully to the end; this was because his *virtù* so impressed the soldiers and the people that the latter were continuously left astonished and stupefied and the former stayed respectful and content. (109)]

The narrative that follows fails to distinguish persuasively Severus's conduct from the others'; the basis of his success was simply his *virtù*, which the text cannot really concretize. The *virtù* remains an absolute, impervious to description or even to understanding.

> A Caracalla, Commodo e Massimino [fu] cosa perniziosa imitare Severo, per non avere auta tanta virtù che bastassi a seguitare le vestigie sua. (53)

> [It was fatal for Caracalla, Commodus, and Maximinus to imitate Severus, since they lacked the *virtù* to follow in his footsteps. (114)]

We seem on the brink of a tautology wherein *virtù* obtains success and success results from *virtù*. The close of this long chapter can add little to this semantic circle.

The following chapter 20 foregrounds a factor that will complete the subversion of a prescriptive political science—the factor of the unique set of circumstances, the unpredictable, asystematic *kairos*. Should the prince disarm his subjects, deliberately antagonize them, foster divisons among them, build fortresses?

> Di tutte queste cose non si possi dare determinata sentenzia se non si viene a' particulari di quelli stati dove si avessi a pigliare alcuna simile deliberazione. (54)

> [It is impossible to give a final verdict on any of these policies, unless one examines the particular circumstances of the states in which such decisions have had to be taken. (114)]

Despite this impossibility Machiavelli states his intention to discuss each question in general terms, but each discussion tends to appeal finally to "i particulari," "i tempi." The appeal implicitly calls into question the analysis and the counsel of the preceding chapters, since these have been presented as transcending concrete occasions and as generally valid. Here rather in the dominance of circumstances lies the vindication of that instinctive *virtù* that will seize upon the essentials of each concrete occasion and manipulate them with daring and imagination. Just as the writer ends his treatment of the fortresses by commending those who build them and those who do not, so his choice of able advisors is a choice beyond rules: "Good advice, whomever it comes from, depends on the shrewdness of the prince who seeks it, and not the shrewdness of the prince on good advice" (127) ["Li buoni consigli, da qualunque venghino, conviene naschino dalla prudenzia del principe, e non la prudenzia del principe da' buoni consigli" (61)]. The closing sentence of chapter 24, the last ostensibly analytic chapter, seems to offer the only version of closure the book is now capable of.

> Quelle difese solamente sono buone, sono certe, sono durabili, che dependano da te proprio e dalla virtù tua. (63)

> [The only sound, sure, and enduring methods of defence are those based on your own actions and *virtù*. (129)]

The activity of the prince is now fundamentally improvisatory. All courses of action are risky in the nature of things ["l'ordine delle cose"]. The prince as we last view him is profoundly lonely, extemporizing strategems and precautions to extend his hazardous rule, unable to count on his people, his allies, his advisers, or on ancient models of achievement. He must adapt himself ceaselessly, restlessly, to the caprice of changing circumstance, as the penultimate chapter 25 affirms, but to do this is to be extravagantly, inhumanly volatile.

> Se uno che si governa con respetti e pazienzia, e tempi e le cose girono in modo che il governo suo sia buono, e' viene felicitando; ma se li tempi e le cose si mutano, e' rovina, perché non muta modo di procedere. Né si truova uomo sí prudente che si sappi accomodare a questo. (64)
>
> [If a man behaves with patience and circumspection and the time and circumstances are such that this method is called for, he will prosper; but if time and circumstances change he will be ruined because he does not change his policy. Nor do we find any man shrewd enough to know how to adapt his policy in this way. (132)]

The lonely ruler, shifting his balance and his policy, remaking his own character as he remakes his style, listening for each whisper of change in the times, will nonetheless falter in the end from a tragic insufficiency of pliancy.

This failure of the prince betokens the failure of the analyst whose admission of circumstance has caused his conceptual space definitively to implode. Stage by stage, he has withdrawn from dogmatism to qualification to contradiction to a surrender before pure contingency. The text, unable to perpetuate its order, unable to validate imitation, acts out its own version of the prince's failure. The analyst has been unequal to the volatility of his own subject and if, in his penultimate chapter, he leaves open, or tries to, the struggle between Fortune and *virtù*, his own rational power seems defeated by Fortune. Counsel based on experience is impracticable; success lies in the harmonizing of conduct with occasion; and this book, by maintaining ostensibly its function as manual, has evidently denied itself any meaningful statement. The final conclusion, given this collapse of system, would appear to be necessarily confessional or duplicitous. The only real question, apparently, is how much failure to admit.

IV

The final chapter of *The Prince* ("Exhortation to liberate Italy from the barbarians") may have been written well after the others, as though the writer were dissatisfied with his original close. It radically alters the rhetorical mode from deliberation to apocalypse. A desperate urgency, heretofore barely discernible, produces calls for a redeemer like Moses, Cyrus, or Theseus, and the very prostrate condition of Italy, personified pathetically, becomes an argument for her future salvation. Stylistic restraint gives way to oratorical melodrama, and the scorn for myth gives way to the invocation of a savior. In this last chapter the repressed visionary in the author returns to life, the visionary of the *capitoli* and the *Asino d'oro*. The strained hope of the vision results in ironies beyond his control: irony in the evocation of "unheard of wonders" [*estraordinarii, sanza esemplo*], in the predicted defeat of the Swiss and Spanish infantry by newly trained Italians, in the identification of the Medici with the hypothetical redeemer, in the concluding quotation from Petrarch, 150 years old, predicting a speedy victory of native *virtù* over the barbarians. The desperate urgency of this chapter apparently derives from the ruinous military situation, but one wonders whether the deeper cause is not the deterioration of the writer's enterprise. If in fact he had established with calm logic the prescriptive science his book had seemed to promise, there would be no need for miracles and messiahs. This conclusion could not properly be called either confessional or duplicitous, but it does not seem free from a degree of self-deception.

To say this, however, is not seriously to deal with the problematic question of the book's closure, nor to determine ultimately what we are left with. One way to respond to these questions would be to point to the text's increasing dependence on a single signifier, *virtù*, which possesses at once too much and too little significance. The meanings of this word as derived from context "go round in an endless series of incompatibilities," according to one critic,[3] and from this circular plethora of meaning, stable meaning might plausibly be seen to leak away. Thus it might be argued that Machiavelli's book is progressively usurped by a signifier that is essentially vacant, pretending to denote a referent that cannot be shown to exist. Historical analysis and political analysis would stand revealed as dependent on a term that is radically blurred, so that the text as a whole could be said to reach an impasse or to move around endlessly in that vortex of incompatibilities. This account would postulate, then, a helpless closure of decentered or hollow statement, feebly circling around its weakness.

An alternative account would recognize in the messianic close an admission that the book had begun by misrepresenting its own character and that it truly belongs to that flow of cultural production it had initially wanted to repudiate. The close restores the book to cultural discourse, "literary" discourse, as against that ulterior, detached, purely analytic discourse it had seemed to claim for itself. The "Exhortation" reveals a mode of imitation that breaks down the segregation of rhetorician and activist, that accepts models from poetry as well as from praxis. The ruler/reader is no longer situated side by side with the writer, engaged in a common *operazione*, but rather opposite the writer, the object of his exhortation. In this view of *The Prince*, the presumption of scientific, systematic closure would be regarded as a distraction that the book gradually, then dramatically dispels. The text could thus be understood as acting out the discovery of its authentic goal, which is the goal of "literature" and all culture, namely the fabrication of a vulnerable construct. The prince Machiavelli fabricates, the conniver with a hundred faces, belongs to the realm of the mythical, which the text has never exorcised, and the prince's *virtù* retains that potent and volatile opacity that is the property of imaginative fictions.

The construct of *The Prince* is of course ungrounded like all cultural constructs. It achieves the shaky validity of an extemporized invention that is exposed, precarious, *bricolé*, conative. If the signifier *virtù* is vulnerable through its simultaneous superfluity and emptiness of meaning, then like other problematic signifiers it calls for the intervention of the reader to drain and fill it, to penetrate its opacity and grasp the emergent integrity of its "incompatibilities." If in the politico-geographic realm the fragmentation of Italy invites a redeemer, in the textual realm the fragmented meanings invite more plausibly the intrusion of the reader's synthesizing and flexible understanding. The invulnerable construct, if such a monster could be conceived, the construct lacking this text's polysemous density, would be condemned to sterility. *Virtù* as a signifier is incontestably imprecise, but it makes demonstrably a somber, obsessive aggression upon the mind that could not be propelled either by pure precision or pure vacancy. *Something* is there in the text, something not wholly unstable, that sort of thing we look to culture to provide. As a scientific concept, *virtù* blurs; as an otherwise unnamable, explosive, newly isolated property of experience, it can be received as seminal. Machiavelli's book does open up a clearing of space, not so much for analysis as for the historical imagination, a space of suggestive uncertainty surrounding a word, and this space becomes a constitutive element of the text, perhaps the most valuable element.

From this view of the book, *The Prince* reaches its close when, having discovered its own mystery and mythicality, it comes at last to admit and proclaim them. This mythical dimension does not cancel out the play of analytic intelligence which has governed earlier chapters. It does not discredit the effort to generalize political action and to read performatively all history as a text. But it does seal the analogy between writer and ruler more firmly, since the writer like his most prestigious models is a prophet, a *profeto*. His book can end decorously when he accepts the role of prophet, and if his crudest concluding prophecy invites irony, we can find in the body of his work a prophetic vision of bitter dignity, a composite image of brilliant, beleaguered fury that cannot effectively be deconstructed. He dismisses in a famous aphorism the role of unarmed prophet: "All armed prophets have conquered, and unarmed prophets have come to grief" (52) ["Tutti e profeti armati vinsono, e gli disarmati ruinorno" (18)]. This dismissal does not really affect his own role. As a prophet, Machiavelli is not totally disarmed: he is armed with that fury of *virtù*. Closure then is not a matter of completing a design; it fulfills no ideal proportions; it does not allow an intellectual order to expand to its outermost limits. Closure in this case constitutes rather a recognition that the text belongs in the sphere of other texts, the sphere of human society—improvisatory, groundless, metamorphic, fictive—the sphere of tragic conation where it finally places and joins its hero.

Notes

1. Quotations in Italian from *Il principe* and the *Discorsi* are taken from Niccolò Machiavelli, *Opere*, ed. Ezio Raimondi (Milan: Mursia, 1969). This passage from the *Discorsi* appears on page 253. Future page references to Raimondi will appear parenthetically after the quotation.
   Quotations in English from *The Prince* are taken from the translation by George Bull (New York: Penguin Classics, 1980). Quotations from the *Discourses* are taken from *The Prince and the Discourses*, intro. Max Lerner (New York: Modern Library, 1950). The passage quoted appears on page 397. The parenthetical page references will refer to these English editions. I have however taken the liberty throughout of substituting the Italian word *virtù* for its supposed English equivalent, since the argument of this essay depends upon the reader's recognition of this term.
2. *Tutte le opere di Niccolò Machiavelli*, ed. F. Flora and C. Cordié (Milan: Mondadori, 1950), 2:768–69. The translation is by the writer.
3. Sydney Anglo, *Machiavelli: A Dissection* (London: Gollancz, 1969), 236.

5. READING RABELAIS:
VARIATIONS ON THE ROCK
OF VIRTUE

■

TERENCE CAVE

THE PROBLEM of Rabelais continues to be a problem: that is of
course its interest, although one may wonder whether this is the
moment for giving it a new twist. It is also a problem for literary
criticism in general, since the focal issue is whether the fictions of
Rabelais can be made to yield a coherent, univocal meaning. Perhaps this *is* a good enough moment insofar as there are signs that
the deadlock has eased slightly. The historical, "positivist" commentators of whom Michael Screech is the doyen now acknowledge
that the nature and function of language form a central thematic
thread in the *Chroniques,* and that the linguistic theory Rabelais
draws on embodies such notions as the conventional nature of the
linguistic sign and the fundamental ambivalence of human uses of
language. On the other hand, *nouveaux critiques* who used to scorn
the pedantry of those who patiently attempt to restore Rabelais's
meaning by reference to its intellectual context are now aware that
their freedom from such chores can easily become a fool's paradise.

It is thus worth making a fresh attempt to specify the interaction
between the two kinds of approach, to look for the common ground
(and the real differences). The first—and last—thing to say is that it
is not a question of a choice between a work with a single, intended,
moral, historically demonstrable meaning and a work that can be
made to mean anything. The principal theme of this essay will be
the coexistence of precise reference, context-bound articulation of
topoi, controlled allusiveness, with a fundamental instability that is
acknowledged thematically and has its own historical grounding.
One can argue, in fact, that Rabelais is encountering in his comic
writing the problems that anyone will encounter when the limits

and limitations of language are explored (be he Plato, Montaigne, Pascal, Mallarmé, or Derrida), but that the problems assume a configuration wholly and crucially specific to the period: a Pauline *topos*, for example, which Rabelais would no doubt have vehemently acknowledged to be the embodiment of sacred wisdom, functions in a manner analogous to the way a different kind of "limit"—taboo, censorship, authority, political commitment—might function in another era.

The question is best approached through a specific instance: a textual fragment. The glossing of a fragment is somehow, for everyone, a necessary condition of reading Rabelais. It is possible, of course, to articulate general propositions about the meaning of the text as a whole, but generality is more pernicious, less convincing in readings of Rabelais (or Montaigne) than in texts that—however speciously—offer their own coherence, even their own coherent gloss. The difficulty is not to know where to begin but where to stop: in the *Quart Livre* especially, where the complexity and imaginative richness of the text are most fully developed, the episodic nature of the voyage allows one to intervene at almost any point; but once one is in, the possible itineraries multiply with each step forward. This is particularly true of the "Gaster" episode, since—as Screech points out—it is the only one in the *Quart Livre* which does not come to a positive narrative end: it drifts, as it were, with the current of *topoi* until the movement is arrested by an image of the fleet becalmed. In the present analysis, it will be the beginning that provides the momentum: a figure of the Rock of Virtue, labeled "Hesiod" by the text itself, but belonging to a topical tradition of which Jean Lemaire de Belges's *Concorde des deux langages* is the outstanding contemporary example, perhaps the first to be composed in French.[1]

I

Like the "frozen words" and many other figures of the *Quart Livre*, Rabelais's Rock of Virtue is presented first as a marvel ("une isle admirable entre toutes aultres")[2] encountered on a fabulous journey: it is like the discovery of something wholly new *or* of an antiquity or relic. In Jean Lemaire's account of the *topos*, these elements are quite explicit: the narrator, amid his "loingtains voyages et erreurs plus que vagabundes," hopes to find "aulcune chose estrange, merveilleuse et anticque"; is rewarded by sighting "un rochier treshault et tresmerveilleux"; and then forgets his previous labours "par affection de nouvelleté."[3] Eventually, the description of the Rock is presented by Lemaire as an *inscription* on the Rock itself (38). One can easily imagine Pantagruel's company coming across such an inscription and deciphering it. Indeed, this is in effect what happens: when they arrive at the top, the narrator-as-character ("je") thinks it is the Garden of Eden, while Pantagruel makes the guarded assertion that it is "le manoir de *Areté* (c'est vertus) per Hesiode descript." For the characters, the Rock may be a real place, perhaps the one described by Hesiod, but, for the reader at least, it is a textual fragment of uncertain provenance, dredged up from the past and pointing towards a possibility of ethical meaning. It is also, by the same token, an enigma, a phenomenon that raises questions but does not wholly answer them.[4]

The configuration recalls earlier episodes: the deciphering of inscriptions amid the ruins on the Isle des Macraeons; the discovery of the "Enigme en prophétie," as if it were an antiquity, in the course of the excavation of Thélème; or the enigma that accompanies the genealogy of Gargantua (itself an archaelogical "find") at the beginning of *Gargantua*. The possibility of a cross-reference to Thélème is endorsed by the fact that the inscription on the gate of the abbey describes it as "le sejour d'honneur," a phrasing that recalls Jean Lemaire's "grand vergier d'honneur et le sejour royal" (40) and, more generally, the tradition of allegorical scenarios carrying a moral message.[5]

This pattern of references, internal and external, carries with it the theme of a lost or unattainable utopia. The Thélème inscription establishes an antithesis between virtue and vice, inclusion and exclusion, inside and outside; it is also temporally removed, into the past or the future. The Isle des Macraeons is the embodiment of a vanished glory: the temples are in ruins, the heroes are dying. The Rock of Virtue retains its antithetical character initially (rebarbative slopes, idyllic summit), but proves to be very much a latter-day Eden: if it is the place described by Hesiod, it is no longer as Hesiod described it, since the "Manoir de *Areté*" has been usurped by Gaster, who has also, it seems, displaced Porus, god of spiritual abundance, as the spouse of Penia.[6]

In its character as a dubiously utopian inscription, *Quart Livre* 57 points back, through the archeological layers of Rabelais's text, toward another group of *loci*. Panurge's notorious encomium of debts already conscripts Hesiod's Rock as an emblem of the happy state of the debtor and of his singular perseverance in achieving that state:

> Et pensois veritablement en debtes consister la montaigne de Vertus heroicque descripte par Hesiode, en laquelle je tenois degré premier de

ma licence, à laquelle tous humains semblent tirer et aspirer, mais peu
y montent pour la difficulté du chemin, voyant au jourdhuy tout le
monde en desir fervent et strident appetit de faire debtes et crediteurs
nouveaulx.

Toutesfoys il n'est debteur qui veult: il ne faict crediteurs qui veult. Et
vous me voulez debouter de ceste felicité soubeline? Vous me de-
mandez quand seray hors de debtes? (*Tiers Livre* 3; *TLF*, 40)

[And I truly thought that debts were the substance out of which was
formed the mountain of heroic Virtue described by Hesiod, on which I
held the first degree of my licentiate, and to which all human beings
appear to aim and aspire, but few climb it because of the difficulty of
the ascent, seeing that today everyone has a fervent desire and crying
hunger to make new debts and creditors.

Nonetheless not everyone who wishes is a debtor, not everyone
who wishes can make creditors. And you wish to cast me down from
this sublime happiness? You ask me when I shall be out of debt?]

The paragraph division here is modern and, I think, misleading.
The gloss on the *topos* must surely begin at "voyant" and continue
through the sentence "Toutesfoys . . . veult": all men strive to
climb the Rock, but few succeed; *likewise* everyone nowadays wants
to be in debt, but the wanting is not enough. Panurge *has* reached
the top—from which Pantagruel seems to wish to cast him down
("debouter")—and thus enjoys sublime felicity.[7] His speech is full
of mock utopian commonplaces; it is a rhetorician's counterpart of
Thélème, displaying with particular clarity the mechanism by
means of which such flimsy dream-worlds can be constructed out of
the debris of classical allusions and neoplatonist or scholastic *loci*.
The Rock of Affluence is explicitly, in this instance, a figure of the
speaker's desire, of his clamorous appetite. Indeed, Panurge himself, as a fictional character, is fabricated out of such desires and
appetites: he is always in search of new utopias to invade and an-
nex, be they alimentary, pecuniary, or sexual (the three are not really
separable, as the vocabulary of this passage shows).

This is not the first time that Panurge uses the phrase "strident
appetit." It appears at the very moment when he enters Rabelais's
fiction, in *Pantagruel* 9. Here he is already the embodiment of a fallen
state, an exile from utopia. He is at once a survivor of Babel and an
avatar of the ingenious but devious Odysseus—like Gaster, a kind
of *daimon*.[8] He imitates Odysseus in not speaking until he has
eaten; appetite is an unyielding tyrant (it is here that the phrase
"strident appetit" appears in its literal sense); the stomach has no
ears.[9]

This last adage, no doubt gleaned (together with other similar ones) from Erasmus,[10] recurs in the *Tiers Livre* but only comes into its own in the *Quart Livre* with the sequence of "alimentary" episodes. And so we return to Gaster, who personifies the adage, turns it into narrative. Just as, in *Tiers Livre* 3, the *locus amoenus* that crowns the Rock is a place where appetite (desire for money) reigns, so too in *Quart Livre* 57 the well-known itinerary through thorns and stony paths leads to the kingdom of inflated desire.

The fragments thus come together momentarily in order to display the cracks, to invoke the ghost of a broken fable. The exercise no doubt has powerful moral implications. A "straight" reading of the episode (if straight readings are possible when the episode is so strikingly crooked) might suggest that Rabelais is satirizing the scholastic and monastic notion that prescribed mortifications automatically lead to spiritual bliss; they are more likely, he might argue, to nurture appetite precisely by trying to repress it. This psychological insight, developed in the overtly satirical account of the Gastrolâtres and their extravagant menus, is central to the Erasmian and evangelical attack on observances in general and fasting in particular.

On the other hand, the glimpsing of some such message through the cracks, or amongst the topical twists and turns, is an activity made possible by the way Rabelais writes, and therefore should not be allowed to short-circuit the interest of the writing itself as a medium in which thematic possibilities are at once manifold and provisional. Gaster is a personification, bringing a moral theme to life; but he is also a proverbial text curiously implanted on another such text. One might ask oneself *how* this figure was drafted into an allegorical scene having an apparently quite different function and import,[11] but whatever intertextual hypothesis one might propose, it remains evident that the usurping of the Rock of Virtue (and of the marriage-bed of Porus) by a stomach without ears creates a pattern of stress or conflict within the episode. Hesiod and Plato are no sooner invoked than they are displaced; these venerable textual "sources" speak from a long-lost time of fullness, their message distorted by the superimposition of other messages, other textual echoes. The utopia invaded by Gaster may be—is—a moral and spiritual one, but it is also a half-effaced inscription the meaning of which can only be imperfectly glimpsed or pointed to.[12]

II

The character of this agonistic confrontation of texts could be further revealed by an analysis of the composition of the episode as a whole.

But the process would be a lengthy one: the outgrowth of adages, borrowings, quotations, allusions, and echoes is enormous. Like an overfull belly, the six chapters describing the rule of Gaster are nothing if not distended. Two or three comments will have to suffice for the purpose of showing the strains and pressures at work in the text.

The first is the observation that Rabelais's Rock is given very little space in which to establish itself as the decor for the Gaster episode. Panurge's allusion in *Tiers Livre* 3 is after all only an allusion; *Quart Livre* 57, on the other hand, begins with a topographical fiction that could easily have been the scope of Jean Lemaire's or François Habert's (see section V). Thélème, after all, provides a precedent, as does the Isle des Macraeons. But the initial description is allowed no more than a couple of lines, after which (without a break in the sentence) the direction is shifted by a reference to the "mons du Daulphiné," which is claimed to be even more difficult of access than Hesiod's: only one man, a soldier of Charles VIII's army, has made the ascent, discovering at the top an old ram.[13] The digression is a good deal longer than the reference to the Rock, so that the ancient *topos* is eclipsed by a modern allusion, a fictitious marvel by an exploit passing for a fact, a serious moral fable by a semicomic anecdote (the dwelling-place of Virtue is *first* usurped, it would seem, by the "vieux belier"). Marichal, who does not mention this passage in his commentary, would no doubt use it to endorse his argument that Rabelais is *parodying* the Rock of Virtue, and it is hard to avoid this conclusion, provided that one does not infer that the result is simply to reverse the traditional values associated with the Rock. The various elements of which the episode is made up are engaged in a much more nuanced and unresolved conflict. One might also note that Rabelais is here writing, in comic terms, the sort of gloss that many humanists would have understood: an excavated fragment of ancient wisdom is assimilated into the world of the commentator by means of a contemporary allusion.[14] Parody, assimilation, distortion, and displacement are the inevitable consequences of the humanist practice of imitation, and Rabelais is here visibly repeating the process within the conventions of a comic narrative.

A tiny detail in the subsequent presentation of Gaster shows how "allusive shift," as one might term this kind of effect, can be present in a single phrase. To call Gaster "Messere Gaster" is, as Marichal points out, to confer on him pejorative associations: the trick is done by means of a xenophobic distortion of the Italian title.[15] The appelation is an act of aggression, drawing the nonspecific allegory of the belly (which could simply be a figure of Gluttony) into the realm of nationalistic prejudice. The hint will not be developed directly in this episode, but the satire of the Gastrolâtres and Engastrimythes in chapters 58 through 60 rejoins the topical satire of the Homenaz episode to remind one that the moral themes of the 1552 *Quart Livre* are articulated in terms of a conflict-ridden world of ecclesiastical policy and doctrinal dispute.

A rather different but analogous effect is produced a page or two later, where the pilot of Pantagruel's ship tells the story of the unsuccessful rebellion of the "Somates" (limbs) against Gaster. This is in fact the well-known fable recounted by Aesop and Livy (the fable of Menenius Agrippa), and the narrator indicates this by claiming that the Somates followed the example of the limbs in Aesop's fable; but the claim has the effect of suggesting that what was only a fable has taken place in reality. A doubled fiction offers the mirage of a practical possibility, an event that might, here and now, come to life. And since the fable specifically evokes a challenge to authority, it is arguable that its intercalation into the sequence beginning with Gaster's usurpation reinforces a sense of aggression latent in both theme and textual composition.

III

These various kinds of verbal or topical juxtaposition are thus fraught with tension at more than one level. At the center, no doubt, is the writer's desire to construct his own discourse out of existing materials, the prestige of those materials being often so great that something like an act of aggression or willful subversion is necessary in order to escape their constraint while profiting from their authority. In the overall economy of the episode—which is in this respect wholly characteristic of the 1552 *Quart Livre*—the reader is, however, likely to perceive the tension first as a constant shifting of ground and of register. *Topoi* are half-sketched, then abandoned or given a sudden twist; substitution and modification are prominent enough to dominate the act of reading. Rabelais is thus constructing what Ong has called a "commonplace rhapsody," a topical *copia* that confers on the materials of a humanist miscellany an associative order, transforming them from an inert catalogue into a dynamic mode of expression, a *rhetoric*. He is also, as suggested above, performing a sort of commentary without a single master text, very much in the manner of Budé in the *De asse*, where precise glosses on antique monetary values slide imperceptibly into moral, political, and religious observations on the world of the commentator.[16] And, just as the modification and substitution of ancient commonplaces and venerable citations create a predominantly agonistic dialogue with the past, so too the forays into the contemporary world are motivated by commitment and aggression. No one would deny that Rabelais is a satirist; he is also an apologist—for his own writings,[17] and no doubt also for certain national policies (Gallicanism) and evangelical humanist doctrines (the attack on mortifications). These two modes of motivated rhetoric (attack and defense) are dependent on a textual structure that is itself a defense and an attack, an appeal to textual authority and a rejection, disowning, and dismemberment of that very authority.[18]

Yet the agonistic mode of composition is of course present in the form of a narrative, whether at the global level (an episode in a fictional voyage) or at a local level (the insertion of secondary fables and anecdotes). The reader can therefore hardly avoid attempting to link the fragments, to derive from them a coherence of some kind; he cannot simply read them as a collection of the various things that have been said on the exigencies of appetite and its moral and material consequences. By opening the episode with a well-known allegorical schema that suggests an easy reading ("virtue requires self-discipline," or something of that kind); by placing the whole episode under the aegis of an allegorical personification ("this is an episode about the belly, i.e., about appetite, gluttony, material concupiscence"); by inserting adages, Aesopic fables, and quotations from Scripture, which all seem to have a clear message; by these several means Rabelais exploits the reader's conditioning or "competence," his presupposition that if he presses the right buttons, a certain overall meaning will automatically be printed out.

On the other hand, the economy of shift and substitution, and the construction of a narrative *dispositio* that disperses or dissociates just when one might expect continuity and integration,[19] constantly outwit the reader's desire for stability and certainty: in this respect, Rabelais's writing has profound affinities with Montaigne's. The presence of certain dominant moral themes and emphases is undeniable: the worship of Gaster is presented as pernicious, the Gastrolâtres are subjected to aggressive ridicule, and the quotation from St. Paul at the end of chapter 58—unquestionably the most venerable borrowed fragment in the episode—sounds a moral note powerful enough, one might think, to polarize all the other materials.[20] It is, as Screech argues, a master-source, a transcendent authority, a limit.[21] Yet the reprobation of belly-worship is followed, as Rigolot points out, by the chapters in which Gaster is seen as the "master of arts"—ambivalent, no doubt, but still leading toward superior

realms of wisdom (see the end of chapter 62). Rigolot is also right, I
think, in suggesting that the exuberance of the language in which
Rabelais presents ostensibly pernicious activity (the gastronomic
inventories in chapters 59 and 60) suggests a conflict at the heart of
Rabelais's own text between subconscious desire and the conscious
acknowledgment of moral imperatives.[22] One might restate this
point by saying that the proliferation of *topoi,* figures, anecdotes,
and lexical items is always in excess of what is required for the
transmission of a didactic or moral intention, excess being linked
here with the economy of substitution in such a way as to prevent
any moral injunction, however venerable, from establishing itself as
an interpretative key. It is crucial also to recognize that the "excess"
cannot be domesticated and dismissed by the strategy (used from
time immemorial by those who are suspicious of literature) of char-
acterizing it as a "sugaring of the pill" or as a smoke-screen designed
to protect the writer from official disapproval: the sugar and the
smoke are precisely those elusive substances that constitute the
chemistry peculiar to literature and cannot be siphoned off except,
speciously, in authorial and editorial prefaces.

IV

At this point, it may be helpful to characterize four different readings of the episode; the exercise will at least serve to demonstrate its
complexity and the extent to which the reading of Rabelais is still a
problem.

Marichal's commentary, which is chiefly concerned with demonstrating and elucidating textual allusions, emphasizes the element
of parody (particularly antiplatonist parody): he suggests that
Rabelais is mocking facile or artificial ethical commonplaces, beginning with the Rock of Virtue. He also brings out the extent to which
Gaster is an ambivalent figure, a *daimon* or mediator who is the
source of both good and evil. But in the end he opts for the hypothesis of an evangelical allegory, following Saulnier's reading.[23] His
commentary *ends* with the Pauline injunction, thus changing the
order of the text in order to make the evangelical text appear as the
touchstone for a stable and coherent meaning.

Screech demonstrates the links between the Gaster episode and
those that precede and follow it by analyzing the themes of eating
and excess but also, and more particularly, the themes of language
and its relation to moral action.[24] The question of "signs" (verbal
and nonverbal) thus emerges as a dominant element, and it is clear
from what Screech says here and in his commentary on the "frozen

words" episode that he is fully aware of the extent to which the realm of signs appears, in Rabelais, as a shifting and uncertain one. Yet he is convinced that Rabelais wishes us to believe that some fragments of language—those that can be designated as "revealed truth"—are immune to the general flux, so that, presumably, if one listens to the scriptural quotations, all the rest is superfluous, a kind of comic window-dressing (or at most a demonstration of how one can be misled). On the Rock of Virtue, Screech comments: "Rabelais gives it his own forceful twist by making want and hunger the driving-forces which gave man the force to struggle onwards and upwards to virtue. Once he has done so, Hesiod's fertile plateau of virtue stretches out delightfully before him" (444). And later, on almost the last page of his book, he speaks of the "manly moral strivings symbolized by the *Manoir de Areté*" (460). It seems to me that this reading does not fit the text. If we follow Rabelais's narrative and climb the Rock by means of "manly moral strivings," we find the fertile plateau of virtue, but we find it usurped by Gaster. Is Gaster at the bottom of the Rock, encouraging us to ascend, or at the top? In either case, there is a moral and topical complexity here— rightly noted by Marichal—which Screech ignores by the device of compartmentalizing the *topoi*, suppressing their mutual contamination.

Jeanneret's elegant exposition of the later chapters of the *Quart Livre* also connects the alimentary and linguistic themes, but with a different emphasis.[25] He clarifies the opposition between images of material opacity and inertia and images of spiritual transparency and mobility, associating the negative set with an excessive dedication to the *signifiant* at the expense of the *signifié*. Pantagruel represents a superior insight into the nature, function, and limitations of language. For Jeanneret, this—rather than some evangelical moral message—is the import of the sequence, in which Gaster "ne cautionne aucune thèse particulière, mais illustre à son tour l'ambivalence des signes et la nécessité d'une vision dialectique. . . . Gaster *bifrons:* voilà qui devrait suffire à invalider, d'entrée, les lectures univoques" [does not support any particular thesis, but illustrates for its own part the ambivalence of signs and the necessity of a dialectic vision. . . . The *double-visaged* Gaster: here is what ought to suffice to invalidate, from the outset, any univocal reading] (21). Ambivalence is endemic, then; the search for a single meaning is ill-conceived (the article contains some mild polemic against positivistic historical readings).[26] Yet Jeanneret's version still seeks to "déchiffrer" (14) the sequence; it is itself a kind of allegory that stabilizes the sense. He respects the multiple thematic levels of the text by making it interpret itself: reflexivity is the key to coherence. Such an account would also, one could add, allow for a more strictly "literary" reading that would confront the thematic elements with the restless mobility of the writing itself (whether one sees the themes as determining the mode of writing or vice versa).

Rigolot's version has already been referred to. It maintains the ambivalence noted by Marichal and Jeanneret, and perceives the conjunction of the Rock of Virtue with Gaster as being problematic, but goes further in that it makes allowance for a counterpoint—even an antithesis—between language and theme. It thus comes nearer than the others to coping with the problem of "excess" referred to above: unconscious or semiconscious intentions, visible in the equivocations, tensions, and excessive proliferation of Rabelais's language, must be predicated in order to account for the intermittent and, as it were, asymmetrical presentation of the "consciously intended" moral themes. It is singularly appropriate (although Rigolot does not quite say this) that Gaster is the figure of a desire that cannot be bypassed; it can be repressed, limited, partially or temporarily tamed by moral and evangelical *topoi*, but it inevitably leaves its traces, visible in the disruptions of thematic and figurative continuity and in the libidinous rhetoric that asserts its own right to repetition by means of anaphora.[27]

V

Other readings could be brought into play,[28] but this set of variations on the apparently immovable Rock of Virtue is sufficient to set in motion a further critical excursion.

It is easy to agree with Screech and Marichal that a great deal of historical evidence, as well as the exploitation of stylistic registers and structural emphasis within the text, suggests that one of the dominant vectors of Rabelais's fiction—what we perceive as its inscribed intentions—is a complex of evangelical humanist topics. The argument that his comedy discredits all such topics (again deliberately or intentionally) by parodic subversion is now virtually untenable. It is also easy to accept the contention of Screech and Jeanneret that the Gaster episode participates in the thematization of language that characterizes the later (1552) version of the *Quart Livre*. Since the problem of the linguistic sign, far from being a post-Saussurean theme, is already well known and much debated in the late Middle Ages and Renaissance, its contemporary phase can be elucidated—as Screech brilliantly elucidates it—in order to clarify the conjunction of semiological *topoi* which, in these chapters, provides an inbuilt mode of exegesis (a metalanguage written into the fiction). The quest for the *Dive Bouteille* must, according to any such reading, be a sinuous and interrupted itinerary, a groping amid half-darkness for glimpses of a plenitude that is always above or beyond. But it follows, for example, that Pantagruel's speculations on the origin of the frozen words is not, as Screech would have it, Rabelais's opinion on language, but a plausible and attractive opinion, offered together with others, an insight that allows the quest to go forward precisely because it is provisional rather than final. Finality, in this sense, would destroy the fiction and contradict everything the text *seems* to mean.[29]

Rabelais's allusions and quotations, then, are extraordinarily precise, or precisely deformed; but it should not, at all costs, be inferred that they may be neatly aligned in order to produce some single intended sense. Their quirks and vicissitudes, their refusal to let themselves be so aligned, are not a consequence of slapdash composition or of an indeterminate *verve comique:* they compose the text as an amalgam of Christian doctrine, humanist learning, popular legend and lore, and an insatiable appetite for language. The precision and the imaginative richness of the work lie in the configuration thus produced, which is of course quite different from saying that *any* reading is possible. The Gaster episode, like the whole of the fiction, is a "plural" text, but its plurality operates within strict limits. Its agonistic structure is dependent on these limits, since there can be no tension, no conflict, no serious game, unless the elements of which it is composed have an identity and a rhetorical function. A permissive reading of Rabelais (or of any literary work, for that matter) is simply not interesting.

One need only look briefly at François Habert's *Temple de Vertu* of 1542 to grasp the enormity of any critical move that risked reducing Rabelais's fiction to a didactic handbook spiced with *gaulois* humor.[30] Habert's temple is built on the Rock of Virtue: at each point, the reader's path is signposted so that he knows exactly what value, positive or negative, to assign to the emblematic figures he encounters and so that he emerges with a clearly and explicitly articulated evangelical message. Of course the decor is functional; it is indeed strictly functional, in that its rhetoric is as little as possible disturbed by superfluous desires. If the style is bare and prosaic, that is no doubt deliberate, since it corresponds to an evangelical preference for austerity (and a distrust of humanist stylistic pretentions) characteristic of poets in the entourage of Marguerite de Navarre. Nowhere is Gaster or any cognate figure let off the leash; nowhere does the articulation of the text deviate; nowhere is the hermetic seal broken to allow the contamination of desire.[31]

Jean Lemaire's Rock is a different matter. In its oscillation between moral *topoi* and themes of poetic composition, it reveals the uncertainty of a writer engaged in a cultural struggle, the agon of a poet caught between ambition and a sense of inadequacy; the uneasy relation between the two temples—Venus's and Minerva's—allows one to glimpse a drama of desire and its frustration, just as the naturalization of the *terza rima* and the illustration of the *alexandrin* compose a conflict at once textual and nationalistic. But even here we know in general, once we are launched on our itinerary, where we are going: we don't meet old rams or bellies when we get to the summit, and the author-narrator tells us clearly enough what he *thinks* he is doing.

Rabelais's variant is of quite a different order. We are first presented with what looks like an easy riddle. From the first lines of description of the Rock, we already know, if we are at all familiar with such *topoi*, what we shall find at the top. But the easy solution proves to be wrong: the riddle becomes an enigma, a complex amalgam; the path to Virtue becomes a labyrinth at the center of which sits a distinctly disquieting figure (he, too, would be easy enough to tame in some stories, but not in this one). Gaster monstrously disrupts the simple relationship between a fable and its meaning; he is an obstacle, not to be bypassed or maneuvered out of the way. It is certain enough that he is not to be treated as a *telos:* that way leads only into Antigonus's chamber-pot. He is a mediator, perhaps, a fallen cousin of Eros; he is also an originator, a primal and ineradicable desire that grounds the quest for knowledge and mastery of nature. And so the episode composed by chapters 57 through 62 ends with a movement outward into enigmas and marvels: it forms a kind of chiasmus, in which the articulated meaning (presided over by a personification, be it Virtue or Gaster) is suspended equivocally at the center, enclosed between unresolved figures. The riddle or fable is normally a complex structure that yields a simple solution; in Rabelais, that order—proffered momentarily at the outset—is reversed, so that a simple allegory becomes the libidinous origin of an ever-proliferating superstructure of invention.

The Rock of Virtue, then, proves difficult indeed to climb. The reader is likely to feel that he spends most of his time half-way up the prickly slope, goaded on by glimpses of what may or may not be the summit. The utopia in which Pantagruel and his companions temporarily think they find themselves gives them a point of reference, as Thélème provides a point of reference on a larger scale in *Gargantua*, but it comes dangerously close to appearing, in retrospect, to have been a mirage. This is because it is quite strictly a *textual* utopia, and all textual utopias—being a product of human language and human desire—are, as Rabelais very well knew, a kind of mirage. The words of Scripture, admittedly, may be a true oasis for an evangelical humanist, but in Rabelais's fiction they are dependent on the kaleidoscopic *topoi* that surround them. The utopias of the logos can no longer be disentangled from the Babel of the fallen world; if they could, Rabelais's writing would be superfluous, pure excess.

Modern poetics may thus, arguably, be particularly appropriate for the analysis of certain Renaissance texts, reaching parts that positivistic readings cannot reach. On the other hand, a modern critical reading that took no precise account of historical data would be merely arbitrary. It is essential neither to succumb to the fear of unresolved problems and force the text to yield a reassuringly univocal meaning, nor to throw the baby out with the bath water by being too permissive. To move in the space between these options is to sustain a kind of diplomacy of which Rabelais's diplomat patrons would no doubt have approved.

The uncertainty inscribed in Rabelais's fictions is, then, a *precise* uncertainty, an inability to piece together a fully coherent account of contemporary moral, religious, and linguistic problems—an epistemological impasse. It is not reducible to the serene uncertainty of a Christian sceptic,[32] although the possibility of such a serenity is perceived intermittently in the *Tiers* and *Quart Livres*. It characterizes a moment in history when the nature and structure of knowledge were notoriously in question, when the image of a total encyclopedia was still tantalizingly close, but when the items that might compose it simply would not cohere to form a stable whole. There are, of course, no stable wholes in the history of ideas; imaginative works thrive on the instabilities and insufficiencies of their contemporary ideologies, which is why literature is a fundamental medium for historical understanding. But in Rabelais, the sense of instability and uncertainty dramatized by the text is particularly moving because it operates within the constraints of a sensibility for which certainty might be, ought to be, possible. The epistemology of Rabelais's text is not nihilistic, nor is it wholly subversive: it recognizes authorities, limits, and constraints, but it also recognizes and capitalizes on the limits of textual authority. Its desire for utopia is obsessive and exuberant; but so is its love of change, diversity, Heraclitan flux—the pleasure of uncertainty being very precisely the pleasure of the text.

And so the Hesiodic Rock, apparently so stable, looms for a moment with its promise of a solution; then it begins, as it were, to waver and fade. The tide of *topoi* rises around it, until the reader sees that what looked like an island on which a landfall might be made is only a singularity in the endless shifting movement of the text. Like Pantagruel and his crew, we are committed to a voyage for which no completely reliable map will ever be drawn.

NOTES

1. For a detailed comparison of Rabelais's text with Jean Lemaire's (which he must have known), see R. Marichal, *"Quart Livre:* Commentaires," *Etudes rabelaisiennes* 1 (1956): 185–86. A concise history of the topos is provided by Henri Franchet, *Le Poète et son œuvre d'après Ronsard* (Paris: Champion, 1922), 103 ff.
2. François Rabelais, *Le Quart Livre,* ed. R. Marichal (Geneva: Droz, 1947), 230. All subsequent references to Rabelais's work will be given in abbreviated form, indicating chapter numbers and the page number of the edition in the *Textes littéraires français* series (*TLF*). For the Gaster episode, chapter numbers only will be provided, since this paper presupposes a detailed reading of the episode (quotations will for the same reason be brief and infrequent).
3. Jean Lemaire de Belges, *La Concorde des deux langages,* ed. Jean Frappier (Paris: Droz, 1947), 36–37.
4. Cf. the citation of "authorities" in the same chapter on the question "Who was the original 'master of arts'?" The multiplication of possibilities here both undermines the decision in favor of Gaster and associates Gaster by implication with the other figures mentioned—including "Amour" in the ensuing allusion to the neoplatonist myth of Porus and Penia, since Love was for Ficino the master of arts (see below, note 6).
5. On the "rhétoriqueur" antecedents of Thélème, see R. Lebègue, "Rabelais et les grands rhétoriqueurs," *Les Lettres romanes* 12 (1958): 10–12. Cf. also the reference to the "Manoir de vérité" (the utopian source from which, according to Pantagruel, the "paroles gelées" may perhaps emanate) in *Quart Livre* 55, *TLF* 226.
6. On the neoplatonist provenance of this allusion, see Marichal, "Commentaires," 190–92. It has recently been shown that Rabelais probably borrowed the reference from Celio Calcagnini (see M. A. Screech, "Celio Calcagnini and Rabelaisian Sympathy," in *Neo-Latin and the Vernacular in Renaissance France,* ed. Grahame Castor and Terence Cave [Oxford: Oxford University Press, 1984], 34–35); but it is patently Rabelais who has transformed the myth by substituting Gaster for Porus, and indeed by inserting a neoplatonist allegory without warning into his idiosyncratic version of the Rock of Virtue.
7. The phrase "en laquelle je tenois degré premier de ma licence" is obscure; none of the critical editions provides a wholly satisfactory gloss. Might it be a satirical reference to the notoriously rigorous discipline of the College de Montaigu (although the topic would have seemed rather dated in

1552)? The analogy between *Tiers Livre* 3 and *Quart Livre* 57 is sharpened by the fact that Gaster's consort "Penie" is a commonplace sixteenth-century personification of poverty (cf. the last paragraph of *Quart Livre* 57); for further analogies, see Marichal, "Commentaires," 189.

8. On Gaster as a *daimon*, see Marichal, "Commentaires," 193 ff. See also Ludwig Schrader, *Panurge und Hermes* (Bonn: Romanisches Seminar der Universität Bonn, 1958): Schrader's comparison of Panurge and Hermes shows that Panurge has many of the ambivalent features one associates with the *daimon*.

9. The parallel between Panurge and Odysseus has been analyzed in detail by Gérard Defaux, *Le Curieux, le glorieux et la sagesse du monde dans la première moitié du xvie siècle: l'exemple de Panurge (Ulysse, Démosthène, Empédocle)*, (Lexington, Ky.: French Forum, 1982), chs. 1 and 2; see also Terence Cave, *The Cornucopian Text: Problems of Writing in the French Renaissance* (Oxford: Oxford University Press, 1979), 111–15 (on Panurge and Babel), and "Panurge and Odysseus," in *Myth and Legend in French Literature*, ed. Keith Aspley, David Bellos, and Peter Sharratt (London: Modern Humanities Research Association, 1982), 47–59. It should be noted that, in the Homeric passage alluded to in *Pantagruel* 9, Odysseus unashamedly proclaims the priority of appetite in a setting (Alcinous' palace) that is idyllic, if not quite utopian: the incongruity is one that would no doubt have appealed to Rabelais's imagination and may be distantly echoed in *Quart Livre* 57.

10. Erasmus, *Adages* 2.8.84 ("Venter auribus caret"); for a list of other adages on this theme, see M. A. Screech, *Rabelais* (London: Duckworth, 1979), 443–44.

11. It is conceivable that the conjunction results from a yoking of two passages from Hesiod, the well-known *topos* from *Works and Days* (287–92) and a brief allusion to "things of shame, mere bellies [gasteres]" in *Theogony* 26 (the context includes the notions of poetic inspiration, prophecy, and the telling of lies and truth). A brief search in the most likely intermediary texts produced no such instance, but Rabelais could of course have collated them himself. The provenance of Gaster is in any case not a purely learned one, since *Quart Livre* 59 contains a reference to an analogous figure from popular carnivals (see Screech, "Celio Calcagnini," 33–34).

12. Themes such as these—especially the notions of fragmentation and conflict implied by the humanist theory and practice of *imitatio*—are developed at greater length in *The Cornucopian Text*, but the specific conception of an agonistic intertextuality in Renaissance writing is brilliantly developed by Thomas M. Greene, *The Light in Troy: Imitation and Discovery in Renaissance Poetry* (New Haven: Yale University Press, 1982), to which I owe certain of the emphases of the present essay.

13. Marichal's note on this passage in the *TLF* edition points out that it was not Doyac but Antoine de Ville who climbed the mountain, and that it was not a ram that he found there but some chamois. As a modern rectifying gloss, it cannot be read without a touch of irony, and demon-

strates at the most that the purpose of Rabelais's digression is strategic, not informative; it is reminiscent, on a miniature scale, of the confrontation of fantasy and commonplace reference in "the world in Pantagruel's mouth" (*Pantagruel* 22). The exploit, in its reference to "engins mirificques," also anticipates the ingenuities inspired by Gaster (*Quart Livre* 61–62).

14. See Jean Céard, "Les Transformations du genre du commentaire," in *L'Automne de la Renaissance, 1580–1630*, ed. Jean Lafond and André Stegmann (Paris: Vrin, 1981), 101–15.

15. See Marichal, "Commentaires," 192.

16. See J.-C. Margolin, "De la digression au commentaire: pour une lecture humaniste du *De asse* de Guillaume Budé," *Neo-Latin and the Vernacular* (see above, note 6), 1–25.

17. See the concluding passage of the Prologue of the *Tiers Livre*, and especially the 1548 Prologue and the dedicatory epistle (1552) of the *Quart Livre*.

18. Marichal notes the strident, aggressive tone that characterizes certain passages in this episode ("Commentaires," 189). But in referring to the rhetoric of apology, I am thinking in particular of Margaret W. Ferguson, *Trials of Desire: Renaissance Defenses of Poetry* (New Haven: Yale University Press, 1983), in which rhetorical theory in the manner of Kenneth Burke and psychoanalytic theories of defense are fruitfully brought to bear on Renaissance texts.

19. Examples are given elsewhere in this essay; another is provided by the interpolation, in the account of the Engastrimythes (chapter 58), of the story of the ventriloquist Jacoba Rhodigina, which is presented as an eyewitness account. The shift here has a function similar to the "Doyac" anecdote at the beginning of the episode.

20. The end of chapter 58 and the end of chapter 60, where the pointed fable of Antigonus and his chamber pot is recounted, together provide a powerful moralizing framework for the activities of the Gastrolâtres. This segment, taken on its own, would thus seem to be virtually unequivocal.

21. Screech, *Rabelais*, 446.

22. See François Rigolot, *Les Langages de Rabelais* (Geneva: Droz, 1972), 152–60. A similar tension seems to me to be apparent in Erasmus's essay *Lingua*, where the condemnation of pernicious chatter (and related vices) is proffered in a singularly self-indulgent and copious language.

23. Marichal, "Commentaires," 201–2; cf. V.-L. Saulnier's general interpretation of Rabelais's works as an evangelical allegory in *Le Dessein de Rabelais* (Paris: SEDES, 1957); also, by the same author, *Rabelais II: Rabelais dans son enquête* (Paris: SEDES, 1982).

24. Screech, *Rabelais*, 439–41.

25. Michel Jeanneret, "Les Paroles dégelées: Rabelais, 'Quart Livre,' " *Littérature* 27 (1975): 14–30. See also the same author's "Quand la fable se met à table," *Poétique* 54 (1983): 163–80.

26. Defaux (*Le Curieux, le glorieux et la sagesse du monde*, 158, note 29) takes sides with Screech and rejects Jeanneret's "plural" reading.

27. See the two sequences on Gaster as "master of arts" (ch. 57, "Et tout pour la trippe!" and chs. 61–2, "Est advenue . . . ," "Attendu que. . . ."); also the lists of dishes in chs. 59 and 60, in which repetition takes the form of synonymy.

28. See for example Saulnier, *Rabelais II*, ch. 21; Alfred Glauser, *Rabelais créateur* (Paris: Nizet, 1964), 264–67.

29. The dual character of Rabelais's theory of language is persuasively demonstrated by François Rigolot in "Cratylisme et Pantagruélisme: Rabelais et le statut du signe," *Etudes rabelaisiennes* 13 (1976), 115–32. Rigolot suggests that Rabelais explores in his fiction the notion of a language grounded in truth and thus pregnant with meaning, while constantly dramatizing the arbitrary nature of linguistic signs: it would thus be wrong to interpret Rabelais's text by reference to one or other pole of the antithesis taken separately. I have developed a similar argument (the copresence of "plenitude" and "emptiness") in the sections on Rabelais in *The Cornucopian Text*. See also Dennis Costa, *Irenic Apocalypse: Some Uses of Apocalyptic in Dante, Petrarch and Rabelais* (Saratoga, Calif.: Anma Libri, 1981), ch. 5; and David Quint, *Origin and Originality in Renaissance Literature: Versions of the Source* (New Haven: Yale University Press, 1983), ch. 6. Costa and Quint admit the play of ambivalence but subordinate it in the end to Rabelais's recurrent themes of Christian teleology and eschatology; they thus revert to what is essentially an allegorical—even anagogic—reading.

30. François Habert, *Le Philosophe parfaict et le Temple de Vertu*, ed. Henri Franchet (Paris: Champion, 1922).

31. I concede that this is a risky generalization: no doubt one could get one's knife in somewhere if one tried hard enough, since no piece of writing is wholly invulnerable to such operations.

32. Defaux shares with Screech the view that Rabelais espoused a form of Christian scepticism. For a summary of this view, prefaced by a quotation from Screech, see Defaux, *Le Curieux, le glorieux et la sagesse du monde*, 135–42. Defaux does, however, also stress the tensions and ambivalences inherent in such a position.

6. GUNPOWDER AS TRANSGRESSIVE INVENTION IN RONSARD

■

ULLRICH LANGER

Dapoi fra me pensando, che non puoco biasmo merita quel huomo, qual, over per scientia, over per sua industria, over per sorte ritrova qualche notabil particolarità, & chi solamente lui solo ne voglia esser possessore, perche se tutti li nostri anciani il medesimo havesseno osservato, poco dalli animali irrationali al presente saressimo differenti adunque per non incorrere in questo biasimo o deliberato di volere tai mei quesiti, over inventioni mandar tutto in luce.
— NICCOLÒ TARTAGLIA, prologue of
the *Quesiti et inventioni diverse*

At homini nulla fera perniciosior, quam homo. Rursum illae cum pugnant, suis pugnant armis: nos praeter naturam arte cacodaemonum excogitatis, instruimur homines in hominem perniciem.
— ERASMUS, *Dulce bellum inexpertis*

THE ASSOCIATION of gunpowder and the devil is a commonplace in the Renaissance. It figures as the satanic double of the invention of printing: knowledge of good entails knowledge of evil.[1] In his little instruction manual devoted to gunpowder, the *Feuerwerkbuch von 1420*, the anonymous author recommends a specific diet for the future soldier (e.g., moderate use of wine, avoidance of vinegar, eggs, and all dry and hard substances), and he urges above all assiduous religious devotion.[2]

Des ersten sol er got eren und vor allen dingen vor auge haben mer dann ander reisig leütt Dann wann er mitt dem pulver oder mit der püchss umbgat so hat er seinen grossen und allergrösten feind vorhanden.

[First of all he should honor and consider God before all other things, more than other armed people, for when he handles powder or a gun he has his great and greatest enemy in his hands.]

Similarly the master technician of artillery, Niccolò Tartaglia, cannot help but question the consequences of his calculations, which, after all, permit men to better kill each other:

> Ma poi fra me pensando un giorno . . . mi parve cosa biasmevole, vituperosa, & crudele, & degna di non puoca punitione appresso a Iddio, a voler studiare di assotigliare tal essercitio dannoso al p[e]ssimo, Imo destruttore della specie humana, & massime de Christiani in lor continue guerre.[3]

> [But then one day I thought . . . it seemed to me a blameworthy, shameful, and cruel thing, and worthy of no little punishment before God, to want to attempt to refine such a practice which is extremely damaging, even destructive of the human species, and especially of Christians in their continuous wars.]

In spite of these doubts he publishes his treatise; in his later works he will affirm that artillery serves to defend the Christians against the Turks and will thus justify his first publication, the *Nova scientia* (1537).[4] In his moral reflections, Tartaglia does not insist on the diabolical nature of gunpowder itself, but instead concentrates on the catastrophic effects of the new weapons. These reservations finally succumb to the vertigo of his demonstrations and calculations.

However, the initial remorse of the supreme geometrician of artillery indicates the persistence of a network of symbolic associations centered on gunpowder: the man who captures fire in an iron cylinder imitates the Father who alone possessed lightning. More importantly, the creation of the gun permits its owner to escape the imitation of the Father and to constitute himself as an independent creator. This independent creation resembles a self-generation of man who is finally freed from the previously necessary mediation through the Father as model.

Gunpowder represents above all a hyperbolic Promethean transgression. The theft of fire is surpassed by the theft of lightning. The association between cannons or guns and the sky's lightning is very frequent in the Renaissance.[5] Rather than proceed chronologically by supposing a precise chain of influences and readings, I will attempt to define a network of symbolic associations in a synchrony that might, at first, seem arbitrary. This synchrony is constituted by a set of literary works whose treatment of gunpowder forms a sym-

bolic coherence.[6] The historic point of departure seems to have been
the battle of Ravenna (1512) and the subsequent condemnation of
the harquebus by Ariosto in the *Orlando Furioso*.[7]

All that is connected not only to the murderous use but also to the
fabrication of gunpowder and cannons is represented by images of
depth. In Ariosto, Orlando hurls Cimosco's gun from the top of a
cliff down into the depths of the earth, because it is in those same
depths that the gun originated.[8] The elements necessary to the
production of gunpowder as well as of iron have to be dug up from
the earth. The mining process often inspires a figural terminology
that organizes itself around a return to the womb of Mother Earth.[9]
Excavation is essentially the uncovering and the discovering of the
process of conception in the womb. In a treatise on niter (essential to
the production of saltpeter) William Clarke makes explicit exactly
this association:

> The Generation of Natural Bodies is done in secret, which may seem to
> be not only for the preserving of heat, being a chief instrument in
> natural productions, but that so sublime and curious a Mysterie might
> not vulgarly be prostituted, but to her most intellectual Observers,
> who by the Eye of Reason can investigate, what cannot be discovered
> by the outward sense. Hence the manner of the Generation of Miner-
> als, Vegetables, and Animals are as obscure, and hid, as the dark
> subterraneous Mines, the impervious earthly Vegetable, and female
> animal Matrix, being the places of their formation. . . . No less obscure
> is *Nitre* in its Birth, and as difficult to be explained. . . . *Nitre, with other
> Minerals, in the beginning of the World,* was first *created* in the Earth; and
> by the power given to it from the Creater, hath preserv'd and *multiply'd
> itself.* And so from the Creation, not only the formation of its own body,
> but its propagation and perpetuation proceeds. . . . For, although it be
> extracted out of *Nitrous* Earth, yet out of the *Mater Nitri, vel Petrae,* the
> seminary principle remaining in the Earth, there is more generated
> and encreased.[10]

Niter, the basis of gunpowder, is conceived from the earliest creation and multiplies secretly in the womb of the earth. Men have the
power to extract this secret of procreation and can thus observe the
repetition of the creating process. However the observation and
appropriation of conception are not neutral. In Clarke's treatise the
triumphant and celebratory tone cannot mask the exclusion of a
sinister *double:* there is an opinion according to which niter is produced from the genitals, from urine or excrement, or from residue of
wine and beer. This opinion is false, according to Clarke, since
excrement and urine only produce heat through putrefaction and

cannot be converted into saltpeter.[11] But the explicit exclusion of the double is also its tacit affirmation.

The diabolical nature of gunpowder is clearly affirmed by Milton in *Paradise Lost*. Satan seems to have found an "invention" that will guarantee victory over the angels in the battle of the heavens. The invention is obviously the cannon and gunpowder, whose production is described in a manner resembling the symbolic associations noted in Clarke:

> . . . in a moment up they turned
> Wide the celestial soil, and saw beneath
> Th'originals of nature in their crude
> Conception; sulphurous and nitrous foam
> They found, they mingled, and with subtle art,
> Concocted and adusted they reduced
> To blackest grain, and into store conveyed:
> Part hidden veins digged up (nor hath this earth
> Entrails unlike) of mineral and stone,
> Whereof to found their engines and their balls
> Of missive ruin; part incentive reed
> Provide, pernicious with one touch to fire.
>   (6.509–20)

The discovery of the "conception" under the ground, and the digging in heaven's entrails (similar to earth's) are part of the same symbolism of the womb that contains the principle of creation. The "inventor" ("Th'invention all admired" [498]) of gunpowder permits man to observe directly and to appropriate the principle of creation and procreation.[12]

When man "finds" gunpowder, he literally transgresses the terrestrial order. His "invention" is of course understood also as a rhetorical category. In this context *inventio* similarly acquires the meaning of transgression. If it were only a matter of finding a substance already in the ground beneath our feet,[13] the invention would conform to its traditional rhetorical sense. Yet here the process itself of *invenire* connotes transgression (digging in the womb of the mother) and one is apparently capable of capturing the *principle* of creation: man appropriates for himself the power of generation, a power exercised *against* the original Creation. This power at the same time transgresses the order of pro- or re-creation by model and imitation. From now on man can create without *mediation:* we are no longer children of a Father-model—we are our own children.

The short-circuiting of *imitatio* is manifest in the works of Niccolò

Tartaglia, whose *Nova scientia* I quoted above. In the prologue of his *Quesiti et inventioni diverse* (1554) he offers a poem to his readers:

Chi brama di veder nove inventioni
Non tolte da Platon, ne da Plotino,
Ne d'alcun altro Greco, over Latino,
Ma sol da Larte, misura, e Ragioni,
Lega di questo le interrogationi.

[Whoever desires to see new inventions not taken from Plato or Plotinus, nor from any other Greek or Latin, but solely from Art, measurement, and reason(ing), may he read the inquiries of this person.]

Plato and Plotinus, Greeks and Romans, will no longer be necessary for his geometrical calculations; one can avoid mediation by concentrating totally on oneself. Tartaglia's sense of invention is analogous to the transgression of poetic imitation: the new invention confers on the poet the power of remaking the models, of remaking Creation. In Ariosto the virulent condemnation of the harquebus in canto 11 of the *Orlando Furioso* includes a curious description of this creative power at work. Germany first learned this "cruel" art, then Italy and France, where one "forms" different guns and gives them different names:

Alcuno il bronzo in cave *forme* spande
che liquefatto ha la fornace accesa;
búgia altri il ferro; e chi picciol, chi grande
il vaso *forma*, che piú e meno pesa:
e qual bombarda e qual *nomina* scoppio,
qual semplice cannon, qual cannon doppio;
qual sagra, qual falcon, qual colubrina
sento *nomar*, come al suo *autor* piú agrada.
(11.24–25; my italics)

[One spreads into hollow forms the bronze which the burning furnace has liquified; another pierces the iron, and forms small or large recipients which weigh more or less: and I hear this one named a "bombard," that one a "scoppio," that one a "simple" cannon, another a "double cannon," this one a "sagro," the other a "falcon," another a "culverin," as it pleases their author.]

After having "formed" guns, the "author" gives them different names, partly technical, partly zoological. Thus the Adamic function of naming is added to the creation of forms: the author enriches our lexicon with technical terms (*bombarda, scoppio*) or catachreses (*sagro, falcone, colubrina*) which correspond to the new forms. The terrible destruction caused by gunpowder (cf. especially 11.26–27) reflects the imagination's ultimate transgression of human order and of the order of creation.

It is this sense of unmediated invention that underlies Ronsard's treatment of the gunpowder theme and whose particular aspects are most explicit in two poems from the *Meslanges* of 1555, "les Armes" and "l'Elegie du verre," both dedicated to Jean Brinon, his liberal friend and patron.[14]

The most explicit treatment of modern weaponry by Ronsard is found in "les Armes." The poem was written in response to a gift by Brinon which consisted of that which the poem condemns, a set of ornamental weapons, a "panoplie." I will return to the problematic nature of the poetic exchange practiced by Ronsard.

The poem's exordium is a quick overview of all possible transgressions that accompany the somber invention or uncovering of iron:

> Quiconque a le premier des enfers deterré
> Le fer, estoit, Brinon, lui mesme bien ferré:
> Lui mesme avoit, ce croi-je, occis son propre pere,
> Tué sa propre soeur, tué sa propre mere.
> Lui mesme avoit au soir à son hoste etranger
> Dessus la table offert ses enfants à manger:
> Et ne croioit qu'au ciel les dieux eussent puissance
> (Car il n'en croioit point) de punir son offence.
> (6.204–5. 1–8)

[Whoever first unearthed iron in hell was, Brinon, himself of iron: he himself had, so I believe, killed his own father, killed his own sister, killed his own mother. He himself had offered to his foreign guest on the table in the evening his children to be eaten: and he did not believe that in the heavens the Gods would have the power (for he did not believe in them) to punish his offense.]

The first two lines are almost a translation of the exordium of an elegy by Tibullus: "Quis fuit, horrendos primus qui protulit ensis? / Quam ferus et vere ferreus ille fuit!" (1.10.1–2). Rhetorically these beginnings are indeed quite similar: the striking *annominatio ferus/ferreus* in Tibullus is reproduced by Ronsard's *fer/ferré*. However the meaning is not quite the same; Tibullus plays on the closeness of *ferreus* (made of iron, insensitive, cruel) to *ferus* (animal-like, cruel, wild) and thus connects the violence associated with iron to animalistic cruelty. Man becomes more like an animal in perfecting instruments of violence. In Ronsard the association *fer* (iron) / *ferré* (made of iron, insensitive) does not include the connotation of *animal*, even though the poet could very well have chosen an epithet using the element *-fer-*: in sixteenth-century French the words *fere, ferin*, and *ferité* were all available to express animal-like cruelty.[15] So Ronsard has *excluded* any association with animals in order to underline the perfectly *human* nature of this discovery (as Erasmus too points out in his adage *Dulce bellum inexpertis*). Man is not imitating any other being on the earth in this invention.

Moreover, in Ronsard's version the *annominatio* not only covers the words *fer* and *ferré*, but is announced by the first line's *enfers*. The discovery of iron is then a hellish invention or, conversely, hell is an invention of those who discovered iron. The *enfer* is literally *en fer*, that is, under the earth where iron is found, and *en fers* in the sense of "in chains," unfree. He who discovers and uses iron is he who gains a control over the principle governing the underworld.

The description of the first finder of iron is characterized exactly by his freedom from dependence of any kind. Amplifying Tibullus's interrogative *quis*, Ronsard designates him by *Quiconque*: he has no name, he is a place that could be filled by whomever, *quiconque*. The inventor of iron possesses himself perfectly. The anaphoric use of *lui mesme*, the repetition of *propre*, point to an absolute "ipséité," self-sameness, of the inventor. His creation is of course simultaneously a destruction, since he must kill all of those who might partake of his identity. He guarantees his own freedom from filiation of any kind—no one precedes him and no one succeeds him. He expels all dependents in a reverse parody of the gods' attempts to eternalize their reigns: instead of eating his sons or incorporating his children, he prepares banquets of Thyestes where he offers his progeny to be ingested by *others* (*à son hoste etranger*). Finally of course he does not believe in the gods, which means that they do not exist, just as their obverse, hell, is only a reflection of his nature, the *ferré*. The radical expulsion and self-sameness of the inventor of iron represent a significant change from the wily intermediary Prometheus whose success is always the product of his double nature, a Titan who was also a friend of the Olympians.

Death, discord, and destruction characterize the sad age into which the world enters with the uncovering and retrieval of iron.[16]

> Mais si tost que le fer par malheur fut trouvé,
> Qu'au fond de ses rougnons Pluton avoit couvé,
> Par tant d'espaces d'ans là bas dessous la terre,
> Au jour aveques lui la discorde & la guerre,
> Et le meurtre sortit, & sortirent dehors
> Ces mots de tue, assomme, & mile horribles mors.
>
> (21–26)

[But as soon as, by misfortune, iron was found, which in his loins Pluto had incubated during so many years there under the earth, along with iron discord, war, and murder came out to the light of day, and those words of kill, slaughter and a thousand horrible deaths came out as well.]

Penetrating Pluto's body man appropriates the faculty of reproduction (*rougnons*) and forces the earth to excrete death and numerous words designating violence among men. The process of generation envisaged is a sinister parody of Venus's procreation of terrestrial species—it is essentially transgressive, as sodomy is a transgression of conception. However, the transgressive reversal of procreation becomes the only *effective* imitation of the gods:

> Qui pis est, des humains les races trop cruelles
> N'ont fait tant seulement roidir en alumelles
> Le fer en long batu, mais du grand Jupiter
> Ont osé par le fer le tonnerre imiter,
> Et imiter sa foudre en du fer entonnée,
> Bien d'une autre façon que ne fit Salmonée.
> (43–48)

[What is worst, the too cruel human races not only made into rigid swords the beaten iron, but dared to imitate great Jupiter's thunder by iron, and dared to imitate his lightning enclosed in iron, in a very different way than Salmoneus.]

The Renaissance, with its invention of gunpowder, provides a daring imitation of Jupiter's thunder and lightning, more effective than Salmoneus's feeble attempts at reproducing the sound of thunder. Again the underworld provides the basic tools in this reverse procreation, and Ronsard insists on bodily excretion and expulsion in order to express the process of gun-making:

Ils ont fondu premier l'homicide metal,
Souflé d'une furie, au brasier infernal
Que vomit Flegeton: ils ont mis en la fonte
Le son, la peur, l'horreur, l'ire, & la flame pronte
Pleine de puanteur: ils ont apres cherché
Le soufre, que nature avoit à part caché
Dans les venes de l'eau, puis le long des murailles
Des estables de Circe, ou dedans les entrailles
D'une grotte relente, ou d'un mont reculé
Ilz sont allés chercher le salpestre gelé.

(49–58)

[First they melted the homicidal metal, blown by a Fury in the infernal blaze which Phlegethon vomits; they put into the melting pot the sound, the fear, the horror, the anger, and the rapid flame full of stench: then they looked for sulphur which nature hid away in the veins of water; then they looked for frozen saltpeter along the walls of the pigsties of Circe, or in the entrails of a stinking cavern, or of a hidden mountain.]

The "vomit" of Phlegethon, the "stinking" flame announces the transgressive search for sulphur and saltpeter in the bowels of the earth. As the entrails and the anus are the hidden parts of the body, sulphur is found in the earth where nature had hidden it, or it is found in pigsties symbolizing vast, indifferent excretion. Infernal excretion is the corporeal sign of the death wish: "Pourquoi, chetifs humains, avés vous tant d'envie / A grands cous de canon d'acoursir vostre vie?" (87–88) [Why, little humans, do you have so much desire to shorten your life with great cannon shots?]. But the production of death is still production, engendering. As Ariosto before him, Ronsard insists throughout the poem on the new lexicon engendered by iron and gunpowder (17.25–26.107–8); the excretion of violence is also the excretion of words and poetic production. The evocation of the hidden, distant place where the radical inventor finds new and effective material ("caché," "reculé," "elongnées") strangely recalls the distance and foreignness of the source of inspiration, Narcissus's "bord étranger" (6.76.44).

The hints of Ronsard's positive interpretation of weaponry are given in the terms used to describe its effects. The cannonball flies so fast that "l'enfer s'en crevace & prent clarté nouvelle" (64) [hell cracks open and receives a new clearness]. The iron mines are "mise en lumiere" by the "artizan avisé" (116–17, correction of 1584). The new light is not without its humanistic resonance and the vehement condemnation of guns cannot competely hide a certain satisfaction with the literally illuminating effects of these weapons. However, all in all, modern invention at its most dramatic is inevitably a transgressive, alienating parody of original procreation.

One of the consequences of gunpowder is the destruction of hierarchy and the (re)turn to a chaotic horizontality. There are no more singularized epic combats and there is no more gradation in the value of warriors. The implication for the poet is that all epic writing has to refer to the ancient past, since guns have eliminated the possibility of any contemporary heroic deeds:

> Par lui [the inventor of guns] come jadis
> on ne voit plus d'Hectors,
> D'Achilles, ni d'Ajax, hé Dieu! car les plus fors
> Sont aujourduy tués d'un poltron en cachette
> A cous de harquebuze, ou à cous de musquette.
> Au tems qu'on batailloit, sans fraude, main à main,
> On congnoissoit au fait celuy qui estoit plain
> De peur ou d'assurance, & ne vouloit-on croire
> Que Thersite au combat meritast tant de gloire
> Qu'Achille en meritoit, mais Thersite aujourduy
> Tue Achille de loin, & trionfe de luy.
> (77–86)

[Because of him one no longer sees Hectors, Achilles, nor Ajax, oh God! for the strongest are nowadays killed by a coward in hiding by the harquebus or the musket. In that time, when one fought, without trickery, hand to hand, one knew by his deed the person who was full of fear or assurance, and one did not want to believe that Thersites merited as much glory in combat as Achilles, but today Thersites kills Achilles from afar, and is triumphant over him.]

Contrary to the ancient style of combat, one no longer knows one's opponent, one fights with cunning and tricks, and great heroes can be killed by the least worthy. Ruse has of course never been absent from the arsenal of the weaker, but the generalization of combat *en cachette* and *de loin* is troubling. The hiddenness and distance of deadly fire recalls its transgressive, infernal origin. The fact that one does not know one's opponent's qualities adds an element of unpredictability: it is essentially by chance that men are killed, since they can be killed by anyone at any time. Epic hierarchy and predetermination are replaced by the horizontal, temporal narrative of chance.

God's abandonment of man at the end of the poem is only an extension of the destruction of hierarchy implied by guns:

> Toutesfois je plain tant du commun le domage,
> Que je voudroi (croy moy) que celuy qui l'usage
> Trouva premier du fer n'eust jamais esté né,
> Et n'avoir eu tes dons, car Dieu n'eust detourné
> Son visaige de nous, & la paix violée
> N'eust point abandonné la terre desolée
> Pour s'en voler là hault laissant le monde icy
> S'entre-piller, fraper & tuer sans mercy.
>   (123–30; last two lines added in 1567)

[However I so much pity men for the damage they suffer that I wish, believe me, that he who first found the use of iron had never been born, and I would like not to have had your gifts, for God would not have turned his face away from us, and violated Peace would never have abandoned the desolated earth in order to fly above, leaving men here to pillage, to beat and to kill without mercy.]

The world is left to its own indiscriminate violence; the string of infinitives in the final line of the poem denotes a continuous, senseless activity of humanity deprived of historical teleology.

"Les Armes" is one in a series of poems written as thanks for gifts by Ronsard's generous Maecenas, Jean Brinon: a statue of Bacchus, a glass, a set of weapons, and a hunting dog. The guns and swords are the most problematic of these gifts. The poet adds a brief palinode to his condemnation of iron and gunpowder in order to acknowledge a gift that obviously would have been impossible if iron had not been discovered and guns invented:

> Mais que di-je, Brinon, qui n'auroit la miniere
> Du metal & du fer jadis mise en lumiere,
> Et qui ne se seroit brusquement avisé,
> En fondant le canon, de l'avoir pertuisé,
> Et d'avoir asserré l'alumelle trampée,
> Tu ne m'eusses donné ny dague ny espée,
> (Car le fer n'eust usage) & ne m'eusses, Brinon,
> Donné ny pistolet, ny rouet, ny canon.
>   (115–22)

[But what am I saying, Brinon, if someone had not brought to light the mine of metal and iron, and if someone had not suddenly decided, in melting metal of cannons, to puncture it, and to harden the wet sword, you would not have given me dagger nor sword (since there would be no usage of iron) and you would not have given me pistol, harquebus, or cannon.]

The poet accepts the gift, yet blames its inventor in the poem accepting the invention. This paradoxical exchange can be explained by Ronsard's unwillingness to offend a generous donor; on the other hand, the detailed treatment of the invention and its resonances invite speculation on the status of poetry in this exchange.

If gunpowder constitutes the "bad" invention, then poetry presumably is a "good" one; that is, in exchange for an instrument of destruction, the poet creates an instrument of preservation. The diabolical invention is the pretext, the first cause, of a good invention. Moreover the poem is in some ways "innocent"; since it was not there *first*, the price of radical newness is paid, as it were, by another ("Quiconque"). The poet also *possesses* the product of newness, self-sameness, just as the ancient poets possessed new subject matter about which to compose their epics. "Les Armes" is then a poem that pretends to be (serenely) secondary, condemning yet accepting a necessarily transgressive invention.

If "les Armes" is a most explicit treatment of diabolical *inventio*, "l'Elegie du verre" is a subtle manifestation of its consequences for *imitatio*. The praise of glass is connected, understandably, to the praise of Bacchus, who incarnates certain poetic ambitions of Ronsard and his period.[17] In this poem the glass contains the wine that comes from Bacchus. But the glass ends up containing the god not only metonymically, but literally: Jupiter kills the pregnant mother Semele with his lightning, and Bacchus must be washed of blood and powder before being placed into Jupiter's thigh, from which he will be reborn.[18] Ronsard has Bacchus washed in the glass.

Before this myth is alluded to, however, Ronsard praises the glass given him by Brinon:

> O joly verre, oseroi-je bien dire
> Combien je t'ayme, & combien je t'admire?
> Tu es heureux, & plus heureux celui
> Qui t'inventa pour noyer nostre ennuy.
> Ceux qui jadis les canons inventerent,
> Et qui d'Enfer le fer nous aporterent
> Meritoient bien que là bas Rhadamant
> Les fist punir d'un juste chatiment,
> Mais cestuy là, qui d'un esprit agile

Te façonna, fûce le grand Vergile,
Ou les nochers qui firent sans landiers
Cuire leur rost sur les bois mariniers,
Meritoient bien de bailler en la place
De Ganimede à Jupiter la tasse,
Et que leur verre inventé de nouveau
Alast au ciel, & fait un astre beau
. . . .
Non, ce n'est moi qui blasme Promethée
D'avoir au ciel la flame derobée:
Il fist tresbien: sans le larcin du feu,
Verre joly, jamais on ne t'eust veu.
                    (6.166–67.11–34)

[O pretty glass, will I dare say how much I like you, and how much I
admire you? You are happy, and happier is he who invented you to
drown our sorrows. Those who earlier invented cannons and who
brought us iron from hell deserved being punished there by Rhada-
manthus, but he who with an agile mind fashioned you—was it the
great Virgil, or the boat pilots who without andirons roasted meat on
wood from the seashore—they deserved to give the glass cup to
Jupiter in place of Ganymede, and deserved to have their glass, newly
invented, rise to the sky and become a beautiful star. . . No, it is not I
who blame Prometheus for having stolen the flame from the sky: he
did very well: without the theft of fire, pretty glass, one would never
have seen you.]

Two inventions figure in the context of Virgil, Jupiter, and Prometheus: glass and guns. The latter originate in hell and are connected
to *iron* (*fer*); glass, on the other hand, comes from heaven and fire
(*feu*). The invention of glass is not without its double—guns. Yet the
distinction fire/iron is not really a distinction: we have seen that it is
exactly the conjunction of fire and iron which lends guns their
power and which defines the invention as such. The gun is at the
same time the theft of lightning and a raping of the earth. The
apparent exclusion of guns—that is, their condemnation and connection to iron—serves to purify fire and the resulting glass by
limiting the symbolic associations. Yet their explicit exclusion also
grants guns a place in the poem.

Ambivalent invention repeats itself in a different form: Ronsard
compares and opposes glass to gold, especially to gold vessels or
cups. The "joly" glass is preferable to the "monstrueuses taces" of
gold, such as the gold cup of Nestor (168.64–66). The preference is
explained by the fact that gold is mined, just as, we may add, iron

and niter (and thus guns): "Premierement d'avant que les tirer / Hors de leur mine, il faut plus dessirer / L'antique mere" (69–71) [First of all, before taking them / out of their mine, one must tear up / the old mother]. Gold engenders violence: when men drink too much, a gold vessel can split "par sa grosseur epaisse / Le chef de ceux qui nagueres amis / Entre les pots deviennent ennemis" (84–86) [by its thick size, / the head of those who, until recently friends / among the vessels became enemies]. Finally the praise of glass seems to constitute an attempt to dissociate the theft of fire by Prometheus, or the invention of glass, from their violent double, the mining of metal, or implicitly, the invention of guns.

However, the very fact that glass is praised by condemning metal suggests that one is necessary to the other. The fire of heaven implies the iron of earth. These elements are not only symmetrical opposites, but structurally indistinct from each other, as both represent the appropriation of radical invention.

As we have seen, Ronsard connects the invention of glass to poetic invention: "Mais cestuy là, qui d'un esprit agile / Te façonna, fûce le grand Vergile" (19–20). The words *esprit* and *façonner* recur at the end of the poem; this time the fabrication of glass can be read as an allegory of poetic creation:

> C'est un plesir que de voir renfrogné
> Un grand Cyclope à l'oeuvre enbesongné,
> Qui te parfait des cendres de fougère,
> Et du seul vent de son aleine ouvriere.
> Come l'esprit enclos dans l'univers
> Engendre seul mile genres divers,
> Et seul en tout mile especes diverses,
> Au ciel, en terre, & dans les ondes perses:
> Ainsi le vent duquel tu es formé,
> De l'artizan en la bouche enfermé,
> Large, petit, creux, ou grand, te façonne
> Selon l'esprit & le feu qu'il te donne.
> Que diray plus? par espreuve je croi
> Que Bacus fut jadis lavé dans toi,
> Lors que sa mere atteinte de la foudre,
> En avorta, plein de sang & de poudre.
>   (97–112)[19]

[It is a pleasure to watch a great brooding Cyclops hard at work, who perfects you in the ashes of ferns and by the sole wind of his industrious breath. Just as the spirit enclosed in the universe engenders

alone a thousand different genera, and alone in all a thousand different
species, in the sky, on the earth, and in the blue waves, so the wind by
which you are formed, enclosed in the artisan's mouth, fashions you
wide, small, hollow, or large, according to the spirit and the fire he
gives you. What more will I say? As proof I believe that Bacchus was
formerly washed in you when his mother struck by lightning expelled
him full of blood and powder.]

"L'aleine ouvriere" and "l'esprit enclos dans l'univers" (100, 101)
are allusions (as Laumonier points out) to the *Aeneid* where the
spiritus (6.726) is described as a seed as vigorous as fire and of divine
origin ("igneus est ollis vigor et caelestis origo / seminibus.")[20] Ronsard insists on the singularity of the creator-spirit ("Engendre
seul. . . . Et *seul*. . . .") who creates a multiplicity of species in the
sky, on the earth, in the waters, with varied forms ("Large, petit,
creux, ou grand"). These forms are *fashioned* (*façonnées*, 107) by him
who possesses the "esprit" (101), just as Virgil "d'un esprit agile /
Te [the glass] façonna" (19–20). The description of the *spiritus* by Virgil
is at the same time a fashioning by or of the *spiritus:* in other words,
the fact of describing the process, of discovering that which is "enclos," is already its appropriation. Virgil, who has described the
spiritus, creates forms by its virtue; Ronsard's description is then an
imitation of Virgil and his appropriation of the creative spirit.

Yet this implicit imitation is an insufficient account of Ronsard's
rewriting of Bacchus's birth. Whereas Virgil fashions the glass in
which Bacchus will be washed, Ronsard associates himself with that
which *necessitates* his washing: Jupiter's lightning. The mother Semele is "atteinte de la foudre," torn and covered with powder.
Gunpowder, excluded at the outset, returns here in its symbolic
manifestations, first by the tearing of the Mother Earth (70–71) by
mining and then in a direct way through Jupiter's lightning. The
Renaissance invention, present through its explicit exclusion, returns through lightning and is placed *before* the glass. The false
distinction between cannons, iron, mining (on the one hand), and
glass, fire, heaven (on the other), permits gunpowder to place itself
at the very cause of the "avortement" of Bacchus, before the glass
created by the Virgilian *spiritus*. The rewriting of Bacchus' "first"
birth is thus an attempt to define the poetic autonomy of the Renaissance vis-à-vis Virgil.

After the *avortement* of Bacchus, the praise of the glass continues
through the praise of wine:

> Et [je crois] que des lors quelque reste du feu
> Te [au verre] demoura, car quiconques a beu

> Un coup dans toi, tout le tems de sa vie
> Plus y reboit plus a de boire envie,
> Et de Bacus toujours le feu cruel
> Art son gozier d'un chaut continuel
>   (113–118)

[And (I believe) that since then some rest of the fire was left in you (the glass), for whoever has drunk from you wants to drink more and more all during his life, and the cruel fire of Bacchus always burns his throat with a continual heat.]

The *feu* (113) that remains in the glass may designate either the rest of the lightning/powder, or the fire that was part of the glass's fabrication (108). Instead of maintaining Virgil as the only source of inspiration, Ronsard has the fire of lightning coexist with the Virgilian fire, and thus places himself at the source. He will be able to engender himself, a power that he will describe openly elsewhere, as in the 1584 correction of the "Odelette à luy mesmes": "De moy-mesmes je me veux faire / L'heritier, pour me satisfaire" (6.104) [I want to make my own / inheritor of myself, to satisfy myself].

Fire, the cause of thirst, is the sign of the desire of its contrary, water or wine. Thirst for wine is also poetic thirst, that is, the state of lack that the Renaissance poet feels at the "fontaines" of the Muses. The problem of an imitation that can only be degeneration haunts Ronsard's poetry: the ancients have emptied the Muses' source, and there remains not a drop for the thirsty Renaissance:

> [Les Grecs] beurent à longs trais
> Toute l'eau jusque au fond des filles de Memoire
> N'en laissant une goute aux derniers pour en boire,
> Qui maintenant confus à-foule-à-foule vont
> Chercher encor de l'eau de-sur le double Mont:
> Mais ilz montent en vain, car plus ilz y sejournent,
> Et plus mourant de soif au logis s'en retournent.
>   ("Hymne de la Mort," 8.163)

[(The Greeks) drank in long draughts to the bottom all the waters of the daughters of Memory, leaving not a drop for the last ones who now, lost, in crowds, go to look for more water on the double mountain: but they climb in vain, for the longer they are there, the more dying of thirst will they return home.]

These words of despair are contradicted elsewhere by Ronsard's sense of his own poetic inexhaustibility: his epigones drink of his infinite source.[21]

In either case fire, cause of the thirst that is the sign of the quench-
ing source, is at the origin of the creative process and lays bare the
problematic relationship between epigone and model, a relationship that seems endlessly to repeat its dilemmas. However, the
representation of the "diabolical" invention of gunpowder opens
this schema of mediated creation: the self-same inventor can place
himself outside of literary filiation, paradoxically before the ancient
models.

In the "Hinne de Bacus" the power of the "cuisse-né" god is
defined in a semantic chiasmus: "Alme pere Denys, tu es beaucoup
à creindre, / Qui contrains un chacun, & nul te peut contraindre"
(6.188.229–30) [Nourishing father Dionysius, you are to be feared
greatly, / you who constrain everyone, and no one can constrain
you]. The "Elegie du verre" seems to constitute just such a "constraint" of Bacchus: the glass (i.e., Virgil's *spiritus*) contains the violent god. Yet Ronsard is at the origin of these constraints; he has
found the secret of lightning.

Notes

This chapter is a revised and expanded version of an article that appeared
in *Romanic Review*, May 1982, 184–94.

All translations, including these two epigraphs, are by the author.

> [Then I thought that he who by science, hard work, or chance finds
> something remarkable and who wants to be its sole possessor merits
> no little blame, for, if all the ancients had done the same, we would
> hardly be different from the irrational animals now; so, in order not
> to incur this blame I have decided to bring my inquiries and in-
> ventions to the light of day.]

> [No beast is more pernicious to man than man himself. Also, when
> beasts fight, it is with their own arms; we men use unnatural arms
> invented through the art of demons in order to kill other men.]

1. Cf. Rabelais, *Pantagruel*, 8: "Les impressions tant élégantes et correctes en
usance, qui ont esté inventées de mon aage par inspiration divine, comme, a contrefil, l'artillerie par suggestion diabolique."
2. Ed. W. Hassenstein (Munich: Verlag der deutschen Technik, 1941), 4;
similar dietary restrictions are found in the *Büchsenmeÿsterei* (Strasbourg:
Chr. Egenolphen, 1529), vi.
3. *Nova scientia* (Vinegia: Sabio, 1537), viii–ix.
4. In the prologue to the *Quesiti et inventioni diverse*. Cf. also John R. Hale, *The
Art of War and Renaissance England* (Charlottesville: University Press of
Virginia, 1961).
5. Cf. for example Ariosto, *Orlando furioso*, IX, 88; Ronsard, "les Armes," VI,
p. 207, vv. 45–47 (all references to the works of Ronsard are taken from the

Oeuvres complètes, ed. Paul Laumonier [Paris: Hachette, Droz, Didier, 1914–75, 20 vols.); Milton, "In inventorem Bombardae" (1626) and *Paradise Lost*, VI, vv. 490–91; William Clarke, *The Natural History of Nitre, or, a Philosophical Discourse of the Nature, Generation, Place, and Artificial Extraction of Nitre, with its Vertues and Uses* (London: E. Okes, 1670), 78–79: "But it hath been doubted whether so ingenious and dreadful a *Machine* could be a humane Invention, which, when it was first published, the World thought she had lost all her strength; for what more terrible or violent could humane Wit invent to its own destruction, than this *artificial Lightning* and *Thunder*." The troops of Fabrizio Colonna declare, in the battle of Ravenna, when they are attacked by artillery, "Cuerpo de Dios! somos matados del cielo: vamos combater hombres" (quoted by Sir Charles Oman, *A History of the Art of War in the Sixteenth Century* [London: Methuen, 1937], 140). Cf. also S. Gabriel Busca, *Della espugnatione et difesa delle fortezze* (Turin: G. Dominico Tarino, 1598), 2d. rev. ed., 18 (1st ed. 1585); Daniel Davelourt, *l'Arcenal et magazin d'artillerie* (Paris: s.n., 1610), 78 ff., 96; Robert Norton, *The Gunner Shewing the Whole Practise of Artillery* . . . (London: H. Robinson, 1628), 38; Casimiro Simienowicz, *Vollkommene Geschütz Feuerwerck un Büchsenmeisteren Kunst*, trans. L. B. Thoma (Frankfurt a. M.: J. D. Zunner, 1676), translator's prologue, f. 4 ro.

6. Cf. Ariosto, *Orlando furioso*, IX, 88–91, XI, 24–28; Spenser, *The Faerie Queen*, I, vii, 13; Rabelais, *Pantagruel*, VIII, XXVIII; Maurice Scève, *Microcosme*, III, vv. 911–22; Ronsard, "Les Armes," VI, pp. 204–11; T. Tasso, *Gerusalemme liberata*, XII, 42, 45; A. d'Aubigné, *L'Hécatombe à Diane*, IV, X, XII, etc., *Stances* VI, *Ode* XIII, *Tragiques*, "Misères," *passim*; Cervantes, *Don Quixote*, I, 38; Milton, *Paradise Lost*, VI, vv. 469–523. I am thankful to Gérard Defaux and David Quint for valuable suggestions concerning this topic.

7. Concerning the attitude of Ariosto to the wars of the Este family, cf. Giorgio Padoan, "L'*Orlando furioso* et la crisi del Rinascimento," in *Ariosto 1974 in America*, ed. Aldo Scaglione (Ravenna: Longo, 1976), 1–29, and Angelo Cerri, "L'Ariosto e la battaglia di Pavia," *Giornale storico della letteratura italiana* 152 (1975), 551–56.

8. "O maladetto, o abominoso ordigno, / che fabricato nel tartareo fondo / fosti per man di Belzebú maligno / che ruinar per te disegnò il mondo, / all'inferno, onde uscisti, ti rasigno. - / Cosí dicendo, le gittò in profondo" (IX, 91; all quotations from the *Orlando furioso* are taken from ed. Lanfranco Caretti [Torino, Einaudi, 1966]). Cf. also Spenser, I, vii, 13: "that divelish yron Engin, wrought / In deepest Hell. . . ."

9. For a discussion of objections to mining in the Renaissance, cf. Walter M. Kendrick, "Earth of Flesh, Flesh of Earth: Mother Earth in the *Faerie Queen*," *Renaissance Quarterly* 27 (1974), especially 537–41. The fabrication of gunpowder can evidently be associated with "traditional" alchemical processes, but is distinct from the latter in the fact that it is a practical and effective invention. For mining and alchemical symbolism cf. Mircea Eliade, *Forgerons et alchimistes* (Paris: Flammarion, 1956), 175 ff.

10. Clarke, *History of Nitre*, 16–18; italics are in the text. Cf. also Davelourt, *L'Arcenal*, 35.

11. Clarke, *History of Nitre*, 20–21. Johann Kunckel, *Oeffentliche Zuschrifft von dem Phosphoro mirabili und dessen leuchtenden Wunder-Pilulen sammt angehängten Discurs von dem weyland recht benahmten Nitro, jetzt aber unschuldig genandten Blut der Natur* (Leipzig: M. Rustwurm, 1678), 31–51, has similar problems with urine.

12. Satan speaks of niter before its discovery in "dark nativity . . . pregnant with eternal flame" (vv. 482–83).

13. "[E]ach [rebellious angel] how he / To be th'inventor missed, so easy it seemed / Once found, which yet unfound most would have thought / Impossible. . . ." (vv. 498–501). There is an abundant recent literature on imitation in the Renaissance; the most useful for this study are G. W. Pigman III, "Versions of Imitation in the Renaissance," *Renaissance Quarterly* 33 (1980): 1–32, especially 16 ff. on emulation; Claude-Gilbert Dubois, *Le maniérisme*, (Paris: Presses universitaires de France, 1979).

14. Cf. I. D. McFarlane, "Ronsard's Poems to Jean Brinon," in Frieda S. Brown, ed., *French Renaissance Studies in Honor of Isidore Silver* (*Kentucky Romance Quarterly* 21, suppl. 2, 1974), 53–68.

15. Ronsard's uses of *ferin* and *fere* are quoted by E. Huguet in his *Dictionnaire de la langue française au XVIe siècle*.

16. Cf. Elizabeth Armstrong, *Ronsard and the Age of Gold* (Cambridge: Cambridge University Press, 1968), 19–21; Daniel Ménager, *Ronsard: Le Roi, le Poète et les Hommes* (Geneva: Droz, 1979), 75.

17. Cf. especially Terence Cave, "The Triumph of Bacchus and Its Interpretation in the French Renaissance: Ronsard's *Hinne de Bacus*," in A. H. T. Levi, ed., *Humanism in France at the End of the Middle Ages and in the Early Renaissance* (Manchester: Manchester University Press, 1970), 249–70.

18. Thus the epithet "deus fois né" in the ode 38 in the 4th book of Ronsard's *Odes* (ed. of 1557), VII, 192.

19. Cf. also the "Hinne de Bacus," VI, p. 178, vv. 20–23: "Le plus gratieus feu du grand Saturnien / Fist ta mere avorter, & que parmy la foudre / Non encores formé, tu sortis noir de poudre / Hors du ventre brulé. . . ."

20. Cf. also D. P. Walker, *Spiritual and Demonic Magic from Ficino to Campanella* (Leiden: Warburg Institute, 1958), ch. 1, especially pp. 12–13.

21. "Vous estes mes ruisseaux, je suis vostre fonteine, / Et plus vous m'espuisés, plus ma fertile veine / Repoussant le sablon, jette une source d'eaux / D'un surjon eternel pour vous autres ruisseaux" (1563) from the *Responce aux injures* . . . (XI, p. 169, vv. 1039–42).

7. MONTAIGNE AND THE SUBJECT

OF POLITY

■

TIMOTHY J. REISS

I sent your Grace
The parcels and particulars of our grief,
The which hath been with scorn shoved from the court,
Whereon this Hydra son of war is born,
Whose dangerous eyes may well be charmed asleep
With grant of our most just and right desires,
And true obedience, of this madness cured,
Stoop tamely to the foot of majesty.
　　　—SHAKESPEARE, *2 Henry IV*, 4.11 (c. 1597–98)

IT MIGHT seem that the question of the subject (of any subject) in the work of Montaigne lies on such well-worn terrain that it is scarcely worth the trouble to cover it again. Indeed, much has been said regarding the "ambiguities" and "contradictions" of Montaigne in this regard. He has been seen sometimes as the precursor of the voluntarist Cartesian subject, and other times as the sign of a moment in which something like a "subject" still remains to be constituted. There have been disputes between those who emphasize the all-too-famous phrase, "Each man bears the entire form of man's estate" (3.2.611,782)[1] and those who favor another, less well-known, one, "I do not share that common error of judging another by myself" (1.37.169,225), or the warning that follows it immediately: "I have a singular desire that we should each be judged in ourselves apart, and that I may not be measured in conformity with the common patterns." At times Montaigne is viewed as a conservative, as the loyal and even intolerant subject of his prince; at others he is praised as a (secretly) radical or even revolutionary thinker—the intrepid successor of what is then interpreted as the "leftist" text of his friend La Boetie, the *Discours de la servitude volontaire*. Thus it is that recently (we need not venture into the interpretive tradition) there has been talk of Montaigne's "dialectic" of the self (which is no dialectic at all), of the "wager" of exemplarity that is taken to inform his thought, or again, to avoid the suggestion of extremism in this latter, of the "paradox" of this appellation, "Michel de Montaigne," which names a "universal being" one minute, but which cannot name anything at all the next.[2]

I do not want to extend this field of ambiguity, of contradiction, of paradox and extreme. Such views seem to me to emerge from a refusal to situate Montaigne in a specific historical moment, and from a desire to read him as an exemplary representative of the "human"—as if this concept of the human were not itself the product of a certain history (a matter to which I will return). Yet it is not a question here of situating him in any "social" or "biographical" sense (this latter work having already been accomplished magisterially by Donald Frame).[3] Rather, I want to consider Montaigne insofar as he belongs to a certain moment of what is called more and more nowadays "the history of mentalities"; and this with reference to a particular field of thought—that of political theory. Thus I shall attempt not only to cut across the question of the subject in Montaigne and that of a certain political thought, but as well to place the problem with relative precision in a current of political thought leading from the Middle Ages through a "first" definitive questioning (dating from the period of Machiavelli's work) toward an eventual consolidation of the liberal theory of the state in Hobbes and Locke.

In a general fashion, though without special reference to political theory, this development has been examined more closely in my *Discourse of Modernism*. There I make considerable use of Michel Foucault's work in order to analyze a certain textual corpus to show how what he calls the *episteme*, what I prefer to call the sociocultural environment, gradually develops and consolidates into a sphere of action and thought under the sway of what I term the dominant discursive model. Because this analysis seeks to show how contradictions and occultations, emergent and residual elements in one such model force a relatively gradual *transformation* toward another, it differs considerably from Foucault's notion of epistemic rupture, though it can make use of his tools for the analysis of a sociocultural environment once it has in fact been consolidated. The difference from Foucault's analysis, however, goes further than what has just been suggested. For the concept of the sociocultural environment is used to enable us to escape from an analysis that remains essentially bound to a linguistic order and views all human processes as in some fundamental way languagelike. All human actions, I would propose, may be conceived as forms of discourse. But "discourse," here, is positively *not* to be understood as in any way coterminous with language. Rather does it refer to the meaningful process ordering *any* sign material, where language (for example) is simply one such material. With this in mind, once we begin to see all human actions as sociocultural ways of producing meanings, and history as a process of environmental transformations and consolidations, then the very terms of such actions take on new meanings.[4] If Montaigne, for example, is viewed as participating in a period of transformation, then we begin to realize that certain key terms recurring constantly in the *Essays* may well have been fundamentally misinterpreted—in the light of meanings they have taken on under the sway of a discursive model that Montaigne may have helped bring into being but which is quite foreign to his own and his contemporaries' thought and action. Trying to analyze Montaigne in such a light, to fit such terms at once into their particular history and into the practical and theoretical environment that was Montaigne's, will oblige us, I think, to see the *Essays* in a completely new light and as playing an emblematic role in the consolidation of an eventually new discursive dominance of unexpected importance and significance.

Instead of seeing the ambiguities and contradictions, I shall propose simply that in Montaigne there are "two" subjects: one which scarcely constitutes itself as such, which marks an attempt to seize thought in process and which is rigorously "private" (to use a word employed constantly by Montaigne); the other by which the "public" individual is "subject" to his prince—in the first case the private "subject," in the second the social and political subject. It is this double constitution of the subject which I shall pursue briefly. Yet I must stress right away that *in no way* is this duality a question of opposition. On the contrary, one is absolutely essential to the other. If the political subject has a "being," one must find it in the constant movement of thought that alone constitutes the private subject; if this latter has an "existence," it is thanks to its projection (in a geometrical or logical sense) into the concrete world of the social.[5] Even more important than this absence of contradiction: we find ourselves here faced with a schema rigorously analogous to that which exists in the case of the sovereign prince. Indeed, in this double subject we find the form of "the King's double body" as symbolized in the phrase of succession, "The King is dead, long live the King," and definitively elucidated by Ernst Kantorowicz. In the king's case it is a question of the "mystical" and immortal body, guaranteeing the stability and permanence of the state, as against the present, particular and mortal body, subject to the laws and punctual relations of a given society and historical moment.[6] This idea is found in Montaigne, as in this addition to the 1595 edition:

> We owe subjection and obedience equally to all kings, for that concerns their office; but we do not owe esteem, any more than affection, except to their virtue. Let us make this concession to the political order: to suffer them patiently if they are unworthy, to conceal their vices, to abet them by commending their indifferent actions if their authority needs our support. (1.3.9,19)

The relationship here is not simply made up out of thin air. The duality of the mystical body and the material body of the king is a concept essential to a certain order of sovereignty. Coming down from the Middle Ages and affirming itself especially in theories of divine right toward the end of the sixteenth century, the theory of the double body is one way of guaranteeing the stability of a certain type of social and political order (in fact, one should speak less of "theory" and more of "mentality," for Kantorowicz's explication of the theory relies less upon great theoretical texts than upon juridical and polemical documents—the reflections of a certain concrete practice). The mystical body guarantees the continuity of the state, the immutable existence of the social. In Montaigne this notion corresponds as well to the public subject, servant of the established political order, maintained by the legitimate government and guaranteed by God through the mystical body of the king. But the king, insofar as he is a living being, has his own real body—a body that by the same token moves, changes, and dies. It is there that we find this "perennial movement" (3.2.610,782) that is proper to everything in the lower world and that is above all the "proper" characteristic of the private person: "Seeing that the slightest pinprick, or passion of the soul, is sufficient to deprive us of the pleasure of being monarch of the world. At the first twinge of the gout, there is no comfort in his being Sire and Majesty" (1.42.192,254). Montaigne is expressing his agreement with Xenophon, who in his *Hieron* (also used by La Boetie) shows the king of the title role affirming that "even in the enjoyment of pleasures kings are worse off than private citizens" (ibid.,195,255).

This state of affairs comes about because the king, as living symbol of the order of state, cannot shed his political role, whereas the specific ("private") individual can easily withdraw: "For anyone who wants to ensconce himself by his hearth, and who can manage his house without quarrels and lawsuits, is as free as the Doge of Venice" (ibid.,195,257). Like Diocletian, a king may indeed want "to retire to the pleasure of a private life" (ibid.,196,258), but he cannot escape from the requirement of being always visibly present in his political aspect. The private being of the king, says Montaigne, is secondary and must be suppressed. All other members of society have a certain choice:

> In truth, our laws are free enough, and the weight of sovereignty scarcely touches a French nobleman twice in his life. The real and essential subjection is only for those among us who go seeking it and who like to gain honors and riches by such service. (ibid.,195,257)

Through this idea of liberty, then, we come back to the double subject. For here we are in fact dealing, on the social level, with the "liberty" and unobstructed movement of thought as a *process*, as ongoing thinking: "Things in themselves may have their own weights and measures and qualities; but once inside, within us, she [the soul] allots them their qualities as she sees fit" (1.1.220,290). But the freedom to withdraw from the social is no more than that, for if this freedom of reason becomes mixed in with the public domain of the sociopolitical, one ends up with complete confusion. I shall cite here a passage that is, to be sure, very famous, but one that permits us to situate Montaigne within a whole itinerary of the political thought of his age:

> I have observed in Germany that Luther has left as many divisions and altercations over the uncertainty of his opinions, and more, as he raised about the Holy Scriptures. Our disputes are purely verbal. I ask what are "nature," "pleasure," "circle," "substitution." The question is one of words, and is answered in the same way. "A stone is a body." But if you pressed on: "And what is a body?"—"Substance."—"And what is substance?" and so on, you would finally drive the respondent to the end of his lexicon. We exchange one word for another word, often more unknown. I know better what is man than I know what is animal, or moral, or rational. To satisfy one doubt, they give me three; it is the Hydra's head. (3.13.819,1046)

This passage follows a long discussion of the multiple interpretations given of the laws by legal theoreticians, and it precedes a long appeal for the simplification of these same laws as well as the elimination of learned glosses that only augment "doubts and ignorance" (ibid.,817,1044) and lead to "an irregular, perpetual motion, without model and without aid" (ibid.,818,1045). For this reason the very "commandment" of the laws, he says, is "confused and inconstant" (ibid.,821,1050).

We find a whole series of preoccupations thrown together here: the question of right and law, that of religious opinion and thus of the civil wars, a question concerning language and its relationship to things and concepts, another regarding inconstancy and yet another, implicit, on the subject and what it is capable of knowing. It will be useful to link this passage immediately with another dating from the same edition (1588)—a passage that addresses the same series of questions and which, like the one above, will facilitate my insertion of Montaigne into a certain theoretical "development" concerning the state and power, the subject and sovereignty. I believe I can show that Montaigne occupies a place at once interesting and important in this development, to which the literary criticism normally concerning itself with Montaigne has paid little or no attention.[7]

This time Montaigne speaks explicitly of the civil wars to the extent that he is considering those who seek to "upset the state":

> All sorts of new depravity gleefully draw, from this first and fertile source, examples and models to trouble our government. Men read in our very laws, made for the remedy of this first evil, an apprenticeship and excuse for all sorts of wicked enterprises; and we are experiencing what Thucydides says of the civil wars of his time, that men baptized public vices with new milder names to excuse them, adulterating and softening their true titles. (1.23.87,119)

This well-known passage by the Greek historian had become a sort of cliché in the political thought at the close of the wars of religion and we will return to Montaigne's use of it very soon. But let us move on, for a few moments, to other writers known by Montaigne, some of whom played considerable roles as much in public life as in what Pierre Mesnard has rather felicitously called the launching of political philosophy.[8] Then we shall be able to situate more easily Montaigne's considerations on the subject, on sovereignty and the relationships of force within the state.

In August of 1570 Louis Le Roy signed at Saint-Germain-en-Laye the dedication to his *Exhortation aux Francois pour vivre en concorde, et iouir du bien de la Paix.* The text is dedicated to King Charles IX, who, at the same place and in the same month, had signed the pact known as "The Peace of Saint Germain," putting an "end" to the second war of religion. In his work, Le Roy stresses that a single sovereignty, concretized in the person of the king, is essential to the continued existence of "all the Kingdom" (2 ro). The stability that necessarily follows such sovereignty (an idea possibly culled from Bodin's *Method for the Easy Comprehension of History,* published in 1556—but the question was in any case becoming a burning one) he sets against the complete upheaval resulting from political sedition, a principal consequence, he says, of the discontent of the nobles (10 ro). The major sign of this upheaval is the complete confusion of the sense of language: on this subject he quotes at great length the passage from Thucydides which we have just seen mentioned by Montaigne (44 vo–46 vo). We shall come back to this, not only because we will find the reference elsewhere, but because the relationship between political sedition, the overthrow of state sovereignty, inconstancy of the subject, and linguistic confusion is no less central for Montaigne. This relationship is closely linked to all the debates surrounding the question of sovereignty and political power.

Louis Le Roy, in 1570, sets the concept of the prince's unique sovereignty against another—that of a dispersed sovereignty represented at the time by the discontent of the nobles. It had already become clear that the so-called wars of religion masked a completely different struggle: the one between an old "feudal" concept of relations of force and a new concept yet to be found. In the meantime a confusion reigned which all found disquieting, but by which few commentators were deceived: what was at issue, the complaint ran, was not at all the religious question, or not primarily, but rather the "interest" of one side or the other. The diversity of these interests sowed confusion. At the level of political relations this confusion was perceived as a question of sovereignty. For, affirms Montaigne, it stems from according an unwonted identity and privilege to the private subject: "Society in general can do without our thoughts; but the rest—our actions, our work, our fortunes, and our very life—we must lend and abandon to its service and to the common opinion. . . . For it is the rule of rules, and the universal law of laws, that each man should observe those of the place he is in" (1.23.86,117). Or, again, he adds, "it takes a lot of self-love and presumption to have such esteem for one's own opinions that to establish them one must overthrow the public peace and introduce so many inevitable evils" (ibid.,87,119). Anyone who opts to place the private realm first, "meddles with choosing and changing, usurps the authority to judge" (ibid.,88,120). Montaigne thus considers the intervention of the private into the public domain as a usurpation of sovereignty.

I would like to take another example whose considerable interest for the case of Montaigne we shall see shortly. In his *Second Discours sur l'Estat de France*, published in 1593, Michel Hurault de l'Hospital denounces the ambition and self-interest of the house of Lorraine. According to him, it has resulted in 30 years of war: "For religion was not yet at stake; they took it only for want of a better pretext."[9] He continues with a short history of the civil wars, shortly thereafter giving a specific example of struggles between various interested groups which shows how, concretely, these struggles were played out. He stresses that what is at stake is indeed sovereignty:

> Just man, if at this moment you wanted to see the image of confusion and disorder, you would find it clearly painted in that party. To begin with, the Duke of Mayenne calls himself *Lieutenant general of the Royal State and of the crown of France*. This is a great illusion: can there be a *Lieutenant*, if there is no head? And who is head if not the King? Yet the majority of their party doesn't want any king. *As to the State*: formerly one heard talk of the States of France, but never of the State: or if one heard it named it was when one said, "the King and his State." In that case the state was named in terms of obedience and not of command: and these madmen place it at the head. (*SD*, 146)

Montaigne, who is doubtless less interested by the Huguenot party in and of itself than by the idea of a legitimate king, leans in the same direction in a passage added in 1595:

> See the horrible impudence with which we bandy divine reasons about, and how irreligiously we have both rejected them and taken them again, according as fortune has changed our place in these public storms. This proposition, so solemn, whether it is lawful for a subject to rebel and take arms against his prince in defense of religion—remember in whose mouths, this year just past, the affirmative of this was the buttress of one party, the negative was the buttress of another; and hear now from what quarter comes the voice and the instruction of both sides, and whether the weapons make less din for this cause than for that. (2.12.323,420)

The question being debated is indeed that of rebellion and sovereignty. Furthermore, we find ourselves manifestly at a moment of change in the very concept of the state: this is not a new finding, but it is important to notice that this change takes place not simply on the basis of some theoretical abstraction. It does so through reference to actual conditions and applies itself *immediately* to concrete life.

According to Hurault, the Catholic League affirms that the head of state is nothing more than the guardian ("lieutenant general") of *a state that is itself sovereign*. It would be easy indeed to find examples of the phrase "State of France" before this date: the argument proposed by Hurault is that this phrase had always signified the king's domain over which he is sovereign—an inalienable domain in some sense the "proper" characteristic of the immortal body of the king. This is the meaning of the doctrine of the king's two bodies. If sovereignty is characteristic of the state itself (thus an abstract concept, not personified by the king, which will eventually need the ascendency of the doctrine of contract in order to fix and explain the relationship of the sovereign state to its individual members), then what counts is the immortality of the state, so to speak, and not that of the mystical body of the king. The consequence of this, says Hurault, is very serious: the complete confusion of a state that no longer has a language. Since there is no longer a sovereign prince, the officers of the ex-king no longer know "how to pronounce, they dare not speak in the name of the King [i.e., Henry IV], they do not want to speak in the name of the people and even less in that of Monsieur de Mayenne, for by the statutes of the Kingdom they can recognize no one but he who has absolute command" (*SD*, 147).

Thus one is up against a fundamental disorder and confronts a "divided multitude of authorities" (*SD*, 147). It is the birth of anarchy in the strictest sense of the term: the loss of a single head leads in the long run to an infinite multiplication. And so Hurault complains of the creation of kinds of communes ("councils of certain persons of low degree in whose hands all authority has been placed") in the cities, saying that this "new democracy has undermined" the principal "Royal column," which is "justice": "Following the example of the capital city of Paris, all the other cities are doing the same thing; we have a Republic in every town" (*SD*, 148). If events continue to unfold in this way, all the other cities, big and small, will do the same: "And thus by degrees there will eventually be no village in France that has not made itself into a sovereign state" (*SD*, 149). It is worth following a bit further the interesting perspectives opened up by Michel Hurault's commentaries (which were of a type quite widespread at the time). They have a certain importance regarding the interpretation of Montaigne that I shall propose, especially, as concerns the historical role I shall attempt to show him playing.

Hurault thus argues that the League finds itself in a contradictory position. On the one hand it assumes the total sovereignty of the state, while on the other it confronts a real splintering of this very same state, a disintegration of the country's local units into a bunch of tiny sovereignties. His argument turns around the essential idea that the state and its prince are inextricably linked. Royal sovereignty (inherent in the immortal and mystic body) forms the keystone of the state as a single unit: remove this stone (by denying the king or his unique sovereignty) and the state disintegrates. Each part is driven into independence, and chaos ensues—whence the constant call of a Montaigne for "natural and simple obedience," an obedience that must be through "subjection" and not through "discretion" (1.17.51,73).

Such an obedience is essential: "The ordinary discipline of a state that is in a healthy condition does not provide for these extraordinary accidents; it presupposes a body that holds together in its principal parts and function and a common consent to its observance and obedience" (1.23.89,121). And in 1595 he adds that: "The law-abiding pace is a cold, deliberate and constrained one, and is not the kind that can hold up against a lawless and unbridled pace." One of the principal merits of the Christian religion is its "precise recommendation of obedience to the magistrate and maintenance of the government" (1.23.88,119). To this statement from 1588 he adds in 1595 that it seems

> very iniquitous to want to subject public and immutable institutions and observances to the instability of a private fancy (private reason has only a private jurisdiction), and to attempt against divine laws what no government would endure against civil laws. These last, although human reason has much more to do with them, are still supremely the judges of their judges; and the utmost ability serves at best to expound and extend their accepted use, not to turn it aside and innovate. (ibid.,88,120)

Divine laws, social laws, sovereignty of the "magistrate"—together these form a network, a "coherent body" that dissolves under the pressure of any usurpation "of mastery" (1.17.51,73: addition in 1595), of any usurpation of the "authority to judge" (1.23.88,120). For him as for Hurault the consequence of such usurpation is concretely visible on all sides: "the unity and contexture of this monarchy, this great structure, having been dislocated and dissolved" (ibid.,87,118: addition in 1588).

The doctrine of sovereignty as it is found in the *Six Books of the Republic* (1576) of Jean Bodin does not differ fundamentally from this type of argument. It lies at the base of every response given to the question posed most clearly by La Boetie regarding what he calls "la servitude volontaire": How can one explain the fact that millions of people obey one? This question was asked both by the Huguenots following the Saint Bartholomew Massacre and by the League following the death of Henry III (as we have seen Montaigne lament: 2.12.323,420) as a way of justifying sedition. The final response of a Hobbes would be the same as Montaigne's: to give free rein to "private fantasy" already assumes that the state does not exist, that there is no legitimate order and hence no society, since, as Hobbes says in his *Behemoth*, the latter depends upon the former. For the one as for the other the response would thus be to place the accent on the *volontaire*, rather than the *servitude*. Thus sovereignty lies for Hobbes (though not for Montaigne, since for him voluntary obedience has nothing to do with people's "rights" but instead with their "duties") not in the prince as an individual but in the state as a collective enterprise *represented by* princely authority. It will be Locke, soon after in his *Treatise of Civil Government* (1689), who will confirm the idea that sovereignty belongs to the state, whatever forms of representation it may now take (thereby giving the necessary theoretical support to the effects of the 1688 revolution).[10]

At the time of the close of the religious wars, we are still very far from any such solution, even if we are at the center of the debates that will lead to it.[11] Moreover, Hurault seems to perceive such a solution, though he disputes it and considers it impossible:

> This is not all, for even when the capital cities of the provinces have chased out the King, killed all the nobles, conquered each their own province and bailiwick, they will still have to form some sort of government afterwards and some judiciary link will have to be found to hold them together. (*SD,* 149)

This idea of a "judiciary link" [*lien de justice*] is interesting indeed, for what can such a "link" be if it is not a contract? Equally interesting is the fact that Hurault describes it as an abstraction. Indeed, he does not say "they will have to find" (the construction one would expect considering what precedes it), but "will have to be found." The phrase *qu'il se trouve* implies that the link will, so to speak, find itself.[12] The formula suggests that in Hurault's eyes the question is not one of a concrete alliance or of a person but of an abstract doctrine that would permit the return of an ordered civil structure. Equally "Hobbesian" is his idea that the lack of such a link leads necessarily to evil, since malice is the chief characteristic of natural man en masse: "I do not believe that they could ever agree on anything except doing evil; for good action is not to be found amid such confusion." And he adds that "the nature of man is malicious [*meschant*]" (*SD,* 150). Confusion, disorder, malice, and finally death ("you won't last long this way" [*SD,* 151]) will of necessity follow the destruction of the "ruling lord's" sovereignty (*SD,* 151). I cannot but recall Hobbes's famous phrase from the beginning of *Leviathan* (1651), according to which in the state of nature "the life of man is solitary, poore, nasty, brutish, and short."

This is why, according to Hobbes, voluntary surrender of the individual's power to a central authority is absolutely essential. Hurault says nothing else. According to Hobbes the absolutely fundamental natural right is the protection and conservation of one's own life. It follows, for a rational being, that the fundamental natural law is the law of peace (*Leviathan,* 1.14). For Hobbes the "natural" consequence of this is the contract that founds civil society and which emerges from a rational accord among individuals possessed each of the same free will and, at least until the moment they relinquish it freely and willingly, of their own complete power. For Hurault exactly the same condition depends upon an act of the king and the subject's recognition of the advantage of obedience: this is the difference I noted earlier between a will linked to right and one linked to duty. Hurault transforms a call to peace directed at all combatants in the present wars of religion into an affirmation of the king's sovereignty within his state. Let the king think of peace, he says,

> for perhaps this is one of the great secrets of his state. Peace offers the advantage that subjects necessarily bring their will and assent into obedience of the Prince, otherwise there would be no peace. War and force cannot achieve this end. For true obedience relies upon free will and not force. When a king commands peoples who are voluntarily obedient, he possesses in himself alone the force of his scepter and needs no one else but himself. (SD, 192–93)

He underscores the fact that the king will hence have no need of the many kinds of officers, captains, princes, nobles, and so on to whom he would then owe the maintenance of his crown, and he will thus provide no element that could lead to the present confusion, the cause of the loss of sovereignty and of chaos. On his subjects' part, will corresponds to duty, and this duty appears as the mark of a fixed position within a social hierarchy. Such difference in rank in no way affects the equality of the subjects with regard to royal sovereignty, provided only that the sovereignty be absolute. This notion of mutual dependence and utility seems to contain something "proto-contractual" (in the Hobbesian sense of the contract, a sense having little to do with the Huguenot contractual theory, which implies a kind of constitutive accord between two separate entities, people and prince, ratified by their mutual relationship to God).

For both Hurault and Montaigne it is duty that cements this mutual relationship of utility and dependence. When he speaks of the teacher's need to train his pupil for his social obligations, Montaigne affirms: "If his tutor is of my disposition, he will form his will to be a very loyal, very affectionate, and very courageous servant of his prince; but he will cool in him any desire to attach himself to that prince otherwise than by a sense of public duty" (1.26.114,154). This idea is no mere theoretical abstraction. It answers a real need for mediation between extremes, between the Huguenot party of Henry of Navarre and the League, between Protestantism and Catholicism (an opposition treated increasingly by commentators of the period as a hypocritical pretext), between the old high feudal nobility and the new high (often ennobled) bourgeoisie, between a desire to maintain a fragmentation of centers of power—be they Protestant cities or the great old fiefs—and an ever stronger tendency toward the centralization of power and the consolidation of the state into a nation. The perfect symbol of this last tendency will be the transformation of Henry of Navarre into Henry IV, his conversion for political reasons from Protestant to Catholic (which corresponds perfectly to Montaigne's oft-repeated idea that public duty requires the suppression of "private fantasy"), his passage from the Béarn and Pau, his native city, to the Île de France and Paris, capital of the country.

The theoretical notion of duty finds its practical counterpart in that group of thinkers, statesmen, highly placed functionaries, and lawyers known as the *Politiques*. They functioned in fact not only as mediators between opposing parties but also between old and new conceptions of the state. The case of the man I have just cited at such length is in many ways exemplary. Michel Hurault de l'Hospital was grandson of the chancellor of France. Both men must have been well known to Montaigne. As regards his relationship to the great chancellor (himself a friend of La Boetie long before Montaigne), we have the essayist's own testimony, as well as others'. As for the grandson, circumstances are sufficient indication: he had been chancellor to Henry of Navarre. Among other tasks, he had undertaken missions to Holland and Germany on his behalf. His duties were such that he was obviously suspected of Calvinism, though no one could discover exactly which religion he followed. We know that Montaigne, on missions for Henry, had to undergo the same kind of annoyances. When Henry became King of France, Hurault was named governor of Guillebeuf. He died in 1592. Montaigne's relations with Henry of Navarre, his court, his diplomacy, and his political interventions are today well known (even if not in every detail), so we should not be surprised if there are profound coincidences between his thought and Hurault's.

This situation is not simply of anecdotal interest. What is at issue are discussions and struggles that led directly to the modern concept of the liberal state. In this light we may look at the specific case that we have seen both Hurault and (though less explicitly) Montaigne consider: that of the Duke of Mayenne. Mayenne was the second son of François of Lorraine, Duke of Guise and brother of Henry of Guise. Following the assassination of his brother in 1588 (on order of Henry III), Mayenne sparked a revolt in Burgundy and Champagne, then entered Paris on February 15, 1589. Once in the capital he organized a local government, called the *Conseil general d'union*—the very pattern for the disintegration of sovereignty deplored by Montaigne and Hurault. Throughout this entire period, or at least for the duration of the Estates of Blois in 1588, which ended with the assassination of Mayenne's brother, Montaigne was present—along with Etienne Pasquier, who mentions him in this context.[13]

To show these personal connections is important, for one may describe all these personages—Pasquier, Hurault, Montaigne, Henry IV himself—with the words Horkheimer uses in speaking of Bodin:

> The tendency to remain neutral in religious questions, and to subordinate religion to reasons of state, the recourse to a strong state which would be the guarantor of the security of commerce and exchange, corresponds to the conditions of existence of the *parvenue* bourgeoisie and its alliance with absolute monarchy.[14]

The question is thus first of all one of stability and certitude. When Le Roy speaks of sedition, of the dispersal of sovereignty and of the confusion of language, he cites at length the passage from Thucydides in which the historian comments upon the false use of language as both symptom and cause of the social upheaval of the civil wars. For Le Roy, the sovereignty of the principal subject, the king himself, is on the one hand set against the disintegration of sovereignty among the nobles and in the city councils, but it is also opposed on the other to the uncertainty of a language that false usage is destroying—along with the social fabric.

I spoke earlier of a cliché, and indeed the idea of a rapport between language and the social realm is very widespread. Le Roy's own work enjoyed an international renown. Already in the 1580s the Englishman Gabriel Harvey stated that it would be difficult to find a scholar who was not reading "Le Roy on Aristotle or the *Six Books* of Bodin."[15] But the relationship in question goes way back. In texts from the close of the sixteenth century one finds quotations, not only from Thucydides, but also from, among others, Plato, Aristotle, and Xenophon. Let me take up another instance in which Thucydides is quoted, because it is relatively short and especially because it appeared the year before the edition of the *Essays* containing the first appearance of both the reference to Thucydides and the famous passage that I cited toward the outset of this essay comparing the multiplicity of linguistic interpretations with "the Hydra's head." I am referring to the *Discours politiques et Militaires* of François de la Noüe (1587):

> The wise historian Thucydides describes summarily how the Greeks governed themselves during civil discord. . . . As soon as an insolent remark was made somewhere, he says, everyone else found the nerve to say something worse, either in order to do something new or to show that they were more assiduous than the others, or more insolent and eager to avenge themselves: and all the evils which they committed they disguised with praiseworthy titles, calling temerity magnanimity; modesty pusillanimity; precipitate indignation virility and boldness; consultation and prudent deliberation pale tergiversation. In this way, whoever showed himself always furious was reputed a loyal friend; and whoever contradicted him was held suspect. . . . Today I ask if in similar actions we have not equalled the Greeks?[16]

La Noüe was obviously a considerable personage; he was a famous soldier (known as "Iron Arm" [*Bras de fer*]) and one of the chief lieutenants of Gaspard de Coligny. Still, he deserves a place alongside the other "mediators." Although he was one of the leaders of the Huguenots, it was to him that Charles IX turned in order to attempt a reconciliation with his party after the Saint Bartholomew Massacre. Thus, like Montaigne or Hurault, he was perceived at least potentially as a mediator, as a participant in the launching of a different kind of future. And like them he understood the confusion of language, of social relations, and of political life as one and the same problem.

The same can be said of the Duke of Alençon (Henry III's brother, the fourth son of Henry II), who, complaining of foreign (i.e., Italian) influence at court, allied himself with the Protestant forces at Dreux on September 15, 1575. He, too, could thus be presented as a mediator, one to whom Innocent Gentillet can address his "Souhait pour la France" at the end of his *Anti-Machiavel* of 1576: "That he will extinguish the fires of our civil wars in the countryside and the cities: And like a French Hercules cut off the heads of this monster who still today shows itself sworn enemy to our laws."[17] Twenty years earlier in his *Arraisonnement* of 1569, François de Belleforest had called these confusions "the tortuous hydra of rebellions."[18] In his text of 1593, Hurault would apply this same metaphor very precisely to the League:

> It is thus that we must consider generally the Party of the League today, this monster having been formed of many members which, for having been ill-proportioned from the outset, have rendered it so terrifying that it is no wonder if it has been seen to have several heads, like a serpent engendered out of the earth's putrescence. (*SD*, 153)

We have seen this same idea expressed by Shakespeare in my epigraph taken from 2 *Henry IV,* especially if we recall that the archbishop's commentary (concerned with a rebellion, though of course he pretends otherwise) precedes a whole series of deceptions, traps, and even an apparent betrayal: that of John of Lancaster toward the rebels and that of Hal toward Falstaff and then his father, Henry IV, when he "removes" his crown.

The metaphor is thus applied at once to the disintegration of the political and linguistic orders. Pasquier applies it to a situation of most specific interest to us because it concerns the actual case of the Guises of which I spoke before: it again links Montaigne and himself, Guise and Mayenne, the real situation of France to this metaphor concerning state and language and thus to a particular political-theoretical movement. In a letter written to "Monsieur Airault Lieutenant Criminel d'Angers," Pasquier speaks of the assassination of the Duke of Guise and of his uncle the Cardinal during the meeting of the Estates-General at Blois. This is how he explains the situation:

> You should know that the King was enraged by several matters which occurred to his disadvantage during our assembly, and which he thought were only due to the direction of these two Princes. He felt that the more flexible he showed himself toward our members, the more intractable they became toward him (such that it was truly a Hydra, one of whose heads cut off gave birth to seven others; so much so that three or four days before Monsieur de Guise had quarrelled with him both about his status as Lieutenant General and about the town of Orleans [which was *ligueur*]). He thus decided [*il se delibere*] to have the two Princes done to death, considering that their death would also be that of all these new Councils.[19]

The comparison is here of enormous significance, not simply because of the complexity of the elements mentioned before and which it composes together, but because it links in detail the birth of political factionalism with the birth of too many words (*nouueaux Conseils, une dispute, il se delibere,* and so forth): not to mention that the Estates of November and December 1588 were themselves a matter of discussions. The use of the hydra metaphor thus coincides with the use made everywhere of the passage from Thucydides: subject, sovereignty, power, language, right, law, war, and peace are thus all so many concepts concealed within these texts of Montaigne. And he is a link of prime importance in the discussions that eventually lead to the solution of certain of these issues. In Montaigne's eyes one cannot separate language from reason, and both share in the inconstancy proper to all human things: " 'We reason rashly and inconsiderately,' says Timaeus in Plato, 'because, like ourselves, our reason has in it a very large element of chance' " (1.47.209,276). Montaigne says in fact that human reason, "ridiculous" and "risible" as it is, cannot guarantee language, on which the sociopolitical order nonetheless depends. But neither is the opposite the case, for language too takes part in this constant movement. Only *the law* (itself, however, prey to a multiplicity of interpretations) can resist: "The commonwealths that kept themselves regulated and well governed, like the Cretan and the Lacedaemonian, made little account of orators" (1.51.222,292).

In opposition to the law, speech (the use made of language) serves to "manipulate and agitate a crowd and a disorderly populace"; it serves to persuade "the herd" and "the ignorant" in a state where "things were in perpetual turmoil." In such a case, speech *can* offer itself as "a medicine," though a very dangerous one, for it appeals precisely to the constant oscillation of the private being and not to the loyalty of the public one. Either it sets off anarchy (Mayenne in Paris, for example) or it is of use only where anarchy already reigns, for instance in Rome at the time of the civil wars, "when affairs were in the worst state and agitated by the storm of civil wars" (1.51.222,293). So we come back again to the commonplace of Thucydides. Thus Montaigne affirms that the best way to obstruct these pernicious developments is to secure the power of one man: "it is easier to safeguard him, by good education and advice, from the effects of that poison" (ibid.). This power "of a monarch" will in turn guarantee the "good government" of the state.

The law and the order of the state thus rest on the king's unique sovereignty, itself "situated" in his mystical body, whose guarantor is God himself and God's reason. The latter's stability stands in direct opposition to human reason: "Now our human reasons and arguments are as it were the heavy and barren matter; the grace of God is their form; it is that which gives them shape and value" (2.12.326,424–25). The plenitude of divine reason stands in opposition to "the inanity, the vanity and nothingness of man" (ibid.,327, 426). "Divine majesty" stands as the only true reason over against the nothingness and instability of human reason: "It is to this alone that knowledge and wisdom belong; it alone that can have some self-esteem, and from which we steal what we account and prize ourselves for" (ibid.).

We should not believe that we are dealing here with scepticism pure and simple. On the contrary, we are faced with a complex schema of the human situation in the natural, social, and divine orders. On one side stands weak human reason, largely useless except in that it allows reasoning individuals to come to an awareness of their own universal weakness; on the other side—but not infinitely removed—stand God and his reason. Between the two lies the space occupied by the society of the organized state, which is best guaranteed by a king who partakes to a certain degree of both divine permanence and reason (the doctrine of the mystical body) and the domain of the human (the real body). The king's participation in both of these realms assures the functioning of the law: the divine secures the role of duty, the human leaves a space for "will." What is lacking in this schema for the moment is the placing of the ordinary person, characterized by inconstancy and incertitude. This question can be answered by means of a discussion of the subject, the notion of a "self."

We are all familiar—too familiar—with Montaigne's statement, quoted at the outset, according to which "each man bears the entire form of man's estate." But considerable difficulties arise when we seek to understand it, and even more appear when we try to extricate *the* sense of it. Three and a half centuries of a certain mode of thought have led us to believe that, essentially at least, the human being is everywhere and always the same. And we have a strong tendency to place this sameness and its essence at the level of a subjectivity that, even if it cannot always be located, is always solidly grounded. Such is the case even if we believe that ontologically it is unseizable in "itself" (the case of the Sartre of *Being and Nothingness*, for example) and psychologically unable to be held onto (by Freudian psychoanalysis). The existence of this subjectivity, as such, nonetheless presents itself in the form of a clear and distinct concept. It is human being in itself, given as the origin of all human activity, of whatever kind. And all other activity always appears as posterior to it.

It is true that Marxism thought it had escaped from such a concept of subjectivity. Yet perhaps the most considerable crisis of Marxist theory (at least in the West) has come precisely from the perception of a renewed need to make room for such a concept—while comprehension of it has not yet found a way to move beyond Hegel. This is to say that our concept of the subject still remains in a line stemming directly from Cartesianism.[20] And if I am compelled to mention the name of Descartes here it is just because he marks the moment at which Western philosophy took on a certain inflection.[21] Now Montaigne may indeed be one of the precursors of this inflection, but he has not yet reached it; and one must beware before launching into anachronism. Let me say right away, and with a certain abruptness, that this Cartesian idea of the subject is not to be found in Montaigne.

The context of the affirmation of this "entire being" (*estre universel* 3.2.611,782), of this "entire form," which Montaigne could easily "dislike" (as he says himself, ibid.,617,791), seems to leave no doubt regarding its signification—though the English translation, changing the terms, loses it entirely. The essential characteristics of this universal condition of the "human" are indeed the "perennial movement," this "stability itself" which is "nothing but a more languid motion." Montaigne could never paint this universal "being," because in itself it exists nowhere; he can only paint the "passage." He insists that "we go hand in hand and at the same pace, my book and I" (3.2.611–12,782–83); the phrase was added for the 1595 edition, as was this other one: "I have no more made my book than my book has made me—a book consubstantial with its author" (2.18.504,648). All of this is old hat. Still, one can only conclude from it that the "universal being" is universal by virtue of its movement and inconstancy. The universal character of the world, of "all things," is indeed this constant instability. The universal being is universal because it conforms to this universal character of the world. The movement of being, the passage that is thus painted by Montaigne, is the essential form of the human: whence also follows, precisely, the fact that one can "tie up all moral philosophy with a common and private life just as well as with a life of richer stuff" (3.2.611,782).

The sentence, then, that "each man bears the entire form of man's estate," so often used as proof of Montaigne's discovery of the modern concept of subjectivity (that of the willful and self-possessive subject, doubtless, but above all of a self that is always and everywhere the same and constant in itself) is entirely caught up in contradiction in the very passage where Montaigne introduces it. To be sure, something like a "confirmation" of this concept of the self seems to present itself a little later: "There is no one who, if he listens to himself, does not discover in himself a pattern all his own [*une forme sienne*], a ruling pattern [*une forme maistresse*], which struggles against education and against the tempest of the passions that oppose it" (3.2.615,789). A ruling pattern, therefore, a deep self that struggles not simply against customary forms and those imposed by education—against the social—but even against all those irrational passions stemming from the very humanity of the individual of which this subjectivity would compose the "still, quiet center of being." To the modern mind this seems quite admirable: here we are before an almost Cartesian subject.

Yet here we are again in complete contradiction, for the very next paragraph insists on "corruption and filth," on disease, guilt, sin, vice, and ugliness, the constant companions of humankind (2.2.616,789), that is to say on the fact that humans in their social relations never escape the rule of passions nor everything vicious in their social relations. In practice, therefore, the "ruling pattern" remains quite hidden, fitfully glimmering perhaps as a kind of hope—what we might nowadays call a *desire*, but a permanent and forever unsatisfied desire. Far from some innate structure of mind, this would be a sign of the *absence* of such a subject rather than one of its presence. In Montaigne's text itself its idea is explored only through contradiction and opposition.

I am tempted indeed to suggest that in the *Essays*, the "subject" is glimpsed only by these signs of its *absence*. In Descartes the subject is *there* by the certainty of its *presence*. When Montaigne affirms that even "conscience" itself is "born of custom" (1.23.83,114), he removes from the subject (before the fact, of course) one of the elements central to its modern concept: the moral sentiment that, for subsequent thought, will be one of the fundamental marks of the human, central to the thinking of Montesquieu and Rousseau as it will be to that of Adam Smith and Kant. One can even wonder whether it is questioned at all by Freud, since the moral sense is then lodged in the superego as the presence of a socialization fully assumed in and by the psyche, and such an assumption presupposes the psyche's identity, its presence to itself.

Two types of movement govern both "the earth, the rocks of the Caucasus, the pyramids of Egypt" and the human being: they move "both with the common motion and with their own" (3.2.610,782). The sentence is obscure: from external and internal motion? From the social motion and the universal motion that is characteristic of all things? For my present concern, there is no difference between the two interpretations. As far as human beings are concerned, the exterior *is* the social, and the interior *is* the private—and thereby the universal. The private *is* movement, thought in process that is not yet reason since it is by definition disordered. The freedom of the individual resides in keeping a space for the private while at the same time lending oneself to the social order, to the requirements of the law—which moreover is the condition *sine qua non* for maintaining this private freedom. One must learn not to mix the two, and what Montaigne says about inheritances in this respect can be applied generally as well: "it is abusing this liberty unreasonably to make it serve our frivolous and private fancies." One must instead follow "the common and legitimate arrangement" (2.8.289,377). Thus do we avoid "the natural instability of our conduct and opinions" (2.1.239,315).

On this question Montaigne does not hesitate: on the social level the private (and universal) subject has no function; nor does the language that accompanies such a "subject":

> I have the same opinion about these political arguments: whatever part they give you to play, you have as good a chance as your opponent, provided you do not bump up against principles that are too plain and obvious. And therefore, to my mind, in public affairs there is no course so bad, provided it is old and stable, that it is not better than change and commotion.

He says this in spite of the present corruption:

> The worst thing I find in our state is instability, and the fact that our laws cannot, any more than our clothes, take any settled form. [Because of the (false) freedom granted to the private] It is very easy to accuse a government of imperfection, for all mortal things are full of it. It is very easy to engender in a people contempt for their ancient observances; never did a man undertake that without succeeding. But as for establishing a better state in place of the one they have ruined, many of those who have attempted it have achieved nothing for their pains. (2.17.498,639)

The sole means whereby things become a bit more stable (or continue so, if one has the good luck to be in some stable state) is custom, *la police*, and the recognition that in the realm of public affairs "frivolous and private fancy" must be replaced by a public subjectivity: "I give my prudence small share in my conduct; I readily let myself be led by the general way of the world" [*l'ordre public du monde*] (ibid.). It is only the authority of political power—and its acceptance by everyone—only the state in the power of a single individual which can guarantee a certain constancy: this is what law is. It does not concern the private subject, which is characterized only by "inconstancy" and about which law can do nothing, but a public subject, which secures itself through appurtenance to an order of custom.

This law of state assumes then the acceptance by the subject, as sociopolitical function, of a certain order—both out of a ("voluntary") duty and out of interest. This law will guarantee not only the material well-being of the subject in question, but also its ordered use of reason, which without law is mere directionless wandering unable to help anyone except "by accident" (2.6.272,358). This is doubtless why Montaigne insists upon the movement of the *Essays* and upon the fact that they do not concern his public being: "It is not my deeds that I write down; it is myself, it is my essence" (ibid.,274,359). He may indeed set himself forth as an example of the universal being, but social and political being depend upon an order of custom which is visible (at least in principle) to all.

Thus, like the entire group of the *Politiques* (they were never exactly a party), Montaigne affirms that obedience to accepted custom, to law, and to familiar authority is essential: "In this controversy on whose account France is at present agitated by civil wars, the best and soundest side is undoubtedly that which maintains both the old religion and the old government of the country" (2.19.506,650–51). For him what dominates is the concept of a local, particular society.[22] The notion of a society that would correspond to some concept of universal justice is impossible: the universal is either human inconstancy or a divine constancy to which the human has no access: "Justice in itself, natural and universal, is regulated otherwise and more nobly than that other, special, national justice, constrained to the need of our governments" (3.1.604,773). A utopia founded upon this universal justice remains forever unobtainable, and any attempt to reach it will lead only to anarchy; and even tyranny is preferable to anarchy. The worst of evils is not the failure to attain "universal" justice—that in any case belongs to God; it is disorder. And yet natural human reason is only a disordered drift of no possible use to the social domain (even though the "grace of God" could give it a "form" directing it toward his universality)—whence the "Machiavellianism" of Montaigne, which leads him to affirm, for example, that under certain conditions the prince may find himself obliged to give up "his [private, and thus universal] reason to a more universal and powerful reason [here, that of the state]" (3.1.607,777).

The comparative "more" here signals clearly the three following steps: (1) universal nature, private subject, inconstant reason; (2) society ordered and customary, public subject, reason of state, king sovereign by virtue of his "human body"; (3) God, divine reason, king sovereign by virtue of his "mystical body." The private subject is related to the second step by will; the public subject is related to the third by duty, with the king functioning as mediator. The order of law is obviously essential in this schema: "It is neither handsome nor honorable . . . to keep oneself wavering and half-and-half, to keep one's allegiance motionless and without inclination in one's country's troubles and in civil dissension" (3.1.601,770). The individual has a social obligation to maintain this order. For a certain period this type of relationship will remain central to the concept of divine right and to the (official) theory regarding the relationship between the social realm and the individual, the king and the divinity. The royalist poet Abraham Cowley will articulate this notion clearly in 1639, after the Pacification of Berwick and the consequent peace between England and Scotland, in a poem to Charles I: "Welcome, great Sir, with all the joy that's due / To the return of *Peace* and *You*, / Two greatest *Blessings* which this age can know: / For *that* to *Thee*, for *Thee* to Heav'n we ow."[23]

So the state, coherence, law, and ordered reason form a whole. The corruption of reason, visible for example in the "false" use of language, leads to the ruin of the state—in fact it signals it. Since mutual understanding is brought about solely by way of words, whoever breaks a promise betrays human society. Speech is the only instrument by means of which our wills and thoughts communicate; it is the interpreter of our soul. If it fails us, we have no more hold on each other, no more knowledge of each other. If it deceives us, it breaks up all our relations and dissolves all the bonds of our society (2.18.505,650). A good linguistic order guarantees a reasonable subject, and this subject is thus inseparable from the sociohistorical situation; whence derives Montaigne's insistence upon participation in government and in "public society," as he says that "our very life—we must lend and abandon to its [public society's] service and to the common opinions" (1.23.86,117). To accept "treachery, lewdness, avarice, and every sort of inhumanity and cruelty" (3.6.695,889) as the French did during the wars of religion and as the natives of America were forced to do by European conquerors is to accept a condition counter to ordered reason since it goes hand in hand with the acceptance of anarchy and the destruction of discourse.

Thus the social subject itself becomes guarantor of a well-ordered society and historical process to the precise extent that it denies its own "universality." This subject is in no way Cartesian; it could never remove itself from the here and now, either politically, socially, or temporally. Reason and social equity conform strictly to each other—so says a remonstrance addressed to Henry III in 1593 which Montaigne and the *jurats* of Bordeaux all signed.[24] In Montaigne there is no concept of anything like a "self" that can grow into self-realization. There are two subjects: one is nothing more than an inconstant passage; the other is reasonable and is defined only by its insertion into the sociopolitical realm. He says this himself, in fact, in a passage added to the 1595 edition:

These supple variations and contradictions that are seen in us have made some imagine that we have two souls, and others that two powers accompany us and drive us, each in its own way, one toward good, the other toward evil; for such sudden diversity cannot well be reconciled with a simple subject. (3.1.242,318)

If by the word "good" here we understand *order*, and by "evil" we understand *disorder*—a change authorized by the text—we come back to my own argument. For order in Montaigne is always that which conforms to what he calls the "well-governed" [*bien policé*] state, whereas evil, disorder, is always anarchy, a release of human passions and desires, always drawing us toward extremes that are necessarily vicious. On the level of the state we have seen the terms into which this opposition is translated. As Shakespeare's Henry V says with reference to precisely such a political context: "Every subject's duty is the King's, but every subject's soul is his own" (*Henry V* [1598–99], 4.1).

In speaking of the normative grammars of the second half of the seventeenth century, Michel Foucault writes that "it is in the very nature of grammar to be prescriptive, not because it would like to impose the norms of language, beautiful and faithful to the rules of taste, but because it ascribes the radical possibility of speaking to the setting in order of representation."[25] I have myself affirmed that the nearly "metaphysical" necessity of such grammars at that time (recalling the demand for order that one finds in all realms of knowledge) responds to a loss of order in the world—or more precisely to the loss of a certain type of order, an order owing nothing to humans and whose guarantor lay "elsewhere," as "divine will," or the "world-soul." As long as people and the world of which they are a part are subsumed into an order that transcends and contains them, human classifications can go on being diverse, multiform, and polysemic at will. The disappearance of such an order, however, imposes the need for a will to order that is properly human.[26]

The sixteenth century lived through the progressive loss of such an external order: and first of all there where it had been at once the most "visible" and the most closely experienced—in the social and political domains. The Machiavellian analysis of political practices and realities had driven aside any need for divine intervention, a development of which Cardinal Reginald Pole had warned Charles V as early as 1539. The French religious wars raised the same problem in the most acute of forms: a close reading of commentators of the age quickly convinces one of the influence of Machiavelli's analysis—even when the contrary is affirmed.[27] In the domain of the *res publica*, as it was called, civil war, ever increasing inflation, constantly expanding unemployment, the collapse of feudal bonds, and the uncertainty of mutual obligation between monarch and subject were all strikingly patent signs, lived in the very flesh, of the recognized order's dissolution.

One of the responses brought by the next century would be the hypostasis of the subject into a willful and possessive individual, with its own recognized rights, a subject that would succeed in imposing *its* order. The new knowledge would be nothing but the imposition of the individual's own power onto nature. All the forces necessary to the social disposition would be invoked by the new centralized state, eventually legitimized by the concept of the contract and of its presupposition: the cession of the power of each in favor of one who, since he represents all, will guarantee the peace and good order of the new civil society. Such a solution was unavailable to the thinkers of the sixteenth century. If, as early as 1576, Jean Bodin could elaborate the theoretical bases of an absolute sovereignty (and, as we have seen, he was followed by a whole swarm of writers), it would be a very long time before the arrival of a sociopolitical conjuncture that could respond to his formulation. In France it came with the age of Louis XIV—once he had won his victories in the Frondes—built upon terrain prepared by Richelieu. In England it would come with the brief "dictatorship" of Cromwell in the mid-1650s and then the short reign of James II leading up to his expulsion in 1688. These, however, are only the extreme forms of a model built upon a concept of the subject as fixed, as the originator of all action, of all knowledge, of all power, and so on.

Without the constitution of such a fixed subject, disorder could not be eliminated in this way: "I paint the passing"; "stability itself is nothing but a more languid motion" (and so many other famous lines from Montaigne). A private subject (such as that of seventeenth-century individualism will be, but then in a quite different manner) could never fix itself, could never take a position once and for all—let alone impose itself. Thus Montaigne offers a particular response to the question of his friend La Boetie: Why do millions of people allow themselves to be crushed by the power of a single man, when one only need do nothing to bring such power tumbling down? Even such an abstention, Montaigne implies, would suppose that these ("voluntary," La Boetie would say) slaves, these "serfs" could fix themselves as subjects. If they could act in such a way, then they would no longer be the subjects of a prince, but rather his equal—a status already at least implicit in Machiavelli. But for Montaigne, as we have seen, the political subject receives its being from its relationship to a sovereignty incarnate in the person of the prince. This subject of the state may in some sense "keep," free and "for itself," the inconstant and constantly mutable subject, but as a constant subject one has a duty toward society and the common good. In the private realm the "individual" *is not properly speaking a subject*, nothing but this constant motion. As a subject one becomes in some sense the "function" of the prince. In a letter to Henry IV, dated January 18, 1589, in which he counsels the new king on the proper comportment to exercise toward his new "subjects," Montaigne makes this idea explicit. One need only be a little attentive, he writes, for "popular inclinations go in waves; if the leaning in your favor is once established, it will gather its own momentum and go all the way" (1092,1398). It is enough for the king to show his people "a paternal and truly royal affection" (ibid.).

If the private being could constitute itself as a fixed subject, it would necessarily go against the civil order—whence come the commentaries of Hurault, Le Roy, Montaigne, and many others regarding the members of the House of Lorraine and sovereign cities; whence also doubtless (at least if the tradition upholding the story is well founded) Montaigne's reputed advice to Henry of Navarre following his victory at Coutras not to follow the forces of Henry III and thus take on a rebel's status. The king need not abuse his subjects; he has only to show himself. The metaphor of the father/son relationship that we have just seen Montaigne use is rigorous and exact: whence as well the horror of the Saint Bartholomew Massacre. In that case the king had completely perverted his relationship to the people. Until that date it had always been possible to maintain that violence was being perpetrated only by those seeking to oppose the legitimate power of the king on the grounds of religion, by the overthrow of feudal obligations, and so forth. The massacre risked bringing on total confusion and cutting away all possible points of stability. This explains why Montaigne constantly extols a "return" (which would in fact be no return at all), the recovery of the old stability, of the old union of church and state, the establishment of a royal sovereignty and a well-defined state power.

Contrary to what Richard Sayce has suggested, there is no contradiction between the concept of the subject's inconstancy and the desire for a stable political order in Montaigne.[28] Nor is it simply the case, as I have just suggested, that the latter guarantees the possibility of the former. It is just as much that the lack of fixity of the private subject guarantees the stability of the state and the place of the public subject: for that becomes the *only* possible place in which something like an "individual" with a more or less secure status can situate itself. In the face of a political and social crisis, Montaigne seeks to keep from losing his footing by redeeming a certain number of elements placed at his disposal by the political theory and practice of his age which seemed pertinent to the stabilization of civil life. It becomes clear that it is an anachronism to argue (as the critical tradition continues to do) about the conservatism, the liberalism, or the radicalism of Montaigne. It makes little sense either to speak of a "democratic" Montaigne (as Donald Frame and many after him have done), and still less to speak (with Sayce and others) of a "revolutionary" Montaigne. He is resolutely of his age and can be inserted fully into a current running from Machiavelli to Locke.

Montaigne affirms the necessity of obedience to the laws and customs of a particular local society. At the same time he is convinced that what guarantees the functioning of voluntary duty and of the political subject's loyalty to the sovereign prince is the conformity of sociopolitical reason and equity. We have seen a moment of mediation in this conjuncture. In synchronic terms it is a question of opening a path between two extremes of political thought. In diachronic terms the point is to pass between two different concepts of universal order: one that would be external to the human and to which it would submit, and another that would in some sense be due to humanity. One manifestation of this latter concept at the close of the seventeenth century would be the quest for a universal grammar, conceived as conforming exactly to the structure of human reason, universal but at the same time individual and particular—Cartesian "good sense."

Now it happens that there is an intermediary theoretical step, quite widespread and typified by Montaigne, leading directly to this new concept of order. For the essayist, we have also seen, the only point of solid anchorage for the political subject lies in a constant, fixed public order. The close of the sixteenth century was in fact precisely a moment of passage when jurists and historians believed that they had found the certainty of universal reason in the political and legal order itself instead of in a divine system or in individual reason: I am referring to the movement known as "neobartolism." In a commentary on the *Anti-Tribonian* of François Hotman (1567), J. G. A. Pocock has noted that the jurist "proposes a project for legal apprenticeship in which students undertake a comparative study of all known and valued juridical systems with the aim of extracting from them the essential principals of juridical reason common to them all." We have here, he adds, "the principle known by the name of 'neo-bartolism' which came to dominate French juridical thought toward the end of the [sixteenth] century, and whose fundamental principle is that of discovering the basic principles of all systems of law."[29]

We can see clearly here the conceptual resemblance between this project and the attempt that will develop three quarters of a century later to find a universal grammar capable of providing for the constants of reason and human discourses. The difference between them, however, is no less essential. The neobartolists (and Montaigne with them) envisage a sociopolitical and juridical universal. Universal grammar assumes instead *the universality of the structure of individual reason:* for Montaigne such a structure could never be found nor literally even imagined. Montaigne—and I insist upon this essential fact—considers that the sociopolitical order, the reason of state, is a "superior reason," since individual reason in the Cartesian sense does not even really exist yet. It seems to me that this is the sense of the "universal reason" in terms of which the prince sometimes finds himself obliged to act.

For Hobbes and Locke, this superior reason will become the "function" of individual reason, which could in effect be characterized according to the laws furnished by a universal grammar. And indeed, those are the very terms with which Hobbes prefaces the *Philosophical Rudiments Concerning Government and Society:* "not to point which are the laws of any country, but to declare what the laws of all countries are."[30] Such general and universal laws will then be possible because they stem from a single rationality, from a human mind whose act of creating civil society is exactly equivalent to the divine *Fiat* of the Creation in *Genesis*—as Hobbes will himself write in the Introduction to *Leviathan*. The double "subject" of Montaigne then easily generates a more general and even more central reading. The subject as "passage" (though, as I have indicated, we cannot really yet use the term "subject" for it) will be transformed into cognitive reason (though it is not yet such for Montaigne); it will be that reason conscious of the continuity and certainty of its own functioning—in short, the *cogito* of Descartes. The political subject will take instead the form of the Cartesian or Baconian "provisional morality," which renders possible the social being's action while keeping aside the being of "method" and of the "new reason," which is not yet in a position to oversee a change in the political or social order. For the time being such a separation doubtless seemed essential. It has been well understood by Max Horkheimer who, in a comparison of Montaigne to the Protestant thinkers of his age, notes their shared notion of the weakness of human reason: "Both of them reject reason only to the extent that it enters into opposition with what is legally established, with the existing order, they don't reject science as such."[31]

Thus there are, so to speak, two types of thought. One represents the movement of the private realm, transported into the social domain; it is upon this base that La Boetie would have liked to situate his (utopian) society founded on what he called amicable "mutual recognition" [entrecognoissance]—the very idea of which Montaigne rejects (for him, in a rather untypical anti-Ciceronian move, friendship is a *private* affair). The other represents what will become the provisional ethics of Descartes. The question for the future became that of articulating the two together. Once again, it was the theory of the contract that succeeded in doing so, making possible the combination of the two subjects into one. The thought in process of the *Discourse of Method* or of the *Meditations* would become the voluntary subject of the *Passions of the Soul*, and *this* subject would become the fixed subject able to enter into the Hobbesian (and then Lockean) contract.

The concept of universal laws in the sociopolitical and juridical domain—a necessary concept given the permanent inconstancy of private reason on the one hand and the gradual disappearance of belief in direct divine intervention into human affairs on the other— would be replaced by the conception of universal laws that govern individual reason and *produce and create* the civil society of the state. Thus reason would become *originative*. The neobartolist idea had hardly been satisfactory, since it was difficult to perceive the fundamental unity of social systems whose diversities were more striking than their similarities. Once individual reason had been raised to an originative position, the whole thing became much "easier," and after Locke the way is opened to the *Spirit of Laws*, to the exploration of diversity subject to a human thought that is structurally everywhere and always identical with itself. For Montesquieu the relationship between this thought and the sociopolitical structure would be, in an ideal system, of the most immediate kind—and thus superior to what one finds elsewhere. Within this development the complex thought of Montaigne occupies a place both representative and important.

NOTES

1. Michel de Montaigne, *Complete Works*, trans. Donald Frame (Stanford, 1957). All references will quote this edition. The first two roman numerals indicate the Book and Essay number, these being followed by page num-

bers referring first to the English translation, then to the French text of the *Oeuvres Complètes*, ed. Albert Thibaudet and Maurice Rat (Paris, 1962). A rather different version of the present essay was originally published in French in *Montaigne*, ed. Steven Rendall, Jr., *Oeuvres & Critiques*, 8.1–2 (Tubingen, 1983), 127–52. The translation is by Timothy Hampton and has been revised by the author.

2. The texts to which I refer here are, in the order presented: Frederick Rider, *The Dialectic of Selfhood in Montaigne* (Stanford, 1973); Marcel Gutwirth, *Michel de Montaigne ou le pari d'exemplarité* (Montreal, 1977); Antoine Compagnon, *Nous, Michel de Montaigne* (Paris, 1980). If I name them here, it is essentially because they are recent. It is obviously useless to try to list, even partially, the critical works treating the question of the subject in Montaigne—especially when we consider the fact that every work written on the *Essays* consecrates at least a chapter to the problem. For me, one basic book remains Hugo Friedrich's *Montaigne*, trans. Robert Rovini (Paris, 1968); the chapter devoted to Montaigne in Terence Cave's work, *The Cornucopian Text: Problems of Writing in the French Renaissance* (Oxford, 1979), is very important for showing how the "copious text" (Erasmus) produces an outpouring tending to disclaim any possible formation of the subject. In his recent *Montaigne and the Introspective Mind* (The Hague, 1975), Glyn P. Norton maintains the old notion concerning "the emergence of modern psychological man in the *Essais*," such that "in the lines of Montaigne's self-portrait" he sees the "figure of ourselves" (17, 211). But he is definitely bucking a trend toward rereading Montaigne. Richard L. Regosin (*The Matter of My Book: Montaigne's "Essays" as the Book of the Self* [Berkeley and Los Angeles: 1979]), viewing Montaigne's presentation of the self essentially as a process of making metaphors, leans away from any monolithic concept, yet nonetheless ascribes to the "movement and action" that compose the human self the eternal reality of the human as its self expression in language, "the authentic materialization of the immaterial" (249). Certain recent studies go much farther. Jules Brody argues strongly that close analyses of the actual textual forms of the *Essays* remove interpretation from emphasis on the self and stress that their meaning is produced in the reader's interaction with it—indeed, the traditional view of the self in Montaigne then becomes largely untenable: "Les Oreilles de Montaigne," *Romanic Review* 74, no. 2 (1983), 121–35. John O'Neill's recent work is a fine presentation of such a view: *Essaying Montaigne: A Study of the Renaissance Institution of Writing and Reading* (London, 1982). I should also mention Edwin M. Duval's two recent essays: "Montaigne's Conversions: Compositional Strategies in the *Essais*," *French Forum* 7 (1982): 5–22, and "Lessons of the New World: Design and Meaning in Montaigne's 'Des Cannibales' (1.31) and 'Des Coches' (3.6)," *Yale French Studies* 64 (1983): 95–112. One comment from this last is worth quoting for its proximity to what I am here maintaining and to what I will be arguing at the end of this essay: "Reason, it would appear, is a far less uniform and universal faculty than Descartes would later maintain" (103). Finally, in

her, "'Sur des vers de Virgile' (3.5): Antinomy and Totality in Montaigne," *French Forum* 2 (1977), 3–21, Erica Harth argues how the *Essays* make a synthesis of traditional opposites, thus marking a cultural moment of pivotal passage—a view somewhat akin to that offered in this essay, although in different terms and seen from a very different angle. The implications of such views as these diverse essays express seem clearly in line with the present essay: the concept of the monolithic, or even ambiguous subject is a consequence of a particular reading. This is not to deny the importance of some notion of something like "subjectivity" in Montaigne (the words we are forced to use are a serious trap here). Dalia Judowitz has explored Montaigne's "self" as different from and leading toward Descartes's "subject" in the first chapter of her *Subjectivity and Representation: The Origins of Modern Thought in Descartes* (Cambridge, 1986). Her discussion—like most of those just mentioned— strikes me as peculiarly disembodied, as though the whole matter could be reduced in some way to a linguistic effect. It certainly *is* that, but to make such effect primary seems retrogressively perverse, as though 1960s "structuralism" on the one hand and Heideggerian poetizing on the other had provided us with an incontrovertible and complete model of knowledge. The importance of expression and communication should not blind us to the fact that (a) there are other ways of making meaning than through the material of natural language, and (b) history and society *are* composed of many other human activities that create our understandings and the elements making possible such understandings. All this is to say that to comprehend the broader implications of the *Essays*, we need to insert these matters into their particular sociocultural environment, and thus have some hope of understanding their role in a discursive formation. For some guidance concerning works dealing with Montaigne and his political thought, the simplest recourse is to general bibliographies; articles, especially, proliferate on this subject, not to mention chapters of books. The works of Frieda S. Brown, *Religious and Political Conservatism in the "Essais" of Montaigne* (Geneva, 1963), and Manfred Koelsch, *Recht und Macht Bei Montaigne: Ein Beitrag zur Erforschung der Grundlagen von Staat und Recht* (Berlin, 1974) furnish more ample bibliographies. These works base themselves on the traditional notion of the subject, as does the chapter on the matter in Jean Starobinski's *Montaigne en mouvement* (Paris, 1982), 293–367. It is also the case for Anna Maria Battista's chapter, "Sul 'Machiavellismo' di Montaigne," in her book, *Alle origini del pensiero libertino: Montaigne e Charron* (Milan, 1966), which argues on the basis of the idea that the essayist values social phenomena "in function of his primary investigation into the true essence of human nature" (9). She asserts that Montaigne offers a variety of diverse sociopolitical concepts then available for use in other more systematic theories, though, she concludes, these concepts do provide a political logic eventually able to be used by the politics of a centralized, absolute power (50). As we will see, arguing on the basis of a discussion of the "self" in Montaigne which radically escapes from the tradition, I will assert that Montaigne plays a far more vital and subtle role in the transformation of mind toward the modern mentality—in particular with regard to sociopolitical theory and practice (itself an opposition that holds up no more nowadays than it did in Montaigne).

3. Donald M. Frame, *Montaigne: A Biography* (New York, 1965). See also his *Montaigne's Discovery of Man: The Humanization of a Humanist* (New York, 1955).

4. Ithaca, 1982. The concepts referred to here are explored in two current books: *Discourse and Society* and *The Meaning of Literature*, of which the second will doubtless appear before the first, though it is the first that presents the general theory—the second exploring a particular case. The development of political discourse will itself be considered in a long work in progress.

5. These terms of "being" and "existence" are of course anachronistic here in this sense, but they serve to underline the relationship that seems to be at issue. F. Rider comments on the relationship between private and public "world" (*Dialectic of Selfhood*, 8–11), though without giving it any particular attention, and F. S. Brown discusses the same question from a completely different point of view (*Religious and Political Conservatism*, 72–81). The opposition also appears in (e.g.) the *Vindiciae contra tyrannos* (1579) and elsewhere. I do not seek to imply it is unique or original in Montaigne.

6. Ernst H. Kantorowicz, *The King's Two Bodies: A Study in Medieval Political Theology* (Princeton, 1957). This "mystical" body not only guarantees the stability of the "body" of the state, but it is identical to it, coextensive with it—as the English poet Thomas Carew indicates so well at the time of the last illness of King James I, around 1624: "Entring his royal limbs that is our head, / Through us his mystic limbs the paine is spread, / That man that doth not feele his part, hath none / In any part of his dominion" (*The Poems of Thomas Carew*, ed. Rhodes Dunlap [Oxford, 1949], 35, quoted in C. V. Wedgwood, *Poetry and Politics Under the Stuarts* [1960; rpr. Ann Arbor, Michigan, 1964], 29).

7. With the exception, especially, here of Manfred Koelsch's book, *Recht und Macht bei Montaigne*, which also considers what he calls "der 'gedoppelte Mensch'" (91–97), though in a way somewhat different from mine.

8. Pierre Mesnard, *L'Essor de la philosophie politique au XVIe siecle*, ed. 3, (Paris, 1969).

9. Michel Hurault, *Second Discours sur l'Estat de France*, in *Quatre excellens discovrs sur l'estat present de la France . . .* , (Paris, 1593), 99–243: this citation, 116. All references to this text will be signaled by the letters *SD*, followed by the page.

10. On this question see particularly Julian H. Franklin, *John Locke and Theory of Sovereignty: Mixed Monarchy and the Right of Resistance in the Political Thought of the English Revolution* (Cambridge, 1978), 87–126. These views had already culminated in the paper arguments just before the trial of

Charles I. These were of such a kind that Samuel Hartlib, the probable author of a pamphlet entitled *Rectifying Principles* (1648) expressing the Army's views, could insist: "The State at large is King, and the King so-called is but its steward or Highest Officer" (quoted by C. V. Wedgwood, *The Trial of Charles I* [London, 1964], 88). Such a view remained doubtless a minority one even in England, at least until the Glorious Revolution and the publication of Locke's *Second Treatise*.

11. For the relation between the wars of religion in France and English political thought, see J. H. M. Salmon, *The French Religious Wars in English Political Thought* (Oxford, 1959); as well as two older works: John Neville Figgis, *The Divine Right of Kings* (Cambridge, 1914); G. P. Gooch, *History of English Democratic Ideas in the Seventeenth Century* (London, 1898).

12. In view of the importance I am ascribing to this passage, it seems necessary to give the French: "Ce n'est pas tout, car quand bien les villes capitales des Provinces auroient chassé le Roy, auroient tué tous les nobles, conquis chacune son ressort & son bailliage, il faut encores qu'entre elles, apres elles prenent quelque forme de gouuernement & qu'il se trouue vn lien de iustice qui les tienne ensemble."

13. Estienne Pasquier, *Les Lettres d'Estienne Pasqvier Conseiller & Advocat general du Roy a Paris. Contenans plusieurs belles matieres & discours sur les affaires d'Estat de France, & touchant les guerres ciuiles*, 2 vols. (Paris, 1619), 2.379. "We were, [Montaigne] and I, familiars and friends, thanks to a meeting of minds and a common culture. We were together in the city of Blois at the time of that famous assembly of the Three Estates in 1588, whose end brought about so many of France's misfortunes."

14. Max Horkheimer, "Montaigne et la fonction du scepticisme," in *Théorie critique: essais* (Paris, 1978), 276.

15. Quentin Skinner, *The Foundations of Modern Political Thought*, 2 vols. (Cambridge, 1978), 2.300. This text contains a short discussion of Montaigne in this context (275–89).

16. François de la Nouë, *Discours politiques et Militaires du Seigneur de la Nouë. Nouvellement recueillis & mis en lumiere* (Basel, 1587), 55–56.

17. Innocent Gentillet, *Anti-Machiavel*, édition de 1576, ed. C. Edward Rathé (Geneva, 1968), 635.

18. François de Belleforest, *Arraisonnement fort gentil et proffitable sur l'infelicite qui suyt ordinairement le bonheur des grans: Avec un beau Discours sur l'excellence des Princes du sang de France . . .* (Paris, 1569), f. 68 ro (misnumbered, in reality f. 60 ro).

19. Pasquier, *Lettres*, 2.21 (the assassinations occurred on December 23–24, 1588). I am not suggesting the hydra metaphor to be a new one, but that it takes on a new and significant use. J. H. M. Salmon notes an interesting case demonstrating the popularity of the image. He records how Jacques de Crussol, baron d'Acier, became particularly feared during the first civil war "and emblazoned his banner with hydra heads representing cardinals being crushed by a Protestant Hercules" (*Society in Crisis: France in the Sixteenth Century* [1975; rpt. London, 1979], 130). But the concept of

revolt as a hydra head was not new even in postclassical Europe well
before this. John Barnie has recorded a poem celebrating the English
victory over the Scots of David Bruce at the Battle of Neville's Cross on
October 17, 1346, in which it is said that the Scots "are like the many-
headed hydra—when one (head) is cut off, three grow in its place without
any harm to the body" (John Barnie, *War in Medieval English Society: Social
Values in the Hundred Years War 1337–99* [Ithaca, 1974], 51). In the actual
poem in question this passage is entirely isolated from the remainder,
which specifically associates the English cause with that of Christ (who is
named seven times and God once in the lines preceding those para-
phrased here) and their army with the chosen people going against the
infidels. ("On the Battle of Neville's Cross," in *Political Poems and Songs
relating to English History, composed during the period from the Accession of
Edw. III to that of Ric. III*, ed. Thomas Wright, 2 vols. [London, 1859–61],
1.42). In no other of the poems of this collection, which include poems on
the revolts of Jack Straw and the Lollards, do I find this image (those of
foxes or wolves being more common—e.g., 1.232, 249). The opportunity
is not even taken when a poet is asserting "the single head" of the Church
(1.241). There is certainly no connection with language. It is the case that
before parliament in 1344, when Edward III was asking for a war subsidy,
it was claimed he had information Philip VI of France was "fully resolved
to destroy the English language, and to occupy the land of England." This
is cited by Barnie, who notes that the same fear was raised 44 years later
(*War in Medieval English Society*, 102). He concludes that language is now
increasingly identified with the nation. Yet the difference from what I am
discussing is clear. Language is viewed as something able to be deliberately subverted from without. In the later sixteenth century its internal
decay is seen as simultaneous with that of the state, as coterminous with
it, even sometimes as a *cause* of the state's dissolution. Edward III's idea is
utterly different: the cause of linguistic subversion is enemy action—not
to confuse language, but to make it disappear, and with it the English
nation as a separate entity. What happens to language is an *effect* of enemy
action, just as the imposition of Norman French after 1066 was. In any
case, both the example of the hydra image and the (very different) one of
the association of language with the nation's identity, are entirely isolated
cases so far as I am able to determine.

20. The difficulties that this idea poses for a thought aiming to be dialectical
    are obviously considerable. I have indicated some of them with reference
    to the case of Sartre in particular in "La Matière des signes: langage et
    société selon Sartre" in *Sartre et la mise en signe*, ed. M. Issacharoff and J.-C.
    Vilquin (Lexington, Ky., 1981).

21. As to the way in which I understand the particularity of this inflection
    (and also the conceptual context for this essay) I permit myself to refer
    again to *The Discourse of Modernism*, and also to my *Tragedy and Truth:
    Studies in the Development of a Renaissance and Neoclassical Discourse* (New
    Haven, 1980).

22. On this subject see Brown, *Religious and Political Conservatism*, 82–83.
23. Abraham Cowley, *Poems*, ed. A. R. Waller (Cambridge, 1905) 22, cited by Wedgwood, *Poetry and Politics*, 55.
24. The text of this remonstrance has been published by Brown, *Religious and Political Conservatism*, Appendix, 97–100.
25. Michel Foucault, *Les Mots et les choses: une archéologie des sciences humaines* (Paris, 1966), 101.
26. Reiss, *Discourse of Modernism*, ch. 1.
27. The work in progress mentioned in note 4 deals with this question.
28. Richard A. Sayce, *The Essays of Montaigne: A Critical Exploration* (London, 1972). See especially "The Conservative and the Revolutionary," 233–59.
29. J. G. A. Pocock, *The Ancient Constitution and the Feudal Law: A Study of English Historical Thought in the Seventeenth Century* (1957; rpr. New York, 1967), 23.
30. Thomas Hobbes, *The English Works*, ed. Sir William Molesworth, 11 vols. (London, 1839–45), 2.23: "Preface to the Reader."
31. Horkheimer, "Montaigne et la fonction du scepticisme," 274.

8. CERVANTES'S *LABORS OF PERSILES:* "WORKING (IN) THE IN-BETWEEN"

■

DIANA DE ARMAS WILSON

I

THE WORK Cervantes considered his masterpiece—which he twice proclaimed "the great *Persiles*" and once "the best book of fiction composed in our language"—has been until very recently disdained, trivialized, and rigorously excluded from the canon. If the posthumous *Trabajos de Persiles y Sigismunda* (1617) is no longer the "forgotten" text that Rafael Osuna lamented in 1969, the relationship between its sexuality and its writing still offers a major challenge to interpretation.[1] The sterility of Don Quixote's circuitous journey gives way, in Cervantes's late experimental romance, to a rhetoric of generativity: birth, copulation, and parenting are all tactical metaphors within a text whose final word is "posterity" (475). The violent opening scene of the *Persiles*—with its hero being hoisted out of "the narrow mouth of a deep dungeon" into "the light of the clear sky which covers us" (51)—is a literalization of the Spanish idiom for giving birth: *dar a luz.* The central episode of Feliciana's postpartum flight from maternity begins with yet another uterine trope, this one anxiously proferred by the narrator: " 'Pregnant was the oak tree'—let's say it that way" (291). And the closing words of the *Persiles,* perhaps Cervantes's last line of fiction, recant his literary beginnings by extolling the antipastoral "issue" of great-grandchildren (475).[2] This fascination with "things newborn" moves, with admittedly monstrous gait, outside the Greek romance conventions that inform Shakespeare's late plays or even Cervantes's own avowed model, Heliodorus.[3] The *Persiles* reveals its author as a disrupter of sexual norms, of those cherished encodings of Golden Age fiction that survived his earlier assaults on the tottering books of chivalry. Both the teleology and the limits of these hardy norms are unmasked in the *Persiles* through the agency of the Androgyne, a metaphoric figure that subtends the entire verbal body of the text and even divides it into two problematic halves. The nature of this shaping metaphor in the *Persiles*, its place in the discourse of the Renaissance, and its meaning for representation constitute the subject of my essay.

All the mechanisms of generativity in Cervantes's last romance hinge upon the power of naming sexual experience dialogically. Linguistic and biological creativity have become, in this work, parallel paradigms. The creation of a double-voiced or androgynous discourse rescripts Don Quixote's ultimately fatal inability to generate anything beyond his "engendered" Dulcinea (*DQ*, 2.32). All readers recall how she eventually becomes the re-creation of Sancho and, in turn, of the game-playing duke and duchess. The radicalized encounter with sexual otherness in the *Persiles*, however, adumbrates many of our contemporary critiques of systematic thinking. Throughout Cervantes's romance, countless "mouths" and "tongues" and "voices" adduce their gender as ground for commentaries on how the sexes implicate each other. Mutes, polyglots, and even ventriloquists will reiterate the titular "labors" of the protagonists as they struggle to escape the verbal impotence of the "Barbaric Isle," the text's initial landscape. A formal interplay of male and female voices works as a strategy to counter the "voices" of this Barbaric Isle which, in the opening words of the *Persiles*, are barking out orders for yet another sacrificial victim.[4] To move away from the discursive powers of this scapegoating economy—a monolingual world where voice constitutes authority—it is crucial to learn the language of the other. The only female defector from this violent sacrificial community, years after falling in love with a foreigner by "signs," summarizes the couple's long progress toward a mutual bilingualism: "He has taught me his language, and I [have taught] him mine" (82). A complex and uncanonical work that flouts all the Golden Age conventions of genre and gender, Cervantes's text reimagines this androgynous discourse across its main plot and multiple interpolations. The journey of the *Persiles*, as I shall argue, is both a quest for a different sexual economy and for a language with which to name it.

In order to hypothesize a creative and mutual transformation of the polarity masculine/feminine, Cervantes exploits the Androgyne, a figure of ancient if classically debased pedigree. The

Androgyne that informs the *Persiles,* as what follows will elaborate, is a syncretic Renaissance creation that corrects and criticizes its platonic model. By way of formal confirmation of the sexuality it proposes, Cervantes's text is itself metaphorically "an" androgyne—a fiction structured in the shape and by the conjunction of two different halves. This metaphor suggests no irenic escape into some utopian realm where all dualities are left behind. Rather it investigates the laborious journey into a new discursive space that can incorporate them all: a "place," as Cervantes's hero will defend his own story-telling enterprise, "where all things fit and nothing is out of place" (227). The "place" of Cervantes's discourse may be usefully refracted through the modern prism of Hélène Cixous, who, foreseeing a new kind of "vatic bisexuality" in writing, articulates an altered mode of thinking that uncannily echoes the processes of the *Persiles:*

> To admit that writing is precisely *working (in) the in-between,* inspecting the process of the same and of the other without which nothing can live, undoing the work of death—to admit this is first to want the two, as well as both, *the ensemble of the one and the other,* not fixed in sequences of struggle and expulsion or some other form of death but infinitely dynamized by an incessant process of exchange from one subject to another . . . with millions of encounters and transformations of *the same into the other and into the in-between.*

Cixous envisions this kind of writing as possible only in areas not subordinated to the dominant theoretical discourse and—in what could serve as a portrait of the iconoclastic and socially marginal Cervantes—as "conceived of only by subjects who are breakers of automatisms, by peripheral figures that no authority can ever subjugate."[5] To conceptualize "the work of death" in Cervantes is to conjure up, almost automatically, the narrative of *The Curious Impertinent,* in which the word *death* appears with numbing frequency, and in which the scapegoating of Camila's sexuality is metaphorized as disease and death (*DQ,* 1.33–36). Cervantes "undoes" this sequence of death in the *Quixote* (which includes, of course, its hero's pathological horror of sexuality) by exploring the fictional possibilities of sexual otherness in the *Persiles.* When we evaluate this experimental text in terms of its formal, thematic, and linguistic concerns with otherness, Cervantes once again emerges as a breaker of automatisms—only this time in the erotic sphere.[6] By positing gender as socially constructed through cultural fiats—through "laws" or maxims whose errancy is punningly established—the text calls into question a sexual economy that relies on the loudest voices of its "barbarians" and the muteness of its women.

Written during what Philip III's censor eulogized as "the swan-

song of a good old age almost within the grips of death" (41), the
Persiles borrows from Cervantes's youth for its fictive time: a two-
year period sometime between 1558 and 1572.[7] The main plot
focuses on the journey of two royal lovers from Iceland or "Thule"
to Rome. Disguised as brother and sister, the protagonists travel
under the pseudonyms of Periandro and Auristela. Although pi-
ously undertaken, the pilgrimage that structures the main plot is, as
we learn at its end, essentially a stratagem for allowing the protagonists to escape from an inauspicious love triangle. The narrative
itself opens *in medias res* well into this journey, on a "barbaric" island
in the North Sea, moves down to Portugal and Spain at its midpoint,
and concludes in Rome, with the marriage of the protagonists in
front of St. Paul's. Only after he has endured or survived catastro-
phes without number—from fires and falls to shipwrecks and poi-
sonings—can the hero marry the heroine: "with his tongue," as the
text puts it, he "pronounces a *yes*" (474). The multiple "labors" of the
protagonists function as a matrix for some dozen interpolated tales
of sexual vicissitudes, narratives that both rupture and illuminate
the main plot while amplifying its logic of representation. These
inset tales, which constitute about one-fourth of the text, have been
accused of ruining its suspense and *dispositio*.[8] Viewed from a less
canonical perspective, these tales may be seen to subvert and dislo-
cate the sexual economy of the *Persiles'* opening landscape, its emblematic "place" of male primacy: the Barbaric Isle.

As characterized in the first four chapters of the *Persiles*, this island
sustains a community of isolated males whose "Law" or ritual idolatry dictates a continual circulation of women. Purchased "with
chunks of gold ore and extremely precious pearls" (57), these foreign women are then fetishized as incubators for the horde's potential messiah. This male traffic in women, the text is careful to note,
has not *brutalized* the barbarians: whether "purchased or robbed,"
the women are "well treated by them, who only in this show themselves not to be barbarians" (57). The only notable deprivation for
women on the island would appear to be speech. Or as the interpreter Transila explains to the visitors, "these my masters do not
wish me to dilate my speech in anything other than what is pertinent to their business" (62). The Barbaric Isle's mechanisms of sexual
continuity, as disclosed by the potential "slave" Taurisa, are trig-
gered by the "impertinent prophecy" that one of the barbarians will
father a world conqueror on an imported woman. The potential
father of this "king" may be identified by his manly ingestion of the
pulverized hearts of sacrificial victims, since he alone will be able to
swallow them without wincing (55–58).[9]

Into this world of sanctified violence, Cervantes's hero is twice delivered, first as a sacrificial victim and, having narrowly escaped this fate, next as a "woman." In order to rescue the captive Auristela, Periandro has pressed his rival Arnaldo into cross-dressing him so lavishly that, as the narrator explains, "he resembled to all appearances, the most elegant and handsome woman human eyes had yet seen. The sailors were all admiration; Taurisa, speechless; Arnaldo, confused" (60). When Periandro meets up with Auristela, she herself, in male clothing, is being readied for sacrifice. Their tearful embrace, each in gender disguise, inspires a fatal desire in Bradamiro, a barbarian warrior, for the feminized Periandro: "This woman is mine because I want her" (67). The Barbaric Isle's governor instantly punishes Bradamiro's deviancy from the male code with a deadly arrow into his mouth—"stopping the movement of his tongue."[10] One arrow leads to another and civil war breaks out in the all-male kingdom, "son not respecting father, nor brother, brother" (68). After Bradamiro's allies set the island on fire, its inhabitants are turned to "ashes" (70). The protagonists manage to escape in the company of "the interpreter"—the only woman officially admitted to the community for a commodity other than that of her body: her polyglotism.

The major difference between a feminist interrogation and the traditional "doctrinal" readings of the *Persiles* must turn on the status accorded to the symbolic exchange of power and goods that *is* the Barbaric Isle. The text's opening chapters, in fact, focus the narrative insistently upon the economic laws of circulation for women that sustain the "vanity" (58) and guarantee the continuity of the insular patriarchy. At the heart of the social contract inscribed in what has been called the *Persiles'* "long repellent beginning" (virtually an invitation to skip over it) is the legislated traffic in women. Indeed, everything turns on it: the impending sacrifice designed to provide "hearts to burn" for the patriarchal taste-test; the hero's rescue from immolation and his return to the isle as a disguised commodity; Bradamiro's lust for the cross-dressed hero and, as its consequence, the insular civil war and eventual holocaust. The economic particulars of this curious Renaissance landscape can scarcely be lost on readers even faintly familiar with Claude Lévi-Strauss's analysis of elementary kinship structures.[11] Cervantes's Barbaric Isle is a society mediated by chunks of gold, a culture in which the commercial is confounded with the genealogical transaction. A society of bow-and-arrow gesticulators who communicate by "sign language" or by a "clamor" that is "articulately understood by nobody," the barbarians are ever anxious to limit or negate the voices of others (53, 51). Ritually trained to swallow hearts unflinchingly,

Cervantes's agitated barbarians are violent men with an "inviolable" belief in the power of their sacred origins and their manifest destiny: to inseminate a purchased woman with their long-awaited messiah. The only power they lack, in short, is the power of the word: they remain a society whose confusion of language—thrice alluded to in the opening chapter—reflects its confusion of mind (51–53).

The conspicuous subject of male traffic in women, screened out of the domain of most *Persiles* criticism,[12] will be repeated, in variations of increasingly sophisticated barbarism, throughout Cervantes's text. In a double-voiced narration by the barbarians' "interpreter" and her father, we eventually discover that the resourceful Transila had earlier escaped from the *ius primae noctis* or "barbarous custom" (112) of her own country, an Irish culture that legally obliges all its brides to sexually satisfy their eager male in-laws. But Spain too, will be found to have its own "barbarians" who traffic in women while violently "giving forth voices": Feliciana's raging kinsmen, "more like executioners than father and brother," set out to kill her for having foiled their marriage plans by the "infamy" of a pregnancy (291–312). Even in civilized Italy, Alejandro Castrucho will try to force his niece into a cross-cousin marriage "so that the wealth would remain in the family" (402–12). There is little difference, it would appear, between the male traffic on the Barbaric Isle and Castrucho's attempted traffic in his niece. Both narratives stress the "impertinence" of patrilineal descent systems in which women function as bearers instead of sharers of meaning. Cervantes's text will erase Castrucho as cleanly as it did the barbarians: just as they destroy themselves at the sight of an androgynous embrace, Castrucho will suffer a "mortal paroxysm" at the "two yeses" of his niece's union with an outsider (411).

Cervantes's fictive use of the notion of barbarism at the beginning of his narrative is not a culturally self-authenticating device deployed to confirm the value of a Mediterranean civilization at its end. Barbarism and civilization do not appear to function, as various critics have suggested, as binary oppositions. Avalle-Arce's vision of Cervantes's barbary, to cite only one instance of the traditional reading, is that of a kind of Arctic hell opposed to Rome's heaven: or as he puts it, "from the dungeons of the Barbaric Isle to 'heaven on earth' " ["Introducción," 26]. This hierarchical sweep overlooks the fact that Rome itself in the *Persiles* turns out to be a morally corrupt world of sophisticated violence. The civilization represented in the second half of Cervantes's text is a very contested concept: both the main plot and its interpolations contain one elaboration after another of the buying and selling of sexuality that constituted the

Barbaric Isle.[13] As one of the cherished dichotomous oppositions dominating Western metaphysics, the civilization/barbary polarity turns out in the *Persiles* to be illusory—similar, in fact, to the good/evil opposition questioned by the discursive narrator toward the work's end:

> It seems as if good and evil are such a small distance away from each other, that they are like two coincident lines which, although originating from separate and different principles, end up in one place. (464)

Breaking away from a logic of polar oppositions, Cervantes's writing reaches throughout his romance for a "place" from which to speak about love. It is not civilization, in sum, that calls barbarism into question, since they are also "like two coincident lines" in Cervantes's text. Rather it is the Androgyne that radically questions the primordially masculine model of sexuality metaphorized by the Barbaric Isle. It is a double-voiced discourse, each gender hearing the other, that disrupts and dismantles all systems of circulation based on the injunction of silence and the invisiblity of female desire. The systems that fabricate the sacrificial process in the *Persiles* can by no readerly stretch be exonerated as "human society": they are conspicuously emblematized, in the opening chapters of the *Persiles*, as an all-male society bonded in a futile quest for patriarchal permanence.

Various subtexts have been suggested for the Barbaric Isle narrative, including Aristotle's Iphigenia plot and numerous sixteenth-century chronicles about the American Indians. These last dispose us to inveigh against the phenomenon of human sacrifice as morally abhorrent, a perspective already present in Heliodorus, Cervantes's acknowledged precursor.[14] Beyond its capacity to express rhetorical horror or *admiratio*, however, the cannibalism in Cervantes very explicitly functions to streamline a system of sexual circulation: cooked hearts are the required ingredient for validating a world of fathers and sons. It is the *system*, not the cannibalism, that requires a closer look. Moral or rhetorical readings screen out the sexual aims of this scapegoating mechanism. With its literalized male traffic in women, the structures of desire operative on Cervantes's prolegomenous Barbaric Isle anticipate, as did the structures of *Don Quixote*, the European class narrative of triangular desire.[15] The seventy-five chapters of the *Persiles* which follow the destruction of the Barbaric Isle, however, attempt to displace its dominant male vision, to question and expose its powerful assumptions. How might language and literature refocus an erotic tradition that fetishizes its women and cannibalizes its men? Cervantes's first narrative step is to allow that tradition, in and through its own metaphors of penetration, to self-destruct. The conflagration of the Barbaric Isle is strategically represented as the result of one androgynous exchange: all-male bonding is volatile but the Androgyne makes it combustible. It is the emblematic tableau of the transvestite lovers embracing—each in disguise as the other, each containing the two sexes in one—that first unhinges one barbarian and then destroys them all. The survivors of this contrived holocaust will be pushed out to sea from the smoldering island, out into an "economy of fluids" until, in Book 2, they will be "born again into the world out of the womb of [their] galley" (163).[16] Nearly three hundred pages after that "second time" birth, the narrator of the *Persiles*, looking back on the protagonists' many ordeals, will sum up the whole Barbaric Isle experience in one androgynous image: "the Barbaric Isle, when [Auristela] and Periandro found themselves in traded garments ["trajes trocados"], she in the male, and he in the female ones: a very strange metamorphosis" (341).

As a traditionally androgynous hallmark, cross-dressing has blatant significations in allegory, where clothing sharply defines agency and roles. Cervantes's use of cross-dress at the beginning of his narrative may have parodic inferences. Gesturing back to Greek "initiatory androgyny," the double transvestism of the *Persiles'* introductory scenes may be a recuperative technique.[17] The duplex "metamorphosis," in any event, serves to rectify the sexual asymmetry of Renaissance literary cross-dress, whose most demonstrable function was to allow female characters to escape from home and then to keep them safely on the road. The *Persiles* includes one of these conventional transvestites, Ambrosia Agustina, who serves as a drummer's boy in Philip II's army while chasing after her husband (361–66). Her character does not stray too far from a literary inquiry into the social constraints that say women must wait at home while men go off to wars. But some of the sub-characters in the *Persiles* appear in extreme variants of cross-dress, their own "metamorphoses" augmenting the gender reversal of the protagonists in their opening embrace. A young Lithuanian widow, for example, becomes an avenging pirate after hanging some forty would-be rapists from the tackle and yards of her ship. Sulpicia is presented within Periandro's delayed prologue as literally "dressed to kill," with a stiff white corselet and a high-crested helmet, brandishing a javelin before a squadron of pirate-women whom she—as their *"capitana"*—is expertly drilling.[18] For all its sanguinity, this sexual boundary shift is less striking than the bizarre transvestism of Tozuelo, a rustic who impersonates his pregnant girlfriend in order to spare her a possible miscarriage during some country dances in Toledo. With Tozuelo's gender disguise—in fact an act of nurturing on his part—readers may come closer to what Heilbrun calls the "viscerally unbearable" androgynous scenario.[19] The text acknowledges its potential repellency by having the mayor of Toledo berate Tozuelo for the "delinquency" of his cross-dressing—an act that the mayor deprecates as "mucous-like," i.e., of little esteem ["es mocosa la culpa"]. Although Tozuelo is accused of having "profaned" the dances (Toledo's famous *villanas de la Sagra*), all ends well when the authorities give up their "childishness" and marry the couple, the groom still in female garb. As an ad hoc "pregnant male," Cervantes's dancing Tozuelo belongs among the truly liminal figures of the carnivalesque world.[20] The text at this juncture creates a new sign to describe its odd couple: "*los donceles*" (327–30). The normally feminine noun *doncella* [maiden] is altered by the imposition of a common gender ending [-*es*], then modified by a masculine definite article [*los*]. This kind of wild neologizing seems entirely appropriate in a work that radically questions gender codes. Cervantes's nonce word transcends syntax to invoke the Androgyne.

The rebarbative associations of male transvestism, which has canonically represented emasculation, are pointedly addressed in chapter 3 of the *Persiles*, when the cross-dressed hero is described as on the verge of weeping tears "that did *not* arise from an effeminated heart," but rather from a just consideration of other people's sufferings [63–64]. There is, in other words, no loss of masculinity, no loss of "place" for Cervantes's androgynous males, whose fundamental mandate is to dramatize a superior economy of caring in the face of a punitive male solidarity.[21] Losing place or face in any hierarchy of gender, one might add, presents little threat to the main population of the *Persiles:* as self-exiles from their respective cultures, they are far more concerned with being lost at sea. In many ways Cervantes's last romance prefigures the modern "paradigm shift" away from hierarchies, away from dynastic or patriarchal modes of thought. In my view, the "complicated machinery" of the *Persiles* does not rest, as has been argued, on the hierarchical Great Chain of Being but, rather, on the circular Androgyne that refuses all hierarchy.[22] The text asks readers to respond to its blurring of sexual categories with a suspension of the old aversions: androgyny is represented as an enterprise vital to its practitioners, vexing to its critics, and fatal to its opponents. The representation signals toward a different ordering of sexual relations, toward a psychic and sexual economy founded on an ethic of caring. Such an exploration does not *require* transvestism. There are characters in the *Persiles* who experience the reality of the other gender without cross-dressing: the polyglot Transila, based upon the Italian virago-type heroine, is celebrated for her "manly [varonil] *brío*" (69); the putative "adulterer" Rosanio is dubbed "the Knight of the Infant" ["el caballero de la criatura"] because he inherits the care of his son when the infant's unwed mother must flee for her life (290); and Isabela Castrucha, perhaps the most protean figure in the text, is addressed as an obscene "old man" while she successfully feigns—ventriloquizes—demonic possession (409).[23]

Cross-dress is only one way in which the *Persiles* signals its alertness to sexual oppositions as a category for a poetics. The import of the Androgyne, the archetypal sign of the Couple, is suggested to the reader as early as the title page, where the copulative conjunction of Persiles *and* Sigismunda links together a male/female polarity as co-owners of a definite sum of travails.[24] This titular compounding recalls a generic principle of the better known surviving Greek romances: unlike the chivalric and pastoral romances known to Cervantes and named after either heroic or desirable individuals, the Greek romances from the Second Sophistic period (including Heliodorus's *Ethiopica*, whose official title is *The Loves of Theagenes and Chariclea*) are all named after a heterosexual couple.[25] Duplicitous in all senses, Cervantes's wandering heroes have two names apiece and travel, across the text, under their pseudonyms. Persiles' assumed name especially begs for interpretation. When we recall how Cervantes's earlier hero, Alonso Quijano, agonized about choosing "resonant and significant" names for himself, his lady, and his horse [*DQ*, 1.1], the compound pseudonym of *Periandro* acquires its own resonant signification. From the Greek prefix *peri-* (round, around, about) and the noun *andros* (man), we infer a manhood yoked to its own gender qualifier: *Periandro,* a region or place lying around the fixed gender of masculinity (cf., *pericardium*). Periandro likens himself to some anagogic region beyond time and space, as noted above, in response to repeated criticism of his narrative techniques: "I . . . am made like this thing which is called place, where all things fit and nothing is out of place" (227). Speaking from a peripheral reality, Cervantes's ex-centric hero insists on incorporating—both into his narratives and into his questing self—all contradictions.[26] The refusal to limit or bound either gender or speech is characteristic not only of Periandro but also of the narrative that contains him, the *Persiles* itself.

That Cervantes's writing uses gender metaphorically is further shown by the main genealogical transaction of the *Persiles.* Two queen mothers, heads of Thule and of Friesland, engineer a union that will remove the threat of sterility from their respective all-male

and all-female royal lines, isolated in their separate Northern kingdoms. Since one of the notable distinctions of Spanish Golden Age
texts is the almost complete absence of the figure of the mother, the
spectacle here of the absent father (if it can so be called) is an unorthodox touch.[27] To compound this early subversion of the fathers,
the text also chooses to ridicule the sensitive institution of pri-
mogeniture: it appears that Thule's queen regards her eldest son
Magsimino, perennially away at wars, as simply "detestable" (abor-
recible). Since Magsimino is officially engaged to the heroine Sigismunda (who at this prepubescent stage has "no will whatsoever"
[467]), his younger brother's growing passion for the visiting prin-
cess threatens a domestic triangle. In order to foil the absent Magsimino and to aid the young protagonists, Queen Eustoquia packs
the lovers off to Rome under a pretext that is revealed as the pre-text
only in the book's closing chapters. Her plan works when, two years
and many shipwrecks later, the marriage of the protagonists,
blessed by the dying Magsimino, effects a merger between the
gender-specific royal lines. The main genealogical exchange in the
Persiles, then, empowered exclusively by mothers, reverses the
transactions of the Barbaric Isle: traffic in women gives way to traffic
by women. The success of their endeavors gives ultimate validation
to the Androgyne, a figure disseminated throughout the text to
eclipse both patriarchal and hierarchal mechanisms of sexual
control.

The process of the two-in(to)-one reflected in the kinship structures of the protagonists is given rhetorical emphasis at key points
in the narrative. In response to Auristela's long disease of jealousy,
Periandro invokes the Androgyne when he speaks, in alchemical
terms, of producing a compound out of their joined souls: "a compound so singular and so unique [un compuesto tan uno y tan solo] that
death will have much to do in dividing it" (185). This anagogic or
copular metaphor is at work in the Persiles even in ironic form when,
during one of the protagonists' most divisive exchanges, they each
insist aloud that their two souls "are no more than one" and that no
contentment can equal the experience of "two souls who are one"
(414–15).[28] The dynamics of yearning attending this copular metaphor are echoed throughout the text by an ostentatious partitive
construction that focuses rhetorically on the notion of halves. The
hero's first address to the heroine, whispered during their transvestite embrace, underlies the primacy of this structural formula: "O
dear half of my soul!" [¡O querida mitad de mi alma!].[29] Although
Avalle-Arce allows that the formula "abounds" in the Cervantine
canon, he chooses to dismiss it as "of remote Horatian origin,"

thereby editorially consigning this critical phrase to a male preserve of authority. As a classical commonplace, the phrase does indeed appear not only in Horace's ode to his friend Virgil (3.8), but also in Ovid, Augustine, and Petrarch—to note only a sample of Latin writers who employ variants of the vocative *pars* (or *dimidium*) *animae meae* to address their male friends. Cervantes himself used the figure homoerotically at the start of his career: in the pastoral *Galatea* (1585), Timbrio laments that both his male rival and his female love are the "two true and better halves of his soul."[30] The transgressive logic of just such a metaphor may have inspired Aristotle's observation that the idea of Aristophanes' Androgyne appears to be somewhat watery when it embraces more than two persons (*Politics*, 2.1.16f. [1262b]). Such triangulated figurations never occur in the *Persiles*, however, where the "other half" is always the other gender. As such, the phrase signals to origins even more remote than Horace and to notions of otherness less in complicity with male interests. It is the myth of the two *different* sexual halves (andro/gyne) which funds both the thematics and the structures of the *Persiles*.

Focusing on Cervantes's playful use of the two-in-one, his experimentations in anagogy, enables us to take a fresh look at the traditional criticism lamenting the *Persiles* as a "split" text. The majority of serious commentators since Friedrich Bouterwek (1804) have shared a view of it as "split," or as Osuna puts it, "as a work cut into two parts" (*escindida*: cut, divided, separated). Osuna, in fact, speaks of this "scission" (*escisión*) as "without a doubt the most mysterious thing about the *Persiles*." The traditional distinction between the two halves of the work (Books 1 and 2 are set in the Arctic zones, Books 3 and 4 along the Mediterranean) is perhaps best articulated by Atkinson, who writes of the "obvious concern with symmetry in the architecture of the novel, which, as it balances the action between North and South, unknown and known, symbolical and material, introduces too in the first half one significant national of each of the four known countries later to be traversed." But Atkinson refuses to be seduced by all this symmetry. In a study confessedly entitled "The Enigma of the *Persiles*," he concludes abruptly, in a curious non sequitur, that "mere realism was not and could not be Cervantes's concern." The enigmatic notion of two irreconcilable textual halves has led critics to promote one over the other. Atkinson, for instance, sees only the first half as the "vital" one, where "everything is relevant." Menéndez y Pelayo, on the other hand, claims that the *Persiles* "contains in its second half some of the best pages ever written by its author." In a classic summary of opinions on the

Persiles, Osuna notes "the lack of unity in the novel, a problem yet to be studied; if the two parts are so different, what is it that joins them together?"[31] My reading addresses itself to that question. If the "enigma" of the *Persiles* demands to be articulated on the level of theory, such a theory might well begin with the signifying capacity of a pair, an ensemble, of two split halves. The enigma of the "split," in short, asks readers to organize the text in relation to splitting, scission, or division as forces of signification. A split is not a flaw if it can be shown to be a structuring and a strategy. The *Persiles*, as I construe it, is a strategically split or double-voiced discourse—a cunning analogue of the ancient split between the sexes it aims to explore.

II

Where in the world—or at least in his own Renaissance *mundus significans*—could Cervantes have found the organizing metaphor for his last romance?[32] The androgynous tableau of his transvestite protagonists, which exhibits the intentional axis of the narrative, may have been suggested to him by any one of the countless emblems, many linked to alchemical processes, which helped to feed the European mania engendered by Andrea Alciati's first collection of *Emblemata*, published in 1531.[33] It is also likely that Cervantes was familiar with the Androgyne in the "resurrected" form it took within the multiple free translations, reconstitutions, and adaptations of Plato's *Symposium* which came forward in the cinquecento. But the androgynous figuration subtending the *Persiles* is critically different from the Androgyne invoked within the humanist hermeneutics associated with Learned Latin, a tradition whose own "puberty-rite mentality," savoring in some ways of the Barbaric Isle, has recently been well documented.[34] Unlike the gynophobic Ficino, Cervantes does not un-sex his Androgyne. It was Ficino's phrase, we recall, that Don Quixote borrowed to describe his platonic love—his "amores tan platónicos" [2.3]—for Dulcinea. But all traces of the militant asceticism that characterized both Ficino and Don Quixote are erased in the *Persiles*.[35] Cervantes's literary project, from its pastoral start to its byzantine finish, explored one recurrent question: How does one talk about—"give voices to"—*desire?* The pastoral and chivalric romances seemed to talk of little else, but their languages of desire relentlessly turned on the same courtly love *topoi* that maddened and destroyed Don Quixote. His quest for his ideal lady, with its ascetic and triangulated dynamics, was indeed, to recall Cixous' s phrase, "fixed in sequences of struggle and expulsion [and] death." In every way Dulcinea is a literalizing of that "dead-end street" that Sancho imagines her to live on [*una callejuela sin salida*, 2.9]. The *Persiles* tries not only to rectify this failure of Eros in the *Quixote* but also to finish the unfinished *Galatea* (1585), a work that was self-evaluated, during the scrutiny of Don Quixote's library, as "proposing something but concluding nothing" (1.6).[36] In order to conclude his original proposal, Cervantes needed a two-in-one formula that would make a concord of discords, that would account for the "labors" of romance. A model for this kind of synthesis—mutual sexual love and spiritual integration—was already part of the authentic philosophical discourse of the Renaissance: Leone Ebreo's *Dialoghi d'amore* (1535). Within Leone's double-voiced discourse between a man and a woman, Filone and Sofia (Filo/Sofia) enter into a complex dialogical exchange on the nature of love and desire. We are indebted to the third of these dialogues for the most resonant rehabilitation of the myth of the Androgyne within the platonic tradition. Leone's Androgyne, I submit, contains the meaning of the "enigma" of the *Persiles*. That Cervantes had access to Leone's work is established by the prologue to *Don Quixote*, Part 1, in which "a lively, clever friend" of the author's recommends the Hebrew platonist as an authority: "If you should be dealing with the subject of love, with a smattering of Tuscan you can apply to Leon the Hebrew, who will supply you to your heart's content."[37]

Leone's generative retailoring of the platonic Androgyne both criticizes and corrects its platonic model. In the *Symposium*, the Androgyne has its Western literary inaugural as a primordial myth. Aristophanes recalls how the original nature of mankind embraced not two but three sexes: man, woman, and Androgyne (man/woman), all circular beings with eight hands and feet, four ears, two privy members. Zeus punished their insolence against the gods by cutting them all in half, "like a sorb apple which is halved for pickling, or as you might divide an egg with a hair"—amusing kitchen similes that betray the platonic denial of all *difference* between the two halves of the heterosexual Androgyne. There follows in the Aristophanic text a passage whose language of division and reunion, with its well-known metaphysics of nostalgia, will find its way, centuries later, into the *Persiles*:

> After the division the two parts of man, *each desiring his other half*, came together . . . longing to grow into one. . . . so ancient is the desire of one another which is implanted in us, reuniting our original nature, *making one of two*, and healing the state of man. *Each of us when separated . . . is always looking for his other half.*

Despite its echoes of this mathematical language, Cervantes's text cannot be regarded as simply another "footnote to Plato." In the platonic text, it bears recalling, the androgynous sex is roundly disdained: the term *androgynous* signifies "adulterous" men and women and is preserved, Aristophanes is careful to explain, only as "a term of reproach." The deprecation of heterosexual coupling here is reinforced by his teasing endorsement, albeit within an ironic discourse, of the "manly" sex, the sex represented by "the best of boys and youth."[38] In a study of the vicissitudes of Eros in Western culture, Suzanne Lilar laments that "it is to the love of boys that we owe the one and only great Western philosophy of love."[39]

In what amounts to a major literary breakthrough for the *imagination* of heterosexuality, then, Leone Ebreo's text rescues the Androgyne from both Plato's misogyny and Ficino's chastity. Rescripting Aristophanes' merry words of male camaraderie, Leone will identify the specific distortions of Plato's text and provide correctives. Plato's Androgyne appears in the final book of Leone's vast treatise, a work structured as a male/female dialogue and distinguished throughout for its metaphoric use of gender. "A central and persistent feature of Leone's philosophy, perhaps influenced by his readings in Kabbalah" is, according to T. Anthony Perry, "the radical polarization of the entire universe in terms of male and female symbols." These polarities, as Perry argues in his study of the erotic tradition of Continental literature originating from the *Dialoghi*, are integrated by Leone's nondualist stance.[40] Integrative, carnal, and Kabbalistic tendencies all feed into his interpretation of "la fábula del Andrógeno de Platón"—as the 1590 Spanish translation, by Inca Garcilaso de la Vega, rendered Leone's syncretic Androgyne for Golden Age readers.[41]

Even more analogous to the modes of thought we have identified and situated in the *Persiles,* Leone's double-voiced discourse chooses to explore the androgynous aspects of the Creation itself. It is this feature of Leone's Judeo-platonism—his attempt to yoke the platonic myth of the Androgyne with the Mosaic tradition of Genesis—that is fictionally reflected in the "split" structures of the *Persiles,* in its two-in-one merger of erotic odyssey with spiritual pilgrimage. Leone's innovative conflation of two hitherto incompatible traditions would have appealed greatly to Cervantes's certifiably iconoclastic leanings. The Androgyne has never been welcome in orthodox Judeo-Christian circles: it has, in fact, been roundly rejected by the scholastic tradition, doubtless because it threatens their image of a patriarchal God.[42] Leone does not scruple to mediate even these warring polarities.

But let us turn to Leone's text itself. Written "in-between" Moses and the Androgyne, it argues that Plato's fable was actually "translated" from Holy Scripture, from the Mosaic creation story of Adam and Eve. It would seem to Leone that Plato "amplified and adorned" the creation story to make it "conform to Greek rhetoric"—a linguistic manipulation that resulted in "a disordered mixture of Hebrew ideas." Giving Plato his due, however, Leone allows that the Greek version of the Androgyne myth was based, perforce, on some maddening Mosaic "contradictions," namely the two Creation accounts in the Bible: Genesis 1:27, in which God creates humanity ("Adam") in his own image ("male and female created He them"); and Genesis 2:7 ff., in which the creation of Eve out of Adam's rib establishes the priority of the male. These same Mosaic "contradictions" may be the subtext of the *Persiles* when the penitentiaries in Rome, declaring to Auristela the mysteries of the Catholic faith, discourse "over the truth" [*discurrieron por la verdad*] of the Creation story. How Cervantes's penitentiaries *do* in fact handle its contradictions is glossed over in the narrator's account of the "principal and most useful [*convenientes*] mysteries" of the faith (435). But some seven pages later a chapter will close with a remark that unexpectedly reflects upon these undisclosed "mysteries": in his own genesis account of Cervantes's protagonists, the narrator is suddenly compelled to inform us that "nature" created them "as equals and formed out of the same bullet-mold" (442). Cervantes's filiation with Leone, we begin to see, turns on their common subversion of Adam's rib.

For Leone, intentionality is paramount: the "divine Moses" contradicted himself so "manifestly" that he must have meant us to read his "intention" at an allegorical level. Leone claims to be able to interpret the "allegorical significance" of these patriarchal contradictions. In Leone's exegesis of what he has adduced as a Mosaic strategy, the first human being (i.e., Adam) "contained in him/herself [*en sí*] male and female without division." Leone glosses this two-in-one "Adam" with the Chaldean commentaries [*commentarios hebreos en lengua caldea*] that claim that "Adam was created out of two persons, out of one part male and the other female." God's decision that "it was not good for man to be alone" is interpreted by Leone as God's disaffection with "Adam as male and female in one body only, attached back to back, counter-visioned." Thus God put this compound being to sleep and removed one of its sides [*sus lados*], which word, Leone insists, is ambivalent [*equívoco*] and can mean "either side [*lado*] or rib [*costilla*]." By stressing the errancy of the word *rib*— "which here and elsewhere also means *side*"—Leone pluralizes the Bible's mode of signifying. Drawing upon the instability of the

Hebrew language for his reading of Plato's reading of Genesis, Leone's deconstructive reading of that text's "critical difference from itself" separates him from all those "ordinary commentators" who, he claims, "fatigue themselves in making this text agree literally." The errancy of one Hebrew word, in short, empowers Leone to replace Adam's "rib," a trope of male authority, with the Androgyne's "other half," a trope of sexual parity. Thanks to linguistic drift, Eve can become what Moses always "intended": "the side or feminine person who was behind Adam's shoulder."[43] Leone appears to be writing counter to the stubborn Renaissance belief, noted by Thomas Greene, "that Hebrew was a 'natural language' whose names for things corresponded to their true nature."[44] That no "natural" or even neutral language exists for naming sexual experience is also, as we have suggested, one of the governing assumptions of the *Persiles*.

The Androgyne that Plato and the Greeks supposedly derived from Genesis 1:27, we recall, they also deprecated as an "adulterous" entity. Filtered through the rectitude of Moses, however, Leone's retailored Androgyne loses all those suggestions of "reproach" attributed to it by Aristophanes. In Leone, as in Cervantes, the concept of androgyny suggests parity, mutuality, sexuality, generativity, and—what is most unclassical—*difference*. The Hebrew philosopher and the Spanish novelist share an erotic philosophy that signaled, for its age, a new understanding of carnal love and procreation. Leone's rich exploration of the platonic myth reconstitutes the Androgyne as a relation between two vocal modalities of desire—an unorthodox relation between the sexes based upon a "hetero-sexual dialogue" whose discourse we still continue to develop and explore. As "equivocal" as Adam's rib in Leone's commentary, however, the word *androgyny* has been drifting back lately to its classical position as "a term of reproach." In our day the deprecation is most often articulated by radicalized feminist thinkers, who tend to reject *androgyny* as a sign for what Luce Irigaray calls "the old dream of symmetry."[45]

The "shamelessness" of the term androgyny, a perception scarcely confined to Aristophanes and Adrienne Rich, may lie behind the considered historical choices of terms like *hermaphroditism*, with its Olympian distance, or *bisexuality*, with its gender-free prefix. The pedigrees of these terms, however, show them to be no less fraught, no more "faithful to the facts" of the "in-between" sexual thinking we are struggling to describe.[46] Indeed, all three terms bear out Nietzsche's adage that "terms that have histories cannot be defined." Viewed from a rhetorical perspective, however—as the literary metaphor we encounter in both Leone and Cervantes—the term *androgyny* may be regarded, in Hayden White's sense of a trope, as a linguistic "defense" against literality. Leone's text is explicit about androgyny's signifying "something other than the literal": as Sofia baldly puts it, "I do not believe that at any time a man and a woman were in any other way than in two divided bodies, just as they are at present" (223–24). If, as White argues, troping can be understood as "both a movement *from* one notion of the way things are related [in this case, men and women] *to* another notion"—as a deviation from the appropriate use of language towards another conception of what will become appropriate—Cervantes's use of the Androgyne as metaphor becomes clearer.[47] This movement or deviation—from the notion of sexual relations as legislated on the Barbaric Isle toward another not yet "appropriate" conception—constitutes the plot of the *Persiles,* a work that requires us to think our way toward what androgyny could and should be.

That Cervantes recognized such a work would shatter his readers' stable assumptions about "the way things are related" between the genders is illustrated by his authorial intrusion at the beginning of the fourth and final book of the *Persiles* (415–18). As if the text were formally aware of the difficulties of its own future readings, the author steps in to help us with a "commentary." In what amounts to a radical textual strategy, Cervantes himself—or at least a character-author whose capsule autobiography evokes the historical Cervantes—ruptures his narrative with a personal appearance. Once again he comes to posit the problem of the book, this time a book inscribed by his own characters. Thinly disguised as a Spanish man of letters, writing tools and portfolio in hand, he suddenly enters the dining room of an inn outside Rome where the protagonists and their party are lodged. Although he never introduces himself beyond the generic, "I, sirs, am a curious man," he follows this greeting with a thumbnail *vida* that identifies him as yet another image in the Cervantine *obra* of the author as Trickster.[48] This "elegant pilgrim" has a design on the other pilgrims, whom he wishes to enlist in a curious literary project. He asks them all to contribute to an anthology that he is editing, a text entitled *Flor de aforismos peregrinos* [*Posy of Peregrine Aphorisms*]—a parody of Renaissance *Florilegia* of edifying classical maxims. The multivalent pun in the forthcoming book's title (*peregrino* is an errant word meaning *pilgrim* or *palmer* in Spanish, but also *foreign, strange, wonderful*) establishes a formal correspondence between the peregrine aphorisms, the pilgrims-errant, the pilgrim-editor, his "peregrine idea" for this book, and the *Persiles* itself—a text with a pilgrimage frame. The linguistic

errancy of these aphorisms—their tendency to wander, as it were—
advertises their inherent arbitrariness. The dramatic situation of
their *in situ* inscription further indicates how categories of behavior
are all-too-human constructions. The pilgrim-editor's collection,
which he claims to number over three hundred entries already, lifts
our attention from the *Persiles* to the process of its own writing. This
device of a character in search of his "authors" serves, through its
self-reflexivity, to halt and deconstruct the narrative, to move us
abruptly into a scriptive realm. We watch an author asking his
culture to set down the maxims it lives by. We watch him materialize
in his text to show us how authority *is* a fiction.

The distracting image of this text within a text forces an encounter
between two discourses: the *Flor* that explains the *Persiles* that contains it. How do the two texts bespeak each other? Unlike the much-
heralded arrival of the *Persiles*, anticipated as a possible monster but
at no time disowned, the production of the *Flor* is studiously celi-
bate: the pilgrim-editor announces his intention "to produce a book
at the cost of others" [*a costa ajena*]—one that will not appear under
his own name [*no en nombre mío*]. In a narrative stance of disavowal,
he eschews all literary paternity for the *Flor*, yet this orphaned text
exposes both the structures and strategies of the *Persiles*. What do
we read in the *Flor?*

The overwhelming first impression of the collection of maxims is
its gendered arena of production. Like the divided Androgyne,
male and female are represented in this microtext as two split
halves: male aphorisms, conveying general truths, stand in binary
opposition to female maxims, offering moral advice. This is a text
that fictionalizes division and inserts it into the "reality" of a metaphoric pilgrimage. The generic quality of the entries stands out:
none especially fits the character of its contributor, only of his or her
gender.[49] In the masculine entries, inscribed first, desire is exul-
tantly contained in the battlefield (e.g., "Happy is the soldier who,
while fighting, knows that his Prince is looking on"); in the women's
maxims it hovers nervously around the bedroom ("A woman must
be like the ermine, better trapped than sullied"). The male aphorisms inscribe agency and achievement, the female maxims anxiety and admonition. In the masculine ledger, we read postures of
aggression, desires for honor, fame, and death; in the feminine
column passivity, dispensability, and a mania for spotlessness. Cervantes's solicited *Flor* projects, *in nuce*, a world of violence and
complicity—a world where men only desire to seem (be seen as)
heroic, and where women, having fully internalized the reifying
attitudes of their cultures, only desire "not to displease."[50]

As an ensemble, these aggressive/servile discourses represent in boldface the sexual norms that were the ontology of Renaissance fiction. The two mutually uninfluencing currents anticipate, with uncanny accuracy, Freud's theory of sexual difference, his heroic/erotic antinomy.[51] More to our purposes, they stand out as a textbook demonstration of how the sexes are imprisoned in their separate languages, in their own maxims of desire. The positive/privative opposition between the sexes fictionalized in the *Flor*, however, also stands out as a manifest fiction—as a book produced at the "cost" of the author's culture and destined to become, in turn, a producer of that culture. Cervantes's stance of dissociation from his collection of maxims—which he edits anonymously in order to expose—is made explicit at the end of this key chapter, when he recites to the company the one maxim [*sólo uno*] that he claims to know by heart [*de memoria*]: "Do not desire, and you shall be the richest man in the world."[52] This abrupt call for renunciation is pointedly ironic in its context—a clutch of aphorisms telling people what they should desire—and radically calls into question that context. Desire, this closing maxim suggests, need not be organized through an Aristotelian logic of binary oppositions, which habitually divides the masculine from its feminine opposite of privation. Although indirectly conveyed, the pilgrim-editor's patent disaffection for the structures of desire inscribed in his solicited miscellany could not be clearer. Once again in Cervantes the aim is antiliterary. Only here he must commission the text he would subvert. It will be a species of canonized literature, one that the Renaissance invested with power and honorific status: the encoding of their collective wisdom as universal truths of human experience. It would seem that Cervantes is saying, along with George Eliot, that "the mysterious complexity of our life is not to be embraced by maxims." But even closer to our modern sensibility, he is showing readers the subtle mechanisms of gender hierarchization which, as both editor of the *Flor* and author of the *Persiles*, he will repudiate. This pivotal opening chapter of the closing book of the *Persiles* plays out Nancy K. Miller's insight that "the maxims that pass for the truth of human experience, and the encoding of that experience in literature, are organizations, when they are not fantasies, of the dominant culture."[53] By inviting his own characters to encode their gender-marked experience within a chapter of his work, Cervantes creates a paradigmatic text of cultural "fantasies" whose logic of polar oppositions the *Persiles* was written to expose and disrupt. A logic of male violence and female complicity will always break down, as it did on the Barbaric Isle, when it confronts an

170 DIANA DE ARMAS WILSON

androgynous exchange. Both the text and the context of the *Flor* recreate for us the glaring reliance of scapegoat mechanisms upon a logic of polar oppositions. The "fiction" of the *Flor* is that it is a fictional version of these binary habits of thought.

As a work that has until recently remained stubbornly outside of the traditional European literary canon, the *Persiles* demands and is beginning to receive an altered mode of reading.[54] Cervantes's experimental last romance seems to have surmised its future misreadings by exposing its own story-telling hero to the continual carpings of the males in his audience, who regard great portions of his narrative as "not very relevant" [*no muy a propósito* (217)]. Both Periandro's lengthy discourse and the *Persiles* that encloses it beg for noncanonical readings: both are working "in the in-between" in order to mute differences and mediate polarities. Cervantes's androgynous heroes begin their multiple labors by confronting a barbaric all-male culture whose economy, based on exchange of such fungible goods as gold and women, answers that culture's very real fears of sterility. The protagonists then journey across a work that structurally resembles the "unique compound" of the relationship they are questing. Such a text may be read as lamentably split or, taking our cue from its hero, as a place where all oppositions can fit. Organized around the metaphors of splitting, wandering, and reunion, the narrative repeatedly invokes the "two-in(to)-one" as a force, in Periandro's words, "to break the inconvenience of . . . division" (414). This figuration of the Androgyne in the *Persiles*, as I have noted, advertises its filiation to Leone Ebreo's unorthodox challenge to Renaissance notions of male primacy.[55] But Cervantes's Androgyne not only undoes that most ancient of hierarchized oppositions, male/female, but also works overtime to undo every other "split" in its text: Greek romance/medieval pilgrimage narrative; first half/second half; main plot/inset stories; North/South; civilization/barbary; Catholic/Protestant; Madonna/whore; and on and on, transforming the one into the other "and into the in-between." In his first romance, Cervantes began to conceive of the possibility of a narrative designed by "weaving one fabric out of contraries" (*Galatea,* 2.102). As the androgynous completion of this unfinished business, Cervantes's last romance—again like its excentric hero—is a literary universe "where all things fit and nothing is out of place" (227).

NOTES

1. All references to *Los trabajos de Persiles y Sigismunda* cite the edition of Juan Bautista Avalle-Arce (Madrid: Clásicos Castalia, 1969) parenthetically by

page number. Cervantes's prepublication announcements were made, respectively, in *Viaje del Parnaso* (1614), and in the dedications to *Ocho comedias y ocho entremeses* (1615) and to *Don Quixote*, Part 2 (1615). Because of the many editions in use, I have chosen to refer to passages from the *Quixote* by part and chapter number, preceded by the initials *DQ*. All translations of Spanish texts are my own, and all emphasis in quoted passages has been added. For a brief discussion of eighteenth- and nineteenth-century scholars who regarded the *Persiles* favorably, see Rudolph Schevill, "Studies in Cervantes: I. 'Persiles y Sigismunda': Introduction," *Modern Philology* 4 (1906–7), 1–24. In the main, however, Continental criticism has responded to the work with a long silencing tradition. As late as the 1930s, José Bergamín tried to challenge the mystique of a canon that could so serenely ignore its creator's own judgments: "Cervantes, who knew himself very well, and also his qualities as a writer, believed, unfalteringly, that the *Persiles* was his *obra maestra*. *Perhaps the time will come when criticism recognizes it as such*" (*Laberinto de la novela y monstruo de la novelería*). That criticism has finally begun to recognize the *Persiles* as at least worthy of sustained scholarly attention is due to the efforts of such established critics as Rafael Osuna, whose prescriptive essay laments its "forgetting" ("El olvido del 'Persiles' " in *Boletín de la Real Academia Española* 48 [1968]); Avalle-Arce, whose Spanish edition of the *Persiles* has superseded all others (though whose "Introduction," in line with the canonized critical approach, speaks of Cervantes's "hypervalorization" of the work [27]); Tilbert Diego Stegmann, whose German monograph includes a massive bibliography (*Cervantes' Musterroman "Persiles"*: *Epentheorie und Romanpraxis um 1600* [Hamburg: Hartmut Ludke Verlag, 1971]); Alban K. Forcione, whose two studies serve as a quarry for much contemporary work on the *Persiles* (*Cervantes, Aristotle, and the 'Persiles'* [Princeton: Princeton University Press, 1970], and *Cervantes' Christian Romance: A Study of Persiles and Sigismunda* [Princeton: Princeton University Press, 1972]); and Ruth El Saffar, who reads the *Persiles* as "the culmination of a life-time of writing" (*Beyond Fiction: The Recovery of the Feminine in the Works of Cervantes* [Berkeley and Los Angeles; University of California Press, 1983]).

2. In a survey of "the erotic casuistics of the pastoral," Renato Poggioli stresses its "unwillingness to accept fully the realities of the sexual condition of man." The pastoral admits into its "masculine dream world" no copulation, conception, babies, infants, or children: "adolescence and early adulthood are the only important pastoral ages" (*The Oaten Flute: Essays on Pastoral Poetry and the Pastoral Ideal* [Cambridge: Harvard University Press, 1975], 42–63). I discuss Cervantes's perversion of pastoral in my essay entitled "Uncanonical Nativities," in *Masterpieces of World Literature: Cervantes*, Robert Lecker, gen. ed. (Boston: G. K. Hall, 1986).

3. "I offer you the *Labors of Persiles*," Cervantes's official prepublication advertisement declared in 1613, "a book which dares to compete with Heliodorus, if for all its daring it doesn't emerge with hands on its head"

("Prólogo al lector," *Novelas ejemplares,* in *Obras completas,* ed. A. Valbuena Prat, 10th ed. (Madrid: Aguilar, 1956), 770. In his avowed competition with the Greek romancer Heliodorus, lavishly praised by the humanists for his classically correct *dispositio,* Cervantes *did* produce a monster—at least in Jane Gallop's sense of "a being whose boundaries are unclear." The failure of taxonomies to embrace his "monster" bears further scrutiny. Gallop reminds us that feminism is "the defense and validation of such monsters" ("The Monster in the Mirror: The Feminist Critic's Psychoanalysis," English Institute, Harvard University, Sept. 4, 1983). The reference to Shakespeare, in full, reads: "Thou met'st with things dying, I with things new-born" (*Winter's Tale,* 3.3.113–14).

4. "VOCES daba el bárbaro" begins the text, with the direct object "voices" wrenched into primacy through Latin word order. It is instructive to examine the ritual sacrifices of Cervantes's barbarians in the light of Walter Ong's "Latin Language Study as a Renaissance Puberty Rite," in *Rhetoric, Romance, and Technology* (Ithaca: Cornell University Press, 1971), 113–41.

5. "The Laugh of the Medusa," in *New French Feminisms: An Anthology,* ed. Elaine Marks and Isabelle de Courtivron (Amherst: University of Massachusetts Press, 1980), 253–54. On the social marginality of Cervantes, see Américo Castro, *Cervantes y los casticismos españoles* (Madrid: Alfaguera, 1966). Carlos P. Otero has more recently located Cervantes, among others, within a minoritarian counterculture of sixteenth-century Spanish intelligentsia ("Introducción a Chomsky," prologue to his translation of Chomsky's *Aspectos de la teoría de la sintaxis* [Madrid: Aguilar, 1970], xxv–xxviii).

6. Critics who acknowledge Eros as a governing force in the *Persiles* do so tentatively or grudgingly. Mack Singleton, for example, attacking the text for its grave neglect of "existential" issues, laments that the "only" psychological problems it examines are "erotic" —thereby positing Eros as the antithesis of existence ("The *Persiles* Mystery," in *Cervantes Across the Centuries,* ed. Angel Flores and M. J. Benardete [New York: Dryden, 1947], 230). More recently, Cesáreo Bandera (who regards the *Persiles* as deservedly "short-lived") finds it "significant" that Cervantes would have adopted a Greek romance as his working model: "one of those stories of 'erotic sufferings,' *erotika pathemata,*" characteristic of the Alexandrine society (which Nietzsche considered as the antithesis of the epic) and much closer in spirit to the pastoral novel than to the *Iliad* or the *Odyssey* ("An Open Letter to Ruth El Saffar," *Cervantes* 1 [1981], 105; and "Deseo y creación literaria en el *Quijote,*" *MLN* 95 [1980], n. 282).

7. In Book 3, the prophet Soldino, who claims to have served under Carlos V, foresees certain feats at Lepanto by Don Juan of Austria, as well as the death of Don Sebastian of Portugal in Alcazarquivir—events that occurred in 1572 and 1578, respectively, thereby dating the pilgrimage as earlier than 1572. Since the Spaniard Antonio also fought under Carlos V in Germany (ca. 1547), and the Irishman Mauricio claims to have seen the

king after his abdication, all signs point to a fictive time during Cervantes's adolescence.

8. Forcione's thorough analysis of the structure of the *Persiles* in relation to the Aristotelian criteria of unity concludes that most of the interpolated tales, in their length and independence, "divert the reader's attention from the development of the main plot, destroying the effect of suspense which Heliodorus' *Aethiopica* had achieved and which all contemporary theorists set as the goal of dispositional techniques" (*Christian Romance*, 108; see, for the analysis, 13–63).

9. In a passage that sheds light on Cervantes's Barbaric Isle, Dorothy Dinnerstein observes that it is the uncertainty of the paternal relation that drives men to engage in "various initiation rites through which they symbolically and passionately affirm that it is they who have themselves created human beings, as compared with the mere flesh spawned by woman" (*The Mermaid and the Minotaur: Sexual Arrangements and the Human Malaise* [New York: Harper & Row, 1976], 80). The same uncertainty, if not invisibility, of the paternal relation earlier led Freud into promoting paternity under the banner of a general "advance in civilization, since maternity is proved by the evidence of the senses while paternity is a hypothesis, based on an inference and a premise" and, because of its intellectuality, "more important than maternity." For this reason, Freud concludes, "the child should bear his father's name and be his heir" (*Moses and Monotheism: Three Essays*, in *Standard Edition of the Complete Psychological Works*, vol. 23 [London: Hogarth Press, 1964], 114, 118).

10. Death for amorous presumption by an arrow through the tongue will recur later in the *Persiles* with Clodio's killing, judged by the discursive narrator as "a punishment deserved for his many crimes" (203). In an intricate reading of Cervantes's "Barbaric Law," indebted to Gilles Deleuze's *Logique de sens*, Eduardo González provides further insight into Cervantes's metaphors of penetration: the ingestion of the pulverized hearts, for instance, he reads as metaphorizing "the aboriginal sodomite agitation of the Group" ("Del *Persiles* y la Isla Bárbara: Fábulas y reconocimientos," *MLN* 94 [1979], 233), a notion given authority by Forcione, who writes of Bradamiro's "sodomitic passion" (*Christian Romance*, 40), and by Joaquín Casalduero, who gets "an impression of sodomy" from his reading of this episode (*Sentido y forma de "Los trabajos de Persiles y Sigismunda"* [Madrid: Gredos, 1975], 28).

11. I allude here to the circulation of women at the center of the social contract as described by Lévi-Strauss. The anonymous editor of the Espasa-Calpe edition of the *Persiles* (Buenos Aires, 1952) feels a need to apologize for its "largo comienzo repelente."

12. González nudges the problem tangentially, either within footnotes or parentheses. He recalls in order to eliminate, for instance, "the possibility of a perpetual life of isolated males" in the style of Pliny's *Natural History*, a text that describes an all-male community living alone, "sine ulla femina" ("Fábulas," 253n.). Actually, this is a promising conjecture in that Cer-

vantes certainly knew his Pliny: Book 8 of the *Natural History* is cited within the *Persiles* itself (134). The *parodic* possibilities of such an isolated all-male community may very well have inspired the opening chapters of the *Persiles*. In another footnote González briefly wonders about the women who are imported into Cervantes's fictional isle and there "barbarized" (255 n.). And in a summary of his argument about the "bastardized, post-tragic" generic status of the *Persiles*, he parenthetically notes the paradigm supporting the barbaric "Institution": "(man was here before woman . . .)" [*"hubo hombre antes que mujer"*] (233). The implications of these fragmentary insights are never taken up in González's essay. My own reading of the *Persiles* shows how Cervantes's text goes on, after destroying the Barbaric Isle, to reorganize its latent design of male priority.

13. If anything, the concept of civilization in the *Persiles* comes closer to Leslie Fiedler's vision of it, within the American novel, as "the confrontation of a man and a woman which leads to the fall, to sex, marriage, and responsibility." For Fiedler's notion of an unfortunate "fall," however, we must substitute Cervantes's conception of a joint pilgrimage into sexuality and its responsible consequences. Fiedler's description of "the typical male protagonist" of American fiction, however, may be fruitfully applied to *Persiles'* predecessor, Don Quixote: "a man on the run, harried into the forest and out to sea, down the river and into combat—anywhere to avoid 'civilization,' which is to say, the confrontation of a man and a woman" (*Love and Death in the American Novel* [New York: Stein & Day, 1975], 26). The psychology of Don Quixote's midlife sally as an avoidance technique has been compellingly argued by Carroll B. Johnson in *Madness and Lust: A Psychoanalytical Approach to Don Quixote* (Berkeley and Los Angeles: University of California Press, 1983).

14. For the Iphigenia plot as disseminated by El Pinciano in his *Philosophía antigua poética* (1596), see Avalle-Arce's "Introducción," 51 n. Forcione sees Cervantes's cannibalizing barbarians as imaginatively linked "not only with the American Indians but also with the powers of hell," a connection further glossed by his view of the "barbarians' grotesque marriage . . . and its prophetic offspring" as "demonic counterweights of the various Christian marriages which the work celebrates and of the true Messiah" (*Christian Romance*, 38, 38 n.). In Heliodorus's romance, the gymnosophist community decides to give up human sacrifice "once and for all" (*Historia etiópica de los amores de Teágenes y Cariclea*, trans. F. de Mena, ed. F. López Estrada [Madrid: Aldus, 1954], 424).

15. René Girard's noted structures of triangular desire take their point of departure from *Don Quixote*, a work he sees as seminal to "all the ideas of the Western novel" (*Deceit, Desire, and the Novel: Self and Other in Literary Structure*, trans. Yvonne Freccero [Baltimore: Johns Hopkins University Press, 1965], 1–52). Eve K. Sedgwick has examined the effects of triangular desire on women in the recently published *Between Men: English Literature and Male Homosocial Desire* (New York: Columbia University

Press, 1985). On Cervantes's Barbaric Isle, the "detour through the female" is very precisely restricted to her womb, which, as Luce Irigaray notes in her commentary on patriarchal law, remains simply a passive receptacle with no claims on the "product" of sexual union—the womb "itself possessed as a means of (re)production" (*Speculum de l'autre femme* [Paris: Editions de Minuit, 1974], 16).

16. See Irigaray's observations on an economy of bodily fluids in "La 'Mechanique' des fluides," *L'Arc* 58 (1974).

17. Plutarch recounts in various texts that "initiatory androgyny," as suggested by exchanges of clothing, was frequently practiced in ancient Greece as a wedding custom (Mircea Eliade, *The Two in the One*, trans. from *Mephistopheles et l'Androgyne* by J. M. Cohen [Chicago: University of Chicago Press, 1962], 112–13).

18. This pirate-woman has her predecessors in *Don Quixote*, Part 2. About fictional body changes in that text, see Arthur Efron's "Bearded Waiting Women, Lovely Lethal Female Piratemen: Sexual Boundary Shifts in *Don Quixote*, Part 2," *Cervantes* 2 (1983), 155–64. I thoroughly endorse Efron's contention that "any responsive reader of Cervantes will eventually have to learn something about this area [body-text relationship] of theory" (162).

19. Carolyn G. Heilbrun, *Toward a Recognition of Androgyny* (1964; rpt. New York: Norton, 1982), x.

20. See Elémire Zolla for a discussion of "Carnival, when men get pregnant," in *The Androgyne: Reconciliation of Male and Female* (New York: Crossroad, 1981), 90–91.

21. In a discussion of male-into-female gender disguise, Sandra M. Gilbert argues that "to become a female" is "to be 'de-graded' [in the sense of *demoted*], to lose one's place in the preordained hierarchy that the patriarchal culture associates with gender" ("Costumes of the Mind," in *Writing and Sexual Difference*, ed. Elizabeth Abel [Chicago: University of Chicago Press], 198).

22. Avalle-Arce views the *Persiles* as having been conceived by a mind "magnetized" by hierarchy ("Introducción," 20–21). Forcione finds this "chain of being" metaphor spatial and wanting; he prefers a musical (fugue) analogy for his own reading (see *Christian Romance*, 142–48).

23. I focus upon Isabela Castrucha's feigned madness in an essay entitled "Cervantes' Last Romance: Deflating the Myth of Female Sacrifice," *Cervantes* 3 (1983), 103–20.

24. In keeping with Juan de la Cuesta's original printing (Madrid, 1617), the full title of Cervantes's romance is *Los trabajos de Persiles, y Sigismunda, Historia Setentrional*.

25. Of the many romances, chivalric and pastoral, scrutinized in Don Quixote's library, only *The Nymphs of Henares*—whose full Spanish title was *Nimphas y pastores de Henares* [*Nymphs and Shepherds of Henares*], by Bernardo Gonzáles de Bovadilla (1587)—moves toward androgyny (*DQ*, 1.6).

On the titles of the Greek romances, see Moses Hadas, *A History of Greek Literature* (New York: Columbia University Press, 1950), 291–98.

26. Northrop Frye speaks of the anagogic perspective as "a perspective of reality like that of an angel, containing all time and space"; and of the "independence" of that perspective as illustrated by "the poet's attempt to speak from the circumference instead of from the center of reality" (*Anatomy of Criticism* [1957; rpt. New York: Atheneum, 1966], 122). Cervantes's Periandro frequently speaks from a similarly ex-centric reality.

27. On the increasing presence of the figure of the mother across the Cervantes opus, see Ruth El Saffar's recently published *Beyond Fiction*. Elsewhere El Saffar has noted that the journey in the *Persiles* is "conceived of and inspired, for once, by the feminine," a force she traces across the Cervantine canon, from the *Galatea* on, in its association with water, caves, night, the moon, mirrors, and animals ("Fiction and the Androgyne in Cervantes," *Cervantes* 3 [1983], 35–49).

28. The rhetoric behind this mystical mathematics of two-in-one, transcending all syntax and logic, is explored by Patricia Parker in a discussion of the "twain-made-one" as anagogic or copular metaphor at work in four English texts ("Anagogic Metaphor: Breaking Down the Wall of Partition," in *Centre and Labyrinth: Essays in Honour of Northrop Frye*, ed. Eleanor Cook et al. [Toronto: University of Toronto Press, 1983], 38–58).

29. To cite a few other instances of the formula: "Auristela, *mitad de su alma sin la cual no puede vivir*" (57); "*donde iba la mitad de su alma, o la mejor parte della*" (251); "*no la mitad, sino toda su alma* que se le ausentaba" (252); "*¿Qué mudanza es ésta, mitad de mi alma?*" (364); and in what might be a pun on *enterrarse/enterarse* [bury herself/understand herself], "que no hay mujer que no desee enterarse [sic] con *la mitad que le falta*, que es la del marido". (399).

30. *La Galatea*, ed. Juan Bautista Avalle-Arce, vol. I (Madrid: Espasa-Calpe, 1968), 158 (hereafter cited parenthetically). Timbrio, whose best friend has become his rival in a love triangle, anticipates the "curious impertinent" Anselmo (*DQ*, 1.33–36) and, moved into fraternal status, the "detestable" Magsimino (467). Avalle-Arce traces the Horatian origins of *pars animae meae* back to *Ode* 3.8. However, see also Ovid's *Metamorphosis*, 8.406; St. Augustine's *Confessions*, 4.6; and Petrarch's *Epistola Metrica*, 1.1.

31. Forcione observes that "the view of the *Persiles* as a 'split' work survives in its most recent commentators, even in the one study [Casalduero's] which argues for its thematic unity" (*Christian Romance*, 11). Osuna's comments are from his essay "El olvido del *Persiles*," 55–75. William Atkinson's remarks are in *Bulletin of Spanish Studies*, Liverpool, 24 (1947), 248. Menéndez y Pelayo's statement may be found in *Cultura literaria de Miguel de Cervantes y elaboración del "Quijote"* (1905), cited by Emilio Carilla in the introduction to his edition of the *Persiles* (Madrid: Biblioteca Anaya, 1971).

32. I use *mundus significans* here in Thomas Greene's specialized sense of "a unique semiotic matrix," i.e., "a rhetorical and symbolic vocabulary, a storehouse of signifying capacities potentially available to each member

of a given culture" (*The Light in Troy* [New Haven: Yale University Press, 1982], 20).

33. One manuscript illustration of alchemical androgynization, for instance, depicts a dead king and queen who share one crown, one body, and one soul—this last seen flying from them heavenwards (see Arnold of Villanova's *Rosarium philosophorum*, MS 394a, 16th C., Stadbibliothek Vadiana, St. Gallen).

34. Considering Renaissance Latin teaching, as Walter J. Ong does, within the psychological framework of violent puberty rites—involving forcible removal from the maternal world of the vernacular, segregation within a closed male environment, and corporal punishment in order to instill "corage" (courage, heart-iness, strength of heart)—provides a most suggestive pedagogical frame for Cervantes's Barbaric Isle narrative ("Latin Language Study"). Father Ong's argument also sheds a glaring light on the ascetic strain found in certain neoplatonic thinkers, e.g., in Mario Equicola's aversion to "the filth of coitus" (John Charles Nelson, *Renaissance Theory of Love: The Context of Giordano Bruno's "Eroici furori"* [New York: Columbia University Press, 1958], 70); in Baldesar Castiglione's assertion that sensual lovers feel only those pleasures "which unreasoning animals feel" (*The Book of the Courtier*, trans. Charles S. Singleton [Garden City, NY: Anchor Books, 1959], 339); and in Marsilio Ficino's seminal invocation of the Androgyne in his Latin Commentary of the *Symposium* (1469). In this last work, essentially a Christian celebration of chaste male bonding, the Androgyne appears as an anemic personification of *Iustitia* (ed. Sears Reynolds Jayne, vol. 19, University of Missouri Studies 1 (Columbia: University of Missouri Press, 1944), 58 ["aliae secundum *iustitiam, quae promiscua. . . ."*].

35. On the circumstances of Ficino's coinage of "Platonic Love," see Nelson, *Renaissance Theory of Love*, 69 n.

36. The *Galatea* was, in fact, "proposing" sexual equality—one of the staples of Spanish pastoral, as Elías L. Rivers has noted. But bound within that same pastoral's "fictional world of historical contradictions," it could, of course, "conclude" nothing ("Review" of Claudio Guillén's *Literature as System: Essays Toward the Theory of Literary History*, MLN 88 [1973]: 427).

37. Leon the Hebrew (Leone Ebreo) was born Judah Abrabanel, ca. 1460, into an old and illustrious family of Spanish Jewry. He was personal physician to Ferdinand and Isabella of Castille until 1492, when the Abrabanel family marched at the head of the exiles during the expulsion of the Jews from Spain. Leone settled down in Naples where he left the memory of "excellent philosopher and physician." Though legend long had it that he converted to Christianity before his death, he most probably never apostasized and is extravagantly praised in the Hebrew literature of the period. In 1501–2 Leone wrote one of the most famous and popular works of the Italian Renaissance, the *Dialoghi d'amore*, published in 1535 in Rome. (See *The Philosophy of Love*, trans. F. Friedeberg-Seeley and Jean H. Barnes [London: Soncino Press, 1937], the English version I have con-

sulted in addition to my working edition, the 1590 Spanish translation that Cervantes is certain to have read: *Diálogos de amor*, trans. Garcilaso Inca de la Vega, ed. Eduardo Julia Martínez [Madrid: Ediciones Villaiz, 1949]).

38. Plato, *Symposium*, trans. Benjamin Jowett (New York: Bobbs-Merrill, 1956), 30–32.

39. *Aspects of Love in Western Society*, trans. Jonathan Griffin (New York: McGraw-Hill, 1965), 68.

40. In my view, the neoplatonism of the *Persiles* belongs entirely within Leone's tradition of integrative eroticism, a tradition of nonascetic conjugal relations that entirely by-passes the masters of Italian neoplatonism, and that obsessively uses the heterosexual two-in-one metaphor. Perry would include within this tradition: the French platonists Maurice Scève, Pernette du Guillet, and Antoine Héroët, who used Leone's *Philosophy* as their "breviary"; Jorge de Montemayor, the father of Spanish pastoral and noted apologist of marriage; and John Donne, whom Perry regards as an "apostle of mutual love and sane sexual relations." Perry's study, which he claims is "the first to examine in an extensive way the implications of Leone Ebreo's erotic philosophy for literature," has, I believe, a missing chapter: Cervantes's *Persiles* not only belongs squarely in this neglected tradition, but might also serve as its most powerful narrative prose statement (*Erotic Spirituality: The Integrative Tradition from Leone Ebreo to John Donne* [University, Ala.: University of Alabama Press, 1980], 1–2, 37).

41. Leone's Androgyne commentary may be found in the third of his dialogues in the Martínez edition of the *Diálogos* cited above, 211–43.

42. The theory of an androgynous Adam is explicitly refuted by Augustine (*De Genesi ad litteram*, 3.22, PL, 34.294) and by Aquinas (*Summa*, 1a93.4). Such an idea would necessarily imply that God, in whose image Adam was created, was also androgynous. This gnostic idea of an androgynized God may be found in Paracelsus and in marginalized theology. See also the Hermetic treatise *Asclepius*, which argues for a God containing both sexes (*Corpus Hermeticum*, ed. A. D. Nock, trans. A.-J. Festugiere [Paris: 1945], vol. 2, 321 f.).

43. Leone's biblical derivation of the platonic myth had its predecessors in Philo Judaeus and Numenius, who also held that Plato knew Mosaic theology (Nelson, *Renaissance Theory of Love*, 97 n.). A curious reversal of influence may be found in *Genesis Rabba* 1.1, a gnostic gospel whose creation account appears to be an imitation of Plato's myth of the Androgyne (Elaine H. Pagels, "The Gnostic Vision," *Parabola* 3 [1978]: 7). My citations from Leone have all been taken from the *Dialoghi*, 214–20. I have used the term "deconstructive reading" in Barbara Johnson's sense as "the careful teasing out of warring forces of signification within the text itself," which would fit Leone's turn-of-the-sixteenth-century analysis of the Genesis text's "critical difference from itself" (see *The Critical Dif-*

ference: Essays in the Contemporary Rhetoric of Reading [Baltimore: Johns Hopkins University Press, 1980], 5).

44. Greene, *Light in Troy,* 6.

45. Irigaray's reading of Freud's 1933 "Femininity" lecture is called "The Blind Spot of an Old Dream of Symmetry" (*Speculum*), a symmetry (from the Greek *summetros,* "of like measure") in which the two sexes are measured by the same measure, a masculine one, and the woman is found not different but wanting. Shoshana Felman describes the woman within the polarity masculine/feminine (andro/gyne) as "theoretically subordinated to the concept of masculinity," i.e., "viewed by the man as *his* opposite . . . *his* other, the negative of the positive, and not, in her own right, different, other, Otherness itself" ("Woman and Madness: The Critical Phallacy," *Diacritics* 5 [1975], 3). Adrienne Rich includes "androgyny" among words she "cannot choose again" ("Natural Resources," *The Dream of a Common Language: Poems, 1974–77* [New York: Norton, 1978]). And Mary Daly rejects the term as a "semantic abomination," a "misbegotten" word that conveys to her (who once promoted it) "something like 'John Travolta and Farrah Fawcett-Majors scotch-taped together' " (*Gyn/Ecology: The Metaethics of Radical Feminism* [Boston: Beacon Press, 1978], xi).

46. The terms "androgynous" and "hermaphroditic" are often used interchangeably, despite periodic reminders by scholars that the latter is, as Heilbrun reminds us, "an anomalous physical condition" (xii). Eliade, too, has tried to distinguish the idea of the hermaphrodite—an anatomical aberration implying an augmentation of organs—from the ritual androgyne, which he claims only "decadent writers" understand as a hermaphrodite (*Two and the One,* 100). Leone Ebreo is also careful to distinguish the androgyne from the hermaphrodite, whom he defines in his second dialogue as a man who, because of a Mercury/Venus conjunction at his nativity, will be given to "foul and unnatural lust" and will "love men and have no shame to be both active and passive" (*Philosophy,* 159). Spenser, however, refers to the reunited Scudamour and Amoret, embracing, as "that faire Hermaphrodite" (*Faerie Queene,* 3.12.46, 1590 ed.).

47. *Tropics of Discourse: Essays in Cultural Criticism* (Baltimore: Johns Hopkins University Press, 1978), 2.

48. It is curious that Edward C. Riley would see the pilgrim-editor as one of the "few curious and pathetic figures" in the Cervantine canon. Instead of an authorial self-portrait, Riley reads the aphorism-gatherer as proof that Cervantes was "alive to . . . the excesses and abuses of plagiarism" (*Cervantes's Theory of the Novel* [Oxford: Oxford University Press, 1962], 63). But why would a character "plagiarize" a book of collective wisdom? It seems more plausible to regard him as yet another of Cervantes's Trickster figures (see, in this line, Ruth El Saffar's "Tracking the Trickster in the Works of Cervantes," *Symposium* [Fall 1983], 106–24).

49. Even the heroine's entry—"The best dowry an illustrious woman can

bring is her chastity" (417)—which may appear to tally with her obsessive purity, has already been cited by a tavern wench in an earlier episode, who recalls as *her* source of the maxim "the mother who bore me" (332). The ermine maxim is also invoked, in a fit of hysterical moralizing, by Lotario, the sullier-to-be of his best friend's wife in *The Curious Impertinent* (*DQ*, 1.33).

50. Cf. Barbara Johnson, "Teaching Ignorance: *L'Ecole des Femmes*," *Yale French Studies* 63 (1982), 179.

51. "The Relation of the Poet to Daydreaming," in *On Creativity and the Unconscious*, trans. I. F. Grant Duff (New York: Harper, 1958), 47–48. Freud's repressive model for women maintains that their unsatisfied dreams and desires are mostly erotic, whereas those of men are ambitious *as well as* erotic. I owe a debt of gratitude to Peter L. Rudnytsky for reading earlier versions of this essay, and for expert counsel on various Renaissance and Freudian problems.

52. Although editorial tradition considers this maxim as an allusion to the false author of the second part of the *Quixote* (Alonso Fernández de Avellaneda) because his spurious novel appeared in Tordesillas, the shoemaker's hometown (418 n.), this geographical coincidence scarcely sheds light on the maxim itself, or on its privileged status as the most memorable, as well as the most subversive, of all the maxims to which it provides closure. An obvious reference to Plato's *Symposium*, the shoemaker's maxim communicates its derivation from Leone Ebreo's *Dialoghi*, whose opening argument also addresses the platonic theme of desire as lack and even includes its own analogous maxim: "he is truly rich who is content with what he has" (*Philosophy*, 13).

53. "Emphasis Added: Plots and Plausibilities in Women's Fiction," *PMLA* 96 (1981): 46. Miller cites Eliot's dictum from *The Mill on the Floss* (New York: N.A.L., 1965), 348–49.

54. See, for example, González, "Del *Persiles* y la Isla Bárbara"; also the chapter on the *Persiles* in El Saffar's *Beyond Fiction*, a study that traces the increasingly feminine trajectory of Cervantes's prose writings. My argument on the concept of androgyny in the *Persiles* has been greatly enriched by El Saffar's reading of the Cervantine unconscious. My discussion of Cervantes's reading of Leone reading Plato reading Moses is deeply indebted to the strategies of Rachel Jacoff's forthcoming "Models of Literary Influence in the *Commedia*," an essay that addresses not only the issue of gender reversal in remote texts but also its implications in our own contemporary "labors."

55. For the scholastic infrastructures of these notions, see Ian Maclean's *The Renaissance Notion of Woman: A Study in the Fortunes of Scholasticism and Medical Science in European Intellectual Life* (Cambridge: Cambridge University Press, 1980). In a section focusing on Renaissance reactions to Aquinas's systematized account of the creation of woman as "something defective and *manqué*," Maclean concludes that there was "no serious challenge" to this account in the Renaissance: "at best, it might be said that the

issue was of no great interest to the majority of Renaissance theologians" (8–10). Although the issue *was* of great interest to Leone and Cervantes, it is clear that their positive statements against these orthodox and schematic accounts of women's inferiority were destined to be filtered for centuries through a Continental criticism that foreclosed, one way or another, on any reassessment of sexual roles.

9. DEFERRAL, DILATION, DIFFÉRANCE: SHAKESPEARE, CERVANTES, JONSON

■

PATRICIA PARKER

Rather than abandon it, we ought perhaps then rethink the concept of *différer*. This is what we should like to do, and this is possible only if *différance* is determined outside any teleological or eschatological horizon. Which is not easy. . . .

—DERRIDA, *Writing and Difference*

AT THE BEGINNING of "La Différance," Derrida calls attention to the doubled meanings within the French verb "différer," which like its Latin root (*differre*) "seems to differ from itself," indicating on the one hand difference as "distinction" and on the other "the interposition of delay," deferring or putting off, a combination that, when amplified, begets the rest of this much-extended essay and much else in Derrida besides. At the beginning of Shakespeare's *Comedy of Errors*, the father Egeon is commanded to "dilate at full" (1.1.122) the narrative of his life, and when he does so—in a scene that calls attention both to the amplification of his discourse and to the delaying of his death—is granted a deferral of the promised execution or "doom" (1.1.2), an extension of discourse which is also an extension on life.[1]

Derrida's punning "différance" is silent on this third term from that single Latin root, that of *dilatio* or dilation, which in Renaissance usage in its verbal form meant not only to expand, disperse, or spread abroad but also to put off, postpone, prolong, or protract—meanings that still linger in the modern English "dilatory." But it is, as we shall see, this particular term for the combination of temporal deferral and spatial extension which crucially defines the self-reflexive strategies of a wide range of Renaissance texts, in which "dilation" as delay functions as a kind of semantic crossroads, a complex in which constructs rhetorical and narrative, philosophical and theological, judicial and erotic overlap as figures for the space and time of the text itself.

In our own context, it is remarkable how much of contemporary critical and literary theory has focused on the phenomenon of delay, even apart from Derridean "différance"—from Šklovskij's emphasis on the role of "retardation," to Bakhtin's description of the "chronotope" of delay in Greek romance, to Barthes's characterization of the "espace dilatoire" (both dilated and dilatory space) between riddle and answer, beginning and ending.[2] Such similarities between the recurrent figures of contemporary critical discourse and the characteristic terms of particular Renaissance texts have informed much of recent speculation on the potential application of this theory to a rereading of the Renaissance, not the least of which has been the questioning of whether an ultimately Derridean reading of deferral in these texts is finally historically justified.[3] This essay proposes to suspend that larger question for a moment and to look instead at the remarkable reasonance of this complex of deferral, dilation, and "distinction," or difference, within a wide range of Renaissance texts and contexts, before returning to the question of delay in contemporary theory.

I

Let us begin with the easily conflated associations of "dilation" in the Renaissance, as both spatial extension and temporal delay. The request in The Comedy of Errors that Egeon "dilate at full" the story of his life draws on the rhetorical technique of dilatio or amplificatio which Shakespeare and other Renaissance schoolboys would have had drummed into them from the various rhetorical handbooks of the day. Erasmus begins Book 2 of the influential De Copia ("Abundance of Subject-Matter") by describing how to dilate a short sentence or text—how, in other words, to make much out of little—by "partition," or the creation of rhetorical dividing walls, a tradition that Shakespeare reveals he knows only too well when, in the Pyramus and Thisbe play of A Midsummer Night's Dream, he has Demetrius punningly call the character of Wall the "wittiest partition that ever I heard discourse" (5.1.165). Because discourse, like a body, was thus thought to be divided into its parts or members, one form of this dilation by partition was the rhetorical striptease, inventory, or dismemberment known as the blason, as Demetrius's own detailing of a woman's body reminds us somewhat earlier in

this same play (3.2.137–53). So commonplace, indeed, was this rhetorical and narrative context for "dilation" through the detailing of
component "distinctions" (*distinctiones*) that "to dilate" in Renaissance usage became virtually synonymous with "to narrate or tell,"
as in, for example, Spenser's *Faerie Queene* ("Of diverse things discourses to dilate" [3.3.62.4]; "With that he gan at large to her dilate"
[5.6.17.1]; or "Tho gan that shepheard thus for to dilate" [6.10.21.1])
and other Renaissance texts far too numerous to name.[4]

   In the related art of preaching, the principal method of proceeding
was to make a specific short text respond to the rhetorical counterpart of the command to "increase and multiply." In the words of
Donne, whose sermons sum up the entire tradition of the *ars praedicandi*: "Through partition or division, the Word of God is made a
Sermon, that is a text is dilated, diffused into a Sermon," a description that Englishes such Latin descriptions of the dilation of sermon
discourse as Simon Alcok's *De modo dividendi thema, pro materia ser-
monis dilatanda*.[5] And this rhetorical dilation by partition was to be
used by preachers of the Word in precisely that period of the "dilation" of the Church before the Last Judgment, that is, before the
final apocalyptic end both to the dividing "wall of partition" spoken
of in Ephesians (2:14–15) and to the "partitions" of discourse itself.

   This brings us to our second sense and context, one intimately
related to the dilation of the Word. Patristic writers speak of the
period before Apocalypse as the *dilatio patriae*, as a space of deferral
which leaves time for repentance before that Last Judgment or final
"doom." One of the most powerful subtexts for delay in the Renaissance, apart from the *Odyssey* whose narrative dilatoriness made it
the classical prototype of romance, was the Bible, which is filled
with figures for the space and time of this deferred judgment and
ending (the forty-day space between the promise of "doom" and its
execution in the story of Noah's flood; the staying or suspending of
the sun in Joshua; the extended space between a promise and its
fulfillment in the covenant with Abraham, and so on). Indeed, the
threat of ultimate closure or "doom" begins in the biblical narrative
almost as soon as the narrative itself does. The reprieve granted to
Adam and Eve after the Fall, the remnant of Noah and his family
after the almost-final closure of the Flood—these and other defer-
rals of ultimate end or judgment extend both text and time, widening or dilating the space between *Anfang und Ende*, which in Genesis
threatens to be very contracted indeed. The structure of deferral
inhabits even the Bible's own ending, the Book of Apocalypse itself,
where the final lines end in the still-anticipatory mode of an "Even
so, come . . . ," a retreat from a vision of ending into the more

ambiguous threshold time before that ending, one model for the inconclusive end of Spenser's *Cantos of Mutabilitie* where the speaker granted a vision of the final end of "dilation" is still left within the space of its unfolding. But the New Testament like the Old is filled with warnings that such a delaying of "doom" must not lull its hearers into the assumption that the promised end will be endlessly put off. The structure of deferral here remains resolutely teleological—a waiting for the return of the "Bridegroom," of a much-delayed but finally coming Master (*Dominus*) or Lord.[6]

This space of deferred and yet assured ending was also a space and time left open for what Thomas More and others referred to as the "dilating of Christendome." The ultimate origin of both term and tradition was the *dilatare* of the Vulgate, in passages on the extension or widening of the boundaries of Israel—a dilation only too readily assimilated in Renaissance Europe to the expansion of empire, or imperial domination, a Christianized version of the extended boundaries of imperial Rome.[7] At two crucially self-reflexive moments of the *Os Lusiades* of Camoens, both expansionist impulses combine and are joined by the expansionist energies—the dilating *inventio* or *copia*—of the poem itself. Camoens's epic of empire begins with the enunciation of its intention to sing, as a new Homer or Virgil, the "glorious memory of those Kings who went on dilating the boundaries of both the Faith and the Empire" ("E também as memórias gloriosas / Daquêles Reis que foram *dilatando* / A Fé, o Imperio," 1.2) and in the seventh canto renews its praise for the small band of Portuguese heroes who in spite of all perils go forward to dilate or spread abroad the faith that brings eternal life ("Vós, que à custa de vossas várias mortes / A lei da vida eterna *dilatais*" [7.3]). The dilation of the kingdom is translated into the dilation of empire, and thus also of the poem, which celebrates both.

These Renaissance contexts for dilation as both deferral in time and extension in space are joined by a whole host of others that cannot be fully explored here but must at least be mentioned, since they appear in the texts to which we will turn at the end of this prologue. One is the neoplatonic tradition of *dilatio* as the dilation or Emanation of Being, its procession out from and return to the Source or the One—the model for Nature's pronouncement in Spenser's *Mutabilitie Cantos* that all things "their being doe dilate" (*FQ* 7.7.58), and in Derrida's terms the kind of detour or long way round he repeatedly insists must be distinguished from "différance," since deferral here is clearly contained within the horizon of a *telos* or ending. Another is as a synonym for temporality, or lifetime, itself, for the mediate or earthly as distinguished from the

eternal, simultaneous or apocalyptic—from a place where, as Hugh
Latimer put it in a sermon of 1552, God's will is done "fully" and
"perfectly," or in other words, "without dilation."[8] Still another
dilation is the puffing up, or inflation, of pride, a meaning that gives
to the inflated *alazon* figure of Ajax in Shakespeare's *Troilus and
Cressida* the ironic reference to his "spacious and dilated parts"
(2.3.248–51) or stands behind the "dilation" of Satan, father of all
such *alazon* figures, in Book 4 of *Paradise Lost* (4.977–86).

There are finally, to sum up this Renaissance catalogue, two other
signal contexts for dilation as delay which often, indeed, appear
together as figures for the postponed ending of a text. The first is a
judicial one—the tradition of "dilatory pleas" or *Essoins,* which
Hamlet, in a play very much concerned with deferral, calls "the
law's delay" (3.1.72)—an "exception or defence dilatour" put in for
the purpose of deferring the judgment of a case. Hobbes in the
Leviathan (1.16) writes that "the not decreeing Execution, is a decree
of Dilation," its "deferring till another time," a definition that precisely describes the stay of execution granted by the Duke to Egeon
in *The Comedy of Errors'* opening scene. And, as White's *Commentaries
on the Law in Shakespeare* reminds us, it is also the delaying tactic
behind the course taken by Queen Katherine in *Henry VIII,* which
the King complains is nothing but the "dilatory sloth and tricks of
Rome" (2.4.237).[9] The second context is an erotic one, that deferral
of coitus or consummation which Andreas Capellanus describes as
its *dilatio* (the word he prefers to the Ovidian *mora* or delay)—a
specifically feminine strategy raised almost to the status of an erotic
terminus technicus by the time of the "sweet reluctant amorous delay" of Milton's Eve (*PL,* 4.311) and still going strong in Addison's
reference to "women of dilatory Tempers, who are for spinning out
the Time of Courtship" or in Mrs. Peacham's exclamation in the
Beggar's Opera ("O Polly, you might have toy'd and kist. / By keeping
men off, you keep them on").[10] Such erotic deferral or putting off,
indeed, might well remind modern readers of Barthes's eroticized
descriptions of a narrative and rhetorical "espace dilatoire"; and its
focus on the hymen as a dividing wall or partition made it easily
conflatable with the rhetorical tradition of the dilation of discourse
by "partition," as the dividing "wall" of *A Midsummer Night's Dream*
makes only too explicit. Richard de Fournival's *Consaus d'Amours* or
"Advice on Love" not only repeats Capellanus's advice on the advantages of delay but warns against opening a crucial "gate" too
soon, as the Trojans did to their destruction. And the kind of dilation that puts off going through this particular kind of gate easily
joins with the specifically erotic form of postponement that gives,

for example, to the Greek romances so ubiquitously imitated in the Renaissance both their characteristically dilated length and their characteristic, frustrating delays.[11]

What makes these various contexts for dilation so generative in the Renaissance is the ease with which they combine and cross, often within a single text. Marvell's "To His Coy Mistress," for example—coming as it does at the far end of this Renaissance tradition—passes through a veritable lexicon of the contexts for dilation before it turns abruptly to its *carpe diem* plea, for that specifically erotic consummation devoutly to be wished. And it does so in what are rhetorically its own ironically dilated—both expansive and dilatory—opening lines. "I would / Love you ten years before the Flood: / And you should, if you please refuse / Till the Conversion of the Jews" evokes not just the erotic dilation learned from Capellanus but also the space of dilation or delay before the biblical execution of Judgment, that consummation that is history's long-desired apocalyptic end. In the great summoning of figures for the tarrying of the Bridegroom in Matthew 24–25, the time and space of delayed apocalypse is linked typologically with the time before the judgment of the Flood, while the space before the "Conversion of the Jews" is precisely the space before that apocalyptic Second Coming. "My vegetable Love should grow / Vaster than Empires, and more slow" evokes yet another branch of the lexicon, the dilation of empire proverbially associated with the empires of Greece or Rome and, by extension, with the *imperium* of the Lord of Love. The leisurely *blason* that follows ("An hundred years should go to praise / Thine Eyes, and on thy Forehead Gaze; / Two hundred to adore each Breast . . . An Age at least to every part") evokes the rhetorical tradition of dilation by partition in its appropriately eroticized form, the partition of the body not of discourse but of the beloved. And the evoking of the idea of partition through the lady's division into "parts" subtly prepares, before the abrupt turn to *carpe diem* haste, for the image of breaking through the gate of the hymen as another kind of partition in the poem's erotically apocalyptic closing lines:

> Let us roll all our Strength, and all
> Our sweetness, up into one Ball:
> And tear our Pleasures with rough strife,
> Thorough the Iron gates of Life.
> Thus, though we cannot make our Sun
> Stand still, yet we will make him run.

The biblical echoes of the final couplet recall once again the earlier figures for a delayed apocalyptic end, the tarrying but finally com-

ing "bridegroom." "Make our sun / Stand still" summons up the
staying or suspending of the sun from Joshua 10, one of the primary
biblical figures for the protracting of the "day" of history, or what in
the poem's eroticized context would be that "long Loves Day" (4) of
its own dilated and leisurely opening lines. And it opposes this
staying to the hastening of the advent of the bridegroom sun (Psalm
19:5, "as a bridegroom coming out of his chamber . . . to run a
race"), a coming of the "sun" whose traditional linking with the
long-delayed but finally coming Bridegroom of Matthew 25 would
make the Coy Mistress, in her very procrastination and delay, by
implication a very foolish virgin.

Both the dilation and the final summoning of consummation in
Marvell's extraordinarily concentrated lyric virtually epitomize the
structure of delay and its potential conscription to particular ends,
or kinds of ending. The discussion that follows involves more detailed examination of such "dilation," and its circumscription, in
particular major Renaissance texts—in plays of Shakespeare which
explicitly evoke and exploit its various senses; in Cervantes's *Don
Quixote*, which presents its Second Part as a "dilación" of its First;
and finally in the self-conscious poetics of Ben Jonson's Cary-Mor-
ison Ode. This examination is itself part of a much larger work,[12]
and the contraction of such diverse writings into the space of a single
essay simply cannot be done without some loss and ellipsis. But it
may be worth considering each of these different instances separately, and on its own terms, in order first to suggest the implications of this complex in Renaissance texts in which it has not been
interpreted, or perceived, before returning to the concerns of modern theory and to the opposition suggested in our opening epigraph
from Derrida.

II

> . . . a prayer of earnest heart,
> That I would all my pilgrimage dilate,
> Whereof by parcels she had something heard,
> But not intentively [2nd F, "distinctively"]
> —OTHELLO 1.3

Shakespeare criticism has generally confined itself to the simple
footnoting of allusions in various plays to the rhetorical tradition of
"dilation" or amplification—cited either as proof of Shakespeare's
more than little "Latine and lesse Greeke" or as part of a basic
enumeration of the play's rhetorical tropes and devices.[13] But the
plays in which this complex is explicitly evoked suggest a subtle and

pervasive link between the dilation of discourse and other forms of dilation and delay, including the amplification and central preoccupations of the plays themselves.

The Comedy of Errors, to take just one example, not only begins with a self-conscious evocation of rhetorical dilation—when Egeon is asked to "dilate at full" (1.1.122) the narrative of his life and as a result is granted a temporary postponement of his own execution or "doom"—but also exploits a whole range of allusions that suggest that the space of dilated discourse, as of a deferred "doom," is the space of the comedy of "errors" itself. Life time, to borrow Geoffrey Hartman's recent formulation,[14] is in Egeon's case intimately bound up with story time, with the space and time of a dilated discourse: the easy conflation of legal judgment with Last Judgment in the tradition of Essoins or "dilatory pleas" yields a deferral of execution which lasts, indeed, precisely one "day" and which approaches its end in scenes filled with echoes of the space of dilation before Apocalypse, or history's own deferred Recognition Scene. In this middle space of "error" and putting off (emphasized by such apparently gratuitous namings as the ship called "Delay" in act 4), the spouse Adriana is presented as "waiting" for the return of her "Master" and "Lord" who, like the absent Christ in the period before Apocalypse, is described as a "tardy master," both "at hand" (2.1.44) and not yet come. The play itself is set in Ephesus and its echoes of the New Testament Epistle to the Ephesians include not just the injunction to wives to submit unto their husbands—often noted in relation to this play—but also the "wall of partition" from Ephesians 2, which Shakespeare in A Midsummer Night's Dream conflates both with the hymen and with the "partition" of discourse (5.1.165), a dividing wall crucial to dilation as a form of putting off or delay but one that must finally be "down" (MND, 5.1.337) before an anticipated consummation can be reached. In The Comedy of Errors, indeed, it is in fact a wall or partition that keeps the "tardy" but proper master from returning to his spouse, preventing the play of errors from coming to an end much earlier than it finally does. And this wall is kept intact, in the great failed recognition scene of the play's middle act (3.1), by the much-dilated body of a female figure whose blason suggests the dilated parts of Creation or the Globe itself, before she too is finally claimed by her proper betrothed. The whole of the dilated text of "errors" would seem to be, then, not only a kind of dilatory Essoin, a putting off of the play's own time of "execution" (5.1.121), but also an analogue to the dilated space and time before Apocalypse, before that reunion of a divided family and the deferred but assured bringing of all Error to an end.

All's Well That Ends Well, whose *alazon* figure Parolles or "Words" is also the character who counsels the taking of "a more dilated farewell" (2.1.49–56), similarly depends for its own time and space on the opening up of the oppressive sense of closure or ending with which its first scene begins. But as if calling attention to the structure of a deferral, postponement, or reprieve that must, however, finally come to an end, its second act contains an entire comic scene on the theme of "putting off" (2.2), on the means of dilating the space between a "question" and its "answer" (2.2.14–15) through a copious intermediate supply of words—a delay linked through verbal echo to the play's more erotic forms of putting off. The entire scene closes with the Clown's rueful "things may serve long, but not serve ever" (2.2.53), a conclusion that might apply to all of this play's many forms of putting off before an end or "fine," from the empty verbal dilations of Parolles to the extended life, or dilated farewell, of the play itself.

The very debate over the question of how conclusive is the end even of *All's Well,* with its apparently incontrovertibly teleological title, leads us to speculate that Shakespeare's own recourse to the structures of ending on which he calls may also be a radically experimental one, one that produces as well as reflects the differences we ascribe to "genre" and one that potentially ironizes the forms of dilation, as of closure, even as it employs them. The explicit evocation of dilation in *Troilus and Cressida,* as we mentioned, occurs in Ulysses' ironic praise of the *alazon* Ajax's "spacious and dilated parts" (2.3.248–51), in a scene in which Ajax's own inflated size, like that of Achilles, is a reflection of the puffing up, or "enlarding," of his pride. But the very mention of the term calls attention to the other striking multiplications of dilation within this play, from the erotic dilation or "holding off" of Cressida (1.3.291–300)—the plot of "tarried" fulfillment with which the play begins (1.1.15–30)—to the repeated evocation of rhetorical dilation or amplification, in the detailing of the "parts" of Troilus and Hector, in the obscene exchange in the Greek camp where Cressida is embraced first by the "general" and then by an amplifying succession of "particulars" (4.5.19–52), in the wordy railing of Thersites, and in that self-confessed "tale of length" (1.3.136) that is Ulysses' rhetorical set-piece on the theme of difference, or degree. All of these instances of dilation both as rhetorical extension and as delay—including the play's repeated reference to the much dilated or even swollen bodies of its own dramatis personae—are in turn set against the backdrop of the long-delayed ending or "protractive trials" (1.3.20) of the Trojan War, which in Thersites' phrase may itself be nothing but a dilated or even bloated "argument" (2.3.74) before its long-awaited end, a specious much made out of the precious little that is its theme, not unlike the inflation of the "princes orgulous" we read of in the opening lines. And the play ends both on Troilus's prayer that the long-delayed end of Troy might now come quickly (5.10.8–9) and on the projected end, as well, of Pandar, the very representative from the beginning of the space "between," as if the extension of this ironic "problem" play—which evokes the traditional figures of ending, including Apocalypse, but also undermines the very figures with which it works—had itself been all inflated, and infected, middle, or merely dilated "argument."

There are, finally, at least two plays in the canon which explore the dynamics of closure, of the bringing of dilation to its ending, within the context of tragedy. Much editorial effort has been expended over the problem of what is meant by the "dilated articles" of the message that Claudius sends to Old Norway in act 1 of *Hamlet*, but very little explored of the relation between this evocation of dilation and the rest of a play, which is so preoccupied both with verbal dilation and with delay. Shakespeare elsewhere plays with dilation—and deferral—within the horizon of an ending that, though put off, does finally come; but as the rhetorical handbooks of his day suggest, the potential negative counterpart of a properly ordered dilation, expansive but also carefully marshalled to a conclusion, is that "excessive" dilation or dilatoriness that fails to come to an end, decision, or "point." It is this contrast, perhaps, which informs the tension within *Hamlet* between the "dilated articles" of the message Claudius sends to Old Norway at the beginning, a message that efficiently and quickly puts an "end" to the "business" of a rebellious Fortinbras (2.2.85), and the tedious verbal dilations, the virtual inability to come to such a point, of Polonius and later Osric, reflections of Hamlet's own much-emphasized problem of delay, of how himself to deliver the message with which he is charged. Hamlet's transformation en route to England, his commissioning of that message that results in the deaths of Rosencrantz and Guildenstern, would thus become both part of his own ambivalent assumption of the functions of a king ("why, what a king is this!" as Horatio exclaims) and part of the end-directedness or *telos* of tragedy itself.

The question, finally, of the control or teleological orientation of dilation and delay permeates the whole of *Othello*, and the activity of Iago within it, before the "bloody period" of its tragic ending. Rhetorical dilation is once again evoked in the play's opening Act—in Othello's account of Desdemona's plea that he might "dilate" the

story of his life, of events that were not present to her eye. Othello's
dilation of his narrative, his unfolding to Desdemona's "greedy ear"
of a story she had heard only "in parcels" or in parts, takes place
within the comic context of Act 1 and his demanded narrative becomes the means of his acquittal, before the judicial inquiry of the
Venetian Senate, from Brabantio's charge. But in the hands of
Iago—whose plot depends, as he himself reveals, on the manipulation both of haste and of "dilatory time" (2.3.363)—rhetorical dilation is conscripted to the service of a tragic end; and what the Folio
and all the authoritative texts of the play but one term the "close
dilations" of the great Temptation Scene become part of Iago's accusation of Desdemona before *her* judge, a controlled narrative unfolding that tragically catches Othello's own "greedy ear," and a carefully manipulated movement that, in the play's final scenes, closes
off both further delay and further dilation or unfolding.[15]

The control of dilation by Iago, who, like a dramatist, depends
both upon "dilatory time" and upon what brings it to conclusion,
involves in *Othello* a systematic exploration of the kind of end or
"bloody period" (5.2.358) such a rigidly teleological movement may
ultimately lead to. The containment of dilation or delay within the
horizon of ending seems in Shakespeare to involve both a sense of
an ending which can, like that of the play itself, be only temporarily
put off, allowing a space of "play" that is finally bounded or circumscribed, and a perception of the potentially tragic (or in still other
plays, political) uses of such a teleological drive, a foregrounding of
the very structure of dilation which allows us to see the potential
implications of such containment as well.

III

"dilatado, y, finalmente muerto y sepultado"
—*Don Quixote*

"Dilación" and its cognates is used throughout Cervantes's *Don
Quixote* in contexts that evoke not just its position at a semantic
crossroads between "to defer" and "to widen or dilate"—and
hence, as in the tradition of rhetorical amplification, as a synonym
for the act of narration itself—but also the wide range of associations
we have so far traced, from the putting off of marriage or consummation, to the delaying of execution or death, to the dilation of
empires of various kinds of dominion or control.

In its specifically erotic context, "dilación" appears frequently in
the *Quixote*, as in a number of Spanish Renaissance texts akin to or

influenced by the protracted plots of Greek romance. In Part 1, for example, Marcela's uncle will not marry her off without her consent, thus deferring or putting off the time of her marraige ("*dilatando* su casamiento*," 1.3).[16] In the story of Luscinda and Cardenio, Cardenio is forced by duty and self-doubt to defer (only for the moment, as he wrongly thinks) the time of his union with his beloved ("hablé una noche a Luscinda, díjele todo lo que pasaba, y lo mismo hice a su padre, suplicándole se entretuviese algunos días y *dilatase* el darle estado," 1.24). And in the tale of the Curious Impertinent, Lotario reproaches Camila for not giving him what he wants, complaining that she responds with evasive questions "por *dilatarme* la prometida merced" (1.34). When Dorotea, seduced by Fernando, finally catches up with him in chapter 36, she begs to know why he is putting off their marraige ("¿ por qué por tantos rodeos *dilatas* de hacerme venturosa en los fines, como me hiciste en los principios?"), a complaint Shelton's English translation (1620) renders as "Why dost thou . . . *delate* the making of mine end happy?" And in Part 2, in a pastoral context that might well summon echoes of *Daphnis and Chloe*, Camacho is concerned that Quiteria not give her hand to the "dying" Basilio because it would postpone the satisfaction of his own desire ("pues todo era *dilatar* por un momento el cumplimiento de sus deseos" [2.21]).

"Dilación" here recalls at once the erotic *dilatio* of Capellanus and what Bakhtin describes as the Greek romance "chronotope" of delay. But it also crosses with other kinds of dilation in the *Quixote*, which combine to make such "dilación" a self-conscious strategy of the text itself. Sancho Panza, sitting at last as governor and judge of his own dominion, determines to set a model of speedy judgment and is pleased that his first case involves no "dilatory pleas" ("Paréceme que en este pleito no ha de haber largas *dilaciones*" [2.45]). He also objects to the narrative counterpart of such "dilaciones" when the daughter of Diego de la Llana is so agonizingly "tardy" in reaching the end of her tale ("Desesperábase el governador de la tardanza que tenía la moza en *dilatar* su historia" [2.49]). But Sancho himself is guilty of just such prolixity, or narrative *tarditas*, both in Part 1 and in an earlier episode in Part 2 where he is reproached by the priest for the "dilaciones y pausas" of a tediously dilated story (2.31). And the *Quixote* itself—as one would expect—is filled with such narrations, which are not simply the narrative "retardations" that Šklovskij described, but "dilations" that subtly link the dilation of discourse to dilations of other kinds.

As with the dilated discourse of Egeon in *The Comedy of Errors*, the extended tale of the disguised Ana Felix in Part 2 leads, Scheherazade-like, first to the deferral of her execution, and finally, as so often in romance, to an unexpected recognition scene. She begins with an appeal for a "suspension" of execution that would both defer a promised vengeance and allow her to "dilate" the story of her life ("Suspended—dijo el mozo . . . la ejecución de mi muerte; que no se perderá mucho en que *se dilate* vuestra venganza en tanto que yo os cuente mi vida" [2.63]). "Suspended" here, like "sospensos" in Sancho's plea to the daughter of Diego de la Llana for greater haste, is a term that often recurs in the *Quixote*, as in the romance narratives it parodies, as a figure for the holding over—and holding off—of ending. It is, indeed, often just such suspension or interruption that leads both to the dilation of discourse and to the delaying of endings over large stretches of Cervantes's novel: in the course of the unfolding of the story of Dorotea (itself interminably prolonged), there is inserted the tale of the Curious Impertinent, a digression that Don Quixote himself complains in Part 2 had been an unnecessary dilation, since a narrative limited to nothing but the telling of his own exploits would be "big" enough already (2.3). And the *Quixote* itself repeatedly calls attention to its own dilated narrations and repeated delays, as when it announces, in one of its chapter headings (2.41) that it will treat "Of the coming of Clavileno and the end of this protracted adventure" ("con el fin desta *dilatada* aventura"), the story of Countess Trifaldi, which after being drawn out over no fewer than six chapters is in this one finally brought to a close.

There is, however, an increased emphasis on drawing something "dilated" to its ending as the *Quixote* itself begins to set its sights on the close of its own "dilatada aventura." And the "dilación" of the novel's own protracted narratives at times even explicitly recalls the temporal dilation that is all of history, scripture, or discourse before its apocalyptic end, that deferred and much-postponed "judgment" that, like death, will, it is promised, nevertheless finally come. When the priest objects to the "dilaciones y pausas" of Sancho's prolix tale in Part 2, his master is also vexed by his "dilation" and repeatedly adjures Sancho to cut his story short. Several allusions link the "dilación" of Sancho's narrative both to the six days of Creation and to the space of time remaining before death: the Duchess insists that he be allowed to draw out his tale in his own way, "even if it takes him six days to finish," while the exasperated priest complains that at the rate the teller is going, he will not be done with his tale "till the next world" (2.31). Sancho's "dilation," then, is a kind of narrative hexameron, or six-day creation, before its, and his, final "rest." And in a fashion familiar from this biblical context for a dilation, or delay, within the horizon of an assured ending, the end of the *Quixote's* own dilation also involves a final delimiting of it, with echoes both of that end to dilation which is Apocalypse and of the closure, in death, of an individual life.

Let us return, then, to the epigraph to this section. In the Prologue to Part 2 of the *Quixote,* after the author's complaints about the imposter *Don Quixote* who "has been running about the world masquerading as the second part" ("Dedication," 465), we read that what is to follow is the authorized, or authentic, "segunda parte":

> This second part of *Don Quixote,* which I place before you, is cut by the same craftsman and from the same cloth as the first, and . . . in it I present you with the knight at greater length and, in the end, dead and buried (*"dilatado, y, finalmente muerto y sepultado"*). Let no one, therefore, presume to raise fresh testimonies to him, for the past ones are sufficient. . . . For however good things are, an abundance brings down the price, and scarcity, even in bad things, confers a certain value.

The story of *Don Quixote* is in this authentic second part or sequel to be both "dilated"—taken to greater length—and finally brought to an end in death: the syntax nicely blurs life time and story time, promising a burial that will be not only his end, but its. But it is significant that this promise both of further "dilación" and of ultimate ending comes in the midst of a Prologue, and an incipient second part, which calls attention to the dilative function of all seconds or sequels, including the counterfeit double that is the imposter "segunda parte." Terence Cave has signaled an ambivalence within the ideal of *copia* which surfaces in the tension between copiousness and "copy," between a fruitful abundance of *materia* and a mere duplication, repetition, or second edition, a kind of fallen *copia* rendered even more threatening in the Renaissance by the advent of print and its seemingly endless duplicating power.[17] Something like this tension plays around the edges of Part 2 of the *Quixote,* a sequel that extends a story in danger of confusion with its imposter or twin. The relation between that "dilation" that is the provision of a copious second part and the dangers of the multiplication of "copies" is, in fact, raised right from the beginning of Part 2, from Sampson Carrasco's announcement that the story of the Don and his sidekick is already in print in more than "twelve thousand copies" and "will surely be translated into the tongue of every nation" (2.3), to the discussion of the disseminating power—as well as the potentially increased error—of print (2.4), to the whole elaboration on the advantages and disadvantages of second parts when the matter is copious enough for "not only a second part, but a hundred more" (2.4).

It is noteworthy, then, that the reference in the Prologue to Part 2 to a "dilation" that is finally to be brought to an end is combined with a warning against "fresh testimonies" on the ground that "however good things are, an abundance brings down the price, and scarcity, even in bad things, confers a certain value." For the author of the counterfeit second part is the creator of a dangerous dilation, of the proliferation of a "copy" rather than the extended *copia* that is the intent of the authentic author of the first (a claim to control by the authority of authorship that would, of course, eventually produce something known as copyright). The combination of this warning against "fresh testimonies" with the promise in this Prologue to present the story of the knight "dilatado, y, finalmente muerto y sepultado" involves, then, both an announcement of closure and an interdiction of further dilation, beyond that end. Many, indeed, of the references in the *Quixote* to "adding nothing and omitting nothing" (1.9), to faithfully translating an original, and to the difference between a proper second part and a counterfeit "second" or double recall the repeated biblical injunctions (e.g., Apocalypse 22:18–19) not to add or take away from a canonical "book." In the history of biblical commentary and translation this commandment has always lent a sense of ambivalence or suspect *inventio* to the dilation, or dissemination, of the Word, an ambivalence whose rhetorical counterpart frequently emerged in the concern that while a shorter text might be made, by rhetorical *dilatio*, to "increase and multiply" the sense of its original, it not be allowed, ultimately, to stray too far from that origin, and end.[18]

In this sense, the Prologue to Part 2 (of 1615)—both in its anxiety about the *Quixote*'s spurious double and in its announcement of a sequel or addition that will, though "dilating" the original story, finally bring it to a definitive end—needs, in relation to the whole of this novel's reflections on "dilation," to be juxtaposed to the Prologue to Part 1 (of 1605). For the *Quixote*'s very opening is a prologue on the impossibility of writing a prologue, and the initial threat to the text is that of no dilation at all. The writer professes that he was so troubled by the impossibility of producing anything out of his "sterile and ill-cultivated genius" (25), incapable of "invention" or of producing the authoritative sentences, marginal quotations, and other *materia* that fill out other books, that he was inclined not to publish the book at all. And the terms in which he expresses this to his friend include precisely the "sepultado," or "buried," which the Prologue to Part 2 will later recall: "I have decided that Don Quixote shall stay *buried* ("se quede *sepultado*") in the archives of La Mancha till Heaven provides someone to adorn him with all the jewels he lacks" (27). To this premature burial—an ending that would not even allow the text to begin—the friend responds with advice on how to dilate a slender volume, glancing with characteristic Cervantine irony not only at other writers but at the whole rhetorical tradition of the dilation of discourse. But the advice is curiously double—how both to increase the *copia* of his own text and yet to make what is called here his "simple and straightforward story" different from the notoriously dilated, and frequently endless, books of chivalry it is written to overthrow. This imports an irony from the beginning into the "dilación" of the *Quixote* as a whole. Not only is this first prologue increased by advice on how to dilate or pad his text; but his "lean" (Prologue, 25) book is made fat by the very digressions, interpolations, and seemingly interminable stories that the romances are famous for, just as the lean Don Quixote is joined (we might almost say "doubled" as well as followed, as in "sequel") by his famous fat sidekick.

The dilation of the *Quixote* itself, however—whatever the "largas dilaciones" of its interpolated tales—is finally very much under control and, unlike so many of the romances, brought finally to an ending. Reference, indeed, is made right from the beginning to concluding or cutting short something much dilated or prolonged. In the third chapter of Part 1, a matter and discourse potentially long drawn out are countered by the invocation of its opposite *brevitas*, a combination that Cervantes had already played on in announcing, in the Prologue to the *Novelas Ejemplares*, his intention to publish the second part of *Don Quixote*, in lines that subtly juxtapose "dilación" in the sense of narration with something done without delays: "Verás, y con *brevedad*, *dilatadas* las hazañas de don Quixote" ("You will see, with brevity, told the deeds of Don Quixote"). In the midst of this third chapter, we read that "the innkeeper had begun to dislike his guest's pranks, and decided to cut the matter short (*abreviar*) and give him his wretched order of knighthood immediately," then that the Don himself begged his host to "conclude the matter as briefly as possible" ("que concluyese con la mayor *brevedad* que pudiese"), and finally that the innkeeper responds to the knight's rhetoric "with a briefer speech" ("más *breves* palabras"), in order to bring the episode more expeditiously to a close. Similarly, in the famous chapter of the burning of the books (1.6), filled as it is with echoes of that other "conflagration," which is Apocalypse, some (the "elect") are saved, while others are allowed the traditional dilation, or deferral, of the time of judgment, in order that they may

repent and "show signs of amendment." But it is made clear that
something like this judgment, though deferred, will not be indefinitely put off.

The novel's own references to a promise whose fulfillment is long
deferred (like the promise of a kingdom made to Sancho, a promise
linked to the biblical promise to Abraham) or its seemingly endless
stories, which do, however, finally come to an end, have their larger
textual counterpart in the final bringing to both narrative end, and
death, of the "dilación" that is the extended life, and textual time
and space, of the story of Don Quixote. The same Prologue to Part 2
that gives us this "dilatado, y, finalmente muerto y sepultado" also
calls attention to mortality, a reminder of the "passage of time" (467)
which subtly extends both to life time and to story time, in contrast
to the potentially interminable dilation of discourse, or fictional
"seconds." And even Book 1 provides figures of that "segunda
parte" that is to be not just second but the ultimate conclusion. In
chapter 6, the ironic self-reference to the "Galatea of Miguel de
Cervantes" (62) which "sets out to do something and concludes
nothing," so that they will have to "wait for a second part" to see if it
should be burned or saved from destruction, introduces the notion
of a suspension, or waiting, before a second part that will precipitate
both end and judgment. And even more suggestive, in relation to
the dilation of the narrative of the *Quixote* itself and its conclusion in
its own "segunda parte" of 1615, is the interval of incompletion, or
"suspension," between chapters 8 and 9 of Part 1, where the Basque
and the valiant Manchegan are left suspended on the point of dealing the strokes that would mean both their deaths (75), a suspension
that is finally ended when the story proceeds in chapter 9 to *its*
second part, or conclusion. In relation to the multiple suspensions
that inform dilations of so many different kinds in the *Quixote*, this
dilation and conclusion might serve as an epitome of the whole
book, which opens up a space of "dilación" but does not indefinitely
defer its ending.

IV

"What did this Stirrer, but die late?"

Our final Renaissance instance is a lyric one. In the first "Stand" of
his remarkable Pindaric ode "To the Immortall Memorie, and
Friendship of that Noble Paire, Sir Lucius Cary and Sir H. Morison,"
Ben Jonson describes a man whose whole life was simply un-
distinguished temporal prolongation:

> He vexed time, and busied the whole State;
> Troubled both foes, and friends;
> But ever to no ends:
> What did this Stirrer, but die late?
>   (27–30)

The buried English pun on the Latin *dilatio* or "dilate" learnedly and in typically Jonsonian fashion translates the *mora* or delay of the poem's classical subtext, Seneca's ninety-third moral epistle: "A person like him has not lived; he has merely *tarried* awhile in life" ("in vita *moratus* est").[19] And this mere delaying of death becomes in the poem a foil to the early death of Sir Henry Morison, Cary's friend, whose much briefer but more "perfect" life recalls Seneca's dictum, "We should strive not to live long, but to live rightly":

> All Offices were done
> By him, so ample, full, and round,
> In weight, in measure, number, sound,
> As though his age imperfect might appeare,
> His life was of Humanitie the Spheare.
>   (48–52)

It is this contrast—between mere dilation, or extension of life, and a fullness achieved within a shorter space—which brings to the poem those programmatic and pithily epigrammatic statements so often quoted as representative of the lyric Jonson: "For, what is life, if measur'd by the space, / Not by the act?" (21–22), or again, "It is not growing like a tree / In bulke, doth make man better bee. . . . / In small proportions, we just beautie see: / And in short measures, life may perfect bee" (65–74). The simple dilation of the "Stirrer's" life, however, also has its contrasting opposite. The poem's opening stanza tells of a strange case of arrested parturition—of Pliny's "Infant of Saguntum" who, when about to come into the world in the midst of Hannibal's seige and the start of the second Punic War, retreats "hastily" when he perceives how bad things are in the world, thus making his "Mothers wombe" his "urne" (8). There is in the case of this "infant" who chose to end his life before it began no dilation at all, no space of life time between birth and death, beginning and end.

Jonson's preference is a more fruitful middle way between these two extremes. And the poem itself develops a subtle parallel between this middle way of life and the enunciation of what might stand as its own self-reflexive poetic: "In small proportions, we just beautie see." The pun on "die late" in the stanza on the busy Stirrer manages, in its quintessentially Jonsonian crossing between Latin subtext and English verse, to suggest, once again, both the delaying of death and the rhetorical tradition of the dilating of discourse; and the controlled expansion that is the "dilation" of an ideal art as well as of Morison's brief but ample life, to suggest Jonson's simultaneously lyric, and humanist, development of a particular Erasmian strain. True *copia dicendi* in the humanism of Erasmus has, as Terence Cave has pointed out, two negative counterparts: *inopia*, poverty of diction, or no dilation at all; and, at the opposite extreme, a busy *loquacitas*, dilation without variety, or mere prolixity. True plenitude of language is to be found not in simple extension, or quantitative linear prolongation, but rather in that imaginative richness that expands the nuances within a single word or statement, in a balancing of Ciceronian *copia* with a shaping *brevitas.*[20] What appears in the lines on the Stirrer who did nothing but "die late" to be simply a learned or sotto voce pun—on Seneca's description of the man who simply "tarried" in life—has, perhaps, much wider resonances both within this ode and, more broadly, within the context of Jonson's own poetic and career.

The briefly dilated space that is both "ample" and "perfect," then, involves a mean that is neither the extreme of the aged Stirrer who did nothing but "die late" nor that of the infant who did not dilate at all, an infancy, indeed, whose etymological Latin resonance (*in-fans*, without speech) may suggest its own impoverished rhetorical counterpart. But the simultaneous brevity and perfection of Morison's life and the poem's poetic also implicitly contrasts with the notorious "bulk" of Jonson's own much-dilated plays (as perhaps of his own famous bulk or size). The one stanza of the ode that has puzzled critics, partly because of the uncertainty of its addressee, is the poem's second "Stand," whose "masse," "swell," and "long" curiously recall the dilation of the aged Stirrer of the first:

> Goe now, and tell out dayes summ'd up with feares,
> And make them yeares;
> Produce thy masse of miseries on the Stage,
> To swell thine age;
> Repeat of things a throng,
> To shew thou hast beene long,
> Not liv'd.
> (53–59)

The ode, we remember, was written in the same year as the disastrous first performance of the aging Jonson's *New Inn* and soon after the famous "Ode To Himselfe" in which he vows to leave behind the "loathed stage," which prefers a "mouldy tale" like Shakespeare's romance *Pericles*, for the domain of lyric. Not only does this second

"Stand" recall the empty "die late" or mere dilation of the aged
Stirrer of the first: but its "dayes" made into "yeares," its extended
"masse," and its "Repeat of things a throng / To shew thou has been
long" parodically mimic the language of excessive rhetorical copia
or dilation as well—the art of making what is, as we have seen, an
often specious "much" out of "little." If the reference in this stanza
is indeed self-reference, as several recent readers have maintained,
the stanza's ironical tone is not only a scornful dismissal of self-pity
by an aging man able to look back over a now-failing dramatic career
but also an ironic description of the characteristics dilations, or
swellings, of his own dramatic productions.

The possibility of self-address in this stanza on the greater "masse" of the "stage" indeed summons up, in a kind of self-corrective
retrospect, an image of the kind of massive *copia* these dramas did
involve. Jonson's plays are notoriously dilated in various ways—
heavy in their size and complexity, often weighty in their footnoted
erudition (as in *Sejanus* and *Catiline*), copious in their indulgence of
the exuberance of language or mere verbiage (as with the verbal
excesses of *The Alchemist* or the unbearable talkativeness of characters like Juniper in *The Case Is Altered*), and self-consciously dependent on the techniques of amplification or dilation. A play like *Bar-
tholmew Fair*, indeed, seems almost an inventory of all the Renaissance associations of such verbal and rhetorical dilation—from the
fatuously rotund circumlocutions of Adam Overdo, to the parody of
dilated sermon discourse in the interminable harangues of Rabbi
Busy (whose name makes him the discursive counterpart of the
busy Stirrer of the ode), to the punning link between verbal copiousness, fat Ursula's sheer bulk or size, and the fabled "enormities"
of both Fair and stage. Jonson's plays also often depend for their
very life on that dilation which is the self-inflation of the countless
alazon figures within them; and the implulse to shrink the swelling
of pride and illusion often gives them endings whose own reductive
judgments recall the deflation of both in the Last Judgment.[21]

If "Repeat of things a throng, / To shew thou hast beene
long, / Not liv'd," then, in the stanza on the stage restates in a specifically dramatic and potentially self-reflective context the empty dilation of the aged Stirrer whose life is an ironic counter to Seneca's
dictum "We should strive not to live long, but to live rightly," what is
at stake in this ode may be more than the simple rejection of the art
of others (as in the lines on Shakespeare's *Pericles* in the "Ode to
Himselfe") but a rejection of that particular "art of surfeit" which
Jonson indulged in as a playwright even more than the traditionally
more expansive Shakespeare. And its turning towards the briefer

space, and "perfection," of lyric includes not just a subtle recall of
the earlier ode's rejection of those "mouldy" romance tales that
simply "die late" but also the multiple dilations, bulk, and swelling,
of his own dramatic productions.

The resonance of rhetorical dilation introduced through "die late"
nicely parallels, then, the links throughout the poem between its
resonating terms of life and those of art, a blending so striking that
one of its readers, though he does not develop the link, speaks of the
brevity of Morison's life as itself a kind of "anti-Ciceronianism."[22]
The poem's Senecan subtext already suggests a relation between life
time and story time, alluding as it does to the contrast not only
between the old man's mere "tarrying" in life and "living rightly"
within a shorter space, but also between brief but useful books and
those which are simply "heavy," or dilated: "There are books which
contain very few lines, admirable and useful in spite of their size;
and there are also the Annals of Tanusius, you know how heavy the
book is, and what men say of it." The stanza that begins with the
swollen "masse" of the stage ends with that contrasting sense of
smaller "measures," which in the stanza that follows will become "It
is not growing like a tree / In bulke, doth make men better bee" and
the poem's own embracing of the "just beautie" of "small proportions" instead (65–74). And Jonson's poem plays constantly and
subtly on this disproportion between size and worth, even to the
point where the Senecan original of these very lines ("Just as one of
small stature can be a perfect man, so in a life of small compass can
be a perfect life") resonates with the knowledge that the *brevitas* of
Morison's life had its counterpart in Cary's small size, a "small
stature" that, however, as one of his contemporaries remarked,
"was quickly found to contain a great heart."[23] The counterpart,
perhaps, to both is found within the ample brevity of the ode itself,
in what Thomas Greene has called the "quiet expansion" of its
nouns and the subtly "accumulative extensions and fields of reference" of its language, just as its final imagery of fruits and harvest
(127–28) suggests a quiet fulfillment that is neither the Stirrer's protracted but finally fruitless dilation nor the infant of Saguntum's
prematurely terminated life.

It may be also, finally, that the middle way celebrated in the ode is
expressed through the imagery of light within the very name of
"Lucius" Cary, in a way that opens the poem to another kind of
dilation—not one of perfection and completeness but one related
precisely to the element of incompletion, and even "schism," which
readers have seen as implicated in its Pindaric turns and counter-
turns. The "Brave Infant of Saguntum" refuses a life seen simply as

"death, and night" (14), while Morison is described as having "leap'd" directly to the light of "bright eternall Day" (79–81). Jonson's invocation of the myth of Castor and Pollux—the mortal and immortal members of the constellation of the Gemini or Twins— makes it necessary for "Lucius" not to follow his friend into death but instead to "tarry" (91) in life and shine there ("Whilst that in heav'n, this light on earth must shine" [96]). Cary's "tarrying" on earth subtly recalls Seneca's description of the *mere* "tarrying" in life of the old man, the model for that aged Stirrer who did nothing but "die late." The temptation opposed to Lucius's patient tarrying would be the premature end of suicide, like that of the "Brave Infant" who chose not to dilate at all. Once again, as the ode turns from an enclosed and perfect classical ideal to the "schism" between earth and heaven which Fry reminds us would never be far from the eschatological imagination of a poet like Jonson and which erupts in the dramatic enjambments and end-line divisions of these crucial lines, the poem suggests a somewhat different "dilation" that is neither of these two poles, neither the mere tarrying of the old man nor the premature death of the suicidal infant.

It may be no accident, then, that the primary figure of this third "Stand" is the figure of "twi- / Lights" (92–93), suggesting not simply the two separated lights, earthly and heavenly, of the Gemini but also the temporal image of twilight, which is neither simply the final apocalyptic "Day" that Morison "leap'd" to in his "holy rage" nor the earthly "night" (14) created by the thematically opposed, but verbally identical, "rage" of Hannibal (4) in the poem's opening reference to the siege of Saguntum. For "twilight" is the most traditional of figures for an earthly dilation that is neither of these apocalyptic extremes, but rather the space of life—of deferred death, but also of deferred fulfillment—in between, a space both of waiting and of "standing" (Eph. 6:13) in patience (with the possibility, finally, of a pun on the "Stand" in which it appears), a patient forebearance in the midst of that middle state rather than the infant's refusal of any dilation or life time at all.

V

This is possible only if *différance* is determined outside any teleological or eschatological horizon. Which is not easy . . .
—DERRIDA

The very fact that it seems more than a little wrenching to move from the neoclassical diction of a poem such as Jonson's to the contemporary context of Derridean "différance," or to the reasons behind the invocation of delay in modern theory (including, we might add, Owen Barfield's invocation of *Essoins* in a famous essay on the delay of meaning in poetic figure),[24] might well be reason enough for refusing the attempt altogether. The reminder of historical difference and distance, of the undeniable alterity of the Renaissance, is always a necessary reminder, especially when our perception of what is important in the texts of any period is so intimately tied to the preoccupations of our own critical, and historical, milieu. And it may well seem from our tracing of the pervasiveness of "dilation" both as expansion and as delay in such different Renaissance texts and contexts that the similarity of its terms to those of Derridean "différance"—a similarity that has inspired recent attempts to connect the two—leads us rather to distinguish them, to remark chiefly on the distance between a dilation and delay which is finally caught within the horizon of a telos or ending, however tentatively or self-consciously construed, and the kind of unlimited "différance" envisaged by Derrida. Perhaps, however, we can come to our own tentative conclusions on the question suspended from the beginning.

In a number of the Renaissance texts we have considered, "dilation" as both expansion and delay might be seen precisely as that kind of mastery and control, or simple dilative detour-as-return-tour, which Derrida repeatedly distinguishes from a "différance" without origin, *telos*, or *eschaton*. Certainly rhetoric in the Renaissance envisaged *copia* as a matter not only of "increase" but of masterful control, a technique to be hedged about with all the usual warnings against "Excesse."[25] And the envisaged end to dilation, or delay, in either its biblical or its secular erotic context, similarly invokes a consummating limit. Yet it cannot go without remark that this very nervousness about the possibility of excess beyond or outside that limit, about a dilation potentially out of control or a deferral and proliferating difference that might indeed be endless, itself bespeaks the arbitrariness or fragility of these very limiting structures—even the culturally most authorized ones. No generalization can stand equally for the plays of Shakespeare, or for the Jonson whose relation to his famously expansive English precursor was finally so richly ambiguous, much less than for the Cervantes whose irony is so notoriously difficult to pin down, any more than criticism can finally be sure how conclusive is the closure of a play called *All's Well That Ends Well*, or how to read the rejection of potential romance endlessness and errancy which makes possible the dilation and conclusion of the *Quixote*. It may be that what leads us historically from the forms of dilation and delay in the Renaissance to those more recent texts that inform Derrida's invocation of a limitless "différance" is an exclusively post-Renaissance questioning of those very limiting structures, including that Romantic writing in which the envisaged end to history or the anticipated *telos* of meaning began to seem very far off indeed. But it may also be that both a simple Derridean reading of Renaissance texts and a rigorous opposition to it run in their potential one-sidedness the risk of missing the contradictory presence in the Renaissance of both strains at once, the structure and what eludes or exceeds it, and hence of what might be most fascinating of all to theory.

NOTES

1. "La Différance" originally appeared in the *Bulletin de la Société française de philosophie* 62, no. 3 (1968), 73–101, with an initial discussion of "différer" omitted from the version subsequently placed in *Marges de la philosophie* (Paris: Editions de Minuit, 1972), 1–29. Derrida's repeated distinction between "différance" understood without "any teleological or eschatological horizon" and the kind of deferral, or delay, which is simply a prolonged detour between origin and ending, may be found in, for example, "Freud and the Scene of Writing," "Structure, Sign, and Play in the Discourse of the Human Sciences," and "Ellipsis," all available in English in *Writing and Difference*, trans. Alan Bass (Chicago: University of Chicago Press, 1978), especially 203, 291–92, 294–300, 329, and 331. The edition used for *The Comedy of Errors* and in all subsequent references to Shakespeare is the relevant Arden edition of each play.
2. See the translation of Viktor Šklovskij, *O teorii prozy* (1929), by Guy Verret, as *Sur la théorie de la prose* (Lausanne: Editions L'Age d'Homme, 1973), especially 107–46 on *Don Quixote*; Mikhail Bakhtin, "Forms of Time and of the Chronotope in the Novel," in *The Dialogic Imagination*, ed. Michael Holquist (Austin: University of Texas Press, 1982), especially 84–110; Roland Barthes, *S/Z* (Paris: Editions de Seuil, 1970), 81ff. and 215–16, as well as Frank Kermode's *The Sense of an Ending* (London: Oxford University Press, 1966). Delay, of course, is by no means absent from earlier discussions, such as the correspondence of Goethe and Schiller over the distinctions between epic and tragedy, just as "dilation" still figures in its rhetorical sense in the Preface to Mary Shelley's *Frankenstein* and in various nineteenth-century texts.
3. See, for example, Jonathan Goldberg's *Endlesse Worke: Spenser and the Structures of Discourse* (Baltimore: Johns Hopkins University Press, 1981), and the divergent approaches to this question in Terence Cave's *The Cornucopian Text* (Oxford: Clarendon Press, 1979), and Thomas M. Greene's *The Light in Troy* (New Haven: Yale University Press, 1982), together with his essay "Erasmus's 'Festina lente': Vulnerabilities of the Humanist Text," in *Mimesis: From Mirror to Method*, ed. John D. Lyons and Stephen

G. Nichols, Jr. My *Inescapable Romance* (Princeton: Princeton University Press, 1979) includes an earlier version of my own interest in this problem, especially in relation to deferral in the romances of Ariosto and Spenser.

4. See, among many, the instances of "dilate" and its variant "delate" in the Epistle Dedicatory of Twyne's *Phisicke against Fortune* ("I might dilate this discourse with a thousand arguments"); Nashe's *Piers Penilesse* ("Experience reproves me for a foole, for delating on so manifest a case"); or Thomas Howell's *Devises* ("Some . . . with delayes the matter will delate"). For the rhetorical tradition of *copia*, see, in addition to Erasmus, Joannes Sturmius, *De imitatione oratoria libri tres* (Strasbourg, 1574), 3L3 ("Copia, est ex paucis sententiis plures factae, ex paucis membris numerosiora") and the descriptions of amplification, or dilation, and partition, in such English handbooks as Thomas Wilson, *The Arte of Rhetorique* (1553), fol. 64–84, 91; John Hoskins, *Directions for Speech and Style* (1599), ed. H. H. Hudson (Princeton: Princeton University Press, 1935), 17–28; Henry Peacham, *The Garden of Eloquence* (1593), 120–25; Abraham Fraunce, *The Lawiers Logike* (1588), 56–58; and, for the *blason* as "distribution of every part for amplification sake," George Puttenham, *The Arte of English Poesie* (1589), and Fraunce, *Lawiers Logike*, 59. The production of "much out of little" also had its negative counterpart in a specious, empty, or merely "swelling" amplification: see, for example, Hoskins, 24, and Francis Bacon, "Of the Coulers of good and evill, a fragment," reprinted with his *Essayes* (1597).

5. See *The Sermons of John Donne*, ed. G. R. Potter and E. M. Simpson (Berkeley and Los Angeles: University of California Press, 1959), 5.56; and the text of Alcok, ed. Mary J. Boynton, in the *Harvard Theological Review* 34 (1941), 201–26.

6. See, among numerous instances, the parable of the foolish virgins in Matthew 25, or the contrast in Matt. 24: 42–48 between the watchful servant and the evil servant who says in his heart "My Master will differ [i.e., delay] his commynge" (Tindale, 1526); Josh. 10:13 ("The Sonne . . . dyferred to go downe for the space of a whole daye after," Coverdale version, 1535); and reiterations of the biblical figures of debt and ransom in such discussions as Bishop Hall's reference to "long dilations of payments" in *Heaven upon Earth* (1627), section 5. For the space before Apocalypse as a *dilatio* or delay of judgment, see Alanus de Insulis, *Patrologia Latina*, 210.137; Jean Daniélou, From *Shadows to Reality: Studies in the Biblical Typology of the Fathers*, trans. Dom Wulstan Hibberd (London: Burns and Oates, 1960), 250 ff.; and Parker, *Inescapable Romance*, 57–59. The end of Apocalypse and its "Even so, come" has exerted a certain fascination in Derrida's more recent work, in "LIVING ON: Border Lines," *Deconstruction and Criticism*, ed. Harold Bloom et al. (New York: The Seabury Press, 1979), 123–37; *Glas* (Paris: Galilée, 1974), 220 ff.; and "D'un ton apocalyptique adopté naguère en philosophie," in *Les fins de l'homme*, ed. Philippe Lacoue-Labarthe and Jean-Luc Nancy

(Paris: Editions Galilée, 1981), 445–86, translated in *The Oxford Literary Review* 6, no. 2 (1984), 3–37.

7. See More, *Comfort against Tribulation* (1529), III, Weeks 1213/2 and the Vulgate versions of Exodus 34:24 ("dilatavero terminos tuos"), Deuteronomy 12:20 ("Quando dilataverit Dominus Deus tuus terminos tuos"); with Deut. 19:8 and 2 Corinthians 6:13, 10:15. It is worth noting, for the subsequent discussion here, that "dilatare" is also used *in malo* in the Vulgate—for the dilation of the boundaries of hell by the harlotries of Israel (Isaiah 5:14); for the dilating of the harlot's bed (Isa. 57:8), a use in a sexual sense, as in Isa. 54:2, which may help to inform the concluding sexual pun on "open" in Donne's *Holy Sonnet* on the errant Church (no. 179); and for the "dilation" that is the puffing up of pride and self-display (Matt. 23:5).

8. *Sermons of Hugh Latimer*, ed. Rev. G. E. Corrie (Cambridge: Cambridge University Press, 1847), 385. I have discussed this and other Renaissance contexts for dilation in greater detail in "Dilation and Delay: Renaissance Matrices," *Poetics Today* 5, no. 3 (1984):519–35.

9. Edward J. White, *Commentaries on the Law in Shakespeare*, 2nd ed. (St. Louis: F. H. Thomas Law Book Co., 1913), 371–72. "Dilation" as a form of delay had long been a synonym for the dilatoriness of sloth: Spenser directly links *Essoins* or dilatory pleas with the all-too-dilatory figure of Idlenesse in *The Faerie Queene* ("From worldly cares himselfe he did esloyne, / And greatly shunned manly exercise, / From every worke he challenged *essoyne* / For contemplation sake" [1.4.20]).

10. See Ovid's *Ars Amatoria* (2.717–18; 3.473–74, 752); Capellanus's massively influential *De arte honeste amandi*; Addison in *Spectator*, no. 89 (1711); and Gay's *Beggar's Opera*, Air 9. For a highly suggestive linking of this erotic tradition to the dilation of texts, see Lee W. Patterson, "'For the Wyves Love of Bathe': Feminine Rhetoric and Poetic Resolution in the *Roman de la rose* and *The Canterbury Tales*," *Speculum* 58 (July 1983): 656–95.

11. Longus's *Daphnis and Chloe*, for example, almost unbearably protracts the period before sexual consummation, while the sudden plot turns and complications of Heliodorus's *Ethiopian History* and other Greek romances repeatedly put off the losing of the heroine's virginity or her reunion with her beloved. For the thirteenth-century *Consaus d'Amours* and other French translations and adaptations of Capellanus, see Norman R. Shapiro, trans., *The Comedy of Eros: Medieval French Guides to the Art of Love* (Urbana: University of Illinois Press, 1971).

12. Parts of this essay are taken from work on two separate book-length studies, one devoted to Shakespeare and the second including different Renaissance texts (political and rhetorical as well as literary) informed by dilation and partition, hysteron proteron, and other rhetorical structures.

13. See, for example, T. W. Baldwin's survey of *dilatio* and *partitio* in *William Shakspere's Small Latine & Lesse Greeke*, 2 vols. (Urbana: University of Illinois Press, 1944), especially 2.109–14, 315–21; and Sister Miriam Joseph, *Shakespeare's Use of the Arts of Language* (New York: Hafner, 1947). More

recent and interpretive studies of rhetoric in Shakespeare, though not of this particular complex, include Marion Trousdale's *Shakespeare and the Rhetoricians* (Chapel Hill: University of North Carolina Press, 1982), and Jane Donawerth, *Shakespeare and the Sixteenth-Century Study of Language* (Urbana: University of Illinois Press, 1984).

14. *Saving the Text* (Baltimore: Johns Hopkins University Press, 1981), especially 131, 145.

15. I have attempted fuller readings of *Othello, All's Well That Ends Well, A Midsummer Night's Dream,* and *The Comedy of Errors* in relation to much wider interpretive resonances of "dilation" within them than can be explored here, in "Anagogic Metaphor: Breaking Down the Wall of Partition," in Eleanor Cook et al., *Centre and Labyrinth: Essays in Honour of Northrop Frye* (Toronto: University of Toronto Press, 1983), 38–50; "Dilation and Delay: Renaissance Matrices," *Poetics Today* 5, no. 3 (1984): 519–35; and "Shakespeare and Rhetoric: 'Dilation' and 'Delation' in *Othello,*" in Patricia Parker and Geoffrey Hartman, eds., *Shakespeare and the Question of Theory* (London: Methuen, 1985), 54–74.

16. Miguel de Cervantes, *Don Quijote de la Mancha,* ed. Martin de Riquer (Barcelona: Editorial Juventud, 1968). Parenthetical references are to Part (1605 and 1615) and chapter. Unless specified, all English translations are from the relevant page in J. M. Cohen's translation of the *Quixote* (Harmondsworth: Penguin, 1950). I am grateful to Timothy Hampton for his assistance, both here and elsewhere in this essay; and to Ruth El Saffar and Diana de Armas Wilson for their invaluable comments on this section.

17. Cave, *Cornucopian Text,* 4–5.

18. On this anxiety in Erasmus, for example, see Thomas M. Greene, "Erasmus's 'Festina lente'," especially 138–41. For a masterful and illuminating study of the larger problem of the relation to origins, see David Quint, *Origin and Originality in Renaissance Literature* (New Haven: Yale University Press, 1983).

19. Seneca, *Ad Lucilium epistulae morales,* tran. R. M. Gummere, 3 vols. (Cambridge: Harvard University Press, 1970), vol. 3, 2–5. The text of the ode is from the edition of C. H. Herford and Percy and Evelyn Simpson, *Ben Jonson,* 11 vols. (Oxford: Clarendon Press, 1925–51), vol. 8. I am grateful to Mary Nyquist for originally calling my attention to the pun. Criticism of the poem that has influenced my own discussion includes Thomas M. Greene's in *The Light in Troy,* 288–91; Ian Donaldson, "Jonson's Ode to Sir Lucius Cary and Sir H. Morison," *Studies in the Literary Imagination* 6, no. 1 (April 1973): 139–52; Richard S. Peterson, *Imitation and Praise in the Poems of Ben Jonson* (New Haven: Yale University Press, 1981), ch. 5; and Paul H. Fry, *The Poet's Calling in the English Ode* (New Haven: Yale University Press, 1980), 15–26.

20. Cave, *Cornucopian Text,* 5, 21, 25.

21. See the entire discussion of these aspects of the plays in relation to Jonson's own fabled size in Robert M. Adams's "On the Bulk of Ben,"

included in his edition of *Ben Jonson's Plays and Masques* (New York: W. W. Norton, 1979).

22. Fry, *Poet's Calling*, 22. I am indebted to Fry's own later discussion of the "schism" within the ode as well. Peterson, *Imitation*, 226–27, also draws a link, though he does not pursue it, between the ode's "Each stiled, by his end, / The Copie of his friend" (111–12) and the complex of "copy" and *copia*.

23. *The Life of Edward Earl of Clarendon . . . written by himself* (Oxford: Clarendon Press, 1827), 1.36.

24. "Poetic Diction and Legal Fiction," in *Essays Presented to Charles Williams* (London: Oxford University Press, 1947).

25. See, for example, Peacham's *Garden of Eloquence*, 123 ff, and the anxieties attendant on dilation as described by Greene in "Erasmus's 'Festina lente'." Insofar as the attempt to control dilation was in part the enterprise of humanism, one direction any investigation of this "excesse" might take might well be an exploration of the misogynist tradition of women's excessive talkativeness or *copia dicendi*. This investigation might start from something like the vernacular mother tongue of Shakespeare's Mistress Quickly in the grammar lesson of *Merry Wives of Windsor* (4.1) and its interference with the closed economy of translation from the *sermo patrius*, Latin, into English and back again—the schoolmaster's pedagogy described by Father Walter Ong in "Latin Language Study as a Renaissance Puberty Rite," *Rhetoric, Romance, and Technology* (Ithaca: Cornell University Press, 1971), 113–41.

10. PSYCHOANALYSIS AND

RENAISSANCE CULTURE

■

STEPHEN GREENBLATT

AN EXPERIENCE recurs in the study of Renaissance literature and culture: an image or text seems to invite, even to demand, a psychoanalytic approach and yet turns out to baffle or elude that approach. The bafflement may only reflect the interpreter's limitations, the melancholy consequence of ignorance or resistance or both. But I will argue here that the mingled invitation and denial has a more historical dimension; the bafflement of psychoanalytic interpretation by Renaissance culture is evident as early as Freud's own suggestive but deeply inadequate attempts to explicate the art of Leonardo, Michelangelo, and Shakespeare. The problem, I suggest, is that psychoanalysis is at once the fulfillment and effacement of specifically Renaissance insights: psychoanalysis is, in more than one sense, the end of the Renaissance.

Let me sketch what I mean by turning not to a literary text but to a series of documents that constitute the historical record of the case of Martin Guerre. This record, part of which formed the basis of a fine historical novel by Janet Lewis, *The Wife of Martin Guerre*, has recently been amplified and analyzed with great power by the historian Natalie Zemon Davis in a short book called *The Return of Martin Guerre* and dramatized in a French film of the same title.[1]

The story is this: Martin Guerre was the only son of a prosperous French peasant who owned and farmed a property near the village of Artigat, in southwestern France. In 1538, at the tender age of 14, Martin was betrothed to Bertrande de Rols—a fine match for the Guerre family—but the marriage was not consummated: Martin was thought to be the victim of sorcery, and his humiliating impotence continued for eight years until the charm was finally lifted by a series of religious rituals. Bertrande became pregnant and gave birth to a son who was given Martin's father's Basque name, Sanxi.

Martin's problems were far from over. In 1548 he seems to have had a terrible quarrel with his father, a quarrel that was almost certainly over the control and management of the family property. Accused by his father of a theft of grain, the troubled young man turned his back on parents, wife, son, and patrimony and disappeared without a trace.

Years passed. Martin's mother and father died, and in the absence of the heir the property was managed by his paternal uncle. Unable to remarry, Bertrande raised her son and waited. Then, in the summer of 1556, Martin Guerre returned. He had wandered across the Pyrenees, become a servant, then enlisted as a soldier and fought in the Spanish wars in the Netherlands. Now he seemed a changed man, kinder and less troubled. There is evidence that his resumed marriage was more loving—recorded gestures of tenderness and concern—and in the three years that followed Bertrande gave birth to two daughters. But there were also signs of strain between himself and his uncle, once again over the family property, and in 1559 this strain erupted into a series of court battles that culminated in the accusation that this was not in fact Martin Guerre but an impostor.

The extraordinary trial that followed had as its purpose the determination of the identity of the man who claimed to be Martin Guerre. Most of the inhabitants of Artigat and many from the surrounding villages were called as witnesses—from Martin's four sisters who testified that the man on trial was in fact their brother, to neighbors and friends who were divided: some upholding his claim, others swearing that he was an impostor, still others refusing to identify the prisoner one way or another. There were rumors, eagerly backed by the uncle's party, that the real Martin Guerre had lost a leg while serving as a soldier. Bertrande officially joined in the uncle's complaint, but in court she refused to swear that the defendant was not Martin Guerre, and she was seen during the period of the trial ministering to her husband, even washing his feet. It appeared either that she had been forced to become a plaintiff against her will or that she hoped that this trial would settle once and for all the question of identity, and hence authority, in her husband's favor. Her husband himself took the stand and recalled in great detail events from his childhood and adolescence that only the real Martin Guerre could have known.

The case dragged on through this trial, at the end of which the prisoner was found guilty, and then through an appeal before the Parlement of Toulouse. Finally, all the evidence had been sifted, and the court prepared its verdict, which seemed likely to be in favor of the accused and against the uncle. At this point, and without warning, a man with a wooden leg appeared in the courtroom. Bitterly upbraiding Bertrande for having dishonored him, the man declared that he was the real Martin Guerre. The accused insisted that this was someone hired by the desperate uncle, but virtually all the witnesses now agreed that the one-legged man was in fact Martin Guerre. After the court found for the uncle, the accused man finally confessed that he was an impostor, one Arnaud du Tilh, alias Pansette. At first, it seems, he had merely intended to take advantage of his striking resemblance to Martin Guerre in order to rob the gullible household, but he had fallen in love with Bertrande and decided to assume forever the missing man's identity. Bertrande herself denied any complicity, but it is difficult to know where else Arnaud would have gone for the intimate family history, and though in Janet Lewis's novel Bertrande only senses gradually and very belatedly that her returned husband is an impostor, Natalie Davis suggests, with considerable plausibility, that the wife would have known almost at once. This certainly seems to have been Martin Guerre's own bitter conclusion.

On September 16, 1560, Arnaud du Tilh knelt barefoot in a white shirt before the church in Artigat, formally repented of his crime, and asked the forgiveness of all whom he had offended. This ritual of penitence completed, he was led to the Guerre house in front of which a gibbet had been erected. Mounting the ladder, he asked Martin Guerre to be kind to Bertrande who had been, he declared, entirely innocent. He asked Bertrande's pardon. Arnaud du Tilh, alias Pansette, was then hanged and his corpse burned.

This case, which interested Montaigne, among others, seems to solicit psychoanalytic interpretation. Surrounded by his four sisters, his nurse, and his mother, betrothed at an unusually early age, and thrust, with the familiar rowdy folk rituals, toward adult sexuality, Martin had great difficulty establishing himself in his masculine identity. He was only able to consummate the marriage after he had radically externalized the psychic threat by imagining that he had been bewitched and by undergoing a ritual cure. And when his masculinity was finally confirmed by the birth of the son to whom he gave his father's name, Martin evidently felt compelled to try to displace his father altogether—with a theft, significantly, of his father's grain, his seed. But the attempt was a disastrous failure: his father responded violently, and Martin faced an assault not merely upon his fragile masculinity, but upon his entire identity, an identity from which in effect he fled.

Not only are Martin's impotence, oedipal transgression, and flight the classic materials of Freudian speculation, but the subsequent trial seems to confirm a principle essential to the constitution of the Freudian subject: the real Martin Guerre cannot be definitively robbed of his identity, even when he has apparently abandoned it and even when its superficial signs have been successfully mimicked by a cunning impostor. To be sure, this principle of inalienable self-possession would appear far indeed from Freud's characteristic concerns: the subject in Freud is most often encountered in states of extreme alienation. Driven by compulsions over which it has little or no control, haunted by repressed desires, shaped by traumatic experiences that it can neither fully recall nor clearly articulate, the self as Freud depicts it is bound up not with secure possession but with instability and loss. Such articulation of identity as exists occurs in states of self-abandonment—in dreams and parapraxes—and the self seems lost not only to others but to the cunning representations of others within the self. No mere judicial procedure, no simple execution of the impostor, could suffice to make restitution for this theft of identity, for the criminal is already ensconced within the psyche of the victim.

Yet the intensity of Freud's vision of alienation would seem, in much of his writing, to depend upon the dream of authentic possession, even if that possession is never realized and has never been securely established. There is nothing radically new about an anthropology based upon the desire for the recovery of what was lost and yet was never actually possessed: it is already subtly articulated in Augustine for whom fallenness is defined in terms of an innocence from which all existing humans, including infants, are by definition excluded. What needs to be posited is not an actual, historical moment of possession, but a virtual possession, a possession that constitutes a structurally determinative pre-history. The hysteric in Freud may be alienated from her own body—earlier centuries would postulate a demonic agent to account for comparable symptoms—but the alienation implies at least a theoretically prior stage of nonalienation. There are in fact moments in Freud in which he appears to glimpse such a stage actually embodied in the regal figure of His Majesty the Infant. And if the historical impact of Freud is bound up with a sustained lese majesty, that is, with an assault on the optimistic assumption of a centered, imperial self, the network of psychoanalytic scandals—the unconscious, repression, infantile sexuality, primary process—nevertheless confirms at least the romantic assumption behind that discredited optimism: the faith that the child is the father of the man and that one's days are bound each to each in biological necessity.

This necessity secures the continuity of the subject, no matter how self-divided or dispersed, so that the Rat Man, for example, is still himself when he is acting under compulsions he does not comprehend. Identity in Freud does not depend upon existential autonomy; it is far more often realized precisely at moments in which the executive agency of the will has been relinquished. Freud's tormented subjects may lose everything, but, as Freud's narrative case studies eloquently attest, they do not and cannot lose a primal, creatural individuation. This irreducible identity is not necessarily a blessing; on the contrary, it most often figures as a burden. Along with the secret of incestuous fantasy, the Oedipus myth discloses the tragic inescapability of continuous selfhood.

We may propose than that in Freud individuation characteristically emerges at moments of risk or alienation and hence that those moments do not so much disrupt as secure authentic identity. And with this perception we may return to Martin Guerre, for the consequence of his self-loss was to trigger a communal inquiry into the authentic Martin Guerre. This inquiry was based upon—or helped to fashion—a communal conviction that there was an authentic Martin Guerre, authentic even (or perhaps especially) in his moments of flight and eclipse. Had the one-legged man never returned, the impostor would nonetheless have remained an actor, forever at one remove from his role. Arnaud du Tilh can manipulate appearances, he can draw the surrounding world into complicity with a strategy of deception, he can improvise the mannerisms and insinuate himself into the complex social network of Martin Guerre, but he cannot seize the other man's inner life. The testimony of the community is important—in the court of law, indispensable—but the roots of Martin's identity lie deeper than society; they reach down, as psychoanalysis would assure us, through the frail, outward memories of his sisters and friends to the psychic experience of his infancy—the infancy only he can possess and that even the most skillful impostor cannot appropriate—and beneath infancy to his biological individuality.

It is here in the body's uniqueness and irreducibility, and in the psychic structures that follow from this primary individuation, that the impostor's project must come to grief. Two bodies cannot occupy the same space at the same time; my body is mine until I die, and no improvisation, however cunning, can ever overturn that elementary possession. The mind can play strange tricks, but the body will not be mocked. Martin's identity is guaranteed by the same bodily principle that guarantees the identity of Freud's patients, twisting away from themselves in a thousand tormenting ways, alienated and abused more cunningly by their own inward ruses than ever Martin was abused by Arnaud, and yet permanently anchored, even to their own horror, in the lived experience of their unique bodily being.

But these latter conclusions, though they are ones with which I myself feel quite comfortable, are not ones drawn either explicitly or implicitly by anyone in the sixteenth century. They are irrelevant to the point of being unthinkable: no one bothers to invoke Martin's biological individuality or even his soul, let alone an infancy that would have seemed almost comically beside the point.[2] This irrelevance need not in itself discourage us—the universalist claims of psychoanalysis are unruffled by the indifference of the past to its categories. It may in any case be argued that we are encountering not indifference but either a technical exclusion of certain postulates from a legal proceeding where they have no standing or a self-evidence so deep and assured that the postulates quite literally go without saying. But I think it is worth noting that the canniest Renaissance observer of the case, Montaigne—also the canniest Renaissance observer of the self—draws conclusions that are quite the opposite to those we have drawn. Far from concluding that the trial vindicates or rests upon Martin Guerre's ultimate and inalienable possession of his own identity—a possession intensified in the experience of self-loss—Montaigne writes that the condemnation of the alleged impostor seemed to him reckless. He would have preferred a still franker version of the verdict that the Areopagites were said to have handed down in perplexing cases: "Come back in a hundred years." For, writes Montaigne, if you are going to execute people, you must have luminously clear evidence—"A tuer les gens, il faut une clarté lumineuse et nette"—and there was no such clarity in the trial of Martin Guerre.[3]

I do not mean to suggest that psychoanalysis by contrast would have supported the execution of Arnaud; on the contrary, by complicating and limiting society's conception of responsibility, psychoanalysis would seem to have made it more difficult to execute convicted murderers, let alone nonviolent impostors. But diminished responsibility is not diminished selfhood; indeed for psychoanalysis the self is at its most visible, most expressive, perhaps most interesting at moments in which the moral will has ceded place to the desires that constitute the deepest stratum of psychic experience. The crucial historical point is that for Montaigne, as for the judge at the trial, Jean de Coras, what is at stake in this case is not psychic experience at all but rather a communal judgment that must, in extraordinary cases, be clarified and secured by legal authority. Martin's body figured prominently in the trial, but not as the inalienable phenomenological base of his psychic history; it figured rather as a collection of attributes—lines, curves, volumes (that is, scars, features, clothing, shoe size, and so on)—that could be held up against anyone who claimed the name and property of Martin Guerre. The move is not from distinct physical traits to the complex life experience generated within, but outward to the community's determination that this particular body possesses by right a particular identity and hence a particular set of possessions. At issue is not Martin Guerre as subject but Martin Guerre as object, the placeholder in a complex system of possessions, kinship bonds, contractual relationships, customary rights, and ethical obligations. Arnaud, the court ruled, had no right to that place, and the state had the obligation to destroy him for trying to seize it. Martin's subjectivity—or, for that matter, Arnaud's or Bertrande's—does not any the less exist, but it seems peripheral, or rather, it seems to be the *product* of the relations, material objects, and judgments exposed in the case rather than the *producer* of these relations, objects, and judgments. If we may glimpse analyzable services—identities that invite deep psychological speculation—these selves seem brought into being by the institutional processes set in motion by Arnaud's imposture. Psychoanalysis is, from this perspective, less the privileged explanatory key than the distant and distorted consequence of this cultural nexus.

In a remarkable essay Leo Spitzer observed years ago that medieval writers seem to have had little or no "concept of intellectual property" and consequently no respect for the integrity or propriety of the first-person pronoun.[4] A medieval writer would incorporate without any apparent concern the experiences of another into his own first-person account; indeed he would assume the "I" of another. In such a discursive system, psychoanalytic interpretation seems to me crippled: it is only when proprietary rights to the self have been secured—rights made most visible, we may add, in moments of self-estrangement or external threat—that the subject of psychoanalysis, both its method and the materials upon which it operates, is made possible. The case of Martin Guerre is, to be sure, a remarkable oddity, and I could scarcely claim that by itself it secured much beyond the early death of a gifted impostor. But I suggest that the accumulation of institutional decisions and communal pressures of the kind revealed there did help to fashion the historical mode of selfhood that psychoanalysis has tried to universalize into the very form of the human condition.

This attempted universalization is not the result of a mere blunder or of overweening hermeneutic ambition, for there exist, after all,

complex forms of self-consciousness and highly discursive person-
hood in the West long before the sixteenth century. The sense of
identity secured in the trial of Arnaud du Tilh has its roots in an
exceedingly rich and ancient tradition, a tradition so dense and
multifaceted that it provokes simultaneously an historiographical
paralysis and an interpretive license. The judicial decision to termi-
nate the life of a man who has tried to assume the identity of another
is a tiny episode in a vast history, a history without convenient
narrative lines, with too many precedents, with a bewildering network of contributing and limiting factors: theology, philosophy, law,
social ritual, family customs. It is deeply tempting in the face of such
a history to assume that it is, in effect, no history at all, that the self is
at its core a stable point of reference, a given upon which to construct interpretations, psychoanalytic or other. Such interpretations
based upon a fixed value of identity offer the intellectual gratifica-
tion—consoling in the face of a frightening accumulation of traces
from the past or from other societies or from the dark corners of our
own lands—of a totalizing comprehension, a harmonious vision of
the whole.

But this unitary vision is achieved, as Natalie Davis's book makes
clear, only by repressing history, or, more accurately, by repressing
histories—multiple, complex, refractory stories. Such stories become, in effect, decorative incidents, filigrees enchased on the surface of a solid and single truth, or (in subtler versions) interesting
variants on the central and irreducible universal narrative, the timeless master myth.

But what if we refuse the lure of a totalizing vision? The alternative frequently proposed is a relativism that refuses to privilege
one narrative over another, that celebrates the uniqueness of each
cultural moment. But this stance—akin to congratulating both the
real and the pretended Martin Guerre for their superb performances—is not, I think, either promising or realistic. For thorough-
going relativism has a curious resemblance to the universalizing
that it proposes to displace: both are uncomfortable with histories.
Histories threaten relativism, though they seem superficially allied,
because the connections and ruptures with which historians are
concerned sort ill with the unorganized, value-neutral equivalences
that would allow each moment a perfect independence and autonomy. The power of the story of Martin Guerre, as Natalie Davis helps
us understand, lies not in an absolute otherness that compels us to
suspend all our values in the face of an entirely different system of
consciousness, but rather in the intimations of an obscure link between those distant events and the way we are. The actual effect of

relativism is not to achieve a perfect ethical neutrality—as if we could cleanly bracket all our beliefs and lift ourselves off our moral world—but to block a disconcerting recognition: that our identity may not originate in (or be guaranteed by) the fixity, the certainty, of our own body.

But if we reject both the totalizing of a universal mythology and the radical particularizing of relativism, what are we left with? We are left with a network of lived and narrated stories, practices, strategies, representations, fantasies, negotiations, and exchanges that, along with the surviving aural, tactile, and visual traces, fashion our experience of the past, of others, and of ourselves. The case of Martin Guerre offers, in this context, neither a universal myth nor a perfectly unique and autonomous event; it is a peculiarly *Renaissance* story, the kind of story that the age told itself in a thousand variations over and over again. The point of this telling is not to confirm a truth always and already known, nor—as the fate of Arnaud poignantly exemplifies—is the telling without consequences: in the judicial murder of the impostor we witness in tiny compass part of the process that secures our concept of individual existence. That existence depends upon institutions that limit and, when necessary, exterminate a threatening mobility; the secure possession of one's body is not the *origin* of identity but one of the consequences of the compulsive cultural stabilizing unusually visible in this story.

It is important to characterize the case of Martin Guerre as a *story* not only in order to acknowledge the way that a record of these particular lives, out of so many millions lost to our view, managed to survive in the sixteenth-century narratives of Jean de Coras and Montaigne and the twentieth-century narratives of Janet Lewis, Natalie Davis, Jean-Claude Carrière, and Daniel Vigne, but also in order to make the crucial connection between this relatively obscure, local series of events and the larger historical process in which they participate. For it is in stories—above all, literary fantasies—produced and consumed by those who had never heard of Martin Guerre, that the issues raised by his case escape their immediate territorial and cultural boundaries and receive their fullest rehearsal, elaboration, and exploration. And conversely, the trial and execution of Arnaud du Tilh enables us to understand aspects of the social significance of these literary fantasies that would otherwise remain obscure.

Jean de Coras's account of the Guerre case was not translated into English nor did Montaigne's brief recounting have substantial impact, but sixteenth- and seventeenth-century English writers invented, in effect, dozens of versions of this story. The drama is particularly rich in such versions, from the larcenous impersonation of the missing husband in John Marston's play, *What You Will*, to the romantic impersonations in Beaumont and Fletcher's tragicomedies, from Perkin Warbeck's regal pretentions in John Ford's play of that name to the sleazy tricks of Ben Jonson's rogues. ("But were they gulled / With a belief that I was Scoto?" asks Volpone. "Sir," replies the parasite Mosca, "Scoto himself could hardly have distinguished.") Above all, there are the instances of imposture and loss of personal moorings in Shakespeare: the buffoonery of the false Vincentio in *The Taming of the Shrew*, the geometry of the paired twins in *The Comedy of Errors*, the more impassioned geometry of *Twelfth Night*. Even when there is no malicious, accidental, or natural double, Shakespeare's characters are frequently haunted by the sense that their identity has been lost or stolen: "Who is it that can tell me who I am?" crieds the anguished Lear. And in the most famous of the tragedies, the ghost of Old Hamlet—"Of life, of crown, of queen at once dispatched"—returns to his land to demand that his son take the life of the impostor who has seized his identity.

Not by accident is it in the drama that this exploration of the issue at stake in the trial of Arnaud du Tilh is most intense, for the form of the drama itself invites reflection upon the extent to which it is possible for one man to assume the identity of another. Every theatrical performance at once confirms and denies this possibility: confirms it with varying degrees of success depending upon the skill of the actor and denies it because that skill is itself perceived by virtue of the small but unbridgeable distance between the actor's real and fictive identity. All Renaissance drama is in this sense a playful enactment of the case of Martin Guerre: a convincing impersonation before a large audience that is complicit with the deception only to bear witness at the close to the imposture's end. In some instances the impersonation seemed less playful, more dangerous than others: powerful noblemen complained that they were themselves being represented on stage, and they successfully sought a legal prohibition of the miming of living notables. But even with fictive or long-dead characters, the drama continually celebrates the mystery of Arnaud's art: the successful insertion of one individual into the identity of another. And inevitably this celebration is at the same time an anatomy, an exposing to view of the mechanisms of imposture. What is entirely unacceptable—indeed punishable by death in the everyday world—is both instructive and delightful in spaces specially marked off for the exercise of impersonation. For in these spaces, and only in these spaces, there is by a widely shared social agreement no imposture.

It is no accident too that in virtually all of these plays—and there are other instances in Shakespeare's work and the work of his contemporaries—the intrigue that arises from the willed or accidental mistaking of one person for another centers on property and proper names: purse and person are here inseparably linked as they were in the parish records that began to be kept systematically in England only in the sixteenth century. Henry VIII's insatiable craving for money to finance his military adventures abroad and his extravagances at home led him to exact the so-called Loan of 1522, which was based upon a survey undertaken at royal command earlier that year. The survey, whose financial objectives were kept secret, required authorities in the land to certify in writing the names of all the men above the age of sixteen and "whom they belong to." They were to record as well "who is the lord of every town and hamlet . . . who be parsons of the same towns, and what the benefices be worth by the year . . . also who be the owners of every parcel of land within any town, hamlet, parish, or village . . . with the year value of every man's land within the same."[5] The secrecy built into the survey—for were its purpose known, there would have been widespread evasion and concealment—had the effect of naturalizing the relationship between name and wealth. A man's goods were to be recorded not for the specific purpose of taxation but for the general purpose of identification: to enable the kingdom to know itself and hence to know its resources and its strength.

To the momentous survey of 1522 must be added an innovation less immediately spectacular but in the long run more important: the parish records that Cromwell instituted in 1538.[6] The parish chest, which is for demography what the Renaissance English theater is for literary history, signals, along with other innovative forms of Tudor record-keeping, a powerful official interest in identity and property, and identity *as* property. Precisely this interest is voiced, tested, and deepened throughout Shakespeare's career. It is often said, with a sense of irony and resignation, that though we possess a surprising amount of documentary evidence about Shakespeare's life, virtually none of it is of real significance for an understanding of his plays, for most of the surviving documents are notarial records of real estate transactions. I think property may be closer to the wellsprings of the Shakespearean conception of identity than we imagine.

Shakespeare and his contemporaries, to be sure, knew the difference between a complex individual and what the Norwegian captain in *Hamlet* calls "a little patch of ground / That hath in it no profit but the name." Yet I think that in all the literary instances I have cited, identity is conceived in a way that renders psychoanalytic interpretations marginal or belated. For what most matters in the literary texts, as in the documents that record the case of Martin Guerre, are communally secured proprietary rights to a name and a place in an increasingly mobile social world, and these rights seem more an historical condition that enables the development of psychoanalysis than a psychic condition that psychoanalysis itself can adequately explain.

In Renaissance drama, as in the case of Martin Guerre, the traditional linkages between body, property, and name are called into question; looking back upon the theatrical and judicial spectacle, one can glimpse the early stages of the slow, momentous transformation of the middle term from "property" to "psyche."[7] But that transformation had by no means already occurred; it was on the contrary the result (not yet perfectly realized in our own time) of a prolonged series of actions and transactions. The consequence, I think, is that psychoanalytic interpretation seems to follow upon rather than to explain Renaissance texts. If psychoanalysis was, in effect, made possible by (among other things) the legal and literary proceedings of the sixteenth and seventeenth centuries, then its interpretive practice is not irrelevant to those proceedings, nor is it exactly an anachronism. But psychoanalytic interpretation is causally belated, even as it is causally linked: hence the curious effect of a discourse that functions *as if* the psychological categories it invokes were not only simultaneous with but even prior to and themselves causes of the very phenomena of which in actual fact they were the results. I do not propose that we abandon the attempts at psychologically deep readings of Renaissance texts; rather, in the company of literary criticism and history, psychoanalysis can redeem its belatedness only when it historicizes its own procedures.

There are interesting signs of this historicizing—perhaps most radically in the school of Hegelian psychoanalysis associated with the work of Jacques Lacan, where identity is always revealed to be the identity of another, always registered (as in those parish registers) in language. But I want to end with a glance at a much earlier and still powerful attempt to formulate an historical conception of the self, an attempt that significantly locates the origins of this conception in language and more specifically in literary practice.

"A PERSON," writes Hobbes,

is he whose words or actions are considered, either as his own, or as
representing the words or actions of an other man, or of any other
thing to whom they are attributed, whether Truly or by Fiction. When
they are considered as his owne, then is he called a Naturall Person:
And when they are considered as representing the words and actions
of another, then is he a Feigned or Artificiall person. The word Person
is latine . . . as *Persona* in latine signifies the *disguise*, or *outward appearance* of a man, counterfeited on the stage; and sometimes more
particularly that part of it, which disguiseth the face, as a Mask or
Visard: And from the Stage, hath been translated to any Representer
of speech and action, as well in Tribunalls, as Theaters. So that a
Person is the same that an *Actor* is, both on the Stage and in common
Conversation.[8]

Psychoanalysis will in effect seize upon the concept of a "natural
person" and will develop that concept into a brilliant hermeneutical
system centered upon stripping away layers of strategic displacement that obscure the self's underlying drives. But in Hobbes the
"natural person" originates in the "artificial person"—the mask,
the character on a stage "translated" from the theater to the tribunal.
There is no layer deeper, more authentic, than theatrical self-representation. This conception of the self does not deny the importance
of the body—all consciousness for Hobbes derives from the body's
responses to external pressure—but it does not anchor personal
identity in an inalienable biological continuity. The crucial consideration is ownership: what distinguishes a "natural" person from an
"artificial" person is that the former is considered to *own* his words
and actions. Considered by whom? By authority. But is authority
itself then natural or artificial? In a move that is one of the cor-
nerstones of Hobbes's absolutist political philosophy, authority is
vested in an artificial person who represents the words and actions
of the entire nation. All men therefore are impersonators of themselves, but impersonators whose clear title to identity is secured by
an authority irrevocably deeded to an artificial person. A great mask
allows one to own as one's own face another mask.

If we conceive of a mask (as psychoanalysis has, in effect, taught
us) as a defensive strategy, a veneer hiding the authentic self beneath, then Hobbes's conception must seem brittle and inadequate.
But for Hobbes there is no person, no coherent, enduring identity,
beneath the mask; strip away the theatrical role and you reach either
a chaos of unformed desire that must be tamed to ensure survival or
a dangerous assembly of free thoughts ("because thought is free,"
3.37.478) that must—again to ensure survival—remain unspoken.
Identity is only possible as a mask, something constructed and as-

sumed, but this need not imply that identity so conceived is a sorry business. In our culture masks are trivial objects for children to play with and discard, and theatrical roles have the same air of pasteboard insubstantiality. But this is not always and everywhere the case; a man who lived in the shadow of Shakespeare might have had a deeper sense of what could be counterfeited on the stage or represented before a tribunal. In his conception of a person as a theatrical mask secured by authority, Hobbes seems far closer than Freud to the world of Shakespeare and, of course, Arnaud du Tilh.

Appendix

The social fabrication of identity is, I have argued, particularly marked in the drama where, after all, identity is fashioned out of public discourse, and even soliloquies tend to take the form of rhetorical declamations. But nondramatic literature is, in its own way, deeply involved in the prepsychoanalytic fashioning of the proprietary rights of selfhood. Thus even in *The Faerie Queene,* where property seems to be absorbed altogether into the landscape of the mind, Spenser's concern with psychic experience is not manifested in the representation of a particular individual's inner life but rather in the representation of the hero's externalized struggle to secure clear title to his allegorical attributes and hence to his name. If that struggle is itself a vision of the inner life, it is one that suggests that for Spenser the psyche can only be conceived as a dangerous, factionalized social world, a world of vigilance, intrigue, extreme violence, and brief, fragile moments of intense beauty—just such a world as Spenser the colonial administrator inhabited in Ireland.

What does it mean that Spenser looks deep within himself and images that realm as eerily like the outward realm in which he bustled? It means that for him the noblest representation of the inner life is not lyric but epic—hence the compulsion of Spenserean characters to secure their identity by force of arms. And it means too that even the most well-defended existence is extremely vulnerable to fraud—identity may be imitated, misused, falsely appropriated, as Arnaud du Tilh appropriated the name and property and wife of Martin Guerre.

Evil in *The Faerie Queene* has its large-boned, athletic champions, but its most dangerous agents are the impostors, those who have the power to assume with uncanny accuracy all the signs of virtue. Thus when the subtle Archimago wishes to divide the Red Cross Knight from his beloved Una, truth's allegorical embodiment, he contrives "the person to put on / Of that good knight." "And when

he sate vpon his courser free," Spenser concludes, "*Saint George*
himself ye would haue deemed him to be." The disguise is suffi-
ciently effective to take in Una herself—even truth cannot unmask a
perfect falsehood—and the impostor's identity is only revealed after
he is half-killed by the pagan Sansloy. Conversely, Red Cross's own
identity—his name—is only revealed to him when he too has undergone the trials that belong to the signs he wears. And that name,
first disclosed to the reader as the identity that Archimago falsely
assumed, is paradoxically disclosed late in the poem to Red Cross as
his true origin, an origin he can only possess at the *end* of his quest.

With the idea of an origin that is only conferred upon one at the
end of a series of actions and transactions, I return to the notion that
psychoanalysis is the historical outcome of certain characteristic Renaissance strategies.

Notes

1. Natalie Zemon Davis, *The Return of Martin Guerre* (Cambridge: Harvard
   University Press, 1983). Davis's text was originally published in French,
   together with a "recit romanesque" written by the film's screenwriter and
   director, Jean-Claude Carrière and Daniel Vigne (*Le Retour de Martin
   Guerre* [Paris: Robert Laffont, 1982]).
2. The only conspicuous religious element in the story is at best equivocal:
   Bertrande and the false Martin Guerre apparently frequented a Protestant
   conventicle. Natalie Davis speculates that the couple may have been seeking, in the Protestant ethos of the companionate marriage, a kind of
   ehtical validation of their deception.
3. Montaigne, "Des boyteux" [Of Cripples], in *Essais*, ed. Maurice Rat, 2
   vols. (Paris: Garnier, 1962), 2:478–79.
4. Leo Spitzer, "Notes on the Empirical and Poetic 'I' in Medieval Authors,"
   Traditio 4 (1946): 414–22.
5. Quoted in W. G. Hoskins, *The Age of Plunder: King Henry's England, 1500–
   1547* (London: Longman, 1976), 20–21.
6. See William E. Tate, *The Parish Chest: A Study of the Records of Parochial
   Administration in England* (Cambridge: Cambridge University Press,
   1946).
7. It is important to grasp that this transformation is at once a revolution and
   a continuation; "psyche" is neither a mere mystification for "property"
   nor a radical alternative to it.
8. Thomas Hobbes, *Leviathan*, ed. C. B. Macpherson (NY: Penquin, 1968,
   1.16.217.

11. JOHN SKELTON
AND THE POETICS OF
PRIMITIVE ACCUMULATION

∎

RICHARD HALPERN

I

DEFYING the best efforts of critics, John Skelton has valiantly resisted all attempts to provide him a secure place within the English literary canon. Even among minor Renaissance poets he remains quirky and marginalized, partly because of the conjunction of attributes that led Alexander Pope to dub him "beastly." The satires display a brutish energy for obscure vituperation while *The Tunning of Eleanor Rumming* is a paradigm of what Mikhail Bakhtin termed "grotesque realism": swine, hags, chickens, feces, snot, drool, and ale fly about and combine in every conceivable fashion. C. S. Lewis compared Skelton's distinctive meter with "the form used by every clown scribbling on the wall in an inn yard."[1]

In the end, though, Skelton's disturbance of historical, not biological, species has caused the most trouble. Lewis insists that Skelton "has no real predecessors and no important disciples; he stands outside of the streamy historical process, an unmistakable individual, a man we have met" (143). More specifically, Skelton cannot be fitted within the scheme of cultural periodization which characterizes traditional literary history. Ian Gordon delineated the problem in his 1943 study when he wrote that "Skelton fell between two periods, the receding Middle Ages and the advancing Renaissance, without being a part of either."[2] Reverting, Pope-like, to the vocabulary of the monstrous, Gordon calls Skelton "a Mr. Facing-Both-Ways," adding that "seldom has a poet borne the marks of a transition age so clearly as Skelton."[3] His position as a missing link has no doubt contributed to Skelton's relative obscurity, since neither the

Renaissance nor the medieval "camp" feels quite comfortable in adopting him.

Lewis and Gordon ascribe Skelton's historical unassimilability partly to his perverse and obstreperous individualism (as though one could transcend history by sheer force of will or personality), partly to the "transitional" nature of his historical moment. I shall concentrate primarily on this latter aspect, because the terms in which the problem of Skelton has been posed tell us less about the poet himself than about the inadequacy of certain schemes of cultural periodization.

Interestingly, the articulation of the problem has changed very little since Gordon's day. In *John Skelton's Poetry* (1965), Stanley Fish nuances Gordon's formulation but does not fundamentally alter it:

> Skelton's poetry gives us neither the old made new nor the new made old, but a statement of the potentiality for disturbance of the unassimilated. It is a poetry which could only have been written between 1498 and 1530, when the intrusive could no longer be ignored as Lydgate had ignored it and before it would become part of a new and difficult stability as it would after 1536.[4]

Once again Skelton occupies a kind of historical vacuum, and once again (as it had for Lewis) this shifts the focus of attention from the historical to the subjective: "[W]e shall examine a poetry in which the accidents of history provide the raw material for a drama which is essentially interior."[5]

While Gordon describes Skelton as bearing "the marks of a transition age," both he and later critics find it difficult to formulate the concept of transition, if by this we mean a passage, development, or mediation from one historical stage to another. What they call transition is actually a gap between the end of medieval poetry (ca. 1480) and the beginning of Renaissance poetry (ca. 1536). Fish's chronology has a certain local validity, to which I shall turn, but I would argue that the temporal hiatus he posits is really the displacement of a *theoretical* gap, specifically the inability to theorize a transition.

This in turn results from the empiricist periodizations that the transition must bridge; without a theory of history, critics can only list sets of empirical phenomena whose unarticulated conjunctions are dubbed "medieval" on the one hand, "Renaissance" on the other. Thus the lyric poetry of the later Middle Ages is marked by scholasticism, the formalism of late medieval rhetoric, and an otherworldly, devotional stance, while Renaissance poetry arises from the influence of humanism, the reinvigoration of classical rhetoric, and an interest in the secular. On this level the gap described by Fish does appear; he brilliantly describes Skelton's partial break from a rhetorical tradition that was largely played out, as well as his ambivalence toward a humanism that at that time was emergent but not yet dominant in England.

The barrier to conceptualizing this transition entirely from within literary history, however, is the fact that the dominant structuring forces of the transition are not to be found within literary history but rather in the larger sociohistorical field. Gordon adjoins cultural developments to political, economic, and social ones—the rise of a wealthy commercial class, the consolidation of absolutist monarchy, the Reformation—but these elements merely contribute to a larger *series*, not to a complexly articulated totality. Not only is the problem of transition unresolvable under these conditions, but history itself tends to atomize into what Fish calls "accidents."

In reality, then, Skelton reveals the scandal of literary history, not the other way around. To begin to come to terms with his poetry thus requires us to formulate a history that can accommodate him. This does *not* mean to reduce him, to eradicate his genuine originality in conformity to an iron law, to find a history of which he is the "normal" expression. It means to construct a field against which the eccentricity of his productions can at least be mapped and understood. For history, like nature, abhors a vacuum; the same movement that eliminates the gap between historical "periods" will also eliminate that other (and not unrelated) gap between empirical or "accidental" history and an individual subject conceived as the site of a monadic, interiorized drama.

II

The local and practical task of describing Skelton's transitional poetics has as its necessary condition, then, the construction of an adequate concept of the transition itself. Clearly Skelton stands on the brink of that major cultural revolution we know as the Renaissance. Yet this is in turn situated within a larger and more fundamental historical process: the transition from the feudal to the capitalist modes of production, which Marx described as a process of "primitive accumulation":

> The capital-relation presupposes a complete separation between the workers and the ownership of the conditions for the realization of their labor. As soon as capitalist production stands on its own two feet, it not only maintains this relation but reproduces it on a constantly expanding scale. The process, therefore, which creates the capital-relation can

be nothing other than the process which divorces the worker from the ownership of the conditions of his own labor; it is a process which operates two transformations, whereby the social means of subsistence and production are turned into capital, and the immediate producers are turned into wage-laborers. So-called primitive accumulation, therefore, is nothing else than the historical process of divorcing the producer from the means of production. It appears as 'primitive' because it forms the pre-history of capital, and of the mode of production corresponding to capital.

The economic structure of capitalist society has grown out of the economic structure of feudal society. The dissolution of the latter set free the elements of the former.[6]

In short, "primitive accumulation" denotes the process by which the feudal petty producer was converted into the "free" wage laborer, that is, freed from the politico-juridical bonds of feudal relations, but also separated from the means of production by which he could support himself. The story by which this was accomplished— the deracination of the peasantry by enclosure, engrossment, and the commutation of dues, the destruction of the petty artisan by usurer's capital and merchant oligarchies—is too familiar to need recounting here. So is the story of the other half of primitive accumulation: how merchant's and usurer's capital created a concentrated hoard of money that could be used to hire the newly proletarianized workers as wage labor.[7] As Marx makes clear, however, the process of primitive accumulation does not stand between two modes of production; rather it creates the *elements* of capitalist production from within the *structures* of feudalism.[8] Primitive accumulation is in this sense nothing other than late feudalism, distinguished primarily by a large-scale monetarization of the feudal economy.[9]

The spread of money relations under late feudalism led to what Gilles Deleuze and Felix Guattari have termed the "deterritorialization" of the feudal party.[10] Perry Anderson describes the effects of this process on the state:

> Feudalism as a mode of production was originally defined by an organic *unity* of economy and polity, paradoxically distributed in a chain of parcellized sovereignties throughout the social formation. The institution of serfdom as a mechanism of surplus extraction fused economic exploitation and politico-legal coercion at the molecular level of the village. The lord in his turn typically owed liege loyalty and knight service to the seignurial overlord, who claimed the land as his ultimate domain. With the generalized commutation of dues into money rents, the cellular unity of political and economic oppression of the peasantry was gravely weakened, and threatened to become dissociated (the end

of this road was "free labor" and the "wage contract"). The class power of the feudal lords was thus directly at stake with the gradual disappearance of serfdom. The result was a *displacement* of politico-legal coercion upwards towards a centralized, militarized summit—the Absolutist State. Diluted at the village level, it became concentrated at the "national" level.[11]

If the overcoding[12] of local feudal jurisdiction by the state was, in one sense, the outcome of conflicts within the feudal nobility, it was in another sense a way of centralizing feudal exploitation. By deterritorializing the feudal polity, the absolutist state produced a *"redeployed and recharged apparatus of feudal domination,* designed to clamp the peasant masses back into their traditional social position."[13] In England this process was accomplished by the Tudor and Stuart dynasties, beginning with Henry VII's "primitive accumulation" of state power after the Wars of the Roses.[14]

At this same time, moreover, the spread of feudal commerce and merchant's capital dissolved local and particularistic barriers to trade. The development of commodity production tended to decode[15] productive relations and further deterritorialize the polity, though within strict limits set by the dominant (feudal) relations of production.[16] Together with the overcoding operations of the state (with which it was allied), merchant's capital effected what we may call a primary deterritorialization of the feudal polity. While it could not, and did not seek to, totally dissolve the parcellized sovereignty that characterized feudalism, it reorganized feudal territories within an increasingly unified economic field and thus complemented the overcoding operations of the state which subjected these territories to a unified legal and political apparatus. The period of primitive accumulation thus laid the groundwork for the fuller deterritorialization that would accompany the dominance of industrial capital.

III

Comparing the beginning of Skelton's life, sometime around 1460, with its end in 1529 helps to measure the pace of transition during this period. Actually, Skelton's life lacks an origin, at least one that is accessible to us. The problem arises not from a dearth of documents on John Skelton, but from an abundance of them: "Systematic inquiry reveals about two hundred and fifty Skeltons during the fourteenth and fifteenth centuries, of whom one hundred or so are named John. Some twenty of these are found in London in the poet's time, about half a dozen in the neighborhood of the court."[17]

This documentary excess of Skeltons, none of whom can be conclusively identified with the poet, may be taken as emblematic of the
fragmented, incomplete, and parceled condition of the contemporary administrative machinery. But it is not just that the real John
Skelton has eluded identification; in a certain historical sense he
really does not exist. For the centralized apparatus that will definitively record the identity of its subjects also *produces* this identity in a
new way. The administered subject is not just the trace or recording
of a prior subject. It is a new thing.[18]

Identification of Skelton's birth, or lack of same, contrasts profita-
bly with the traditional account of his death in 1529—at Westminster, where he sought sanctuary from the state he had so fearlessly
ridiculed in his later satires.[19] The Church, of course, had had its
own autonomous and sovereign "parcels" within the feudal polity,
of which the right of sanctuary was an expression.[20] But even as
Skelton wrote satires against him, Cardinal Wolsey was trying to
dissolve the power of sanctuary within the extended sovereignty of
the absolutist state.[21]

> For all privileged places
> He brekes and defaces,
> All placis of relygion
> He hathe them in derisyon.
> (1089–92)[22]

So wrote Skelton in *Why Come Ye Not to Court?* (1522). In the final
section of *Speak Parrot* (1521?), where Parrot is urged to "speke now
trew and plaine," he lets fly a catalogue of abuses which situates the
violation of sanctuary within the political and economic processes of
primitive accumulation:

> So many thevys hangyd, and thevys neverthelesse;
> So myche presonment, for matyrs not worth a hawe;
> So mych papers werying for ryghte a smalle exesse;
> So myche pelory pajauntes undyr colowur of good lawe;
> So myche towrnyng on the cooke-stole for every guy-gaw;
> So myche mokkkyshe makyng of statutes of array—
> Syns Dewcalyons flodde was nevyr, I dar sey.
>
> So many trusys takyn, and so lytyll perfyte throwthe;
> So myche bely-joye, and so wastefull banketyng;
> So pynchyng and sparyng, and so lytell profyte growth;
> So many howgye howsys byldyng, and so small howse-holdyng;
> Such statues apon diettes, suche pyllyng and pollyng—
> ....
>
> So many vacabones, so many beggers bolde,

So myche decay of monesteries and relygious places;
So hote hatered agaynste the Chyrche, and cheryte so colde;
So myche of my lordes grace, and in hym no grace ys;
So many holow hartes, and so dowbill faces;
So myche sayntuary brekyng, and prevylegidde barryd—
Syns Dewcalyons flodde was nevyr sene nor lyerd.
                    (477–83, 491–95, 498–504)

Like some later critics, Skelton juxtaposes rather than articulates the
social transformations at work in his day. Yet a certain logic of adja-
cency connects the violation of sanctuary with the proliferation of
Tudor laws, and furthermore connects these developments with an
increasing concentration of wealth. Parrot's speech recalls Raphael
Hythlodaeus's anatomy of abuses in Book 1 of Thomas More's *Utopia*, but here the focus of analysis is more ethical than social. For
Parrot (and Skelton), these social phenomena are bound together by
the moral category of "excess"—excessive wealth, poverty, power,
pride—and the resultant politics are therefore conservative, consisting primarily of a desire to restore the restraint and reciprocity
that characterized feudal social relations. Yet even while it displaces
social contradictions onto an ethical space, the category of "excess"
allows the social process to be grasped as a totality, albeit an ideological and expressive one. The tentacular reach of "excess" enables
Skelton to conceive, in at least a rudimentary way, of a globalized
process of primitive accumulation.

But the topical politics of the later satires, interesting as they are,
are not my primary concern here. For the process of deterritorialization, which reaches an explicit crisis for Skelton in the sanctuary
question, informs even his nonpolitical works. Political topography
forms a subtext against which all of Skelton's poetical practice defines itself, and this practice in turn generates a politics that does not
entirely coincide with his explicitly stated beliefs, but rather provides a radical and utopian counterpoint to them.

IV

While this essay will focus primarily on *Phillip Sparrow*, unquestionably one of Skelton's masterpieces, we will enter that work by way
of another, "companion" poem. *Ware the Hawk* was composed while
Skelton was rector at Diss, presumably around the time when he
wrote *Phillip Sparrow* (1505?). This period witnessed Skelton's peculiar and somewhat inexplicable "break" with the conventional for-
mulas of late medieval lyric. Ian Gordon wrote that "With the

232 RICHARD HALPERN

change from London to the country parish came a revolution in Skelton's thought and poetry":

> The respected priest, courtier and royal schoolmaster broke out into the most disrespectful of verses and continued on his outspoken way for almost a couple of decades, undeterred by criticism or disparagement, writing with the fervour of a man who had at last found a mission in life. It was as if the headmaster of Eton turned to Communist pamphleteering.[23]

Gordon's witticism, I think, has a figural logic that exceeds its intent. Like the pamphleteering headmaster, Skelton ludicrously betrays his social class, and in so doing seems to leap forward into an as-yet nonexistent social formation; or rather, drags it back into his own, with all the scandal that inevitably attends prophecy. The reasons for Skelton's "conversion" remain obscure. Maurice Pollet suggests that Skelton was dissatisfied at being sent from the royal court at London to the "backwater" of Diss. Perhaps, then, the break resulted from Skelton's experience of having his social mobility rerouted by the state machine.[24] In any case, the break was neither final nor definitive. Skelton remained an enthusiastic supporter of Henry's imperial policies, crowed after the suppression of the Scots rebellion, and took a vain delight in his titles of *orator regius* and poet laureate. Nevertheless, his poetry shows a new strain that will culminate in the satires against Wolsey and the court.

Ware the Hawk, which exemplifies the beginnings of Skelton's distinctive poetic, describes and denounces the actions of a neighboring priest who becomes so involved in hawking that he pursues his prey right into Skelton's church at Diss. There the hawks tear a pigeon apart on the holy altar and defecate on the communion cloth, while the priest himself overturns the offering box, cross, and lectern. The poem vents its rage at the desecration of holy places while flinging both crude and pedantic insults at the offending priest.

Ware the Hawk directs its anger at an act of profanation which it understands primarily as the violation of a boundary or territory; it condemns those who

> playe the daw
> To hawke, or els to hunt
> From the auter to the funt,
> Wyth cry unreverent,
> Before the sacrament,
> Wythin the holy church bowndis,
> That of our fayth the grownd is.
> (8–14)

Skelton's church is, of course, the literal as well as the metaphorical "ground" of faith; the hawking priest offends not only because he has intruded on divine territory, but because he has intruded on Skelton's territory.[25] I do not wish to suggest that the concept of the holy place merely expresses property rights, either for Skelton or in general. But the sanctity of the medieval church, which was articulated within the feudal structure of parcellized sovereignty, represents Skelton's primary experience of this structure, its ideological paradigm.[26] Certainly the violation of the Church's boundaries in *Ware the Hawk* seems to threaten its sovereignty:

> Or els is thys Goddis law,
>
> Thus within the wals
> Of holy church to deale,
> Thus to ryng a peale
> With his hawkys bels?
> Dowtles such losels
> Make the church to be
> In smal auctoryte.
>   (130, 134–40)

For Skelton, the whole hierarchical taxonomy of late medieval culture is interwritten with the Church's territorial sanctity. When this is broken, all other structures collapse like a house of cards.[27]

None of this, however, is particularly novel in itself. The interest of Skelton's poem arises from its formal reaction to the trespass. For *Ware the Hawk* responds to the violation of a politico-religious territory by subjecting itself to a strict rhetorical territoriality. The poem is meticulously constructed according to what Stanley Fish aptly calls the "machinery of the artes praedicandi." After a formal exordium (*prologus*), "the text is punctuated by eight hortatory exclamations (*Observate, Deliberate, Vigilate, Deplorate, Divinitate*—probably for *Divinate—Reformate*, and *Pensitate*) which correspond to the development of the *thema* as taught in the manuals."[28] The conspicuous rhetorical formalism of the poem clearly represents a kind of reaction formation to the disturbance of the church's boundaries; the anarchic trajectory of the hawk finds its answering principle in an exaggerated movement of reterritorialization by the poet, thereby producing a striking—and, for Skelton, characteristic—cohesion between political and rhetorical topographies. This coincidence of spaces produces brilliant formal effects in *Phillip Sparrow* and offers the privileged means by which Skelton transcodes history into literature.

But an additional element transforms the nature of the poem's

process: *Ware the Hawk* is "a burlesque in the Chaucerian tradition."
Both the incident itself and Skelton's indignation are highly ironized; despite its obsessive formalism, the poem's rhetoric constantly
undercuts itself, thereby dissolving the seriousness of the priest's
offense.[29] Thus, we may add, the poem's defensive reterritorialization is also ironic, or at least ambivalent. A gay destructiveness in
Ware the Hawk delights in the violation of boundaries and in the
consequent evaporation of the authority constituted by them. Skelton's imagination both enjoys and extends the profanities committed by the neighboring priest, who, the poet claims,

> wysshed withall
> That the dowves donge downe myght fall
> Into my chalys at mas,
> When consecrated was
> The blessyd sacrament.
> (182–86)

The pleasurable onomatopoeia of "dowves donge downe" exemplifies the festive counterlogic of the poem, which can enjoy the
pollution even of that final cultural territory, the blessed sacra-
ment.[30] It is as if Skelton had marshaled the forces of rhetorical
territoriality in a mock-defensive gesture, the better to overthrow *all*
boundaries in one totalizing motion.

V

Like *Ware the Hawk, Phillip Sparrow* is set in a chapel and concerns a
bird whose presence disrupts the sanctity of the church. The first
part of the poem takes place at Carrow Abbey, where Jane Scrope, a
young woman, composes a fanciful elegy for her pet sparrow.[31]
Against the backdrop of the Vespers of the Office of the Dead, Jane
produces a rambling discourse, sometimes reminiscing about Phillip—their physical intimacies, his endearing habits, his death at the
hands (or paws) of Gib the cat—sometimes engaging in reveries that
arise from his death (she imagines Phillip's journey to the classical
underworld, organizes a fanciful bird mass for him, tries to write a
Latin epitaph). Parallels in theme and content suffice to suggest that
the poem continues the project of *Ware the Hawk,* particularly with
regard to the question of rhetorical territoriality. Lewis's evaluation
of the poem is pertinent:

> It is indeed the lightest—the most like a bubble—of all the poems I
> know. It would break at a touch: but hold your breath, watch it, and it is
> almost perfect. The Skeltonics are essential to its perfection. Their

prattling and hopping and their inconsequence, so birdlike and so childlike, are the best possible embodiment of the theme. We should not, I think, refuse to call the poem great.[32]

The fragility of the poem, its tendency to break apart when handled, constitutes an important element of its form; Lewis shrewdly connects this to the birdlike wandering of its discourse, the "inconsequential" arrangement of its topics.

A sense of the poem's method can be gotten from an opening passage in which Jane enumerates her fears for Phillip's soul:

> Of God nothynge els crave I
> But Phyllypes soule to kepe
> From the marees depe
> Of Acherontes well,
> That is a flode of hell;
> And from the great Pluto,
> The prynce of endles wo;
> And from foule Alecto,
> With vysage blacke and blo;
> And from Medusa, that mare,
> That lyke a fende doth stare;
> And from Megeras edders,
> For rufflynge of Phillips fethers,
> And from her fyry sparklynges,
> For burnynge of his wynges;
> And from the smokes sowre
> Of Proserpinas bowre;
> And from the dennes darke
> Where Cerberus doth barke,
> Whom Theseus dyd afraye,
> Whom Hercules dyd outraye,
> As famous poetes say;
> From that hell-hounde
> That lyeth in cheynes bounde,
> With gastly hedes thre;
> To Jupyter pray we
> That Phyllyp preserved may be!
> Amen, say ye with me!
> (67–94)

This lengthy quotation was necessary to convey the peculiarly agglomerative style of the poem, in which literary references, authors, myths, or, elsewhere, body parts or kinds of birds are collected into unstructured catalogues. *Phillip Sparrow* exhibits that interest in literary *copia* which characterizes the roughly contemporary works of Rabelais and Erasmus, and in which a superfluity of reference seems to obey its own autonomous laws. While invoking an epic tradition, Skelton's allusions do not contribute to a unified or allegorical whole as in the works of Dante and Spenser. Rather, they seem inert and ornamental, collected into hoards that serve no larger design. By analogy, one might designate this *copia* as a primitive accumulation of poetic material. Certainly there is something suggestive about the fact that Renaissance literary *copia* flourished under the political and economic dominance of merchant's capital. Such connections must be made with care, however; I shall return to this one later.

While both the internal ordering of catalogues and their succession in the poem follow a loosely associative flow, and on a dramatic or characterological level produce something like a "stream of consciousness," yet individual catalogues exhibit a strong topical coherence. In the passage quoted above, mythological figures collected from the classical underworld obey no evident pattern of disposition, but they do draw fairly clear boundaries between catalogical sections of the poem. The resultant parceling of *Phillip Sparrow* recalls the rhetorical divisions that characterized *Ware the Hawk* and indeed forms one of the many correspondences between the two poems. Yet the formal partitioning of *Phillip Sparrow* is of a much more complete and radical kind. In *Ware the Hawk*, the headings of each section announce the divisions of the *thema*. Thus, at the same time as they divide the poem, they organize its parts into a global rhetorical scheme. The rhetorical headings thus form a kind of sectional exoskeleton for an otherwise unified discourse. Indeed, they imbue the sections with the appearance of a necessary *order*, since the development of the *thema* follows an established sequence.

In the first part of *Phillip Sparrow*, however, the topical parcels are genuinely autonomous and do not unite the poem into a rhetorical whole. Although some of the topoi draw on established literary practices and subgenres—such as the heroic *katabasis* and the medieval bird mass—yet these derive from different and often incommensurable traditions (a fact that becomes an explicit concern of Jane's when she thinks of composing an epitaph for Phillip) and are furthermore interspersed with such heterogeneous materials as Phillip's erotic wanderings, his reactions to various bugs, and Jane's fantasies about torturing the cat. While the poem is punctuated by overheard scraps of the Office of the Dead, these do not organize Jane's discourse; rather, the poem fragments and absorbs the mass.

This parceled form complements a neutralization of cultural authority, in which it also plays a role. When Phillip Sparrow is substituted for the hero of the classical *katabasis* in the passage quoted above, the comic disproportionality of the bird tends to dissipate the grandeur of the epic machinery. Thus C. S. Lewis describes the poem as "mock-heroic, though the term must here be stretched to cover the mock-religious as well," and goes on to compare it with *The Rape of the Lock*.[33] Yet *Phillip Sparrow*'s innocent destruction of authority must be clearly distinguished from parody or satire. Pope depicts the inversion of epic authority precisely in order to reassert it as the measure of a contemporary decadence. His poem thus depends on maintaining hierarchical differences, while Skelton's poem collapses and neutralizes them. Like Jane herself, *Phillip Sparrow* does not mock cultural authority because it is ultimately indifferent to it. Thus the poem must also be distinguished from those forms of inversion through degradation which characterize the popular culture of the time, and which Bakhtin has so brilliantly described. Skelton does employ methods of festive degradation elsewhere, most notably in *Eleanor Rumming*, but also in *Ware the Hawk*, where the church's spirituality is degraded and materialized when the hawk defecates on the altar (defecation being a recurrent element in festive degradation), and where sacred icons and implements are literally inverted in an emblematic representation of "the world turned upside down."

Unlike *Ware the Hawk*, which displays an ambivalent conflict between orthodox and heterodox, hierarchizing and degrading tendencies, *Phillip Sparrow* simply neutralizes both. The poem's resistance to parody or blasphemy is all the more surprising given the opportunities offered by its impromptu mass for a dead bird. But while the poem draws on traditions associated with goliardic parodies of the mass, it never engages in such parodies itself.[34] This in turn results from the failure of the mass (or any other text) to overcode the poem. For to write either a serious or a farcical mass requires that the mass be taken as a formal and ethical paradigm that the text will then necessarily reflect, either in direct or inverted form. In either case, the liturgy would impose the same kind of order on *Phillip Sparrow* that Skelton's rhetorical schema imposes on *Ware the Hawk*. But its failure to do so typifies the nature of the poem: any number of *potential* master codes may operate in localized parcels of the text, but none succeeds in establishing either a temporary or a global dominance.[35] Nor is there any form of dominance that is distributed among an "oligarchy" of master codes or texts.

We have seen how the absolutist state partly deterritorializes the parcellized sovereignty of feudalism, recoding local structures so as to produce the centralized and ultimate form of the feudal polity. Skelton engages this process by establishing a correspondence between political and literary territoriality—in effect, by reviving in its fullness the concept of the literary *topos*. Having done so, however, he does not produce in *Phillip Sparrow* a representational *inversion* of the polity, a "world turned upside down," or, if you will, a pyramid standing on its head. Rather, he throws the deterritorializing machine[36] into reverse; in response to centralized sovereignty, the poem radically relocalizes its own structure and neutralizes cultural authorities. The result can only be described as parceled anarchy in a poem whose autonomous localities resist hierarchical organization both in respect to one another and in respect to their own internal forms. This is obviously not a mere reflection of an historical process, but a utopian strategy within its field.

VI

A complementary though in some sense contradictory logic pervades the libidinal register of the poem, where parcellation gives way to a process of decoding. A territorial field is still at stake, though here it is not directly the form of the poem but rather the human body with its sociosexually inscribed regions. The first publication of *Phillip Sparrow* caused something of a scandal, owing in part to its boldness in depicting what is clearly an erotic relationship between Jane Scrope and her sparrow. To some degree this was simply a result of reviving and extending a Catullan tradition in inappropriate circumstances; but the "beastly" transgressions on both Skelton's and Jane's parts contribute to a larger program of erotic decoding,[37] one that bears a visible relationship to the politics of the poem's form.

While *Phillip Sparrow* returns intermittently to the topic of Jane's and Phillip's physical intimacy, the most extended passage on this matter is the first:[38]

> For it wold come and go,
> And fly so to and fro;
> And on me it wolde lepe
> Whan I was aslepe,
> And his fethers shake,
> Wherewith he wold make
> Me often for to wake
> And for to take him in
> Upon my naked skyn.
> God wot, we thought no syn—
> What though he crept so lowe?
> It was no hurt, I trowe.

He dyd nothyng, perde,
But syt upon my kne.
Phyllyp, though he were nyse,
In him it was no vyse;
Phyllyp had leve to go
To pyke my lytell too,
Phillyp myght be bolde
And do what he wolde;
Phillip would seke and take
All the flees blake
That he coulde there espye
With his wanton eye.
(159–82)

Fish's reading of this and the other erotic passages is instructive, based as it is on the presumed contrast between a sophisticated male reader and the charming but naive figure of Jane:

> [W]e are aware, as [Jane] is not, of the sexual implications of her demonstratio's: . . . . It is perhaps difficult to read these lines without questioning her innocence, but we make the necessary effort and accept her demurral: . . . It is, however, a conscious effort, and Skelton insists that we make it. If his poem is to succeed, we must be continually aware of the distance between what Jane in her innocence would intend and what we would interpolate.[39]

Fish thus arrives at choice partially justified by the text itself: either Phillip's wandering are innocent, or they arouse Jane sexually. Or again (if I am reading Fish correctly), there is a sexual component Jane is not aware of, though "we" (mature, male readers) know it is there. But what exactly do we "know" that Jane does not? That the relationship is erotic *and therefore transgressive.* But if we take Jane at her word, she does not deny that Phillip's actions may be erotically pleasurable, only that there is anything wrong with this. Nothing has been transgressed ("It was no hurt, I trowe," "In him it was no vyse"). Recourse to Freudian negation ignores the fact that Jane's denials are secondary and formal compared with the pleasurability of the erotic narrative. Fish's analysis is not explicitly psychoanalytic, but it does rely on a supposed latency, the pressure of a not-said.

A "transgressive" reading would garner its strongest support from the passage's thematic parallels to *Ware the Hawk:* just as the hawk's errant flight leads it to violate the sacred territory of the church, so Phillip's wanderings violate the sacred territory of the virgin's body, which doubles with the sanctified host as a holy and hence forbidden ground. Phillip's search for fleas provides a delicate, comic, and titillating parallel to the passage in which the priest's hawk murders pigeons on the sacred altar. In both cases, animal instinct proves sublimely indifferent to the boundaries of cultural taboo. But while *Ware the Hawk* summons up at least a mock-horror at this outrage, *Phillip Sparrow* regards only its pleasures (emblematically, the poem's opening word is *placebo,* its closing phrase *rien que playsre*).[40] Phillip's libidinal nomadism does not transgress the sociosexual inscriptions of the body, therefore; rather it erases them, and thus decodes the body's territoriality.

Phillip Sparrow can thus be understood best in terms of the anoedipal, schizophrenic sexuality described by Deleuze and Guattari in the *Anti-Oedipus:* a regime in which desire flows (or rather, break-flows) between machinic part-objects, unchanneled by oedipal law and the rule of the phallus. It is thus inappropriate to view Phillip as a "phallic symbol," a substitute for a genital satisfaction that is lacking.[41] For this is to fall into the teleology of the Oedipus, to interpret the desiring production of part-objects as the secondary effects of a dominant, "mature," and genital sexuality, governed by the unitary structures of the phallus. Jane's body is composed of desiring-machines—the toe, the knee, the tongue, the breast—all of which produce pleasure, and all of which are connected *not* by the globalizing stroke of the Oedipus (which would organize the parts into a whole inscribed with taboos), but only by Phillip's random and nomadic wandering, which is the movement of desire itself.[42] This process has no *telos*—reproduction or even genital orgasm—nor does it hide or repress anything, nor does it substitute for something lacking; it is simply a decoded and polymorphous flow of desire.

Here it is well to recall Deleuze and Guattari's observation that "global persons do not exist prior to the prohibitions that found them," prior, that is, to their establishment as structural points on the oedipal triangle, which is in turn constituted by subjugating the diverse break-flows of desire to the law of the phallus or castration (78). In her libidinal functioning, then, Jane should not be regarded as a unified subject but as the site of polyvocal and decoded flows. Her desiring-production resists subordination to the Oedipus in much the same way that the parceled anarchy of the poem resists subordination to the unitary rule of a master code. The utopian and schizophrenic alternative to overcoding thus proceeds simultaneously on political, sexual, and formal levels. Yet while mutually implicated, these levels do not bear an expressive relation to one another; the "same thing" does not happen on each. Formally, the poem reterritorializes itself into autonomous parcels, while its libidinal register is characterized by a deterritorialized nomadism, not autonomy but an unchanneled flow between part-objects. This deterritorialization does not, however, correspond to that carried out by the state; it does not unify the body in order to subject it to the rule of the despot. If the libidinal flows have their historical counterpart, it is to the vagrancy of the deracinated classes, that dangerously destructuring flow that it was the function of the state to recode.

VII

We have thus far discussed separately the issues of poetic form and of Jane's desiring-production; but these two converge, for Jane desires to be a poet, and a good third of her discourse concerns her attempt to write an epitaph for Phillip. Here Jane fulfills her eminently *practical* critique of the metaphysics of lack, as all her supposed deficiencies conclusively evaporate. In particular, this section of the poem turns on a witty and, for Jane, quite conscious contradiction between an abundance of poetic material and the "lack" of a disposing style. On the one hand, Jane falls most completely into the alibi of insufficiency, and on the other she refutes it in the practice of her discourse:

> Yet one thynge is behynde,
> That now commeth to mynde:
> An epytaphe I wold have
> For Phyllyppes grave.
> But for I am a mayde,
> Tymerous, halfe afrayde,
> That never yet asayde
> Of Elyconys well,
> Where the muses dwell:
> Though I can rede and spell,
> Recounte, reporte and tell
> Of the *Tales of Caunterbury*
> Some sad storyes, some mery,
> As Palamon and Arcet,
> Duke Theseus, and Partelet;
> And of the Wyfe of Bath,
> That worketh moch scath
> When her tale is tolde
> Amonge huswyves bolde,
> How she controlde
> Her husbandes as she wolde,
> . . . .

> And though that rede have I
> Of Gawen, and Syr Guy,
> And can tell a great pece
> Of the Golden Flece
> How Jason it wan,
> Lyke a valiaunt man;
> Or Arturs round table,
> With his knightes commendable.
>   (603–23, 628–35)

And so on. In the succeeding list of "though" clauses her productivity reaches its zenith as she reels off a miniature encyclopaedia of classical and medieval fables. But then the "though" clauses reach their conclusion, at which point there appears the "lack":

> Though I have enrold
> A thousand new and old
> Of these historious tales,
> To fyll bougets and males
> With bokes that I have red,
> Yet I am nothyng sped,
> And can but lytell skyll
> Of Ovyd or Virgyll
> Or of Plutharke,
> Or Frauncys Petrarke,
>
> . . . .
> For as I tofore have sayd,
> I am but a yong mayd,
> And can not in effect
> My style as yet direct
> With Englysh wordes elect.
>   (749–57, 769–73)

What Jane has, then, is matter—enough to "fyll bougets and males"—but she cannot "direct" her "style." Here, for purely tactical reasons, the poem does succumb to a phallic symbolization. A "bouget" is a pouch, bag, or wallet; the word, related to "bulge," comes from the Latin *bulga*, a leather bag or a womb. A "male" is also a leather bag or wallet, but the word lends itself to witty associations with the testicles.[43] Jane thus bulges with the necessary matter for a poem but cannot "direct" her "style"; that is, she cannot subject her materials to a unitary disposition or mode of expression. But also, she cannot direct her stylus or writing-stick, with its all-too-obvious symbolization: she cannot wield the phallus, she is a maid, she lacks that with which she could subject her materials to a unifying stroke. Jane thus comes to "know" herself in the void of castration.

Yet Jane's lack is ironized, not because she eventually manages to scribble a few Latin verses, but because she has been speaking prodigious poetry all along. Her lack is assigned to her only retroactively, as a kind of phallic *ressentiment*, by the ideal of a unified style that her own productivity continuously exceeds and overflows. The strength of her practice defeats the weakness of her alibi; thus the momentary but intensely phallic symbolization of the passage was not only provisional but in some deeper sense derisory. Like the defensive reterritorialization of *Ware the Hawk* it was invoked only in order to accomplish a more thorough decoding.

Just as *Phillip Sparrow* avoids a unity of form, then, so it avoids a strict unity of style. While Jane is granted a characteristic voice, the poem opens by celebrating polyvocality:

> *Pla ce bo,*
> Who is there, who?
> *Di le xi,*
> Dame Margery,
> *Fa, re, my, my.*
>   Wherfore and why, why?
> For the sowle of Philip Sparowe,
> That was late slayn at Carowe
> Among the Nones Blake.
> For that swete soules sake,
> And for all sparowes soules
> Set in our bede rolles,
> *Pater noster qui,*
> With an *Ave Mari,*
> And with the corner of a Crede,
> The more shal be your mede.
>   (1–16)

From this initial chaos of voices a provisional order can be derived. The Latin is from the Office of the Dead, which Dame Margery, a senior nun, recites. A whispered exchange of voices between Jane and someone else in their attempt to ascertain who is singing mass and why gives way to Jane's long and private devotion for Phillip.[44] Yet the dramatic coherence of the scene does not prevent a linguistic confusion. On the one hand, language seems about to disintegrate; the Latin, first broken into syllables, cedes to the nonsense syllables of the gamut and then to asyntactical fragments. Even the first English phrases form an imperfect and confused dialogue. On the

other hand, phrases enter into promiscuous and "forbidden" connections, allowing the reader to construe statements like "*Di le xi,/*
Dame Margery" ("I have loved Dame Margery"). This linguistic
babble is abetted by the initial confusion of the speakers themselves.

Phillip Sparrow thus arises from a primordial and demiurgic language, break-flows of discourse which lack a defining subject or
speaker.[45] Even the dramatic situation can be construed only *post
festum* and imposed only imperfectly on this original chaos—a term I
use advisedly, for the opening of the poem must be read as a rewriting of the first verses of Genesis, paradoxically superimposed on the
Office of the Dead. From this *prima materia* of discourse emerges the
voice of Jane and its encyclopaedic prolixity. But this is a genesis of a
different kind from the Biblical one, for no ordering *logos* issues forth
from a paternal deity to still the waters. In place of the divine command *fiat lux* comes the *placebo:* this universe will obey only the
order of *jouissance.* No Father, no Law, no State, no overcoding
Phallus, no organic Form. Both the *placebo* and the *dilexi* expel their
completing *dominus,*[46] thus excluding Lordship, though this is not
felt as a lack. For chaos does not admit of voids; only structures have
spaces for a lack.

And yet *Phillip Sparrow* is, in some sense, founded on the void,
specifically that left by the disappearance of its namesake. Elegy is
supremely the genre of lack; Jane's creativity may seem intended to
refill a universe that has been hollowed out by her sparrow's disappearance. But Jane lacks Phillip only in the sense that she lacks a
style. As the extraordinary digressiveness of the poem shows, Jane's
verbal cosmos is not "sparrow-centric." Which is only to say once
again that Phillip is not the phallus; his disappearance does not
overcode the text.

In fact, it does the opposite. The death of a sparrow recalls not
only Catullus's poem, but—especially in this liturgical context—
Jesus' words to his disciples: "Are not two sparrows sold for a
farthing? and one of them shall not fall to the ground without your
Father" (Matth. 10:29). The providential fall of the sparrow sym-
bolizes the total saturation of the cosmos by God's law, its complete
structuration down to the smallest portion; in short, the totalizing
efficacy of the *logos.* Yet the poem neutralizes this like so many other
signs, for Jane's grandiose execrations on Gib the cat, and her comic
hope that

> Phyllyp may fly
> Above the starry sky,
> To treade the prety wren
> That is our Ladyes hen
> (598–601)

only reinforce our sense of the triviality and meaninglessness of the event. The desymbolization of Phillip's death thus destructures the poem's universe instead of reordering it. What has disappeared is not a phallus but a lynchpin, and the removal of this "weak link" allows an entire structure to collapse.

VIII

To return to an earlier point: it is only in reference to the poem's destructuration that its "primitive accumulation" of materials can begin to be understood. We are still dealing with an analogy here, for the structures of material production do not express themselves directly in literary production. Still, this is an analogy of which the poem takes account when Jane compares her stored fables to the bulging contents of a wallet or purse. Even here the analogy to money is ambiguous: do these catalogues represent a hoard or a sudden disbursement? If they form a hoard, how does the poem intend to invest it? Does it await the arrival of a new productive regime?

Temptations to cultural allegory abound here: the poem sings Vespers for the evening of medieval culture, recites the Office of the Dead for a disintegrating mode of production. Significantly, Jane possesses the fables and authors of the medieval tradition, but lacks the stylistic models of Renaissance poetry—Vergil, Ovid, Petrarch. Perhaps the poem sees itself as occupying a void after all, hoarding its materials while an old poetry dies out and a new one awaits birth. It is not impossible that Skelton plays with an allegory of this sort, but its suggestions of a poetic vacuum should not be taken any more seriously than should the other alibis that the poem delivers up.

The poem's "primitive accumulation" becomes clearer if we compare its disposition of poetic raw material with that of another and very different work. The Faerie Queene is in many ways the antitype of Skelton's poem precisely because it strives to be expressive of the structures of absolutist monarchy, both in its doctrine ("For truth is one and right is only one") and in its structure. The globalizing allegories, the subordination of materials to master narratives, produces a totalized form that in turn reflects the total rule of the state. Even though Spenser is equivocal toward the state's power, and even though the poem accommodates an oppositional logic of free errancy and dissemination, still, these are always articulated in relation to the idea of a totalized whole, which is thus always preserved in its countermovements by a kind of Hegelian "negation of the negation."

So too for the poem's use of raw materials. Like *Phillip Sparrow, The Faerie Queene* also has encyclopaedic tendencies, but its materials are articulated within the allegorical structure of the work so as always to produce a "surplus meaning" of either elaboration or contradiction. By contrast, the parceled and partly decoded form of *Phillip Sparrow* deprives its materials of symbolic resonance precisely by rejecting an overarching structure. If in one sense this frees an unchanneled discursive flow, in another it imparts a certain inertness to mythic and generic materials. Neither decoded flows nor autonomous parcels are conducive to meaning; hence interpretive or hermeneutic questions are out of place here. We can only observe what the poem *does*, how it engineers countermovements to the historical process of primitive accumulation.

IX

This, at least, applies to the poem's first part. But Jane's discourse makes up only half of the original poem; the second half, consisting of Skelton's "commendations" of Jane, follows far different rules.[47] Drawing on materials from the cult of the Virgin and on the formulae of courtly love poetry, Skelton constructs an intense but sometimes routinized praise of his beloved.

The first and second halves of the poem exhibit clear stylistic contrasts. As Fish observes, "Artificiality and innuendo replace the ingenuousness of the first section," where Jane's monologue was "conspicuously free of the studied stylization of aureate rhetoric."[48] Jane's speech contains primarily figures of amplification and few of the "difficult figures," but "the statistics reverse themselves in the commendations."[49] Meanwhile, Jane's digressiveness is replaced by Skelton's fidelity to his subject. In general, a more restrained and frugal economy of style pervades the second part.

Setting sophistication against naivete, difficulty against simplicity, and male against female in this way, the second half of the poem quite clearly tries to master the first, as evidenced by the rather disquieting entrance of Skelton's authorial persona. At the end of Jane's section, when she finally manages to write an epitaph for Phillip in "Latyne playne and lyght," Skelton suddenly manifests himself in the midst of her compsition:

> Per me laurigerium
> Britanum Skeltonida vatem

> Hec cecinisse licet
> Ficta sub imagine texta.
> (834-37)

[It was permitted that this should be sung by me, Skelton the laureate poet, in the guise of a fictive image.]

By this epiphanic entrance, Skelton disperses the imaginary voice of Jane and appropriates the whole of the poem for himself. Not only the second half, but also Jane's discourse was an effect of Skelton's rhetorical mastery, which henceforth becomes the poem's ultimate referent.[50] The Skelton-persona thus reorganizes the poem's territoriality so that it is entirely expressive of his rule.

Not surprisingly, "Skelton's" poetry emphasizes symmetry and stasis, and reduces Jane to the commonplaces of the medieval *blazon:* her face is as white as orient pearl, her cheeks are like rose buds, her lips are like cherries, her mouth is "sugred" (1031–40). Her otherwise formalized appearance does contain a blemish, though, which draws the poet's most sustained attention:

> Her beautye to augment
> Dame Nature hath her lent
> A warte upon her cheke,
> Who so lyst to seke
> In her vysage a skar
> That semyth from afar
> Lyke to a radyant star,
> All with favour fret,
> So properly is it set.
> (1041–49)

The wart is a random excrescence, a surd element that resists the poet's efforts to cleanse and spiritualize his beloved. Hence it must be subjected to the most strenuous kind of poetic sublimation and, more important, *fixed* within a structure. The wart is

> set so womanly,
> And nothyng wantonly,
> But right convenyently,
> And full congruently,
> As Nature cold devyse,
> In most goodly wyse.
> (1067–72)

As if the wart were threatening to wander or had already reached its position by an aleatory movement, Skelton makes it into a fixed locus of chaste fascination, and thus into an antitype of Phillip, the libidinal nomad. The wart transgresses no boundaries on a body that has been precisely and definitively inscribed.

This thematic project of overcoding Jane has its formal counterpart in the structural and stylistic unity of the second part. While the commendations are formally divided by the periodic repetition of a refrain, yet the regions produced thereby are essentially homogenous, as they were in *Ware the Hawk*. The second part of *Phillip Sparrow* thus truly forms a whole, into which it tries to incorporate, retroactively, the first part as well.

Yet despite his initially absolutist claims, the Skelton-persona's powers are not unlimited, for his rhetorical mastery of Jane balances an equally powerful erotic submissiveness. Each repetition of the refrain incorporates different paraphrases of the Psalms, such as *Quomodo dilexi legem tuam, domina!* ("How I have loved your laws, o mistress!") and *Legem pone mihi, domina, in viam justificationem tuam!* ("Set laws down for me, mistress, in your just ways!"). Skelton addresses Jane as if she were a sixteenth-century leather lady and asks her to bind him down. Unlike Phillip, the poet will walk only in "just ways"; the second part of the poem is a virtual web of obligations, decorums, entreaties, restrictions, and taboos.

It is clear, then, that the Skelton-persona does not emerge merely to master Jane. She also ironizes his neurotic obsessiveness, his sadistic instrumentality, his stiff formalism, his emptiness of invention. "Skelton" unwittingly illustrates his shortcomings in his very first English phrase, when he promises to devote his "hole imagination" to praising his mistress. If this persona organizes things into wholes, he also reduces them to holes. Nor are the two terms of the pun disparate, for "Skelton" unifies by draining the copiousness of localized difference. The phallic organizer who pretends to totalize and complete the poem proves to be precisely the space of its "hole" or lack.

X

But if the second half of *Phillip Sparrow* does not entirely succeed in subsuming the first, neither is its attempt to do so completely neutralized. At best the poem achieves a balance of forces; "Skelton" reveals the fragility of Jane's poetic, the susceptibility of its anarchic logic to a subsequent structuration and mastery. The project of the poem's first part is thus shown to be utopian in a bad sense as well. Radical as they are, the poem's localizing and destructuring movements depend on a localized freedom, the private imaginings of a young woman whose daydreams flow unimpeded only because they confront nothing outside of themselves. Here is the truth of Lewis's remark that *Phillip Sparrow* is "indeed the lightest—the most like a bubble—of all the poems I know." Not just the structural soundness but the utopian logic of the poem proves evanescent.

It is no accidental irony that the opening word of the poem— *placebo*—also designates a flatterer or sycophant. Thus the very sign that announces the poem's flight from absolutism also suggests its possible capitulation to it. In later and more dangerous days, Skelton would chastise those who

> occupy them so
> With syngynge *Placebo*,
> They wyll no farder go.
> They had lever to please
> And take theyr wordly ease
> Than to take on hande
> Worshypfully to withstande
> Such temporall warre and bate
> As now is made of late
> Agaynst holy churche estate,
> Or to maynteyne good quarelles.
> (*Colin Clout*, 906–16)

These lines may be taken as a retrospective critique of *Phillip Sparrow* as well, which did "no farder go" than to outline a regime of pleasure. Of course, there was no way to withstand the "temporall warre" that not only dissolved the autonomy of "holy church estate" but ushered in a whole new historical era. The deterritorializing process of primitive accumulation was to be thorough enough that Skelton's oppositional project could take form only within its limits; hence the logic of his poetry becomes clear only by way of reference to a total process of transition it had tried to switch into machinic reverse.

NOTES

1. *English Literature in the Sixteenth Century* (New York: Oxford University Press, 1954), 136.
2. Ian A. Gordon, *John Skelton: Poet Laureate* (Melbourne: Melbourne University Press, 1943), 9.
3. Gordon, *John Skelton*, 45.
4. Stanley Fish, *John Skelton's Poetry* (New Haven: Yale University Press, 1965), 249.
5. Fish, *Skelton's Poetry*, 26.

6. Karl Marx, *Capital*, vol. 1, trans. Ben Fowkes (New York: Vintage Books, 1977), 874–75.
7. See, for instance, Maurice Dobb, *Studies in the Development of Capitalism*, rev. ed. (1947; New York: International Publishers, 1963), chaps. 2–5.
8. See Etienne Balibar, "The Basic Concepts of Historical Materialism (especially part 4, "Elements for a Theory of Transition") in Louis Althusser and Etienne Balibar, *Reading Capital*, trans. Ben Brewster (London: New Left Books, 1970), 199–308.
9. This is true of primitive accumulation as a concept. Historically, it took place alongside the emergence of capitalist relations and may be said to have ended when capitalism became the dominant (though still not exclusive) mode of production.
10. *Anti-Oedipus*, trans. Robert Hurley, Mark Seem, and Helen R. Lane (Minneapolis: University of Minnesota, 1983), especially 222–40.
11. *Lineages of the Absolutist State* (London, New Left Books, 1974), 19. Since feudalism was characterized by the unity of the direct producer with the means of production, the ruling class could not appropriate an economic surplus from the production process itself (as in capitalism) but only by means of direct politico-legal coercion—hence the "unity of economy and polity" Anderson attributes to feudalism. See also Nicos Poulanzas, *Political Power and Social Classes* (London: Verso Editions, 1978).
12. "Overcoding is the operation that constitutes the essence of the State" (Deleuze and Guattari, *Anti-Oedipus*, 199). To "overcode" is to subject unorganized or locally coded elements to a global master code. In the case of the absolutist state, this included replacing particularized and often incommensurable local jurisdictions with a unified national code of law— a process that was not merely a rewriting but an operation of power as well. In this it exemplifies the process of overcoding in general, as applied to political, economic, linguistic, or sexual fields.
13. Anderson, *Absolutist State*, 18. While this essay will treat the deterritorializing actions of the absolutist state primarily in spatial and "formal" terms, it should be kept in mind that these are merely the expressions of class struggle.
14. Under Henry VII,

> Centralized royal government was exercized through a small coterie of personal advisers and henchmen of the monarch. Its primary objective was the subjugation of the rampant magnate power of the preceding period, with its liveried gangs of armed retainers, systematic embracery of juries, and constant private warfare. . . . Supreme prerogative justice was enforced by the use of the Star Chamber, a conciliar court which now became the main political weapon of the monarchy against riot and sedition. Regional turbulence in the North and West (where marcher lords claimed rights of conquest, not enfeoffment by the monarch) was quelled by the special councils designed to control these areas *in situ*. Extended sanctuary rights and semi-regalian private franchises were whittled down; liveries were

banned. Local administration was tightened up under royal control by vigilant selection and supervision of JPs; recidivist usurper rebellions were crushed. . . . The royal demesne was greatly enlarged by the resumption of lands, whose yield to the monarchy quadrupled during the reign; feudal incidents and custom duties were likewise maximally exploited. (Anderson, *Absolutist State*, 119)

15. "Decode," in this sense, does not mean to interpret a message or elucidate its code, as in the practice of cryptography. Instead it means to erase or dissolve a code. The "decoding" of feudal productive relations meant the destruction of their concrete social imbrication (in, e.g., the particularistic obligations of feudal land tenure or the paternalism of the guild system) and their replacement by the abstraction of the wage contract.

16. While the succeeding analysis emphasizes the progress of deterritorialization and decoding rather than their limits, these latter must be kept in mind in order to avoid serious theoretical difficulties. In particular, it must not be thought that commodification and trade were by themselves capable of "dissolving" feudalism. If merchant's capital tended to rework local production into a larger web of market relations, yet as a system of "profit upon alienation" it remained dependent on feudal territoriality. Merchant's capital was "continually speculating with the maintained territorialities, so as to buy where prices are low and sell where they are high" (Deleuze and Guattari, *Anti-Oedipus*, 227). Moreover, since feudal production did not allow for the extraction of a surplus from the production process itself, merchant capital could exploit the direct producer only by means of territorial monopolies over the flow of raw materials and finished goods (this was expressed politically by the rule of the "merchant oligarchies" in the towns). Thus while merchant's capital could accommodate itself to the overcoding of the feudal polity carried out by the absolutist state, it came into conflict with the total deterritorialization demanded by capitalist production—hence the tendency for merchant's capital to align itself with the monarchy against the manufacturing bourgeoisie. The full decoding of productive relations had to await the arrival of abstract labor and the wage contract, while the full deterritorialization of the polity (expressed, e.g., in the movement for "free trade") demanded a situation in which profit could be derived, not from the marketplace directly, but from the productive process itself. This condition was met only by industrial capital.

Even the commutation of dues, which Anderson stresses, did not of itself dissolve feudal relations in agriculture (For a detailed discussion of this question, see Dobb *Development of Capitalism*, ch. 2.) At stake here is the conflict between the Smithian view that the market economy alone destroyed feudalism, and the Marxist view that a change in the productive relations was decisive, with trade and money playing only a catalytic role.

17. Maurice Pollet, *John Skelton: Poet of Tudor England*, trans. John Warrington (London: J. M. Dent & Sons, 1971), 6.

18. See Michel Foucault, "What Is an Author?" in *Textual Strategies: Perspectives in Post-Structuralist Criticism*, ed. Josué V. Harari (Ithaca: Cornell University Press, 1979), 141–60.

19. Strictly speaking, the account is not true. Skelton resided at Westminster at his death, but he had by that time reconciled himself with Wolsey and was back in the court's good graces. On the other hand, Skelton had made some use of sanctuary privilege following the publication of *Colin Clout*, and, for similar reasons, left London entirely to stay with aristocratic families in the North in 1523 (Pollet, *Poet of Tudor England*, 130–62).

20. Privilege of sanctuary was "purely secular and jurisdictional, but long before the Tudor period opened, circumstances had given it a false ecclesiastical color" (Isabel D. Thornley, "The Destruction of Sanctuary," in *Tudor Studies*, ed. R. W. Seton-Watson (London: Longmans, 1924), 183–84. The Church, which held about one-third of the land in England, enjoyed a jurisdiction at least partially independent of the king's law. See G. R. Elton, *England under the Tudors* (1955; London: Methuen, 2nd ed. 1974), 103.

21. The fact that Wolsey rather than Henry initiated these policies is beside the point, since it is not the monarch but the state that is at question here. Yet Wolsey allowed Skelton to resolve his ambivalence toward the state into an imaginary dyad, heaping execrations on the lord chancellor while fawning on the king. Nor was Skelton alone in this. Wolsey was, to be sure, more the "type" of the state functionary, and he in fact ran England's domestic and foreign affairs during this period. By taking on the new functions of the state, he allowed the king to remain the object of feudal loyalty.

22. All quotations of Skelton's poetry are taken from John Scattergood, ed., *John Skelton: The Complete English Poems* (New Haven: Yale University Press, 1983).

23. Gordon, *John Skelton*, 21, 26.

24. Skelton was Prince Henry's tutor at court until the death of Prince Arthur in 1502. At that point, when Henry became heir apparent to the throne, another tutor was found for him as part of a general shake-up at court. While older legends that Skelton left in disgrace have been refuted, and while there is no evidence that he was unhappy at Diss, still the rectorship must have seemed disappointing after his former position. In any case, once Henry acceded to the throne Skelton was anxious to be recalled to court. He sent the young king a copy of the *Speculum Principis*, which he had written for him in 1501, and included two poems. "These he had linked together with an identical prayer, repeated in each case: 'May Jupiter Eretrius grant that I languish not by the Eurotas.' He was comparing his sojourn at Diss to Ovid's exile." Pollet, *Poet of Tudor England*, 60.

25. "For sure he wrought amys / To hawke in *my* church of Dys" (41–42, my emphasis).

26. "[W]hile protective jurisdictions in the hands of laymen slowly dwindled and disappeared, except in special cases, those held by abbots and

bishops were left in their integrity." Thornley "Destruction of Sanctuary,"
84. Significantly, Henry VII's first major assault on sanctuary privilege
was designed to suppress a threat of political sedition. In 1486, the Yorkist
Thomas Stafford was dragged from sanctuary and taken to the Tower.
The king's bench then ruled that "sanctuary was a common-law matter in
which the Pope could not interfere . . . and that the privilege did not
cover treasonable offenses." (Elton, *England under the Tudors*, 21–22).
27.

> [E]vangelia,
> Concha et conchelia,
> Accipiter et sonalia,
> Et bruta animalia,
> Cetera quoque talia
> Tibi sunt equalia
> (311–16)

[The Gospels, vessels and vestments, a hawk with its bells
and unreasoning animals and other such things are all the
same to you (Scattergood trans.)]
28. Fish, *Skelton's Poetry*, 89.
29. Fish, *Skelton's Poetry*, 89–98.
30. Cf. Deleuze and Guattari, *Anti-Oedipus*: "The revolutionary pole of
group fantasy becomes visible . . . in the power to experience institutions themselves as mortal, to destroy them or change them according to
the articulations of desire and the social field, by making the death instinct into a veritable institutional creativity" (62).
31. There was a real Jane Scrope, with whom Skelton was apparently infatu-
ated. She, her sisters, and her mother took up residence at Carrow Abbey
in 1502, after her stepfather, Sir John Wyndham, was beheaded by order
of the king for his (rather distant) association with a Yorkist conspiracy.
While the widow's move to Carrow was made for reasons of economy
rather than security, the whole affair casts a political shadow over the
poem's formal and ideological project. For the most detailed account of
Jane Scrope, see H.L.R. Edwards, *Skelton: The Life and Times of an Early
Tudor Poet* (London: Jonathan Cape, 1949), 102–14.
32. Lewis, *English Literature*, 138.
33. Ibid., 139.
34. This, at least, is the opinion of Fish (*Skelton's Poetry*, 102–3) and of F. L.
Brownlow ("*The Boke of Phyllyp Sparrowe* and the Liturgy," *ELR* 9 [Winter
1979]: 5–20, especially 9–10). Gordon insists that the poem is parodic, in
the spirit of the Goliards, but even he wavers on this point (*John Skelton*,
132–33), and in any case, Brownlow makes a much stronger argument.
35. Brownlow, who has done the most careful study of liturgical influences
on *Phillip Sparrow*, writes that "the liturgical frame gives the poem an
objective, external form, but it does not have the internal, organic unity of
form we are trained to recognize. . . . The wholeness of the poem is like
the wholeness of the liturgy it imitates, being a wholeness of tone and

purpose rather than of form" (*"Boke of Phyllyp Sparrowe,"* 6). I would go one step further and claim that the liturgy fails to provide a consistent external form as well as a consistent tone or purpose.

Taking another tack, Stanley Fish analyzes the form of the poem not in terms of the liturgy but in terms of Ciceronian and medieval rhetoric. While he isolates certain local rhetorical structures, though, he fails to elevate any rhetorical schema into an overarching master code (*Skelton's Poetry,* 98–125).

36. Here and elsewhere, "machine" must be taken in its broadest sense to avoid both analogy and anachronism.

37. See note 15.

38. But see also the following:

> [M]y byrde so fayre,
> . . . was wont to repayre,
> And go in at my spayre [opening or slit in a gown],
> And crepe in at my gore [part of a skirt]
> Of my gowne before,
> Flyckerynge with his wynges!
> . . . .
> How pretely it wolde syt
> Many tymes and ofte,
> Upon my finger alofte!
> I played with him tytell-tattyll,
> And fed him with my spattyl,
> With his byll betwene my lippes,
> It was my prety Phyppes!
> Many a prety kusse
> Had I of his swete musse.
>   (343–48, 354–62)

39. Fish, *Skelton's Poetry,* 111–12.

40. The latter phrase ends the original poem, not counting the "adicyon" that was tacked on after 1509.

41. R. W. Mc Conchie argues that the poem "develops the bawdy possibilities of Phillip, especially the phallic ones, through the innocent voice of Jane herself. . . . Clearly Phillip is a kind of sexual surrogate, and more particularly a phallic symbol" ("Phillip Sparrow," *Parergon* 24 [August 1979]: 31–35). This is a masterful bit of oedipal ideology: since Phillip gives erotic pleasure, he must be a "surrogate" or "symbol" for the phallus. In other words, all sexuality is phallic.

Interestingly, some of the contemporary texts that Mc Conchie cites to prove his case actually refute it. For instance, a madrigal by Gascoigne (E. H. Fellows, *English Madrigal Verse, 1588–1632,* 3rd ed. [New York: Oxford University Press, 1967], 358–59) clearly refers back to Skelton's poem, but alas, here Phillip is female:

> She never wanders far abroad,
>   But is at home when I do call.

If I command she lays on load
With lips, with teeth, with tongue and all.
(17–20)

In *Magnificence*, Skelton himself uses the phrase "Phillip Sparrow" to refer to a woman (l. 1562). Thus the tradition sometimes portrays Phillip as feminine and as a "symbol" of oral, not phallic, sexuality. Or rather, the conjunction of name and attributes tends to confuse sexual difference.

Phillip's sexual ambiguities help to lay bare the real mechanisms of jealousy behind the Catullan sparrow tradition. If the sparrow were really only a sexual surrogate or phallic symbol, then the male poet could easily displace it (being the bearer of the "real thing"). But it is the bird's non-phallic characteristics—its wanderings, its gentle oral stimulations—which make it potentially more satisfying to women than men are. If anything, the sparrow rewrites men as surrogates for women and thus signals the repressed (or not so repressed) possibility that female sexuality is essentially lesbian.

The male poet's (or critic's) tendency to read the sparrow as a phallic rival thus exemplifies the very thing whose absence makes the sparrow such a dangerous rival in the first place. The interpretative fixations of the Oedipus merely reproduce the genital fixations of "normal" male sexuality; despite the surface despair that it generates, to see the sparrow as a phallic rival is actually comforting to the male, because it opens up a possible line of identification and displacement *via* the reductive teleology of the Oedipus. This is not to say that Phillip *never* assumes a phallic role, but merely that the poem never privileges this particular symbolization over others.

42. Interestingly, Skelton claimed to have translated a work from French into English entitled "Of Mannes Lyfe the Peregrination."

43. Chaucer's castrated (?) Pardoner carries a compensatory "walet . . . in his lappe, / Bretful of pardoun, comen from Rome al hoot" (General Prologue, 686–87), and this wallet is referred to a few lines later as his "male."

44. Brownlow ("*Boke of Phyllyp Sparrowe*," 9–10) provides some invaluable explanatory material:

> There is no parody of the service at all. It pursues its own course, sung by a nun called Dame Margery. Only in Jane's mind is it a service for her sparrow. In the Middle Ages the Office of the Dead was frequently recited as an addition to the Divine Office, and in religious communities it was (and is) prayed as a suffrage for a deceased member. . . . Jane, in the priory church, following the service in her primer, transforms it into something quite different; but in doing so she is fulfilling, like Dame Margery, a proper liturgical role. For it was customary for lay people to use their primers for private devotion during the recitation of either the Divine Office or the Mass.

45. *Speak Parrot*, which Pollet calls "offensively polyglot" (*Poet of Tudor England*, 121), employs a similarly fragmented and various language.

46. Placebo Dominus in regione vivorum (Ps. 114:9). Dilexi quoniam audies Domine vocem deprecationis meae (Ps. 114:1).

47. "In the second part of the poem, Vespers being ended, Skelton speaks in his own voice. Using the same book of devotions he 'commends,' not the departed soul into the hands of God, but the living person of Jane Scrope" (Brownlow, *"Boke of Phyllyp Sparrowe,"* 10).

48. Fish, *Skelton's Poetry*, 114.

49. Ibid., 116–17.

50. See ibid., 112–16.

12. PUTTENHAM'S PERPLEXITY:

NATURE, ART, AND THE SUPPLEMENT

IN RENAISSANCE POETIC THEORY

■

DEREK ATTRIDGE

I

IN THE ENDLESS STRUGGLE to obtain some understanding of the ways in which our thinking is simultaneously constrained and facilitated by the structures of discourse we use, and have no option but to use, it is obviously important to do everything we can to establish some distance from the associations, distinctions, limits, metaphorical habits, and other systematic features that condition our discursive practices, whether in the criticism of literature or across much wider cultural domains. Many strategies are available for doing this, none of them immune from the charge of being itself necessarily constituted by the available modes of thought and utterance, and all of them liable, sooner or later, to absorption by the infinitely generous embrace of the doxa against which they try to establish a contrary perspective. Reading the texts of the past in an attempt to do justice to their existence as products of different discursive (and sociopolitical) systems has frequently been advanced as one such strategy, though the real difficulties of the exercise, and the impossiblity of verifying any of its results, have often gone unacknowledged,[1] while hindsight has frequently revealed "historical" readings to be little more than the enlisting of past texts in a current theoretical/ideological battle.

In reexamining one aspect of Renaissance aesthetic theory, using George Puttenham's *Arte of English Poesie* as a representative example,[2] I have no illusion of stepping outside the field that provides the structures of my thought and writing (Barthes has argued that literary theory can do no more than make alignments among the discur-

sive systems available at a given moment[3]). But it is perhaps the case
that the arena of conflicting discourses in which I find myself at this
juncture in cultural history holds out possibilities for reading a text
of this kind which have not hitherto existed. Puttenham's treatise,
which has often been regarded as a charming but unsophisticated
and inconsistent potpourri of Renaissance commonplaces,[4] may be
read as an attempt to articulate certain crucial problems having to do
with the status of poetic language within a linguistic and cultural era
continuous with our own but distanced from it in certain important
ways, and as offering a clearer view than a more recent text might do
of the tacit assumptions and conceptual parameters that both make
possible and set boundaries to our confrontations with the same
issues. In particular, to the degree that it appears fissured or self-
contradictory it may reveal inconsistencies or blind spots in our own
thinking over which there lies a veneer put down by the passage of
later intellectual history. Puttenham's treatise is especially useful in
this respect because it does not exercise to the full the rhetorical and
persuasive powers that are, in part, its subject—as is not the case,
for instance, with Sidney's roughly contemporary *Apologie for Poetrie*, where tensions and contradictions tend to disappear under the
immaculate surface of courtly *sprezzatura*.[5]

Although we no longer automatically divide the world around us,
or the actions of men and women, into the broad and exclusive
categories of nature and art, the traces of this mental habit are everywhere to be found, from theories of poetic language to the theological debate over contraception. The distinction between nature
and art was, of course, a classical and medieval commonplace as
well as a Renaissance (and post-Renaissance) one; and it has been
frequently documented and discussed. Its history, its ubiquity, and
its importance in sixteenth- and seventeenth-century English literature have been conveniently and ably surveyed by Edward William
Tayler,[6] and we may begin with some of his formulations of the
relationship between the terms. Tayler finds that although the pairing of nature and art is to be met with at every turn in Renaissance
writing, the relationship between them is presented in remarkably
varying terms: "Nature and art were combined, according to a writer's temperament, training, and purposes, in innumerable and
sometimes contradictory ways" (27). The contrast between the two
most characteristic views of the dichotomy could hardly be more
extreme: "When Art is viewed eulogistically—as the product of
man's 'erected wit,' of a faculty not entirely impaired by the Fall, of a
faculty capable of rational creativity—then Nature usually signifies
the unformed, the inchoate, the imperfect, or even the corrupt. . . .

When, on the other hand, Art is viewed pejoratively—as mere imitation, falsification, reprehensible counterfeit, or even perversion—then Nature signifies the original, the unspoiled, the transcendent, or even the perfect" (36).

Yet in spite of the contradictory uses to which the pairing was put, there appears to have been widespread agreement on its validity as a means of dividing the entirety of human experience: Tayler calls it "indispensable to the thinkers of the Renaissance," and adds, "The use of one term seems automatically to suggest the other, as if the absence of one of the words must betray the fact that the subject has been examined incompletely" (21). Universal assent as to the dichotomous character of experience, the appropriateness of these terms to label the divisions, and their absolute mutual dependence was attended by widespread disagreement as to the significance of the division and the meaning of the terms themselves. This phenomenon is made even more curious by the fact that contradictory positions are often to be found within a single author. "On one occasion," writes Tayler, "a writer may maintain that Art perfects Nature, on another that Art perverts Nature" (30); and among the writers who betray inconsistencies in their various accounts of the distinction Tayler includes not only Renaissance poets and theorists but Plato, Aristotle, Seneca, and Cicero. Nature, then, in Tayler's survey, appears as *both* the principle of perfection and the principle of imperfection—and so does art, in a contrary or complementary relationship. How are we to characterize such an unstable and apparently self-contradictory distinction? Is it sufficient to refer to the changeableness and variety of opinion, and to attempt to extract some "balance" between nature and art as representing the best possible Renaissance position on the matter, or is the radical instability in some way intrinsic to the distinction, and to its function within the discourse of the period?[7]

The opposition of nature and art is, of course, related to several other divisions typical of Western thought, among them the literal versus the figurative, wisdom versus eloquence, dialectic (or logic) versus rhetoric, object versus sign (or representation), speech versus writing, and nature itself versus nurture, or convention, or culture. Jacques Derrida, in discussing several of these dualisms as they occur in a variety of texts, literary and philosophical, from Plato to Ponge, has sought to show that they do not, and cannot, function as stable, given, mutually exclusive oppositions, of which one member is simply primary and self-sufficient and the other secondary, exterior, and dependent. These deconstructive readings do not by any means invalidate the distinctions in question or find fault with

the texts that rely on them; on the contrary, they enhance the significance of the texts as cultural indices by tracing within them much
more than the writer's conscious intentions. As Derrida puts it,
"The writer writes *in* a language and *in* a logic whose proper system,
laws, and life his discourse by definition cannot dominate absolutely. He uses them only by letting himself, after a fashion and up
to a point, be governed by the system. And the reading must always
aim at a certain relationship, unperceived by the writer, between
what he commands and what he does not command of the patterns
of the language that he uses."[8]

As tools to employ in the task at hand, I wish to take two of
Derrida's best-known strategic terms, or *brisures*. These are not critical or philosophical *concepts* (the concept of the "concept" is one of
the questions at issue), but words taken from texts under discussion
which offer, in their own peculiar double allegiances, levers to shift
some of the Western mind's most fixed assumptions. (Derrida, we
must remember, is using a rhetorical and not a logical or dialectical
method: we are not being shown a previously veiled "truth," but by
a certain kind of persuasive language are being freed from the narrow mental paths we have hitherto traveled. We must also remember that the distinction between rhetorical and logical which I
have just made is itself subject to deconstruction, and that Derrida's
practice is not absolutely different from the way philosophy has
always functioned.)

One of these hinge-words Derrida finds at a number of crucial
junctures in Rousseau's writing: the word *supplément* (together with
its related forms), a word that can mean both that which *supplements*
something already complete in itself, and that which *supplies* what is
missing from something incomplete in an important respect—"two
meanings," writes Derrida, "whose cohabitation is as strange as it is
necessary" (*Grammatology,* 144). (The English word is not quite as
self-divided, but will serve as the most convenient translation:
Think of the two ways of perceiving the *O.E.D. Supplement,* as an
addition to a work that has long stood as complete and exhaustive,
and as that which *makes* the *O.E.D.* complete and exhaustive.) These
two meanings are, of course, completely contradictory according to
normal logic, and one would assume that, in any given occurrence
of the word, only one meaning would be possible. But Derrida
demonstrates that certain central dichotomies in Rousseau's writing
are related in a way that renders both these meanings appropriate at
the same time: what is offered as mere addition, in other words, also
makes up for an important lack—and is seen as threatening because
of its tendency to usurp that to which it should only be peripheral

(see *Grammatology*, 144–64). Thus education, for example, which is for Rousseau inherently secondary in that it adds to the perfect, innocent development of nature, is called upon to perform a crucial function in making up for weaknesses in the "natural" constitution of every child. (In trying to think about this elusive knot of relations, it is important to hold on to the fact that *reason* can never grasp the structure of supplementarity because reason is constituted by the *rejection* of supplementarity, the rejection of any possibility that an entity can be both itself and not itself—a rejection that goes back to the beginning of the Western philosophical tradition.) In "Plato's Pharmacy,"[9] Derrida offers a reading of the *Phaedrus* in which the word *pharmakon* is seen to operate in a similarly double way: as that which is added to the natural organism, it can mean both poison *and* beneficial medicament, and, rejected as the former, it inevitably returns as the latter, restoring perfection to the naturally flawed body. Something of its self-contradictoriness exists in the connotations of the word *drug*, an artifical addition to the body's natural intake which can be either a vicious or a remedial supplement.

II

The stability and mutual exclusiveness of the opposition between nature and art would seem to be a necessary foundation for Puttenham's enterprise: the composition of a manual setting out in detail what can be said about English poetry as an art of language. At first sight the distinction, as it operated for an Elizabethan like Puttenham, seems solid enough: "nature" refers to that which occurs *naturally*, or by *kind*, by virtue of what a thing is in all its fullness and self-sufficiency; "art" to that which is contrived by an *artificer* working upon the materials of nature. Every object or piece of behavior that is not natural is artificial (or "artful"), and vice versa. Human beings behave naturally by following *instinct*, and artificially by learning and following the rules of the art in question. The connection between art and rules is always very close: Puttenham gives as the accepted definition of art, "A certaine order of rules prescribed by reason and gathered by experience," and states that poetry was not an art "untill by studious persons fashioned and reduced into a method of rules and precepts" (5).[10] (Although this may seem completely foreign to later conceptions of art that regard "artifice" and "rules" with hostility, we shall see that the difference is not as large as first appears.) An art is therefore by definition *teachable*, and an "Art" of English poetry is designed to teach (and to further) that art by setting out its rules and precepts.

The first of the three books of Puttenham's *Arte*, entitled "Of Poets and Poesie," is not strictly speaking of this kind—it is partly a defense, partly a description and a history of poetry; but Book 2, "Of Proportion," and Book 3, "Of Ornament," set out, without stinting on detail, the two methods by which natural language is altered by the art, or artifice, of the poet: by being organized into lines of regular verse and stanzas, and by being enriched with rhetorical figures. Puttenham's definition of poetry is a strictly formal one, unlike, say, Sidney's, whose treatise is primarily an apology for *fiction*, whether in verse or prose.

Again and again Puttenham stresses the artificiality of art and its distance from nature. Book 2 deals with intricate rhyme-schemes, complex stanza-forms, highly intellectualized visual devices, and the adoption of the elaborate forms of classical versification into English. It uses a metaphoric language that is not at all that of the natural world but that of other craftsmen, the skillful musician dealing in harmony and cadence, for instance, or the fine jeweler; Puttenham is full of admiration for the Oriental verse that he has had described to him as "engraven in gold, silver or ivorie, and sometimes with letters of ametist, rubie, emerald or topas curiousely cemented and peeced together" (92).

Book 3, "Of Ornament," begins with an image designed to fix firmly the distinction on which the entire discussion depends: Just as "great Madames of honour . . . thinke themselves more amiable in every mans eye, when they be in their richest attire, suppose of silkes or tyssewes and costly embroderies, than when they go in cloth or in any other plaine and simple apparell. Even so cannot our vulgar Poesie shew it selfe either gallant or gorgious, if any lymme be left naked and bare" (137). The costly embroideries of poetry are, of course, "figures and figurative speaches, which be the flowers as it were and coulours that a Poet setteth upon his language by arte" (138). Nature is to art as the naked is to the clothed, the literal to the figurative, or the prosaic and everyday to the poetic. This third book is largely taken up with Puttenham's engaging catalogue of the figures of rhetoric, according to his own scheme of classification: the "auricular," which delight the ear alone, the "sensable," which inveigle the mind, and the "sententious," which bring pleasure to both.

Puttenham's poetics would seem to represent a view of art as something defined *against* nature, which he would tend to associate with the instinctive, the savage, the uncivil, the ignorant—a view for which there is a great deal of evidence at this time, and which retained at least a degree of force until the later eighteenth century, when art begins to claim for itself those "natural" qualities, renaming them "spontaneity," "sincerity," "innocence," and so on. But to read Puttenham only as a representive of this Renaissance commonplace is to ignore much that is present in his text, and it is worth pausing on a few of the places at which something more complex—and much less easy to describe—is happening.

In the second chapter of Book 1, Puttenham announces in general terms the position that the entire work is going to defend and elaborate: the chapter is entitled "That there may be an Art of our English Poesie, as well as there is of the Latine and Greeke" (5). In substantiating this claim, Puttenham is faced with the same problem that faced all defenders of vernacular poetry in the Renaissance: the prosody of the modern language verse traditions, as far as it was understood, seemed to lack the intense degree of organization of Latin and Greek verse, by which every syllable was weighed and measured and given an appropriate place in the line. One response, repeated all over Europe throughout the sixteenth century, was to attempt to create similar metrical forms in the vernacular. The other was to look for organizing principles of equivalent intricacy and reliability in the vernacular tradition itself. It is typical of Puttenham's open enacting of the contradictions within his age's intellectual fabric that he attempts both, scarcely making an effort to reconcile the two radically different solutions, and unintentionally providing evidence both for the impossibility of a quantitative system of meter in English and for the prevailing lack of insight into the structures of English verse.[11]

But the problem goes deeper than this. It is one aspect of a more generalized dilemma that lies at the heart of the humanist program of *imitation:* the only goal vernacular verse can set itself, given the controlling assumptions of humanism, is to match its model, classical verse; yet because that model is taken to be the absolute standard, the perfect exemplar, vernacular verse is necessarily condemned always to fall short.[12] This is our first example—one we need not dwell on—of the problematic of the supplement: vernacular verse is necessarily only an addition to the already complete and fully realized body of classical verse, and if it appears to be making claims to be an improvement on, or a substitute for, classical verse, which it must do in order to escape perpetual secondariness, it constitutes a threat to the classical verse's exemplary status, and therefore to its own *raison d'être*. Any assertion of the merits of modern as compared with classical verse, therefore, must somehow at the same time involve a counter-assertion, or the humanist program will disintegrate.

In his attempt to deal with this issue early in Book 1, Puttenham calls on the opposition between nature and art in order to argue that English versification is quite different from, and as good as (but, significantly, not better than), that of Latin and Greek. The argument is that the English rhyming type of verse, to judge from historical evidence and reports of travelers, is "the first and most ancient Poesie, and the most universall, which two points do otherwise give to all human inventions and affaires no small credit." So Puttenham can boast, "Our maner of vulgar Poesie is more ancient than the artificiall of the Greeks and Latines, ours comming by instinct of nature, which was before Art or observation" (10). At the very beginning of his art of English poetry, Puttenham seems to be privileging nature over art, instinct over rules. Not surprisingly, he quickly adds a qualification: such priority is only priority in *time*, like the priority of the naked over the clothed, or the ignorant over the learned. This would now seem to go to the opposite extreme, and to demolish the case for the vernacular by associating it with the naked and the ignorant, but Puttenham is reluctant to let the earlier argument go, and attempts a highly unstable compromise: "The naturall Poesie therefore being aided and amended by Art, and not utterly altered or obscured, but some signe left of it, (as the Greekes and Latines have left none) is no lesse to be allowed and commended than theirs" (10). Naturalness manages to be both an inherent advantage, and, in a metaphor at least as old as Aristotle, a weakness in need of the aid and amendment of art. (Not until Daniel's *Defence of Rhyme* is the argument for the natural superiority of the vernacular versification carried through without flinching—and that entails the abandonment of a large part of the humanist program.[13])

In a later chapter of Book 1, Puttenham firmly reasserts the slightly shaken superiority of the artificial over the natural, sharpening the criticism of his own appeal to nature and its associates, universality and antiquity: poetry is praiseworthy not only "because I said it was a metricall speach used by the first men, but because it is a metricall speach corrected and reformed by discreet judgements, and with no lesse cunning and curiositie than the Greeke and Latin Poesie, and by Art bewtified and adorned, and brought far from the primitive rudenesse of the first inventors, otherwise it might be sayd to me that *Adam* and *Eves* apernes were the gayest garmentes, because they were the first, and the shepheardes tente or pavillion, the best housing, because it was the most auncient and most universall" (32). But *this* now threatens the whole argument in favor of English versification, and nature has to be reintroduced in another attempt to reconcile the irreconcilable: "It is not my meaning that

Art and cunning concurring with nature, antiquitie and univer-
salitie, in things indifferent, and not evill, doe make them more
laudable" (23). Art, it seems, must in some way *agree* with nature,
even though it is defined *against* nature. And lest this should seem
to throw the ball entirely back into nature's court, there is the important qualification: "in things indifferent, and not evill." The role of
the artist, it seems, is to identify what is evil in nature and therefore
not to be followed. It is in this way that nature is "corrected and
reformed by discreet judgements." Poetry is modeled on nature, yet
somehow perfects nature (in the same way that, in the example of
supplementarity we noted earlier, modern poetry is both modeled
on, and yet perfects, classical poetry). The concept of nature is self-
divided (and is therefore not strictly a *concept*): it stands both for that
which is itself, in total self-sufficiency, and that which is necessarily
incomplete and in need of repair.

But there is further difficulty. In so far as art departs from nature
itself (and not just flawed nature), and is constituted as art by that
departure, it is in some sense essentially *unnatural*. The figures of
rhetoric have always been defined as transgressions of the norms of
what Puttenham, like many of his successors to the present day,
calls "ordinary" language. Puttenham is perfectly explicit about
this: "As figures be the instruments of ornament in every language,
so be they also in a sorte abuses or rather trespasses in speach,
because they passe the ordinary limits of common utterance, and be
occupied of purpose to deceive the eare and also the minde, drawing it from plainnesse and simplicitie to a certaine doublenesse,
whereby our talke is the more guilefull and abusing" ("Of Figures
and figurative speaches," [154]). Paradoxically, that which is unnatural and deceitful is able to cure nature of its faults—in a specific
context. Most of these vices, says Puttenham, can in *poetry* be transformed into virtues and occur as such in his lengthy list. Even some
of the deviations he lists unambiguously as vices can on some occasions become virtues, if they are handled in a particular manner by
the poet.

What is it that defines the delicate—yet crucial—balance between
virtue and vice? What is the source of the "discreet judgements"
whereby nature is "corrected and reformed" by art, and not further
depraved? To explain this, Puttenham invokes a completely independent standard, which he calls by a plethora of different names,
their proliferation suggesting both the importance of this moment
within the argument and its elusiveness as any kind of stable concept. Its titles include *decorum* (which I shall arbitrarily favor), *decency, discretion, seemliness, comeliness, agreeableness, seasonableness, well-*

temperedness, aptness, fittingness, good grace, conformity, proportion, and *conveniency.* And in a tight corner, this notion is always waiting to be appealed to by one of its names. If the argument seems to be heading toward a point where virtue and vice, good art and bad art, become indistinguishable—and the whole of Puttenham's enterprise threatens to collapse—decorum can step in to make the vital decision. Decorum is the principle whereby any given poetic device can be judged, according to all the specific, perhaps unique, configurations of its individual situation. It is clearly by far the most important rule in the poet's handbook—without it, he might as well not begin to write. Yet what emerges with surprising clarity from Puttenham's text is that *there is no such rule, and there could not possibly be one.* Decorum is precisely that aspect of the poet's art that is not reducible to rule.[14] And human activity that is not reducible to rule is usually called "natural."

Puttenham does not shy away from this conclusion. When he begins his full and direct treatment of decorum in the third-to-last chapter (having availed himself somewhat surreptitiously of its aid throughout the treatise), he stresses both its central importance and its unamenability to rules:

> In all things to use decencie, is it onely that giveth every thing his good grace and without which nothing in mans speach could seeme good or gracious, in so much as many times it makes a bewtifull figure fall into a deformitie, and on th'other side a vicious speach seeme pleasaunt and bewtifull: this decencie is therfore the line and levell for al good makers to do their busines by. But herein resteth the difficultie, to know what this good grace is, and wherein it consisteth, for peradventure it be easier to conceave than to express. (261)

Puttenham's way of expressing it is by means of an analogy between mind and senses: as, for instance, a sound that is "too loude or too low or otherwise confuse" is displeasing to the ear, so a "mental object" (Puttenham's phrase), if it is disproportioned, can be displeasing to the mind. And whence is this immediate and apparently instinctive response derived?

> This lovely conformitie, or proportion, or conveniencie betweene the sence and the sensible hath nature her selfe first most carefully observed in all her owne workes, then also by kinde graft it in the appetites of every creature working by intelligence to covet and desire: and in their actions to imitate and performe: and of man chiefly before any other creature aswell in his speaches as in every other part of his behaviour. (262)

In order to counteract the side-effects of art's distance from nature— its potential viciousness, ridiculousness, and duplicity—a *natural* principle must be reintroduced. That which the *pharmakon* is designed to cure must itself become a *pharmakon*. Thus in using the analogy of the "Madame of honour" at the beginning of Book 3, Puttenham refers to limbs clad in their *"kindly* clothes and coulours" (137): those clothes and colors which are in some way "fitting" or "natural" for the body.

It follows that the products of art and nature can be very difficult to tell apart. In praising two of his favorite speakers in Parliament and the Star Chamber, Puttenham observes that it "maketh no matter whether the same eloquence be naturall to them or artificiall (though I thinke rather naturall) yet were they knowen to be learned and not unskilfull of th' arte, when they were yonger men" (139–40). He does not really know which it is—and it perhaps matters a little more to him than he admits. Similarly, discussing the question of *style,* he notes that a certain manner of writing is "many times naturall to the writer, many times his peculier by election and arte, and such as either he keepeth by skill, or holdeth on by ignorance, and will not or peradventure cannot easily alter into any other" (148).

But the naturalness of art reaches even further: an artful principle is already present in nature. In discussing "feete of three times," Puttenham observes that apart from the dactyl "they have not hitherto bene made artificiall [not been admitted into the art of English poetry], yet nowe by more curious observation they might be. Since all artes grew first by observation of natures proceedings and custome" (128). And toward the end of the work, Puttenham even blurs the distinction to the extent of tracing the figures of rhetoric—those "trespasses in speach"—back to nature itself: "All your figures Poeticall or Rhethoricall, are but observations of strange speeches, and such as without any arte at al we should use, and commonly do, even by very nature without discipline" (298) (a familiar argument that even Wordsworth was to use in defense of certain figures of poetry). This is perhaps going too far, since art has now disappeared entirely, and Puttenham quickly adds, after noting that different people use these "strange speeches" to differing extents and in differing ways, "so as we may conclude, that nature her selfe suggesteth the figure in this or that forme: but art aydeth the judgement of his use and application" (298). However, we know by now that the art in question—the art of decorum—is in some way a natural rather than an artificial principle. (Wordsworth, too, in trying to achieve a "natural" language for poetry finds he has to *select* from the real language of men, applying his own judgments of what is "truly" natural.)

That art's difference from nature must be controlled by a natural principle is not an unfamiliar point of view, its most memorable expression in English perhaps being Shakespeare's in *The Winter's Tale*.[15] Perdita, it will be recalled, does not grow "carnations and streak'd gillyvors" in her rural garden because of her belief in nature's perfection, and art's viciousness as the dangerous supplement to that perfection:

> I have heard it said
> There is an art which in their piedness shares
> With great creating nature.
> (4.4.86–88)

Polixenes replies, as might Puttenham, though a good deal more eloquently,

> Say there be;
> Yet nature is made better by no mean
> But nature makes that mean: so, over that art
> Which you say adds to nature, is an art
> That nature makes. You see, sweet maid, we marry
> A gentler scion to the wildest stock,
> And make conceive a bark of baser kind
> By bud of nobler race: this is an art
> Which does mend nature, change it rather, but
> The art itself is nature.
> (4.4.88–97)

Only nature, then, can provide the art by which to make good its own deficiencies; or as Derrida puts it, "The supplement comes *naturally* to put itself in Nature's place" (*Grammatology*, 149).

But we need to scrutinize this return of nature a little more closely. As that sentence from Derrida might suggest, what has actually happened in the course of the argument is not that great creating nature, having been excluded by art, is allowed back in the form of decorum to control art; rather, a *supplement* to nature, a surrogate that is more acceptable to Puttenham and his courtly readers, has taken over its role as an alternative to the supplement of art. Although the natural judgment of decorum is equivalent to the ear's dislike of a harsh sound, it turns out not to be as universal a human capacity as that one (remember that it was universality that got Puttenham into trouble in Book 1). "It may be a question," he notes, "who shal have the determination of such controversie as may arise whether this or that action or speach be decent or indecent: and verely it seemes to go all by discretion [i.e., decorum], not perchaunce of every one, but by a learned and experienced discretion, for otherwise seemes the *decorum* to a weake and ignorant judgement, than it doth to one of better knowledge and experience" (263). Decorum, in other words, is what comes "naturally" not to all humanity but to an elite; and members of that elite can be identified by their "natural" sense of decorum. What comes naturally to the majority, who are ignorant and inexperienced, is not *truly* natural.

That this contradiction is something Puttenham simply does not notice is evident from his well-known discussion of the proper variety of language for the poet to use. He defines it extremely narrowly: "that which is spoken in the kings Court, or in the good townes and Cities within the land" (144), and even that geographical generosity shrinks, at least in the case of England, to "the shires lying about London within lx. myles, and not much above" (145). And on what grounds is the poet to favor the language of a tiny minority of English speakers? It is, says Puttenham, "naturall, pure, and the most usuall of all his countrey" (144). "Usual," which is clearly nonsense in terms of statistics, suggests that Puttenham (like Wordsworth after him) is able to assimilate the notion of universality to a politically less troublesome notion of cultural superiority. So the appeal to "a learned and experienced discretion," which sounds like a democratic appeal to merit and effort, marks a prior exclusion of that class without access to learning or to the kind of courtly experience Puttenham has in mind. Hence the "naturalness" of decorum is at a distant remove from universal human nature or instincts; it is an ideological product, a sixteenth-century equivalent of one of Barthes's modern *myths*, whereby a historically specific class attitude is promoted and perceived as natural.[16] In maintaining its power, the ruling elite puts forward, and no doubt believes in, the idea of the "naturalness" of its own behavior and its "natural" self-sufficiency and primacy as a class, as little open to question as nature's own self-defining identity. (Of course, in order to sustain this belief in the face of so much evidence to the contrary, the Elizabethan aristocracy has to have recourse to a number of supplements to its own "natural" superiority—including a highly artificial mode of display—which increasingly threaten to usurp the operation of that superiority.) As his metaphors imply, Polixenes' overarching nature that mends nature in the garden can also be appealed to as justification for selective intermarriage between the (male) nobility and chosen commoners, in the interests of a strong aristocracy.[17]

The problem for Puttenham at this point is that he is writing a *manual,* the only conceivable user of which is the individual who does *not* possess the natural decorum of the few: the would-be poet, who is eager to acquire the necessary learning and experience.[18] But if there are no rules to be adduced as to the essential distinction between successful and unsuccessful poetry, how is he to pursue his aim as an instructor? His solution to the problem is to cite a lengthy catalogue of *examples* of decorum in action (amounting to over a tenth of the book), drawn not from literature but from incidents in court life (264–98).[19] Puttenham assumes, of course, that he belongs to the elite, and that *his* judgment as to decorous speech or behavior—a courtier's excuse for a fart released before Henry VIII, for instance—is not open to question. The neophyte poet is expected to acquire from these vividly depicted exempla a sense of decorum that can then be applied to writing; Puttenham has no qualms about making a direct link between the modes of behavior that sustain political power and the graces of poetry. But his unwillingness to draw up rules of decorum (when he has no hesitation in saying that rules can be deduced by the close observation of nature in its more general sense) points to a wider dilemma: if art—whether the art of poetry or the art of courtly conduct—*were* reducible to rule, it would be available to all who were willing to make the effort. Since the existence of poetry, like the power of the court, is predicated upon its exclusiveness, such a conclusion is unthinkable. Puttenham must therefore produce a manual that is designed to fail.[20]

We have not finished with the dangerous supplement of art, however; it is not to be so easily controlled by being embedded in a social and political context, and granted the status of a pseudonature. Recall that the threat of the supplement is that, since it belies its own secondariness in making good what is lacking in the nature it supplements, it constantly endangers nature's primariness. If the natural body is weak—by nature—and needs the artificial assistance of the *pharmakon,* is not artificiality already presupposed in nature? Although the naturalness of decorum is determined by a minority culture, it must be *believed* to be identical with nature itself; and if art is allowed the role of supplier of nature's wants, that reference point loses its validity.[21]

The source of the problem becomes clearer if we ask what purposes the term "nature" in its most general sense is being asked to fulfill within the discursive system that makes possible Puttenham's writing. It is called upon to stand for a notion of self-sufficiency, wholeness, and plenitude: that which is without self-division or self-consciousness, and without dependence on anything exterior to itself—like the past (in such forms as memory and history), the future (goals, for instance), or rules and codes that preexist and predetermine it. This notion is powerfully operative even (or especially) within Puritan or neoplatonic emphases on the fallenness or secondariness of the nature we experience: fallen nature is, precisely, fallen from its *true self*, what it should have been.[22] But any attempt to ground this notion empirically, or even to give it theoretical or imaginative substance, necessarily fails, caught up as our existence, our language, our thought are in the operation of difference, loss, desire, secondariness, instability, deferral, predetermination, and all the other features of our experience whose inescapability gives rise to our yearning for what we call (among other things) "nature." Art, which is a reaching after, or an echo of, that oneness and self-sufficiency that is nature's alone by right, and which constitutes nature, is called upon at the same time to *produce* the oneness and self-sufficiency of nature by virtue of its own healing and perfecting powers. However, to accept fully that art has this central function, that the apparent supplement has a primary role and not a merely supplementary one, would be to allow the founding notion of nature, of a principle of plenitude and transcendence, to collapse, and with it much of the enabling intellectual (and political/religious) discourse of the time.

In the *Apologie*, Sidney comes close to articulating this view, by arguing that art is the only means of re-attaining, in a fallen world, a glimpse of prelapsarian perfection; but he half withdraws it as soon as he has made it: "But these arguments will by few be understood, and by fewer granted"—a strangely uncomfortable moment in the easy assurance of his rhetoric.[23] Spenser's superb meditations on the relationship of nature and art—in the description of the Bower of Bliss, for example—are suffused with this fear, and it is the same fear that underlies Perdita's brusque rejection of Polixenes' position, at first sight a surprisingly negative response to an eloquent and persuasive argument, one which she seemingly stands to gain by:

> I'll not put
> The dibble in the earth to set one slip of them;
> No more than were I painted I would wish
> This youth should say 'twere well and only therefore
> Desire to breed by me.
> (4.4.99–103)[24]

To allow art—however well-disguised as a greater or subtler nature—to replace nature in the garden would be equivalent, for Perdita, to allowing that most "natural" human response, sexual desire, to be the product of a painted surface (or, we may add, thinking of the end of the play—by which Shakespeare provides a different context for the problem of supplementarity—a painted statue).

The danger that art will supplant nature becomes most acute when art ceases to be distinguishable by its distance from nature and takes on the appearance of nature itself (as threatens to happen, for example, in the Bower of Bliss). Puttenham has accepted that art can come naturally, as does Sidney in the famous passage in the *Apologie* about the "smally learned Courtier" who, "following that which by practice he findeth fittest to nature, therein (though he know it not) doth according to Art, though not by Art."[25] But if art can come by nature, can nature come by art? The whole discussion of decorum tends in this direction and is only prevented from reaching this conclusion by the insistence that decorum is not reducible to rules of art: *natural* art can come only by means of a natural principle. But at the end of his book, after a concluding summary of the whole treatise, Puttenham admits—in what can only be called a supplement—that art does have the power to disguise itself as nature. This assertion is, of course, as old as the notion of art itself; it appears as the classical *ars est celare artem,* or the courtly accomplishment of *sprezzatura,* the ability to present the artificial *as* the natural, but it must always constitute an uneasy place in the discussion of the crucial distinction between art and nature. Puttenham's belated treatment of it is no exception—that belatedness itself being one sign of its potential disruptiveness. In closing the final book, he says he will offer a "principall good lesson for al good makers to beare continually in mind": the lesson of the courtier, "which is in plaine termes, cunningly to be able to dissemble" (299)—in plain terms, because Puttenham is not going to dissemble in presenting us with this unpleasant fact, whose unpleasantness he stresses by going on to quote several nasty examples of courtly duplicity. But the poet— or at least "our English maker"—is an honest man and not a hypocrite (Puttenham forgets that he has described *all* figurative language as deceitful) and is allowed only one form of deception: "When he is most artificiall, so to disguise and cloake it as it may not appeare, nor seeme to proceede from him by any studie or trade of rules, *but to be his natural*" (302; my emphasis). At this point, art, kept in check throughout the book by the operations of nature, breaks loose: if there is an *art* of behaving and writing naturally—and this more than anything else is what seems to constitute the arts of poetry and courtliness—the supplement has indeed put itself in nature's place.

III

Puttenham makes one final attempt, in a kind of supplement to this supplement, to reassert the ultimate primacy of nature, by setting out four kinds of relation between nature and art; but in so doing he succeeds only in articulating once more the instability and undecidability of that relationship. Firstly (I am not following Puttenham's order), art can *imitate* nature, as the painter or sculptor does, or the poet in reporting on the acts of Priam or Ulysses: Puttenham raises here the question of fiction, in which, unlike Sidney, he has little interest (though, as Derrida has shown, the domain of *mimesis* is also inhabited by the structures of supplementarity).[26] Secondly, art can use the stuff of nature, but produce something quite different, as a carpenter does in making a table out of wood: this is what the poet is doing in constructing elaborate stanza forms out of the material of language—the subject of Puttenham's second book, and again not of direct relevance to our discussion.

The other two kinds of relation are directly concerned with the supplementarity of art: it may act either as an *aid* to nature, or as an "alterer" or "surmounter" of nature, so that "her owne effects shall appear more beautifull or straunge and miraculous" (303). As the supplement, art both repairs the deficiencies of nature and adds to a nature that is already complete; as the *pharmakon* it cures nature of its ills, but adulterates it with the artificial. Puttenham uses almost the same terms: "In some cases we say arte is an ayde or coadiutor to nature, and a furtherer of her actions to good effect, or peradventure a meane to supply her wants, by renforcing the causes wherein shee is impotent and defective as doth the arte of phisicke" (303).[27] And in passages Shakespeare might have read, Puttenham compares the poet to the gardener seasoning the soil with "compost" and "costly drugs" to cure the infirmities of nature, or to produce blooms that nature never produces—including the double gilliflower (303–4).

But as we have seen, without the principle of decorum, the principle of "naturalness," art is a vice that distorts nature and makes it ridiculous. Puttenham reiterates the reentry of nature into the argument at this point: since the material of the poet—"language and utterance, and discourse and persuasion, and argument"—are "little lesse naturall than his very sensuall actions," the best poetry, in spite of everything that has just been said in favor of art, is made by "naturall instinct," not "arte and precepts" (305). (This is combined, incidentally, with a preference for "long meditation" over "suddaine inspiration" (305–6): Puttenham, like Wordsworth, is in-

terested only in the kind of spontaneity that comes as the final
product of a long process of meditation.) And in a final assertion of
the overriding claims of nature, Puttenham proposes an idea that
has so far not been fully articulated: "But for that in our maker or
Poet, which restes onely in devise and issues from an excellent
sharpe and quick invention, holpen by a cleare and bright phantasie
and imagination" (when he is at his most creative, we might say), he
is not imitating or perfecting or adding to the effects of nature, "but
even as nature her selfe working by her owne peculiar vertue and
proper instinct and not by example or meditation or exercise as all
other artificers do" (307). Nature is that which, by definition, works
without rules and art, simply by being itself, *natura naturans;* and it is
after all possible—or it is necessary for Puttenham to believe that it
is possible—for the poet to work in this way, too.

The analogy between nature's creativity and the artist's is of
course a familiar and enduring one,[28] and it is a culmination of one
thread that has run through Puttenham's whole argument. But the
counter-thread to this one is still visible too, woven inseparably with
it into the text: the poet, repeats Puttenham in his final sentence
(apart from a last compliment to Queen Elizabeth), should be "more
commended for his naturall eloquence than for his artificiall"; but he
has to add, "and more for his artificiall well desembled, than for the
same overmuch affected and grossely or undiscretly bewrayed"
(307). The ideal is to *be* natural, by being yourself as nature is; but if
you cannot—and the entire manual is built on the premise that you
cannot—you need to supplement your own natural inadequacies by
the exercise of decorum (that "natural" art), so that you may artificially rise to the status of perfect and self-sufficient nature.

IV

Because Puttenham's rhetorical and argumentative strategies are
relatively open, it has been a fairly simple task to trace their contradictions and inner differences. But it would have been possible to
follow the same shifts and rifts in many other accounts, from the
same and other periods, of the distinction between nature and art
(or terms with the same discursive responsibilities thrust upon
them)—because, as should by now be obvious, they arise not from
the diversity of opinion or the vagueness of the terms, but from the
precise demands made upon the distinction, the impossible expectations it has been brought into being to fulfill.[29] A principle of
plenitude, self-sufficiency, self-presence is taken as the necessary
condition for the production of knowledge, or ethics and politics, or

aesthetics; its inevitable failure in these terms results in the positing of a second principle, which is both a perfecting and a displacing principle. This structure of thought is far from being a mere historical curiosity: it continues to underlie most conceptions of knowledge, ethics, politics, and aesthetics. Any attempt to discuss the distinctiveness of poetic language using concepts like "foregrounding" or "deviation" in relation to a norm produces the problems inherent in the impossible logic of supplementarity. Is it possible, we might ask, to enunciate a *consistent* theory of literary language (or art in general) that takes for granted a self-defined "natural" base (whether we call it "ordinary language," "the literal," "the real") against which the special practices of art define themselves? Or will such a theory always and inevitably find itself reintroducing the primary concept—or a disguised (and politically acceptable) version of it—as a way of controlling the otherwise uncontrollable secondary concept, and at the same time discovering the secondary already inhabiting the primary?

The perplexity that Puttenham, as one of our first English literary theorists, evinces in the face of these problems may warn us against expecting too much from the subtler labors of his successors; but his cheerful pragmatism in the face of the perplexing field of discourse may help us, nevertheless, to appreciate the gains to be made from persisting in the impossible project that he, and we, are engaged in.

Notes

1. Among those who have acknowledged the difficulty of the project, and who have offered advice on carrying it out, are Michel Foucault in *The Archaeology of Knowledge*, trans. A. M. Sheridan Smith (New York: Random House, 1972), and Frank Lentricchia in *After the New Criticism* (Chicago: University of Chicago Press, 1980). Two essays that deal specifically with the problem in relation to the Renaissance are Thomas M. Greene, "Anti-hermeneutics: The Case of Shakespeare's Sonnet 129," in Maynard Mack and George de Forest Lord, eds., *Poetic Traditions of the English Renaissance* (New Haven: Yale University Press, 1982), 143–60, and Michael McCanles, "The Authentic Discourse of the Renaissance," *Diacritics* 10.1 (March 1980): 77–87. Sometimes the advice does not amount to much more than "try as hard as you can," although of the above Foucault and McCanles give a clear indication of the intractability of the problem. A comment with interesting implications is made by Blanchot in *L'Espace littéraire:* a work judged to be "good" will be appropriated, but one judged to be "bad" is "set aside, relegated to the inferno by libraries, burned, forgotten: but this exile, this disappearance into the heat of the

fire or the tepidness of oblivion, prolongs in a certain way the just distance of the work" (cited by Greene, 160).

2. I am using the standard edition, ed. Gladys Doidge Willcock and Alice Walker (Cambridge: Cambridge University Press, 1936), which includes a valuable introduction on such problematic matters as authorship and dating—matters that have no direct bearing on my argument here. Page references will be given in the text. I have modernized Renaissance printing conventions and altered "then" to "than" where appropriate.

3. Roland Barthes, "Criticism as Language," in David Lodge, ed., *Twentieth-Century Literary Criticism: A Reader* (London: Longman, 1972), 647–51.

4. The first published reference to it, by Sir John Harington in "A Brief Apology for Poetry" (1591), was derogatory; Harington remarks that "the poore gentleman laboreth greatly to prove, rather to make Poetrie an art," and compares him pointedly with "M. *Sidney* and all the learneder sort that have written of it" (G. Gregory Smith, ed., *Elizabethan Critical Essays* [London: Oxford University Press, 1904], 2.196–97). The note of condescension (and the unfavorable comparison with Sidney) have been echoed by many later commentators; thus Smith in his introduction to *Elizabethan Critical Essays*, after praising Sidney and Daniel, includes Puttenham's work among "essays of less sustained power" (lxx), while Baxter Hathaway opens his introduction to a modern facsimile of Arber's 1906 reprint with a warning that "one must shut one's eyes to the book's many shortcomings" and later complains about the work's "flippancy, its popularization and watering-down of theory for court consumption," applauding it rather weakly as a "more than adequate summation of a traditional approach to poetics" and a "synthesis of commonplaces" (Kent, Ohio: Kent State University Press, 1970, v, xxiii–xxiv). W. K. Wimsatt and Cleanth Brooks refer to Puttenham's "uneven collection of jokes and conceits and the theoretical hints which he musters to introduce them" (*Literary Criticism: A Short History* [New York: Alfred A. Knopf, 1969], 234). The "accuracy" of such assessments is not the issue; more important is what kind of reading such attitudes produce and are produced by.

5. Two readings of the *Apologie* which highlight some of these contradictory processes are those by Ronald Levao in "Sidney's Feigned *Apology*," *PMLA* 94 (1979), 223–33, and by Margaret Ferguson in chapter 4 of *Trials of Desire: Renaissance Defenses of Poetry* (New Haven: Yale University Press, 1983). On Sidney's *sprezzatura*, see also Daniel Javitch, "The Impure Motives of Elizabethan Poetry," *Genre* 15 (1982): 225–38.

6. *Nature and Art in Renaissance Literature* (New York: Columbia University Press, 1964). References will be given in the text. Tayler is, as he acknowledges, building on the work of A. O. Lovejoy and George Boas in *Primitivism and Related Ideas in Antiquity* (Baltimore: Johns Hopkins University Press, 1935).

7. Tayler's emphasis is not on the contradictoriness, but on a reading that will minimize it; thus he writes of the classical authors mentioned: "There

are passages open to primitivistic or even 'naturalistic' interpretations, but the balance in all of these minds falls finally against Nature in the sense of the spontaneous or unreflective" (51). "Finally" refers perhaps to the critics' need to reach a destination rather than to any conclusiveness in the texts in questions that remain, as Tayler says, "open . . . to interpretation." J. W. H. Atkins, in *English Literary Criticism: The Renascence* (1947; repr. New York: Barnes & Noble, 1968), comes to a different conclusion about the same texts, finding that nature (or reason) is the final court of appeal. Thus he quotes a passage from Quintilian (*Inst. Orat.* 9.4.120) in which the writer is advised in matters of rhythm to follow nature rather than art (166), but he omits the last part of Quintilian's sentence, which reads: "none the less there will always be some principle of art underlying the promptings of nature" (Loeb trans.). Madeleine Doran is another who seeks a principle of "balance" to reconcile contradictions in her discussion of "Art vs. Nature" in Renaissance writing (*Endeavors of Art: A Study of Form in Elizabethan Drama* [Madison: University of Wisconsin Press, 1954], 54–70), while Edwin M. Duval, discussing a similar inconsistency in Montaigne's "Des Cannibales," explains it as a deliberate demonstration of the mutability of human judgment ("Lessons of the New World: Design and Meaning in Montaigne's 'Des Cannibales' [1.31] and 'Des Coches' [3.6]," *Yale French Studies* 64 [1983]: 96–112).

8. *Of Grammatology,* trans. Gayatri Spivak (Baltimore: Johns Hopkins University Press, 1976), 158. Further references will be given in the text.

9. In *Dissemination,* trans. Barbara Johnson (Chicago: Chicago University Press, 1981), 61–171.

10. On the importance of rules in Elizabethan conceptions of art, see my *Well-weighed Syllables: Elizabethan Verse in Classical Metres* (Cambridge: Cambridge University Press, 1974), 138–43, and *passim.* Puttenham's association of rules with *reason* marks another dimension of the question, which it is not possible to broach here (though it is implicated, as I suggested earlier, in the very procedures we are using); we may simply note that reason can appear on the side of either nature or art, depending on whether the latter is seen as perverter or perfecter of the former (see Tayler, *Nature and Art,* 27–30 and *passim,* and Duval, "Lessons of the New World," 103).

11. See Attridge, *Well-weighed Syllables,* 217–19. The disparity between the two arguments is usually taken as an indication that they were written at different times (see the introduction to their edition by Willcock and Walker, xliv–liii); if this view is accepted we still have to account for the fact that Puttenham did not correct the earlier argument, but merely added the later one—as a supplement.

12. The tensions within the Renaissance program of imitation have recently been ably brought out by several scholars, notably Thomas M. Greene, *The Light in Troy: Imitation and Discovery in Renaissance Poetry* (New Haven: Yale University Press, 1982); Terence Cave, *The Cornucopian Text: Problems of Writing in the French Renaissance* (Oxford: Clarendon Press, 1979), es-

pecially chapter 2; Ferguson, *Trials of Desire*, especially chapter 2; and David Quint, *Origin and Originality in Renaissance Literature: Versions of the Source* (New Haven: Yale University Press, 1983).

13. See my discussion of Daniel's *Defence of Rhyme* in *Well-weighed Syllables*, 232–34.

14. Whereas decorum in one guise or another has been a recurrent (and necessary) element in the tradition of classical and postclassical literary criticism until this century, since it preserves the authority of those who control literary judgment in the name of "good taste," structuralism can be understood as an attempt to abolish the appeal to any such unformulatable principle.

15. Tayler points out that both Plato and Aristotle make similar comments and also quotes John of Salisbury to the same effect (*Nature and Art*, 79, 135–36). Coleridge, in the course of his disagreement with Wordsworth over the relationship of art and nature, cites the passage from *The Winter's Tale* (*Biographia Literaria*, ed. J. Shawcross [London: Oxford University Press, 1907], 2.50–51).

16. See Roland Barthes, *Mythologies*, sel. and trans. Annette Lavers (New York: Hill & Wang, 1972), especially the essay entitled "Myth Today."

17. Commentators have often pointed out the irony of Polixenes' argument in view of his opposition to his son's courting of an apparent commoner. Shakespeare's late plays by no means offer a summarizable "attitude" to the question of art versus nature, tending rather to dramatize and problematize the opposition.

18. Or the would-be courtier, as recent studies of Puttenham have emphasized; see, for instance, Daniel Javitch, *Poetry and Courtliness in Renaissance England* (Princeton: Princeton University Press, 1978), and Heinrich Plett, "Aesthetic Constituents in the Courtly Culture of Renaissance England," *New Literary History* 14 (1983): 597–621. That *The Arte of English Poesie* can be read as a courtesy handbook does not, of course, diminish its importance as a poetic handbook.

19. Puttenham also mentions a book of his, now lost, entitled *De Decoro* (277), which presumably included many more examples.

20. These are the terms used against Puttenham by Harington, who remarks cuttingly of the former's theory of poetry that "he doth prove nothing more plainly than that . . . it is a gift and not an art" because "he sheweth himselfe so slender a gift in it" (Smith, *Elizabethan Critical Essays*, 2, 197). Puttenham is not, for Sir John, a member of the natural elite.

21. Renaissance writers were not afraid of following through the logic of this position and praising *nature* for its approximation to *art*; as Doran puts it, "Hairs become golden wires or threads, brooks are crystal, water dripping from an oar is a rope of liquid pearl, meadows are enameled or adorned with dainty gems, birds make sweet division" (*Endeavors of Art*, 69).

22. Cf. Derrida's comment: "The speech that Rousseau raised above writing is speech as it should be or rather as it *should have been*" (*Grammatology*, 141).

23. *An Apologie for Poetry*, in Smith, *Elizabethan Critical Essays*, 1.157. Were Sidney to follow this argument through, poetry would replace religion as the way back to God's grace. (There are, of course, related supplementary structures within the religious doctrine involving the Fall and the Atonement.)

24. Shakespeare's critics are sometimes more easily persuaded than Perdita. In a well-known discussion of this passage (reprinted in *The Winter's Tale: A Casebook*, ed. Kenneth Muir [London: Macmillan, 1968], 151–58), Harold S. Wilson asserts that Perdita "cheerfully assents to the figure, if not to the application Polixenes intends" (151). To find "cheerfulness" in Perdita's brief "So it is" is already to have decided that Shakespeare underwrites Polixenes' harmonious view of the distinction in question.

25. Smith, *Elizabethan Critical Essays*, 1.203.

26. See *Of Grammatology*, 203–16, and "The Double Session" in *Dissemination*, 173–285, especially 184–93. Derrida has discussed the complicity between *mimesis* and metaphor, and their relation to a founding principle of nature, in "White Mythology: Metaphor in the Text of Philosophy," in *Margins of Philosophy*, trans. Alan Bass (Chicago: University of Chicago Press, 1982), 207–71; see especially 237–38.

27. Robert Herrick and Robert Burton are among the other Renaissance authors to use the word "supply" in describing art's addition to nature (Tayler, *Nature and Art*, 14–15); and Lovejoy and Boas in their translation of Cicero's account of the same relationship use the verb "supplement" (cited by Tayler, 49).

28. Derrida has discussed Kant's use of this analogy in "Economimesis," *Diacritics* 11.2 (June 1981): 3–25.

29. It is necessary, therefore, to revise Tayler's summary at several points: "When used together the terms represented an almost infinitely flexible and yet 'real' principle of classification that might be used to define the most fundamental relationships within the order of nature" (174). The terms represent a structure far from flexible that operates within the order of discourse; and the "reality" of the classification can only be understood as one of its effects. Renaissance accounts of "savage man," whether documentary or literary, and the genre of the pastoral, to both of which Tayler devotes considerable attention, demand a different analysis in the light of the relations of supplementarity within which, and with which, they operate.

13. HAMLET'S DULL REVENGE

■

RENÉ GIRARD

IN THE portrayal of certain characters, Shakespeare seems deliberately to oscillate between two opposite, really incompatible poles. On the one hand he makes these characters quite distinctive, especially as "villains"; on the other hand he shows these same characters behaving and thinking exactly like their antagonists. In the course of a single play the playwright seems to undo at one moment what he has done the moment before; he builds up and then he undermines the specificity of the same character.

Richard III provides an example. When Shakespeare wrote the play, we are told, the king's identity as a "villain" was well established. The dramatist goes along with the popular view, especially at the beginning. Richard's deformed body is a mirror for the self-confessed ugliness of his soul.

Richard, however, is not alone. Accomplices and enemies surround him. As critics like Murray Krieger and Jan Kott have shown, we are in a world of bloody political struggles and not one adult character in the play has not committed at least one political murder or benefited from one. Most have acted in the past just about as Richard now is acting. Given the slightest chance, they would act again in the same manner. Shakespeare loses no opportunity to demonstrate the point. The two women who have most suffered at Richard's hands cannot resist the temptation of a return to power, even at the cost of an alliance with him, when it is dangled in front of them by the very man who has killed the husband of the first and two young children of the second. The York-Lancaster quarrel, the War of the Roses, functions as a *system* of political rivalry and revenge in which every participant is a tyrant and a victim in turn, always behaving and speaking not according to permanent char-

This is a shortened version of an essay that first appeared in *The Stanford Literature Review*, 1, no. 2 (Fall 1984), 159–200. Asterisks indicate deleted material.

acter differences, but to the position he occupies at any moment
within the total dynastic system. Being the last coil in that infernal
spiral, Richard may kill more people, more cynically than his predecessors but he is not essentially *different*. In the course of the tragic
action, Shakespeare dwells on this nondifference with the same
insistence as he dwelled earlier on Richard's difference as a "villain."

Shylock is another example. A harsh and greedy hater of all Christians, he embodies the mythical figure of the Jew in the medieval
book of antisemitism. The fact cannot be disputed. There are other
facts, however, and they are no less striking. The other Venetians act
exactly as Shylock does. Bassanio's courtship of Portia begins as a
financial gamble, like Antonio's commerce on the high seas, a business venture that could not have been launched without Shylock's
money. There is a constant parallel between all these Venetian enter-
prises:

> *Gratiano*
> Your hand, Salerio. What's the news from Venice?
> How doth that royal merchant, good Antonio?
> I know he will be glad of our success.
> We are the Jasons, we have won the fleece.
> *Salerio*
> I would you had won the fleece that he hath lost.

Even when they banter about the future offspring of the two marriages generated by Bassanio's industriousness, the Venetians manage to sound like Shylock; money is always exchanged against the
flesh and soul of someone:

> *Bassanio*
> Our feast shall be much honored in your marriage.
> *Gratiano*
> We'll play with them the first boy for a thousand ducats.

These mirror effects between Shylock and his antagonists cannot
be fortuitous. Even if we were naïve enough to believe that they are,
we would still have to cope with the famous passage in which
Shylock proclaims the identity of Jews and Christians. They are
alike, he says, they feel the same hunger and the same thirst. They
have the same pleasures and the same pain. Above all, they treat
each other alike, being equally possessed by the spirit of revenge:

> if you wrong us, shall we not revenge? If we are like you in the rest, we
> will resemble you in that. If a Jew wrong a Christian, what is his
> humility? Revenge. If a Christian wrong a Jew, what should his suf-
> ferance be by Christian example? Why, revenge. The villainy you teach

me I will execute, and it shall go hard but I will better the instruction.
(3.1)

What Shylock says here, Shakespeare must believe since the dramatic action abundantly illustrates a reciprocity and an equivalence that are characteristic of all dramatic action in Shakespeare but that in *The Merchant of Venice*, acquire a special significance in view of the popular antisemitism that they contradict implicitly as well as explicitly denounce. And yet all this does not prevent the same Shakespeare from presenting Shylock as a caricatural villain.

The change of emphasis with the beginning is striking but it would be excessive to say that we have two Richards, or two Shylocks, even though like Shylock, Richard, at times, sounds like the only character with an ethical dimension in the entire cast.

The truth is that characters such as Richard and Shylock, after being singled out as very special, even unique villains, turn out to be no more villainous *but no less* than anybody in sight. We have no positive "rehabilitation" in the sense of Rousseau or Lévi-Strauss rehabilitating the "bon sauvage"; what we have, hidden from the absent-minded and the unsensitive, yet strikingly visible to a certain ethical sensitivity is *an equalization in villainy.*

The reciprocity of tragic action makes all characters more and more similar; since the protagonists normally fight each other, they all commit the same actions. The revenge seekers pattern themselves scrupulously on their intended victims, who may become their murderers. Retaliation and reprisals are a form of imitation; how could all the antagonists fail to be morally equivalent since they all turn themselves into perfect copies of each other? This is what Shylock is talking about.

The basic identity of all men is usually obscured, in peaceful circumstances, by those differences that a cultural order exaggerates or invents: differences of age or sex, race, religion, or ideology; functions and dignities, political roles and social hierarchies. Violence and revenge, like love, disregard differences and render them insignificant. When violence holds sway, what appears to matter a great deal at other times simply disappears and becomes almost incomprehensible. The reverse is equally true.

* * *

Hamlet belongs to the genre of the revenge tragedy, as hackneyed and yet inescapable in Shakespeare's days as the "thriller" in ours to a television writer. In *Hamlet* Shakespeare turned this necessity for a playwright to go on writing the same old revenge tragedies into an opportunity to debate almost openly for the first time the questions I have tried to define. The weariness with revenge and *katharsis* which can be read, I believe, in the margins of the earlier plays must really exist because, in *Hamlet*, it moves to the center of the stage and becomes fully articulated.

Some writers who were not necessarily the most unimaginative found it difficult, we are told, to postpone for the whole duration of the lengthy Elizabethan play an action that had never been in doubt in the first place and that is always the same anyway. Shakespeare can turn this tedious chore into the most brilliant feat of theatrical *double entendre* because the tedium of revenge is really what he wants to talk about, and he wants to talk about it in the usual Shakespearean fashion; he will denounce the revenge theater and all its works with the utmost daring without denying his mass audience the *katharsis* it demands, without depriving himself of the dramatic success that is necessary to his own career as a dramatist.

If we assume that Shakespeare really had this double goal in mind, we will find that some unexplained details in the play become intelligible and that the function of many obscure scenes becomes obvious.

In order to perform revenge with conviction, you must believe in the justice of your own cause. The revenge seeker will not believe in his own cause unless he believes in the guilt of his intended victim. And the guilt of that intended victim entails in turn the innocence of that victim's victim. If the victim's victim is already a killer and if the revenge seeker reflects a little too much on the circularity of revenge, his faith in vengeance must collapse.

This is exactly what we have in *Hamlet*. It cannot be without a purpose that Shakespeare suggests the old Hamlet, the murdered king, was a murderer himself. In the various sources of the play there may be indications to that effect, but Shakespeare would have omitted them if he had wanted to strengthen the case for revenge. However nasty Claudius may look, he cannot look nasty enough if he appears in a context of previous revenge; he cannot generate, as a villain, the absolute passion and dedication demanded of Hamlet. The problem with Hamlet is that he cannot forget the context. As a result, the crime by Claudius looks to him like one more link in an already long chain, and his own revenge will look like still another link, perfectly identical to all the other links.

In a world where every ghost, dead or alive, can only perform the same action, revenge, or clamor for more of the same from beyond the grave, all voices are interchangeable. You can never know with certainty which ghost is addressing whom. It is one and the same thing for Hamlet to question his own identity and to question the ghost's identity, and his authority.

To seek singularity in revenge is a vain enterprise, but to shrink from revenge in a world that looks upon it as a "sacred duty" is to exclude oneself from society, to become a nonentity once more. There is no way out for Hamlet and he shifts endlessly from one impasse to the other, unable to make up his mind because neither choice makes sense.

If all characters are caught in a cycle of revenge that extends in all directions beyond the limits of its action, *Hamlet* has no beginning and no end. The play collapses. The trouble with the hero is that he does not believe in his play half as much as the critics do. He understands revenge and the theater too well to assume willingly a role chosen for him by others. His sentiments are those, in other words, which we have surmised in Shakespeare himself. What the hero feels in regard to the act of revenge, the creator feels in regard to revenge as theater.

The public wants vicarious victims and the playwright must oblige. Tragedy is revenge. Shakespeare is tired of revenge, and yet he cannot give it up, or he gives up his audience and his identity as a playwright. Shakespeare turns a typical revenge topic, *Hamlet*, into a meditation on his predicament as a playwright.

Claudius and the old Hamlet are not blood brothers first and enemies second; they are brothers in murder and revenge. In the myths and legends from which most tragedies are drawn, brotherhood is almost invariably associated with the reciprocity of revenge. Close examination reveals that brotherhood, the most frequent probably of all mythological themes, stands for this reciprocity rather than for the specific family relationship it designates. Being the least differentiated relationship in most kinship systems, the status of a brother can become a mark of undifferentiation, a symbol of violent desymbolization, the sign paradoxically that there are no more signs and that a warring confusion tends to prevail everywhere.

This interpretation is confirmed by the large proportion of mythical antagonists who are not merely brothers but identical twins, Jacob and Esau, for instance, or Eteocles and Polyneices, or Romulus and Remus. Twins possess in the highest degree the quality already essential to mythical brotherhood: they are undistinguishable; they completely lack the differentiation all primitive and traditional communities deem indispensable to the maintenance of peace and order.

If everywhere in mythodology enemy twins predominate, if the birth of real twins is a cause of fear, in many primitive communities, and if, very often as a result, one of the children or both are destroyed, the reason lies in the frequent assimilation of biological twins with the cultural twins of revenge and reprisals.

It is surprising, to say the least, that modern anthropology has not yet rediscovered the significance of twins in mythology and primitive religion. Far from pointing to a new direction, the exclusively differential emphasis of structuralism and its offspring constitutes the ultimate fulfillment of the old and most powerful tradition not only of our social sciences and of our philosophy but of religion itself. This tendency minimizes at its best, and at its worst completely suppresses everything essential to the understanding of a writer like Shakespeare, beginning with the mimetic nature of human conflict and the resulting tendency of the antagonists to behave more and more alike as they perceive more and more difference between each other.

If Shakespeare had shared the ignorance of our social sciences and literary critics in regard to mythological twins and brothers, he would never have written *The Comedy of Errors*. The most striking feature of this play is that, thanks to the theme of the undetected twins, many effects that are really similar to the unperceived equalizing effects of tragic conflict can be exploited in a vein of comic misunderstanding.

This significance of twins and brothers, not only in mythology but in a stage tradition that includes, of course, the Plautus of *The Menechmi* must be present to our minds if we are to interpret correctly the scene in which Hamlet, holding in his hands the two portraits of his father and his uncle, or pointing to them on the wall, tries to convince his mother that an enormous difference exists between the two. There would be no Hamlet "problem" if the hero really believed what he says. It is also himself, therefore, that he is trying to convince. The anger in his voice and the exaggeration of his language with its coldly contrived metaphors suggest that he labors in vain:

> Look here upon this picture, and on this
> The counterfeit presentment of two brothers.
> See what a grace was seated on this brow.
> Hyperion's curls, the front of Jove himself,
> An eye like Mars, to threaten and command,
> . . . .
> A combination and a form indeed
> Where every god did seem to set his seal

> To give the world assurance of a man.
> This was your husband. Look you now what follows.
> Here is your husband, like a mildewed ear,
> Blasting his wholesome brother. Have you eyes?

The gentleman doth protest too much. The symmetry of the whole presentation and of Hamlet's own expressions tends to reassert the resemblance he denies: "This was your husband . . . / Here is your husband."

Hamlet begs his mother to give up her conjugal relationship with Claudius. The tons of Freud that have been poured over the passage have obscured its significance. Hamlet does not feel indignant enough to rush out and kill the villain. As a result he feels uncomfortable about himself and he blames his mother because she obviously feels even more indifferent to the whole affair than he does. He would like his mother to initiate the revenge process for him. He tries to arouse in her the indignation he himself cannot feel, in order to catch it second-hand from her, perhaps, out of some kind of mimetic sympathy. Between Gertrude and Claudius he would like to see a dramatic break that would force him to side resolutely with his mother.

It is a generally accepted view nowadays that Gertrude must have felt a tremendous attachment to Claudius. Far from confirming that view, the following lines suggest exactly the opposite:

> Nor sense to ecstasy was every so thralled
> But it reserved some quantity of choice
> To serve in such a difference

Hamlet does not say that his mother is madly in love with Claudius; he says that even if she were, she should still be able to perceive some difference between her two husbands. Hamlet assumes, therefore, that his mother like himself, perceives *no difference whatever*. This assumption is obviously correct. Gertrude remains silent during her son's tirade because she has nothing to say. The reason she could marry the two brothers in rapid succession is that they are so much alike and she feels the same indifference to the one as to the other. It is this overwhelming indifference that Hamlet perceives and he resents it because he is trying to fight it in himself. Like so many other queens of Shakespeare, like the queens of *Richard III*, for instance, Gertrude moves in a world where prestige and power count more than passion.

We are often dominated nowadays in our literary criticism by what might be called an "erotic imperative" no less dogmatic in its demands, and no less naïve ultimately than the sexual taboos that came before. In time, this rebellious child of puritanism will grow old, let us hope, and it may then become possible to recognize that his effects upon Shakespearean irony were no less detestable and destructive than those of his father.

What Hamlet needs, in order to stir up his vengeful spirit, is a revenge theater more convincing than his own, something less half-hearted than the play Shakespeare is actually writing. Fortunately for the hero and for the spectators who are eagerly awaiting their final bloodbath, Hamlet has many opportunities to watch rousing spectacles during his play and he tries to generate even more, in a conscientious effort to put himself in the right mood for the murder of Claudius. Hamlet must receive from someone else, a mimetic model, the impulse he does not find in himself. This is what he tried to achieve with his mother, we found, and he did not succeed. He is much more successful with the actor who impersonates for him the role of Hecuba. It becomes obvious, at this point, that the only hope for Hamlet to accomplish what his society—or the spectators—require, is to become as "sincere" a showman as the actor who can shed real tears when he pretends to be the queen of Troy!

> It is not monstrous that this player here,
> But in a fiction, in a dream of passion,
> Could force his soul so to his own conceit
> That from her working all his visage wanned,
> Tears in his eyes, distraction in's aspect,
> A broken voice, and his whole function suiting
> With forms to his conceit? And all for nothing!
> For Hecuba!
> What's Hecuba to him or he to Hecuba,
> That he should weep for her? What would he do
> Had he the motive and the cue for passion
> That I have?

Another catchy example for Hamlet comes from the army of Fortinbras on its way to Poland. The object of the war is a worthless speck of land. Thousands of people must risk their lives:

> Even for an eggshell. Rightly to be great
> Is not to stir without great argument,
> But greatly to find quarrel in a straw
> When Honor's at the stake.

The scene is as ridiculous as it is sinister. It would not impress Hamlet so much if the hero truly believed in the superiority and urgency of his cause. His words constantly betray him, here as in the scene with his mother. As a cue for passion, his revenge motif is no more compelling, really, than the cue of an actor on the stage. He too must *greatly . . . find quarrel in a straw,* he too must stake everything *even for an eggshell.*

The effect of the army scene obviously stems, at least in part, from the large number of people involved, from the almost infinite multiplication of the example which cannot fail to increase its mimetic attraction enormously. Shakespeare is too much a master of mob effects not to remember at this point the cumulative effect of mimetic models. In order to whip up enthusiasm for the war against Claudius, the same irrational contagion is needed as in the war against Poland. The type of mimetic incitement from which Hamlet "benefits" at this point resembles very much the kind of spectacle governments never fail to organize for their citizenry when they have decided it is time to go to war: a rousing military parade.

But it is not the actor, ultimately, or the army of Fortinbras; it is Laertes, I believe, who determines Hamlet to act. Laertes provides the most persuasive spectacle not because he provides the "best" example but because his situation parallels that of Hamlet. Being Hamlet's peer, at least up to a point, his passionate stance constitutes the most powerful challenge imaginable. In such circumstances, even the most apathetic man's sense of emulation must rise to such a pitch that the sort of disaster that the fulfillment of the revenge demands can finally be achieved.

The simple and unreflective Laertes can shout to Claudius "give me my father" and then leap into his sister's grave in a wild demonstration of grief. Like a well-adjusted gentleman or a consummate actor, he can perform with the utmost sincerity all the actions his social milieu demands, even if they contradict each other. He can mourn the useless death of a human being at one minute and the next he can uselessly kill a dozen more if he is told that his honor is at stake. The death of his father and sister are almost less shocking to him than the lack of pomp and circumstance at their burial. At the rites of Ophelia, Laertes keeps asking the priest for "more ceremony." Laertes is a formalist and he reads the tragedy of which he is a part very much like the formalists of all stripes. He does not question the validity of revenge. He does not question the literary *genre.* He does not question the relationship between revenge and mourning. These are not valid critical questions to him; they never enter his mind, just as it never occurs to most critics that Shakespeare himself could question the validity of revenge.

Hamlet watches Laertes leap into Ophelia's grave and the effect on him is electrifying. The reflective mood of the conversation with Horatio gives way to a wild imitation of the rival's theatrical mourning. At this point, he has obviously decided that he, too, would act according to the demands of society, that he would become another Laertes in other words. He, too, as a result, must leap into the grave of one who has already died, even as he prepares other graves for those still alive:

'Swounds, show me what thou'lt do.
Woo't weep? Woo't fight? Woo't fast? Woo't tear thyself?
Woo't drink up eisel? Eat a crocodile?
I'll do't. Dost thou come here to whine?
To outface me with leaping in her grave?
Be buried quick with her, and so will I.
. . . .
I'll rant as well as thou.

In order to embrace the goal of revenge, Hamlet must enter the circle of mimetic desire and rivalry; this is what he has been unable to achieve so far but here he finally reaches a hysterical pitch of that "pale and bloodless emulation" that constitutes the terminal stage of the ontological disease, so often described elsewhere by Shakespeare, in *Troilus and Cressida* of course, as well as in *A Midsummer Night's Dream*.

These words are a crystal clear expression of the mimetic frenzy that leads to victimage. When we hear them, we should know that the conclusion is near. The explicitness of the passage is comic, really, and crucial to the intelligence of the whole play, coming as it does after all the scenes we have already read and confirming their role as scenes of still half-hearted mimetic incitement. When we recapitulate these scenes, when we place them in the context of similar scenes in other plays, we cannot doubt the existence and paramount importance for Shakespeare of that mimetic cycle that goes from victimage to victimage through the various stages of mimetic integration—ritual, and cultural disintegration—mimetic desire and the "crisis of Degree."

Shakespeare can place these incredible lines in the mouth of Hamlet without undermining the dramatic credibility of what follows. Following the lead of Gertrude, the spectators will ascribe the outburst to "madness."

This is mere madness.
And thus awhile the fit will work on him.
Anon, as patient as the female dove
When that her golden couplets are disclosed,
His silence will sit drooping.

A little later Hamlet himself, now calmly determined to kill Claudius, will recall the recent outburst in most significant words:

> I am very sorry, good Horatio,
> That to Laertes I forgot myself,
> For by the image of my cause I see
> The portraiture of his. I'll court his favors.
> But, sure, the bravery of his grief did put me
> Into a towering passion.

Like all victims of mimetic suggestion, Hamlet reverses the true hierarchy between the other and himself. He should say: "by the image of *his* cause I see the portraiture of *mine.*" This is the correct formula, obviously, for all the spectacles that have influenced Hamlet. The actor's tears and the military display of Fortinbras were already presented as mimetic models. In order to realize that Laertes, too, functions as a model, the last two lines are essential. The cool determination of Hamlet, at this point, is the transmutation of the "towering passion" that he had vainly tried to build up before and that Laertes has finally communicated to him through the "bravery of his grief." This transmutation is unwittingly predicted by Gertrude when she compares Hamlet to the dove who becomes quiet after she has laid her eggs. Gertrude only thinks of Hamlet's previous changes of mood, as sterile as they were sudden, but her metaphor suggests a more tangible accomplishment, the birth of something portentous:

> Anon, as patient as the female dove
> When that her golden couplets are disclosed,
> His silence will sit drooping.

There cannot be a clear-cut answer to the question of Hamlet's "madness." The more acute stages of the mimetic process are more obviously compulsive and self-destructive than the earlier ones. But they are only the full development of what was present as a germ before. That is why these stages are, among other things, caricaturally mimetic. Everything still obscure and implicit until then becomes transparent and explicit. Normal people, so-called, must resort to the "madness" label in order not to perceive the continuity between this caricature and their own mimetic desire. In front of Hamlet's outburst inside the grave, a well-informed psychiatrist must diagnose the type of symptom that belongs to "histrionic schizophrenia," or some such disease. He cannot see anything there but pure pathology, completely divorced from all rational behavior, including his own which he does not perceive as mimetic. The writers of genius never share that illusion. If schizophrenia often imitates "with a vengeance," if it turns to spectacular "histrionics," the reasons may be not that the patient is particularly eager to imi-

tate, or gifted for imitation, but that he is less gifted for the unconscious imitation that is being silently pursued at all times among the
normal people all around him.

The question, "what is the schizophrenic individual trying to
achieve when he engages in his histrionics?" receives an answer in
Hamlet. He is trying to achieve what everybody else seems to
achieve without difficulty. He is trying to be a normal man himself;
he is aping the well-adjusted personality of Laertes, the man who
can draw his sword when he should and who can jump into his
sister's grave when he should, without looking like a madman.

The madman makes us feel uneasy not because his game is different from ours but because it is the same. It is the same old mimetic
game in which we all engage but a little too emphatic for our taste, as
if played with excessive application by a man who lacks a sense of
proportion. This type of madman desperately tries to be like us or
perhaps he merely pretends, in order to put us to shame, to deride
our overwhelming servility. We prefer to leave the matter alone and
not to look at ourselves in the mirror offered to us.

Contrary to what Freud believes, desire, at every stage, learns a
little more about itself. At the stage of histrionic schizophrenia,
desire has learned so much that it knows almost everything, much
more than the psychiatrists do; but far from improving things, superior knowledge, being immediately enlisted once more in the service of desire means a further deterioration of the patient. What the
patient cannot give up is his faith in his model and rival as the
embodiment of being. At every stage of mimetic desire that stubborn faith does not negate experience but takes precedence over it
and uses its lessons for its own purposes, more and more disas-
trously. Thus, mimetic man must finally turn himself and those
around him into a theater of cruelty, as Antonin Artaud would say.

Shakespeare's own ambiguous relationship to the theater is not
unlike Hamlet's relationship to his revenge. But a definition of the
play in terms of the creator's problem as a playwright can be no more
than a necessary first step. Hamlet would not be Hamlet if Shakespeare, as he wrote it, had been contemplating his own scriptural
navel according to the fashion that prevails in the contemporary
script. He would not have created a play of such enduring and
widespread fascination. There must be something in the Hamletian
transposition of the author's lassitude with revenge and its tragedies
that transcends the centuries and still corresponds to the predicament of our own culture.

* * *

The theater still relies on imperfectly detected scapegoat processes for its kathartic effects, much attenuated, of course, but structurally identical to the rituals of primitive religion. This relationship is acknowledged by some critics. In his essay on *Coriolanus*, Kenneth Burke shows that everything in that tragedy is planned with the victimage of the hero in mind and the most efficient strategy of victimage corresponds to the "esthetic rules" defined by Aristotle in his *Poetics*.

Northrop Frye, too, views tragedy as a bloodless and imaginary transposition of sacrificial rites. In order not to exaggerate the difference such a transposition can make, we must remember that sacrificial rites themselves are already a transposition of more spontaneous forms of victimage.

What no one realizes, I feel, is the extent to which Shakespeare himself perceives the theater's dependence on scapegoat phenomena. Shakespeare can reactivate scapegoat effects and allude to this reactivation at the same time. And he goes further than this; he knows that not only *katharsis* but the critique of *katharsis*, the indignant or ironic denunciation of the hunt for scapegoats, may constitute a new kind of scapegoating. The show is no longer on the stage but in the audience. For the knowledgeable few, the real spectacle has become the *katharsis* of the many. Just as the communion of the crowd is obtained at the expense of a tragic hero, the complicity of the knowledgeable few, including the playwright, is obtained at the expense of the crowd, which becomes the real victim in this redoubled and inverted theater.

However subtle and refined theatrical effects may become, they still amount to new displacements of the original scapegoat effects, at the end of which there must still be a real victim who will be effective as a victim in proportion to the satisfaction provided by victimage, in proportion therefore to our inability to acknowledge its arbitrariness. It may well be that traditional cultural forms, such as the theater, can never dispense entirely with victimage. It would be wrong, however, to conclude that the human mind is caught in an endlessly circular process. As far as we can tell, there is something unique in the ability of modern culture to perceive victimage as such, to interpret scapegoat effects, in other words, as psychosocial phenomena rather than as religious or esthetic epiphanies.

* * *

In his essay on ancient Judaism, the sociologist Max Weber correctly observed the biblical tendency to side with the victim. He interpreted this unique perspective as a distortion generated by the historical misfortunes of the Jews, by their failure as empire builders. If historical misfortunes sufficed to account for the existence of the Bible, the world should possess many more such texts. The cultures that can be called successful, over a period of time long enough to make a difference, are certainly very few, whereas innumerable cultures have been even less successful than the Jews. Yet none of them has ever produced anything like the Bible.

The interest of a perspective like Max Weber's is that like all the more recent perspectives, it unwittingly acknowledges the truth. Approval of victimage is the mythical norm, whereas disapproval is the exclusive monopoly of the biblical text. Max Weber sees that monopoly in a purely affective and moralistic light; he does not suspect its momentous consequences for the knowledge of human culture because he is totally blind, as almost everybody else, to the structuring role of victimage in regard not to mythical themes only but to the cultural institutions and values that derive from the myths, including, of course, the belief of Bismarckian Germany in the intellectual virtues of successful imperialism.

Max Weber's interpretation is rooted in Nietzsche's reading of Judeo-Christianity as the resentment (*ressentiment*) of the weak against the strong, the slaves against their masters, the victims against their persecutors. The literal madness of Nietzsche's attitude is that, close as he was to recognizing the truth of human culture, he willfully espoused its lie. He views the rehabilitation of the victim as a futile and destructive rebellion against the iron law of superior strength. The very frenzy of a Nietzsche suggests that the truth of culture is about to burst upon the intellectual scene of the modern world. The forces of repression are really the same as the forces of revelation. The more hysterical the repression becomes, the more visible it must also become *as repression*. Today, of course, primitive mythology is extolled to the high heavens, whereas the biblical text, when it is not completely ignored, is reviled and disfigured. In our world of philosophical hermeneutics and alleged "scientific" interpretation, the biblical text occupies the central position of the undetected scapegoat that secretly structures everything.

Even if the reasons of the biblical writers for siding with the victims were as "bad" as Nietzsche, Max Weber, Freud, and others have claimed, the question of how this attitude was achieved pales into insignificance, really, next to the achievement itself. The critics can overlook the formidable revolution that the biblical perspective represents because they have never suspected what really lies behind mythology.

Even in its most primitive layers, the biblical text already tends to demythologize more effectively than any modern demythologizer. In the Pentateuch, this demythologization still occurs within a mythical framework, as it does, to a certain extent, in Greek tragedy. With preexilic and exilic prophecy, this framework disappears and the prophets openly denounce violence and the idolatry of violence. This Old Testament revelation probably reaches its highest mark with the book of Job, certain psalms, and the Songs of the Suffering Servant, the Ebed Yahveh of the Second Isaiah. One achievement of those texts is to make the role of the scapegoat fully explicit as founder of the religious community, outside of any specific context. Each school of interpreters, Jewish and Christian primarily, has tried to supply its own context and to exclude others, never realizing that, if the first object of the revelation is the generative mechanism of all human culture, all the contexts are equally valid.

In the gospels, similarly, the passion of Jesus must be read, first of all, as a revelation of human violence. The perfect victim does not die in order to insure an immolation that would be perfect in the eyes of a still sacrificial god. The notion means that a victim perfectly nonviolent and just will make the revelation of violence complete not only in his words, but through the hostile polarization of the threatened human community. This victim's death reveals not only the violence and injustice of all sacrificial cult, but the nonviolence and justice of the divinity whose will is thus fully accomplished for the first and only time in history.

To all previous religious laws, the gospel substitutes a single command: "give up retaliation and revenge in any form." This is no utopian scheme, no folksy anarchism dreamed up by a romantic reformer. If the victimage mechanism must be misunderstood in order to remain operative, its full revelation will leave the human community deprived of sacrificial protection.

The traditional reading of many gospel themes suffers from sacrificial distortions. In a nonsacrificial reading, all themes find their place but divested of any reference to a vengeful god. The apocalyptic theme, for instance, at least in the gospels themselves, consists of a purely human threat. Apocalyptic prophecy means no more and no less than a rational anticipation of what men are likely to do to each other and to their environment if they go on disregarding the warning against revenge in a desacralized and sacrifically unprotected world.

Far from being almost exhausted, as many people believe, the impact of the Judeo-Christian revelation may have been lessened so far and retarded by the universal failure to read the texts correctly. Their subversive force was filtered by the sacrificial veils that antireligious as well as religious and traditional readings have thrown over them.

The sacrificial misreading of the gospels made the various phases of Christian culture possible. In the Middle Ages, for instance, gospel principles were superficially reconciled with the aristocratic ethics of personal honor and revenge. With the Renaissance, this edifice began to collapse and Shakespeare is a major witness to that event. Even after the disappearance of blood feuds, duels, and similar customs, Christian culture never disentangled itself completely from values rooted in revenge. Although nominally Christian, social attitudes remained essentially alien to the authentic Judeo-Christian inspiration.

This inspiration never disappeared but it often became too weak to challenge the prevailing compromises, even to take full consciousness of itself. It made its influence felt as a nameless and ambiguous force, a creeping subversion of all social values and attitudes.

Hamlet is certainly no coward; we saw that his inaction, following the command of the ghost, results from his failure to muster the proper sentiments. This failure never receives the direct and unambiguous explanation it demands in terms of a revulsion against the ethics of revenge. We may find this strange at a time when blood revenge was really on the way out and its principle was widely challenged. On the other hand, from a dramatic and literary viewpoint, Shakespeare's silence is not strange at all. *Hamlet* belongs to a genre that demands that the ethics of revenge be taken for granted. A revenge tragedy is not an appropriate vehicle for tirades against revenge.

Outwardly, at least, Shakespeare had to respect the literary conventions of the time. In a revenge tragedy, all eloquence must be on the side of revenge; all the disgust the hero feels for the act of revenge and the creator for its esthetic exploitation, remains a half-formed thought, an almost incoherent feeling that must fail in the end to gain full control of that hero's behavior, not to deprive the play of its official status as a revenge play. The spectators are provided with the victims they expect.

Shakespeare's genius turned this constraint into an asset. The silence at the heart of *Hamlet* has become a major reason for the enduring fascination of the play, its most enigmatically suggestive feature. How is this possible?

If the preceding observations are correct, the dependence of human culture on revenge and victimage is too fundamental not to survive the elimination of the most grossly physical forms of vio-

lence, the actual murder of the victim. If the Judeo-Christian fer-
ment is not dead, it must be engaged in an obscure struggle against
deeper and deeper layers of the essential complicity between violence and human culture. As the struggle reaches these deep layers,
we lack the words to describe the issues; no concept can embrace the
type of subversion values and institutions must undergo. When
language fails, silence can be more suggestive than words.

In *Hamlet*, the very absence of a case against revenge becomes a
powerful intimation of what the modern world is really about. Even
at those later stages in our culture when physical revenge and blood
feuds completely disappeared or were limited to such marginal mili-
eux as the underworld, it would seem that no revenge play, not even
a play of reluctant revenge, could strike a really deep chord in the
modern psyche. In reality the question is never entirely settled and
the strange void at the center of *Hamlet* becomes a symbolic expression of the Western and modern malaise, no less powerful than
the most brilliant attempts to define the problem, such as Dos-
toevsky's underground revenge. Our "symptoms" always resemble
that unnamable paralysis of the will, that ineffable corruption of the
spirit that affect not only Hamlet, but the other characters as well.
The devious ways of these characters, the bizarre plots they hatch,
their passion for watching without being watched, their propensity
to voyeurism and spying, the general disease of human relations
make a good deal of sense as a description of an undifferentiated no
man's land between revenge and no revenge in which we ourselves
are still living.

Claudius resembles Hamlet in his inability to take a prompt and
healthy revenge on his enemies. The king should react more explicitly and decisively to the murder of Polonius who was, after all,
his private councillor; the crime was a personal offense to him. His
reasons for hesitating, then acting only in secret, may be different
from Hamlet's but the final result is the same. When Laertes asks
Claudius why he failed to punish a murderer, the reply betrays
embarrassment.

Even Claudius presents Hamlet-like symptoms. Not Hamlet
alone but the time is out of joint. And when Hamlet describes his
revenge as "sick," or "dull," he speaks for the whole community. In
order to appreciate the nature and the extent of the disease, we must
realize that all behavior we tend to read as strategic or conspir-
atorial, in that play, can also be read as symptomatic of "sick
revenge."

When a certain type of conflict becomes endemic, its reciprocal
structure becomes apparent. The opponents can anticipate each

other's moves. In order to act effectively each one must surprise the other, throw him off balance by doing something the reciprocity does not call for or, on the contrary, he must do what the reciprocity calls for once again: he must make the move now discounted as too obvious by the other side, the move, therefore, that has become the least predictable once more.

Everybody must conceive the same strategic tricks at the same time and the reciprocity that everybody tries to sidestep simultaneously and through the same means must still win in the long run. Strategic thinking, as a result, demands ever-increasing subtlety; it involves less and less action, more and more calculation. In the end, it becomes difficult to distinguish strategy from procrastination. The very notion of strategy may be strategic in regard to the self-defeating nature of revenge which no one wants to face, not yet at least, so that the possibility of revenge is not entirely removed from the scene. Thanks to the notion of strategy, men can postpone revenge indefinitely without ever giving it up. They are equally terrified by both radical solutions and they go on living as long as possible, if not forever, in the no man's land of sick revenge.

In that no man's land it becomes impossible to define anything. All actions and motivations are their own opposites as well as themselves. When Hamlet does not seize the opportunity to kill Claudius during his prayer, it could be a failure of the will or a supreme calculation; it could be instinctive humaneness or a refinement of cruelty. Hamlet himself does not know. The crisis of Degree has reached the most intimate recesses of the individual consciousness. Human sentiments have become as mixed up as the seasons of the year in *A Midsummer Night's Dream*. Even he who experiences them can no longer say which is which, and the critic's search for neat differentiations misses the point entirely. Most interpreters cling to the illusion that differences alone must be real behind deceptive similarities, whereas the opposite is true. Similarities alone are real. We must not be misled by Ophelia's blond hair and pitiable death. Or rather, we must realize that Shakespeare consciously misleads his less attentive spectators with these gross theatrical signs of what a pure heroine should be. Just like Rosencrantz and Guildenstern, Ophelia allows herself to become an instrument in the hands of her father and of the king. She, too, is affected by the disease of the time. Another sign of her contamination is her language and behavior, which are both contaminated with the erotic strategy of a Cressida and the other least savory Shakespearean heroines. What Hamlet resents in Ophelia is what any human being always resents in another human being, the visible signs of his own sickness. It is the

same sickness, therefore, that corrupts Ophelia's love for Hamlet
and debases Hamlet's love for the theater.

* * *

The dilemma has not changed; it has only assumed more extreme
and spectacular forms that should make its perception and definition easier for us than for Shakespeare but, curiously, Shakespeare
is still ahead of us as a "demystificator." We need him, I believe, to
understand better the strange historical situation into which we
have been thrust by the very enormity of our technological power.

I do not intend to be facetious. Technological progress has made
our weapons of war so destructive that their use would defeat any
rational purpose of aggression. For the first time in Western history,
the primitive fear of revenge becomes intelligible once more. The
whole planet has become the equivalent of any primitive tribe but
no sacrificial cult is available, this time, to ward off and transfigure
the threat.

No one wants to initiate a cycle of revenge that might literally
annihilate humanity and yet no one wants to give up revenge entirely. Like Hamlet we are poised on the brink between total revenge
and no revenge at all, unable to make up our mind, unable to take
revenge and yet unable to renounce it. In the shadow of that monstrous threat all institutions dissolve, "degrees in schools and broth-
erhoods in cities," all human relations disintegrate; "each thing
meets in mere oppugnancy." Justice loses its name and "the un-
worthiest shows as fairly in the mask." The enterprise is sick.

Many people curse nowadays the same scientific and technological discoveries they still worshipped a few years ago. The
same biblical god who was blamed earlier for slowing up this progress now that things are beginning to turn sour stands accused of
inciting and promoting this dangerous venture of modern man. We
are still trying to project our own violence against that god but to no
avail, this time, since we no longer believe in him.

In reality, if mankind's domination of the entire world can become
a peril to mankind, it cannot be the fault of some god, it can only be
the human spirit of revenge which is not completely extinct with us.
If we had not decided to exclude the Judeo-Christian scriptures from
our cultural problematic, this fact alone would immediately remind
us of the still unheeded or only partly heeded evangelical warning
against revenge. The Judeo-Christian text may be more relevant to
our destiny, after all, than the oedipal mythology of Sigmund Freud
or the dionysiac mythology of Friedrich Nietzsche. We should sus-

pect by now that there is more to the warning against revenge than utopian anarchism and sentimental moralism.

We should also begin to understand *Hamlet*.

To read *Hamlet* against revenge is anachronistic, some people say, because it goes against the conventions of the revenge genre. No doubt, but could Shakespeare be playing according to the rules of the game at one level and undermining these same rules at another? Has not this ambiguous practice become a commonplace of modern criticism? Is Shakespeare too slow-witted for such a device? Indications abound that in many other plays, he is doing precisely that, still providing the crowd with the spectacle they demand while simultaneously writing between the lines, for all those who can read, a devastating critique of that same spectacle.

If we fear that *Hamlet*, in the present perspective, becomes a pretext, once more, for comments on the contemporary situation, let us look at the alternative. The traditional perspectives on *Hamlet* are far from neutral; their first consequence is that the ethics of revenge are taken for granted. The most debatable question of the play cannot be reached; we exclude it *a priori*.

Hamlet's problem thus shifts from revenge itself to hesitation in the face of revenge. Why should a well-educated young man have second thoughts when it comes to killing a close relative who also happens to be the king of the land and the husband of his own mother? This is some enigma indeed and the problem is not that a satisfactory answer has never been found but that we should expect to find one after our *a priori* exclusion of the one sensible and obvious answer.

Should our enormous critical literature on *Hamlet* fall some day into the hands of people otherwise ignorant of our mores, they could not fail to conclude that our academic tribe must have been a savage breed, indeed. After four centuries of controversies, Hamlet's temporary reluctance to commit murder still looks so outlandish to us that more and more books are being written in an unsuccessful effort to solve that mystery. The only way to account for this curious body of literature is to suppose that, back in the twentieth century no more was needed than some ghost to ask for it, and the average professor of literature would massacre his entire household without batting an eyelash.

Contrary to the official doctrine among us, the insertion of Hamlet into our contemporary situation, and in particular the reference to something as apparently alien to literature as our nuclear predicament, cannot lead the critic further astray than he already is; it cannot distract him from his proper function, which is to read the text. Amazingly enough, the effect is just the opposite. The nuclear reference can shock us back into a sense of reality. It is symptomatic of our condition, no doubt, that we avoid more and more the real issues, and we empty great literary texts of all affective and even intellectual content as we really intend to do the opposite, as we try to concentrate exclusively upon these same texts by excluding only what is extraneous to them.

Let us imagine a contemporary Hamlet with his finger on a nuclear button. After forty years of procrastination he has not yet found the courage to push that button. The critics around him are becoming impatient. The psychiatrists have volunteered their services and come up with their usual answer. Hamlet is a sick man.

From what disease does he suffer? Doctor Ernest Jones, the personal friend and biographer of Freud, has diagnosed the case. Being in the direct line of apostolic succession, so to speak, he is a man most revered and his opinion carries great weight. He is too much a man of science to produce a hasty diagnosis and even after a serious examination of the patient, he willingly admits that he cannot confront the grave symptom of Hamlet's hesitation without hesitating himself between two distinct pathologies: he calls the one *hysterical paralysis of the will* and the other *specific aboulia*. I would personally incline toward *specific aboulia*, which sounds even more forbiddingly technical to my ears than *hysterical paralysis of the will*, but I am only a literary man, easily swayed by the esthetic power of words.

Fortunately for all of us, the Hamletian hesitation of Doctor Jones in regard to the disease has no effect whatsoever upon his conception of the cure. A psychoanalyst never hesitates in regard to the cure. Like Polonius before him, he is absolutely certain Hamlet's problem can be reduced to sex.

The only difference is the shift from the daughter of the analyst to the mother of the patient. That shift makes everything more interesting and modern. Our time being the more disjointed of the two, it should and does produce the more sophisticated Poloniuses it so richly deserves, Poloniuses who can even give a Lacanian twist to their aphorisms. One thing, however, has not changed. The interpreter's satisfaction with his own prosaic cleverness is compounded by the alliance with wealth and power which he contemplates as a result.

If the psychoanalysts could only get the contemporary Hamlet on their couch, if they could only straighten out his Oedipus complex, his *specific aboulia* would vanish; he would stop shilly-shallying and push that nuclear button like a real man.

Almost all critics today stick to the ethics of revenge. The psychia-trist sees the very thought of its abandonment as an illness he must cure, and the traditional critic sees revenge as a literary rule he must respect. Others still try to read *Hamlet* through one of the popular ideologies of our time, like political rebellion, the absurd, the indi-vidual's right to an aggressive personality. It is no accident if the sanctity of revenge provides a perfect vehicle for all the masks of modern *ressentiment*. The remarkable consensus in favor of revenge verifies, I believe, the conception of the play as that no man's land between total revenge and no revenge at all, that specifically mod-ern space where everything becomes suffused with sick revenge.

It is fashionable nowadays to claim that we inhabit an entirely new world in which even our greatest masterpieces have become irrelevant. I would be the last one to deny that there is something unique about our world, but there is something unique also about *Hamlet*, and we may well be deceiving ourselves in order not to face a type of relevance we do not want to welcome.

We must declare irrelevant not *Hamlet* but the wall of conventions and ritualism with which we surround the play, in the name of innovation almost as often as in the name of tradition. As more events, objects, and attitudes around us proclaim the same message ever more loudly, in order not to hear that message, we must con-demn more of our experience to insignificance and absurdity. With our most fashionable critics today we have reached the point when history must make no sense, art must make no sense, language and sense itself must make no sense.

It cannot be a fortuitous coincidence if the world, which four centuries ago wrote *Hamlet* and now finds itself in the strange histor-ical impasse upon which we prefer not to reflect, is also the world whose sole religious law is to renounce revenge, the world that now even refuses to mention it but cannot ignore it any more, the world that finds itself compelled more and more to obey that law . . . or else.

We ourselves forged that situation with no help from anyone. We cannot blame it on some vengeful god. We have no more god upon whom to reject the responsibility we so proudly assumed when it did not appear menacing. Although the situation in which we now find ourselves was eminently predictable, most philosophers and scientists were unable to predict it; the few who did never got a serious hearing.

As modern culture turned to science and philosophy, as the Greek side of our inheritance became dominant, to the point when mythology proper, with disciplines like psychoanalysis, made a kind of intellectual reappearance, the Judeo-Christian text was rejected to the outer fringes of our intellectual life; it is now entirely excluded.

As a result, absolutely no sense can be made of our current historical predicament. We are beginning to suspect something fundamental is missing from our intellectual landscape but we do not seriously dare ask what. The prospect is too terrifying. We pretend not to see the disintegration of our cultural life, the desperate futility of the puppet shows that occupy the empty stage during this strange intermission of the human spirit. A silence has descended upon the earth, as if an angel were about to open the seventh and last seal of an apocalypse.

Terrifying as they are, the possibilities of meaning which lie beyond that stupefied silence are less demoralizing than the current nihilism. We do not have to believe that our culture is a mere aggregate of heterogeneous elements whose imminent disintegration will mean nothing in the vast expanse of the universe. We may not be a product of random forces after all; we may be responsible for what we do, to ourselves and to our world. We do not have to believe that no meaningful language exists between the inhuman equations of science and the crossword puzzles of structuralism and poststructuralism.

Hamlet is no mere word game. We can make sense out of *Hamlet* just as we can make sense out of our world, by reading both against revenge. This is the way Shakespeare wanted *Hamlet* to be read and the way it should have been read long ago. If now, at such a time in our history, we still cannot read *Hamlet* against revenge, who ever will?

14. THE ELIZABETHAN SUBJECT
AND THE SPENSERIAN TEXT

■

LOUIS ADRIAN MONTROSE

"THE ELIZABETHAN SUBJECT" in question is both the Queen's subject, Edmund Spenser, and the Queen-as-subject, subject of and in her subject's discourse, in the Spenserian text. The dynamic principle here exemplified is that, as both the subject and his discourse are shaped by "the Queen"—and here I mean not the person of Elizabeth Tudor but rather the whole field of cultural meanings personified in her—so they also reshape the Queen by the very process of addressing and representing her. It is in such linkages and exchanges that the relations of power between sovereign and subject, between prince and poet, are inscribed and negotiated. In this sense, the various and ubiquitous royal representations may be construed as privileged instances of Elizabethan ideology at work. In this sense, too, there are historically and theoretically sound reasons for continuing to call the society in question, after its reigning monarch, "Elizabethan."

The purpose of this essay is to explore the processes of ideological production implicated in its title, an exploration that necessarily situates the Spenserian text within a larger domain of Elizabethan discourses. In an attempt at methodological consistency, I begin with a brief and explicit programmatic statement intended to situate my own discourse in relation to some current issues in literary and social theory, on the one hand, and to some traditions and trends in English Renaissance studies, on the other.

I

The study of English Renaissance literature has of late been characterized by a renewed interest in questions of "history." In literary studies, "history" has traditionally meant the literary and intellectual histories that, in combination with techniques of close reading, still form the dominant modes of analysis; or, the now-tarnished "world picture" approach that read complex literary works against a supposedly stable, coherent, and transparent "historical background" that enshrined the political and social orthodoxies of the age; or, the erudite but sometimes eccentric detective work of scholars who, treating texts as ciphers, sought to argue one-to-one correspondences between fictional characters and actions, on the one hand, and specific historical persons and events, on the other. Though sometimes reproducing the shortcomings of the older modes of historical criticism, but also often appropriating their labors to good effect, the newer historical orientation is new in its refusal of traditional distinctions between literature and history, between text and context; new in resisting a traditional opposition of the privileged individual—whether an author or a work—to a world "outside." I speak merely of a new *orientation* because those identified with it, by themselves or by others, tend to be heterogeneous in their practices and reticent in their theorization of those practices. In brief, their project is to resituate canonical literary texts among the multiple forms of writing, and in relation to the nondiscursive practices and institutions, of the social formation in which those texts were initially produced—while, at the same time, recognizing that this project of historical resituation is necessarily the textual construction of critics who are themselves historical subjects.

It remains to be seen if the interest currently aroused by this kind of work amounts to more than the ephemeral prestige of the latest academic fashion. In any case, the theoretical and methodological assumptions, principles, and procedures of such a project have yet to be systematically articulated, discriminated, and subjected to scrutiny. All that I offer here are a few tentative reflections on a project in which I myself am engaged. Current invocations of "History" (which, like "Power," is a term now in constant danger of hypostatization) seem to me at least in part a response to (or, in some cases, merely a reaction against) various structuralist and poststructuralist formalisms that have seemed, to some, to put into question the very possibility of historical understanding and historical experience—to dissolve history into what Perry Anderson has recently characterized as an antinomy of structural determinism and destructured contingency.[1] In *After the New Criticism*, Frank Lentricchia links together "the antihistorical impulses of formalist theories of literary criticism" with universalist and teleological notions of "History." (The Marxian metahistorical master-narrative presumably belongs among the latter, although Lentricchia does not say so.) Against this unholy alliance of unifying and totalizing theories, Lentricchia opposes the multiplicity of "histories," characterized by "forces of heterogeneity, contradiction, fragmentation, and difference."[2] Something like this distinction of "histories" from "History" seems to me to be implicit in what has now, for better or for worse, come to be known as the "new historicism" in Renaissance literary studies.[3]

Acknowledging language as the medium in which the Real is constructed, a new historical criticism takes as its subject that interplay of culture-specific discursive *practices* in which versions of the Real are instantiated, deployed, reproduced—and also appropriated, contested, transformed.[4] Integral to this new project of historical criticism is a realization and acknowledgment that the critic's own text is as fully implicated in such an interplay as are the texts under study; a recognition of the agency of criticism in constructing and delimiting its object of study, and of the historical positioning of the critic vis-à-vis that object; and thus a renunciation of the illusory quest of an older historical criticism to recover objective, authentic, or stable "meanings." In brief, to speak today of an historical criticism must be to recognize that not only the poet but also the critic exists in history; that the texts of each are inscriptions of history; and that our comprehension, representation, interpretation of the texts of the past proceeds by a mixture of estrangement and appropriation, as a reciprocal conditioning of the Renaissance text and our text of the Renaissance.[5]

The new orientation to history in Renaissance literary studies (an orientation within which I locate my own insufficiently theorized practice) may be succinctly characterized, on the one hand, by its acknowledgement of the *historicity of texts*: the cultural specificity, the social embedment, of all modes of writing—not only those texts that critics study but also the texts in which they study them. On the other hand, this new orientation is characterized by its acknowledgment of the *textuality of history*: the unavailability of a full and authentic past, a lived material existence, that has not already been mediated by the surviving texts of the society in question—those "documents" that historians construe in their own texts, called "histories," histories that ineluctably and incompletely construct the "History" to which they offer access.[6]

"The Historicity of Texts and the Textuality of History": If chiastic formulations such as this are now in fashion, it may be because they help to figure a current emphasis on the dynamic, unstable, and reciprocal relationship between the literary and the social. This em-

phasis involves a rethinking or wholesale rejection of some dominant alternative conceptions of literature: as an autonomous aesthetic order that transcends the pressure and particularity of
material interests; as a collection of inert discursive reflections of
"real events"; as a superstructural manifestation of an economic
base. Current practice emphasizes both the *relative* autonomy of
specific discourses and their capacity to impact upon the social formation, to make things happen by shaping the consciousness of
social beings. To speak, then, of the social production of "literature"
or of any particular text is to signify not only that it is socially
produced but also that it is socially productive—that it is the product of work and that it performs work in the process of being written, enacted, or read.[7]

By representing the world in discourse, texts are engaged in constructing the world and in accommodating writers, performers,
readers, and audiences to positions within it. In recent years, the
vexed but indispensable term "ideology" has, in its most general
sense, come to be associated with the processes by which social
subjects are formed, reformed, and enabled to perform as conscious
agents in an apparently meaningful world. In this sense, all texts are
ideologically marked, however multivalent or inconsistent that inscription may be. This ideological marking of the text brings me back
to the "subject" of my title, which (following the usage of Foucault
and others) is intentionally—and, I trust, purposefully—ambiguous. I mean to suggest a process of *subjectification* that, on the one
hand, shapes individuals as loci of consciousness and initiators of
action; and, on the other hand, positions, motivates, and constrains
them within networks of power beyond their comprehension or
control.[8]

Perry Anderson has remarked that the "one master-problem
around which *all* contenders have revolved" in the agon of contemporary social theory is "essentially, the nature of the relationships
between structure and subject in human history and society" (*Historical Materialism*, 33). (Variations on this problematic might juxtapose agency, practice, or strategy, on the one hand, to system or
totality, on the other.) The freely self-creating and world-creating
subject of bourgeois humanism is now (at least, in theory) defunct.
The recent trend in a variety of disciplines has been a perhaps over-
compensatory positing of subject as wholly determined by structure. I want to resist this inevitably reductive tendency to think
antinomically, in terms of Subject/Structure. The present study is
concerned with the inscription of subjectification processes in a
variety of Elizabethan texts; these processes I see as dialectically

related to processes of structuration, and thus as intrinsically social and historical.[9] My operating assumptions may be summarized as follows: that the categories of subject and structure are interdependent; that social systems are produced and reproduced in the interactive social practices of individuals and groups; that collective structures may enable as well as constrain individual agency; that the possibilities and patterns for action are always socially and historically situated, always limited and limiting; and that there is no *necessary* relationship between the intentions of actors and the outcomes of their actions.[10] With this much said (and much more left unsaid) regarding matters theoretical, I now turn to matters Elizabethan, mindful as I do that the relationship between "literary theory" and "Renaissance texts" must be made manifest in the Renaissance scholar's critical practice.

II

Shortly before she died in 1558, England's Catholic queen, Mary Tudor, reluctantly designated her Protestant half-sister Elizabeth as her successor. Religious ritual, state ceremony, legal theory, and civic pageantry marked and symbolically effected Elizabeth's transition from Marian subject to ruler of Elizabethan subjects, subjects from whom she now differed not merely in degree but in kind. In her Parliamentary accession speech, Elizabeth declared that although she was "but one Body naturally considered," she was now also, by God's "permission a Body Politic to govern."[11] The political fiction of "the queen's two bodies"—one natural, fallible, mortal; the other, "not subject to Passions . . . nor to death"[12]—occupied a transitional position between the medieval theological doctrine that all Christendom was a collective *corpus mysticum,* and what Quentin Skinner has called "the distinctly modern idea of the State as a form of public power separate from both the ruler and the ruled, and constituting the supreme authority within a certain defined territory."[13] During the second half of the sixteenth century, the monarchical claim to supreme authority within its territories was already securely established both in theory and practice, while formulations of the modern conception of the state as a corporate abstraction had only just begun. At this historical juncture, the body politic inhered in the body of the prince.

Tudor somatic symbolism was culture-specific in two fundamental and interrelated ways: if dominant structures of thought and belief privileged the body of the prince in relation to the body of the subject, they also privileged the male body in relation to the female body. The versions of woman produced by such discourses as those of medicine, law, religion, and domestic economy were almost invariably imperfect versions of man—constitutionally colder, weaker, less stable than he. Almost all modes of authority, domestic as well as public, were invested in positions occupied by men: fathers, husbands, masters, teachers, preachers, magistrates, and lords.[14] The Elizabethan gender-system combined principles of hierarchy and reciprocity, distinguishing male and female as superior and inferior, and interrelating them as complementary. Gender categories interacted with many others—notably those of social estate, age, occupation, and marital status, as well as with religious, economic, educational, and regional distinctions—to produce multiple and shifting coordinates of identity and relationship within which the process of subjectification—the ideological work of fashioning and refashioning selves—was performed.

The dominant Elizabethan ideology inscribed the English commonwealth within a divinely created and providentially directed cosmos. As the governor of a national church, the monarch was the focus of beliefs and loyalties that were sanctioned by and ultimately grounded in God. Perhaps the clearest exposition of the metaphysically legitimated dominant ideology is to be found in the "Exhortation, concerning good order and obedience, to rulers and magistrates," one of a series of homilies devised and disseminated by the regime to be sermoned in state churches:

> Every degree of people in theyr vocation, callyng, and office hath appointed to them, theyr duety and ordre. Some are in hyghe degree, some in lowe, some kynges and prynces, some inferiors and subjectes, priestes, and layemenne, Maysters and Servauntes, Fathers and chyldren, husbandes and wives, riche and poore, and everyone have neede of other. . . . God hath sent us his hygh gyft, oure moost deere soveraygne Lady Quene Elizabeth, with godly, wyse and honorable counsayle, with other superyors and inferiors in a beautiful order and goodly. . . . The scriptures of the holy goste . . . perswade and commaund us al obediently to be subjecte: fyrst and chieflye, to the quene's majestie, supreme head over al, and next, to her honorable counsaile, and to al other noble men, magistrates, and officers, whiche by God's goodnes be placed and ordered.[15]

As the focal point of this hierarchical and homological system, within which her subjects' social positions and interrelationships were constituted, the Queen was represented as not only requiring the collective subjection of her subjects but also guaranteeing their particular subjectivities.

In this sense, of course, Elizabeth Tudor was herself a gendered and socially situated subject. Women were, at least in theory, excluded from the public domain. By virtue of the body politic that she had acquired at her coronation, Queen Elizabeth was the exception to this rule. However, because she nevertheless remained a woman in her body natural, she represented an affront to those very principles of hierarchy of which she was the guardian. As the anomalous ruler of a society that was pervasively patriarchal in its organization and distribution of authority, the unmarried woman at the society's symbolic center embodied a challenge to the homology between hierarchies of rule and of gender. A range of strategies was generated by means of which this ideological dissonance, this contradiction in the cultural logic, could be variously articulated and obfuscated, contained and exploited.

Some of these strategies were Elizabeth's own. At the very beginning of the reign, she was already formulating the discourse by which she would continue to turn the political liability of her gender to advantage for nearly half a century. In 1559, a parliamentary delegation urged their new, young, and female sovereign to fulfill her destiny by marrying and bearing an heir. They reminded her that

> Every one ought to have a care of that place and estate hee hath, and Princes especially, that sithence they are but mortall, the Commonwealth might bee perpetuis'd in immortalitie. Now, this Eternitie you may give unto the English, if (as nature, age, and your beauty requires) you would espouse yourselfe unto a Husband, who might assist and comfort you. . . . Nothing can be more repugnant to the common good then to see a Princesse, who by marraige may preserve the Commonwealth in peace, to lead a single life, like a Vestal Nunne.

In her response (as mediated to us by the official records incorporated into Camden's *Annals*), Elizabeth defended her maidenly freedom and royal prerogative against the promptings of her male advisors that she conform to their patriarchal expectations:

> I have beene ever perswaded, that I was borne by God to consider, and, above all things, doe those which appertaine unto his glory. And therefore it is, that I have made choyce of this kinde of life, which is most free, and agreeable for such humane affaires as may tend to his service onely. . . . And this is that I thought, then that I was a private person. But when the publique charge of governing the Kingdom came upon mee, it seemed unto mee an inconsiderate folly, to draw upon my selfe the cares which might proceede of marriage. To conclude, I am already bounde unto an Husband, which is the Kingdom of England. . . . (And therewithall, stretching out her hand, she

shewed them the Ring with which shee was given in marriage, and
inaugurated to her Kingdome with expresse and solemne termes.)
And reproch mee so no more, (quoth shee) that I have no children: for
every one of you, and as many as are English, are my Children. . . . But in this I must commend you, that you have not ap-
poynted mee an Husband: for that were unworthy the Majestie of an
absolute Princesse, and the discretion of you that are borne my Subjects. . . . Lastly, this may be sufficient, both for my memorie, and
honour of my Name, if when I have expired my last breath, this may be
inscribed upon my Tombe:
> Here lyes interr'd ELIZABETH,
> A Virgin pure untill her Death.[16]

The queen legitimates her desire for autonomy among men by invoking a higher patriarchal authority—not that of her earthly father
but that of her heavenly father, the ultimate ground of her sovereignty. By affirming her absolute self-subjection to God, she re-
affirms her male advisors' subjection to her. She refuses to enact the
female paradigm desired by those advisors: to become the medium
through which power, authority, and legitimacy are passed between
generations of men. (This refusal must be seen as at once an individual preference conditioned by her past experience as a private
person and a political strategy intended to condition her future as a
ruler.) Appropriating and transvaluing her advisors' scornful reference to the "single life" of "a Vestal Nunne," Elizabeth perpetuates
her maidenhood in a cult of virginity; transfers her wifely duties
from the household to the state; and invests her maternity in her
political rather than in her natural body.

As this exemplary instance of Elizabethan self-fashioning makes
clear, Elizabeth does not—cannot—merely deny the cultural constructions of her gender: They are the only terms available within
her culture with which she is able to think herself. In other words,
Elizabeth was more the creature of the Elizabethan image than she
was its creator. Her power to shape her own strategies was itself
shaped—at once enabled and constrained—by the existing repertoire of values, institutions, and practices (including the artistic and
literary conventions) specific to Elizabethan society and to Elizabeth's position within it. She had the capacity to *work* the available
terms to serve her culturally conditioned needs and interests. By the
same token, however, her subjects might rework those terms to
serve their turns.

The authorized version of the queen—variously instantiated in
homilies, proclamations, speeches, pageants, and icons—did not

go uncontested. Not surprisingly, in those alien spaces beyond the boundaries of the realm, the royal image was sometimes subjected to caricature or desecration. For example, on November 17, 1583 (which happened to be the anniversary of the queen's accession), the English ambassador in Paris wrote to Secretary Walsingham to report seeing "a fowle picture of the Queen's majesty sett upp she beinge on horseback her left hande holdinge the brydell of the horse, with her right hande pullynge up her clothes shewinge her hindparte."[17] Such apparently *ad feminam* attacks direct a mixture of national and religious hatreds against the female governor of the English church and state. But cynicism and irreverence are also to be found *within* the boundaries of the realm, and in various social situations. I am not referring to such aberrant cases as that of the religious extremist appropriately named Hackett, who stabbed the Queen's picture through the breast; nor to the notorious discoveries of wax dolls, said to represent the queen, stuck through with hog bristles.[18] What I have in mind are the apparently widespread, often oblique but sometimes quite flagrant expressions of an impulse to demystify or satirize the royal image on the part of Elizabethan subjects.

Let me cite two brief examples, one courtly in origins, the other rural. When, in 1619, Ben Jonson told William Drummond that Queen Elizabeth had "had a Membrana on her which made her uncapable of man, though for her delight she tried many," he was only repeating gossip that, apparently, had already been in circulation at the Elizabethan court before the Armada.[19] If some thought the queen uncapable, others were quite convinced of her capabilities. Thus, in 1580, an Essex laborer named Thomas Playfere was convicted of rumoring that the queen had two children by the earl of Leicester; a year later, a certain Henry Hawkins bettered the report: "the earl hath five children by the queen, and she never goeth on progress but to be delivered."[20] Indictments of aristocratic and courtly immorality are implicit in many extant examples of popular and rural sedition of the period. Hawkins's seditious remark is especially interesting for its cynical explanation of the function of royal progresses. These periodic peregrinations of the court through large areas of England were intended to serve a regime with very limited and unreliable financial, military, and technical resources as a symbolic means of reaffirming its hegemony over an unruly and localized society.[21] For a state that inhered in its sovereign, a state in which the delegation of royal power could be both dangerous and ineffectual, it was of some importance that the queen physically possess her domain and that she be seen to do so. Hawkins's remark—and many others in a similar vein in the records of local Elizabethan courts and in domestic and foreign state papers of the period—could not be dismissed out of hand by a government that relied so greatly upon the charismatic power of the royal personage.

The brief and typical examples I have adduced manifest in what varied and casual ways the royal body—and the royal fiction—might be manipulated by the queen's subjects; and how easily such discursive manipulations might be construed by the authorities as seditious, as potentially threatening to the established order and to be punished accordingly.[22] The fragmentary record suggests that the Elizabethan discourse of sedition often combines religious heterodoxy and a skeptical and materialist attitude toward the authorizing fictions of power with a venerable tradition of misogyny. Like the bawdy subplot of some romantic comedy, a predominantly oral and often scurrilous counter-discourse carnivalized the official cult of mystical royal virginity by insisting upon the physicality of the royal body, the carnal inclinations of the queen.

That the body of the Elizabethan prince was female had a profound impact upon the relations of power in Elizabethan society and upon their representation. Those representations, however, were not merely consequences of the ruler's gender but were themselves particular constructions of it. Let me exemplify the gender-specific resonance of the royal body by contrasting two striking and familiar Tudor icons: one, of Elizabeth; the other, of her father. In his monumental wall painting for the Privy Chamber of Henry VIII at Whitehall (of which only copies and part of the original cartoon survive), Holbein vividly portrays the power of the reigning monarch as manifest in the size, strength, and carriage of his body. (The contrast with his deceased father, Henry VII, who stands behind him, is emphatic.) Roy Strong hypothesizes that the painting was located above the dais, chair, and cloth of state.[23] This suggests a configuration on the analogy of a holy altar: When the king was actually enthroned in the chamber, the icon was made flesh, a mysterious incarnation of the Tudor state was effected. This royal appropriation of sacred space befits the claims to spiritual and temporal dominion made by the Henrician regime against the powers of the Papacy, on the one hand, and those of the English nobility, on the other. The prominence and ample proportions of the king's codpiece—a recurrent feature of Henry's personal iconography—are especially appropriate to the dynastic theme of this particular painting, which

Hans Holbein, *Henry VIII, with Henry VII* (Reproduced by permission of The National Portrait Gallery, London.)

George Gower (?), *Armada Portrait of Queen Elizabeth I* (Reproduced by permission of the Marquess of Tavistock and the Trustees of the Bedford Estates, Woburn Abbey.)

commemorates the birth of Prince Edward, thus guaranteeing (so it seemed) the continuity of the Tudors in the male line. Thus, in its representation of the gendered royal body, Holbein's painting manifests the inseparability of sexual and political potency, virility and kingship.

If Holbein's Whitehall portrait embodies Henrician power in the king's phallic self-assertion, the so-called Armada portraits embody Elizabethan power in the queen's virginal self-containment.[24] In countless Renaissance erotic poems, poet/lovers catalogue their ladies' parts by comparing them to various precious stones and metals. The Armada portrait works rather more obliquely than the blason, by displacing features of the queen's numinous body onto the patterning and decoration of the dress that covers it. In the appropriate spot, at the apex of the inverted triangle formed by her stomacher, the beholder's attention is drawn to an ostentatious bow. Resting upon it are a rich jewel in an elaborate setting and a large teardrop pearl pendant, both of which are attached to a girdle that is also composed of jewels and pearls. This demure iconography of Elizabeth's virgin-knot suggests a causal relationship between her sanctified chastity and the providential destruction of the Spanish Catholic invaders—an event represented in the background of the painting. The royal body provides an instructive Elizabethan illustration of Mary Douglas's cross-cultural thesis that the body's "boundaries can represent any boundaries which are threatened or precarious." She adds that "we should expect the orifices of the body to symbolize its especially vulnerable points."[25] A foreign danger that heightens the collective identity of Englishmen enables the Armada portraits to identify the social body with the body of the monarch. An emphasis on the virginity of that royal body transforms the problem of the monarch's gender into the very source of her potency. The inviolability of the island realm, the secure boundary of the English nation, is thus made to seem mystically dependent upon the inviolability of the English sovereign, upon the intact condition of the queen's body natural.

Like the Armada portrait, the speech that the queen is reported to have made to the troops who were mustered to defend her and her realm at the time of the Armada deploys an identification of corporeal and geopolitical boundaries: "I know I have the body of a weak and feeble woman, but I have the heart and stomach of a king, and of a king of England too." Elizabeth's strategy is to subsume a gesture of womanly self-deprecation within an assertion of the unique power that inheres in her by virtue of her office and nation. Her female honor, the chastity invested in a body that is vulnerable to invasion and pollution, is made secure by the kingly honor invested in her body politic: "And I think foul scorn that Parma or Spain, or any Prince of Europe, should dare to invade the borders of my realm; to which, rather than any dishonor should grow by me, I myself will take up arms."[26] The threat of invasion is here presented in the most intimate and violent of metaphors, as the attempted rape of the queen by a foreign prince. This threatened illegitimate sexual union would contaminate the blood of the lineage and dishonor not only the royal family but the whole nation. Unlike Lucretia, the Roman matron who submitted and was polluted, whose suicide conveniently cleansed the social order, the royal English virgin will defend and preserve herself and her state.

Elizabeth's argument that she had the heart and stomach—the greatness of spirit, the courage and fortitude—of a king was authorized upon the doctrine of the queen's two bodies. Such ideological subtleties were of no consequence to an Essex laborer named John Feltwell, who in 1591 was pilloried for remarking that "the Queen is but a woman." Here the mysteries of state come up against the intransigent common sense of the peasant. What gives this deprecating remark real political edge is its placement within a larger seditious discourse. Feltwell is recorded to have said, when examined, "Let us pray for a father, for we have a mother already. . . . Let us pray for a king. . . . The Queen is but a woman and ruled by noblemen, and the noblemen and gentlemen are all one, and the gentlemen and farmers will hold together so that the poor can get nothing. . . . Therefore we shall never have a merry world while the Queen liveth, and had we but one that would rise I would be the next, or else I would the Spaniards would come in that we may have some sport."[27] The movement of Feltwell's thought is perhaps not altogether coherent but its structural principle is clear enough: a series of opposed identities and interests, between father and mother, king and queen, woman and man, gentle and base, landed and landless, English and Spanish. Initially, his wish for a king/father seems merely antifeminist and not, in principle, antiauthoritarian. It next appears that the queen/mother warrants deposition precisely because she, the putative ruler, has allowed herself to be ruled by men. The men in question, however, constitute a particular socioeconomic class that interposes itself between the prince and her people; both the female ruler and the poor subject are abused. Thus, Feltwell's manifest misogyny quickly modulates into what could be called an intimation of class consciousness: first he indicts the nobility, then the gentry in league with the nobility, and finally the yeomanry in league with the gentry—in short, he locates the common interest of distinct social groups in their ownership of land, an interest that yokes them in a conspiracy against the landless poor. As is characteristic of dissent among the disadvantaged during the period, Feltwell can imagine change only as a heady mixture of holiday and riot. What is striking about his vision of a social apocalypse, however, is that it concludes by creating an opening for the alien: "I would the Spaniards would come in that we may have some sport." In the Spanish violation of the boundaries of the English social body lies the English commons' opportunity to end their oppression by the English elite. Here the strategy of the Armada portraits—the mobilization of loyalty to the regime in opposition to a foreign threat—has, so to speak, been turned inside out.

The rantings of a rural malcontent would perhaps be unworthy of such attention if they did not serve to make a point of larger significance about the relations of power in Elizabethan society. Cultural representations of political authority in early modern Europe, such as those focused upon Queen Elizabeth, are usually discussed in terms of celebration and mystification: as unambiguous expressions of popular enthusiasm or affirmations of collective interests, or as deployments of an apparatus of domination by a ruling dynasty or faction or by the emergent state.[28] These fruitful perspectives may become misleading if they propose to explain such representations of power in terms of a single function; or if they envision power, in essential rather than relational terms, as an exclusive property of those in authority. Foucault has written that "the sovereignty of the state, the form of the law, or the over-all unity of a domination . . . are only the terminal forms power takes. . . . Power must be understood *in the first instance* as [a] multiplicity of force relations."[29] On the other hand, any tendency to disperse power throughout the social body should be tempered by a recognition of the tangible realities of domination—what Foucault himself calls the "institutional crystallization" of power "in the state apparatus, in the formations of the law, in the various social hegemonies" (*History of Sexuality*, 93). We must attend not only to the dynamic relationship between individual or collective subjects and the state—a state personified and gendered in the queen—but also to the dynamic relationships among various status, occupational, and age groups, among numerous political factions, religious sects, and regional loyalties. In other terms, we must attend to the *segmentary* or *sectional* character of power relations in a complex social formation. Not only may groups or individuals with common interests at one level or in one situation have opposed interests at another level or in a different situation, but contradictory interests and pressures may divide individuals or groups within themselves.

The collective discourse of Elizabethan power that we call "Queen Elizabeth" was traversed by multiple and potentially antagonistic strategies. The historical subject, Elizabeth Tudor, was no more than a privileged agent in the production of the royal image. At a fundamental level, all Elizabethan subjects may be said to have participated in a ceaseless and casual process of producing and reproducing "The Queen" in their daily practices—in their prayers, their gossip, their fantasies. But she was also rather more systematically and consciously fashioned by those Elizabethan subjects who were specifically engaged in production of the texts, icons, and performances in which the queen was variously represented to her people, to her court, to foreign powers, and (of course) to Elizabeth herself. Stephen Greenblatt has remarked upon "the Queen's ability at once to fashion her identity and to manipulate the identities of her followers" (*Renaissance Self-Fashioning*, p. 169); my point is that such fashioning and such manipulation were reciprocal. During the course of a long reign, many male subjects of various statuses, skills, and interests were engaged in—and, in various ways, profited by—sponsoring, designing, and executing the representations of royal power. It is in this sense that the ruler and the ruled, the queen and the poet, are construable as subjects differentially shaped within a shared conjuncture of language and social relations, and jointly reshaping that conjuncture in the very process of living it.

III

Few Elizabethan subjects publicly claimed for themselves a more exalted role in the shaping of this conjuncture than did Edmund Spenser. In "A letter of the Authors, expounding his whole intention in the course of this worke," addressed to Sir Walter Ralegh and printed in the first edition of *The Faerie Queene* in 1590, Spenser declares that "the generall end . . . of all the booke is to fashion a gentleman or noble person in vertuous and gentle discipline." This process of fashioning is at once the book's subject and its object: by the rhetorically effective fashioning of artificial persons, the poet may arouse in his readers a process of emulation; the fashioning of the text and in the text may induce a refashioning in and of its audience, a refashioning that can make the gentry truly gentle and the powerful virtuous. The writer who claimed so central a place for himself in literary history and in his own society was of relatively humble origins. It was only by virtue of his M. A. that Spenser, the son of a London artisan, could begin to sign himself a gentleman; and it was by means of his subsidized education and his verbal skill that he gained the aristocratic patronage, state employment, and Irish property that gave substance to his social pretensions. Though acclaimed as a poet and—given his urban, artisan origins—relatively successful in his bid for advancement, Spenser nevertheless always remained on the social and economic as well as on the geographic margins of that community of privilege whom he addressed and presumed to fashion in his poetry.

The Poet claims a moral duty and a rhetorical power to inform and reform the subjectivities of his readers as they read. It is precisely the claim to this duty and power that fashions the Poet himself, that makes the writing subject into what Spenser's text so significantly titles "the Author." When Michel Foucault asks, "What is an Author?" it is to make the vital point that "the author is an ideological product."[30] According to Foucault, "the coming into being of the notion of 'author' constitutes the privileged moment of *individualization* in the history of ideas, knowledge, literature, philosophy and the sciences" (141). His project is to deprive the subject "of its role as an originator," in order to analyze it "as a variable and complex function of discourse" (158, 141). In response, Robert Weimann argues for a necessary correlative analysis of "the discourse as a function of the subject," of the text "as a function of the labor or work objectified in it" and of its "relation to the mode of production and appropriation implicating this labor" (*Structure and Society*, 296, 299). Elsewhere, he writes of the new scope, in the later sixteenth century, for a writer's "own choice of productive strategies vis-à-vis the increasing availability of those means, modes, and materials which, practically and imaginatively (though not necessarily juridically), he can make his own. . . . The study of discourses as '*objects* of appropriation' must be complemented by their study as . . . agencies of knowledge, pleasure, energy, and power."[31]

What I wish to stress in relation to Spenser is the appropriation of the author-function by the signifying subject whose class position excludes him from the direct exercise of other modes of sociopolitical authority. Combining classical and biblical traditions of inspired and prophetic speech with emergent notions of an autonomous fictional space, Spenser synthesizes a new Elizabethan author-function. The "Laureate" authorial persona that Richard Helgerson sees as emergent in Spenser (and fully developed, a generation later, in Jonson) not only professionalizes poetry, it authenticates through print the subjectivity of a writer whose class position might otherwise have rendered him merely the anonymous functionary of his patron.[32] In claiming the originative status of an "Author," a writer claims the authority to direct and delimit the interpretive activity of that elite community of readers by whom he himself is authorized to write. (If this strategy stakes out the imaginative space of the fiction as the writer's domain, it also seems designed to protect him from any imputation of seditious intent; it is, at once, a strategy of power and a defensive tactic.[33]) Spenser's authorial self-fashioning proceeds by the constitution of the writer as a subject of and in his own discourse; and also by the insertion of his text into the economy of courtly service and reward—that is, by its constitution as a *book*, a tangible commodity that functions as a vehicle of the writer's social and material advancement.

The process I have been describing is exemplified—and, indeed, thematized—in the *Aprill* eclogue of *The Shepheardes Calender* (1579), which contains Spenser's inaugural representation of the queen. Of all such moments in the Spenserian corpus, this is invariably regarded as an unequivocal inscription of the dominant ideology of its society, as a text "wholly wedded to the autocratic ruler of the English state"—to quote Stephen Greenblatt's characterization of Spenser's relationship to political authority (*Renaissance Self-Fashioning*, 174). My argument will be that this relationship is equivocal even in the encomium of "Eliza, Queene of shepheardes"; that, by gesturing toward the controlling power of the writing subject over the representation he has made, the *Aprill* eclogue works to suggest that in fact the ruler and the ruled are mutually defining, reciprocally constituted.

The tendency of modern literary criticism to think of *The Shepheardes Calender* merely as a *poem*, and to reproduce and anthologize it as such, obscures what must have been its original intended impact as a printed *book*. The Shepheardes Calender, like the first edition of *The Faerie Queene* (1590), exemplifies the Elizabethan printed book in its tendency toward the proliferation and contamination of genres, toward the inclusion within its covers of a variety of discursive forms characterized by distinctive modes of address to readers. Here I am thinking not only of the multiple poetic forms and styles included within the eclogues but also of such discursive genres as the title page; the address "To His Booke" by "Immerito"; the Epistle, Generall argument, and glosses by "E. K."; the glosses to the individual eclogues; the emblems, woodcuts, and envoy. In such print-specific genres, Elizabethan literary texts manifest a tendency toward the elaboration rather than the effacement of their status as social—and not merely literary—productions. The "apparatus" of *The Shepheardes Calender* is, then, as significant in the constitution of its rhetorical effects, its "meaning," as is the poetry itself. *The Shepheardes Calender* is ostentatiously designed to inaugurate Spenser's career as "our new Poete" (Epistle), an Elizabethan writer capable of shaping the native language into a national vision. The book's reflexive strategies are aimed at instituting it as the founding text of a new English literary canon. That we conventionally date the beginning of the Elizabethan literary renaissance from the publication of *The Shepheardes Calender* is the measure of its success: our project of canon-formation has already been prescribed by Spenser's.[34]

Within the text, the encomiastic song that is the centerpiece of the *Aprill* eclogue is attributed to Colin Clout, "under whose person the Author selfe is shadowed" (Epistle). Colin is in fact absent from the eclogue, withdrawn into melancholy owing to unrequited love. His song is sung by another shepherd for a rapt audience of his peers. All their talk is of Colin; all their admiration is for his skill in making. The eclogue frame thus provides the poem with its own reception: Spenser/Colin's royal encomium is already in circulation, being reproduced and doing its work in society, which is to advertise the author as much as it is to celebrate the monarch.

Colin's song fuses imperial Virgilian, sacred Gospel, and erotic Ovidian traditions into a pastoral consecration of the English, Protestant, and Tudor present. As the gloss points out, the poem appropriates literary traditions for contemporary social uses. An Ovidian etiological myth is reworked into a Tudor genealogical myth: Elisa is "*Syrinx* daughter without spotte, / Which *Pan* the shepheards God of her begot" (April, 50–51). Working here as a kind of referential fiction, pointing outward beyond the poem and its mythographic and literary traditions to concrete historical subjects, the gloss provides an exact correspondence between Pan and "the most famous and victorious King, her highnesse Father, late of worthy memorye K. Henry the eyght." But if Elisa is in some sense to be identified with Elizabeth Tudor, governor of the English church and state, she is also to be identified with a queen already textualized as the gendered and idealized personification of the state, shaped by Elizabethan poets, artisans, preachers, councillors—and by Elizabeth Tudor herself—and functioning as a focus for the collective energies of Elizabethan subjects. In Ovid's text, the outcome of the love chase is the nymph's transformation into the reeds from which Pan, the "shepheards God" (Januarye, 17), fashions his pipes. In the Ovidian logic of Spenser's poem, Elisa becomes a personification of pastoral poetry; she embodies the literary mode of the poem in which she exists.[35] Ultimately, the queen and her various representations are appropriated and recreated in the specificity of Spenser's text as the figurative offspring of the shepherd/poet (himself identified with Pan) and his pastoral muse. Colin's encomium methodically rehearses the poetic engendering of the royal image: The first stanza is an invocation of the Muses; the second stanza expresses the conception of an image through a genealogical procreation myth; in the third stanza, the unfolding of the image commences with the imperative, "See, where she sits upon the grassie greene" (55); in the final stanza, Colin bids his perfected image to go forth into the world, to be received by the queen: "Now ryse up *Elisa*, decked as thou art, / In royall array" (145–46), "Let dame *Eliza* thanke you for her song" (150).[36]

The genealogical myth is repeated in the central stanza of the song:

> *Pan* may be proud, that ever he begot
>   such a Bellibone,
> And *Syrinx* rejoyse, that ever was her lot
>   to bear such an one.
> Soone as my younglings cryen for the dam,
> To her will I offer a milkwhite Lamb;
>   Shee is my goddesse plaine,
>   And I her shepherds swayne,
> Albee forswonck and forswatt I am.
>   (91–99)

The pastoral poet now includes himself within the frame of the image that he is making; this "overlaboured and sunneburnt" (Gloss) rustic bears witness to a Nativity that he himself has brought to pass. Colin offers a lamb to an infant mother-goddess; Spenser offers a pastoral to a queen. The subject's *gift*—both his talent and his offering—is his ability to make the cultural forms in which royal power is not only celebrated but may actually be effected.

Such a poem is not merely the *product* of a received ideology but is itself a distinctive *production* of ideology, which, by representing the queen in a text, ineluctably reconstitutes the queen as a textual product. Thus, the poem may be said to reverse the official relationship of symbolic filiation: To metaphorize Elisa as the poet's offspring is an implicit response to the frequent metaphorizing of the queen as her subjects' mother; it is a contestation of her status as cultural genetrix.[37] What is at issue here is not merely the representation of Queen Elizabeth in Spenser's poem but the representation of that representation, that is, the textual foregrounding of the process of textualization itself. This process does not work to suggest that there is nothing outside the text but, on the contrary, works to locate the text at the conjuncture of various determinations—social, ideological, literary—that have already been transformed within it. By representing itself as an offering to a royal persona produced within it, the poem displays itself in a paradoxical relationship to the structures of power: The cultural work of the subject/poet, his informing power, contributes to the legitimation and implementation of the social and political order within which he himself is subjected. By calling attention to its mediatory relationship to the traditions, conventions, and devices of poetic discourse, on the one hand, and to the social conditions of its own production, on the other, the song of Colin/Spenser works not simply as a royal encomium but as a contextualization from within (so to speak) of its own encomiastic project.

Helgerson has shown how Spenser reworked available cultural models into the distinctive literary role of a "Laureate." But this persona was not only fashioned in contradistinction to those already available to Tudor writers; it was also constructed by analogy to the monarch: As Helgerson himself reminds us, Camden called Spenser "*Angloricum Poetarum nostri seculi facile princeps*" (*Self-Crowned Laureates*, 55). However, if Spenser was regarded by some of his peers as a prince among poets, he was also a mere subject of that prince who is figured within his poem as its muse, patroness, subject, and audience. The subjectivity fabricated by Spenser in writing—his "Author selfe," as E. K. so nicely puts it in the Epistle to *The Shepheardes Calender*—achieves its uncertain sense of mastery, of authorship and authority, not by means of a static analogy with the monarch but rather in an interplay between submission and resistance to the project of royal celebration which ostensibly defines it. By "resistance" I do not mean to suggest any concerted program of sedition, of political opposition or subversion. Rather, it is a matter of the text registering the felt but perhaps not consciously articulated contradiction between Spenser's exalted self-representation as an Author and his subjection to the authority of an other, the contradiction between a specific authorial ideology—that of "the Laureate"—and the social conditions of literary production within which that ideology may be realized in Spenser's historical moment and from his social position within it. In Spenser's text, the refashioning of an Elizabethan subject as a laureate poet is dialectically related to the refashioning of the queen as the author's subject.[38]

In the "Letter to Ralegh," the author declares that "In that Faery Queene I meane glory in my generall intention, but in my particular I conceive the most excellent and glorious person of our soveraine the Queene. . . . And yet in some places els, I doe otherwise shadow her. For considering she beareth two persons, the one of a most royall Queene or Empress, the other of a most vertuous and beautifull Lady, this latter part in some places I doe expresse in Belphoebe, fashioning her name according to your owne excellent conceipt of Cynthia, (Phoebe and Cynthia being both names of Diana)." The emphasis here is not upon the distinction between the mystical office and its creaturely occupant but rather upon the consonance between the public and private virtues of this specifically female monarch. These complementary persons are equally aspects of the queen's body politic and her body natural; she is always already a cultural corpus, a body of texts.

The poet returns to the theory of Elizabethan representation in the proem to Book 3, "contayning the Legend of Britomartis, or Of Chastitie"—a private virtue of obvious political significance in Elizabethan England, and here personified in a female hero. In the opening lines of this book, the poet preemptively asks himself why he has not personified this virtue in Elizabeth herself, and answers that because the queen's virtue and beauty are perfect they are unrepresentable by painters and poets, except by a series of accommodations and displacements. The proem's address to the sovereign concludes by revising the strategy expounded in the "Letter to Ralegh":

> But if in living colours, and right hew,
>   Your selfe you covet to see pictured,
>   Who can it doe more lively, or more trew,
>   Than that sweet verse, with *Nectar* sprinckeled,
>   In which a gracious servant pictured
>   His *Cynthia*, his heavens fairest light?
>   That with his melting sweetnesse ravished,
>   And with the wonder of her beames bright,
> My senses lulled are in slomber of delight.
>
> But let that same delitious Poet lend
>   A little leave unto a rusticke Muse
>   To sing his mistresse prayse, and let him mend,
>   If ought amis her liking may abuse:
>   Ne let his fairest *Cynthia* refuse,
>   In mirrours more then one her selfe to see,
>   But either *Gloriana* let her chuse,
>   Or in *Belphoebe* fashioned to bee:
> In th'one her rule, in th'other her rare chastitee.
>   (3.Proem.4–5)

The process by which Spenser makes the identification of his sovereign with Belphoebe is noteworthy not only for its idiosyncratic representation of the doctrine of the queen's two bodies but for its appropriation of Ralegh as a mediatory figure. It is not Queen Elizabeth but rather Ralegh's Cynthia whose image is split in the mirror of Spenser's poem; and both poets' source is in a complex history of literary and mythographic forms. Thus, in the movement of the proem to Book 3 from the queen to her representations, from referentiality to intertextuality, the male subject/poet puts into question the female monarch's claim to shape herself and her subjects, to personify the principle and power of form. What the poet conventionally deprecates as his inability to produce an adequate reflection of the glorious royal image is the methodical process of fragmentation and refraction by which the text appropriates that image, imposing upon it its own specificity.

Gloriana, the Faery Queen in whose service her knights are fashioned, does not appear as a character in the narrative, whereas Belphoebe is a conspicuous presence in the middle books. I would suggest that this is so at least in part because the beautiful and virtuous lady is more manipulable by the conventions of literary representation—notably those associated with Petrarchism—than is the empress, that erotic conventions structure Elizabethan relations of power in ways advantageous to the writing subject. Petrarchan conventions and the lineaments of the Petrarchan persona are ubiquitous in the courtly culture of the Renaissance. Petrarchism is one of the discourses in which a recognizably modern mode of subjectivity—an introspective egocentricity founded upon the frustration and sublimation of material desires—is first articulated and actively cultivated. The Petrarchan persona is a distinctly masculine subject explicitly fashioned in relation to a feminine other. (It is also, of course, a male subject whose refinements of style and sensibility implicitly mark him off from the common run of men. The gendered discourse of Petrarchism must be understood, then, as already situated within what Fredric Jameson calls "the essentially antagonistic collective discourses of social classes.")[39] The Petrarchan lover worships a deity of his own making and under his own control; he masters his mistress by inscribing her within his text, where she is repeatedly put together and taken apart—and, sometimes, killed.

Placed first among a group of verses that commend Spenser's heroic poem to its royal reader in the 1590 edition is a sonnet in which Sir Walter Ralegh envisions Spenser as overgoing Petrarch—not the heroic poet of the Latin *Africa* but the love poet of the vernacular *Canzoniere* and *Trionfi.* In the sonnet, Laura is displaced by the Faery Queen; Petrarch's female text is displaced by Spenser's. And these displacements are fittingly enacted within a sonnet written by that Elizabethan courtier—Spenser's fellow subject/poet but also his patron and social superior—upon whose "excellent conceipt of Cynthia" Spenser has fashioned his Belphoebe. As Ralegh's sonnet suggests, Elizabethan courtly writers might worship their royal mistress as another Laura, appropriating a Petrarchan language of virtuous desire for a Triumph of Chastity befitting a virgin empress. If such a language provided the ruler with a means of mollifying the authoritarianism of her regime, it also provided her (male) subjects with a flexible medium—at once humble, elegant, and intimate—in which they could supplicate and inveigle their royal mistress, and in which they could project and symbolically master the condition of their subjection to a female ruler.

These Petrarchan politics are aptly demonstrated in the writings of Sir John Harington, a courtier and godson of the queen. In his private "Rememrauncer," he made a note to himself that "the Queene stoode up and bade me reache forthe my arme to reste her thereon. Oh, what swete burden to my next songe.—Petrarcke shall eke out good matter for this businesse."[40] Here the crucial term is "businesse." Alert to any opportunity for the pursuit of self-interest, the purposefully witty Elizabethan courtier ma ᾽ capitalize on a fortunate contact with the royal body by making tl‚e incident the subject of an erotic poem. Elsewhere, in a letter written shortly after the queen's death, Harington reflects slyly and admiringly on her often successful manipulations of her subjects: "Few knew how to aim their shaft against her cunning. We did all love hir, for she saide she loved us, and much wysdome she shewed in thys matter."[41] Harington evokes an image of the court as composed of a mistress surrounded by her suitors, a mother surrounded by her children, and all engaged in a subtle but ceaseless contest of wills. "Few knew how to aim their *shaft* against her *cunning*": A martial metaphor resonates as a metaphor of genital aggression to articulate a frustrated desire for mastery over the sovereign mother/mistress.

Such Petrarchan strategies are evident in the extended blason that introduces Belphoebe into *The Faerie Queene* in Book 2, canto 3. This, the longest character description in the entire poem, repeatedly insinuates a current of sensuality and erotic arousal into its encomium of militant chastity:

> And in her hand a sharpe bore-speare she held,
> And at her backe a bow and quiver gay,
> Stuft with steele-headed darts, wherewith she queld
> The savage beastes in her victorious play,
> Knit with a golden bauldricke, which forelay
> Athwart her snowy brest, and did divide
> Her daintie paps; which like young fruit in May
> Now little gan to swell, and being tide,
> Through her thin weed their places only signified.
> (29)

This rhetorical play between the prohibition and provocation of desire is observable not only in the composition of stanzas but within individual lines. For example, in the comparison of her blushing cheeks to "roses in a bed of lillies shed" (22), the internal rhyme on "bed" and "shed" imparts to the description of her maidenly modesty a subliminal suggestion of her defloration.

Perhaps the most remarkable feature of the blason of Belphoebe is its impairment by one of the poem's very rare unfinished lines, this occurring in the final alexandrine of stanza 26:

> So faire, and thousand thousand times more faire
> She seemed, when she presented was to sight,
> And was yclad, for heat of scorching aire,
> All in a silken Camus lylly whight,
> Purfled upon with many a folded plight,
> Which all above besprinckled was throughout
> With golden aygulets, that glistred bright,
> Like twinckling starres, and all the skirt about
> Was hemd with golden fringe
>
> Below her ham her weed did somewhat traine,
> And her streight legs most bravely were embayld
> In gilden buskins of costly Cordwaine,
> All bard with golden bendes, which were entayld
> With curious antickes, and full faire aumayld:
> Before they fastned were under her knee
> In a rich Jewell, and therein entrayld
> The ends of all their knots that none might see,
> How they within their fouldings close enwrapped bee.
>
> (26–27)

The conspicuous gap at the center of the blason coincides with a conspicuous silence about the center of the body it describes. Moving downward, the narrator's gaze skirts the fringes of Belphoebe's secret parts, displacing them into an intricate description of the "rich Jewell" in which the "knots" of her buskins are "entrayld . . . that none might see." There is a superficial analogy, then, to the representational strategy of the Armada portraits. But, as the royal body is handled ambivalently throughout the blason, so here in particular the symbolic locus of royal power is less a source of the (male) subject's security than an oblique threat to that security.

The narrative within which the blason is incongruously placed concerns the mock-heroic misadventures of the cowardly knight Braggadocchio and his wily servant Trompart. They happen upon Belphoebe while she is hunting in the forest; her description proceeds as Bragadocchio lies hidden in a bush—a debased, voyeuristic surrogate for the male reader. Enkindled with lust, Braggadocchio tries to assault Belphoebe; she threatens him with her boarspear, then turns and disappears from the book. I think this bald summary of the plot sufficient to indicate that the episode is a parodic rewriting of the episode of Diana and Actaeon in *Metamorphoses*, Book 3. In a suggestive essay on Petrarch's reworking of the Ovidian subtext in his representation of Laura, Nancy Vickers has interpreted his descriptive and formal strategies as defenses against the fate of Actaeon: To glimpse the naked goddess in her radical otherness is to transgress "proscriptions imposed upon powerless men (male children) in relation to powerful women (mothers). . . . Petrarch's Actaeon, having read his Ovid, realizes what will ensue: his response to the threat of imminent dismemberment is the neutralization, through descriptive dismemberment, of the threat."[42] Spenser's descriptive dismemberment of Belphoebe conspicuously avoids the danger inhering in the royal body—the body of a virgin goddess and mother. The poet at once evokes and suppresses the darker aspect of the virtuous and beautiful lady, her vengeful power to deform or even destroy her devotees.[43]

An association of the myth with the monarch is suggested by travelers' descriptions of depictions of Diana and Actaeon at two of Queen Elizabeth's residences.[44] Its political import is made explicit in the mythographic commentary of George Sandys's 1632 translation of Ovid: "This fable was invented to show us how dangerous a curiosity it is to search into the secrets of Princes, or by chance to discover their nakednesse."[45] To "discover" the nakedness of the prince is both to locate and to reveal—to demystify—the secrets of state. This exegesis is obviously especially resonant when the prince is a woman whose cult has appropriated the mythology of Diana. In Spenser's blason, the poet protects himself by conspicuously censoring himself, marking the constraint upon his text with a lacuna.[46]

When the poet addresses the queen in the proem to Book 2 of *The Faerie Queene*, he compares his discovery of Faeryland with the contemporaneous discoveries of "the Amazons huge river" and "fruitfullest Virginia" (2.Proem.2). Here Spenser is mapping not only the New World but the Elizabethan psyche. These cultural archetypes—the engulfing Amazon and the nurturing Virgin—are recombined in Belphoebe. The blason in canto 3 concludes with a curiously ominous epic simile:

> Such as *Diana* by the sandie shore
>   Of swift *Eurotas*, or on *Cynthus* greene,
> Where all the Nymphes have her unwares forlore,
> Wandreth alone with bow and arrowes keene,
> To seeke her game: or as that famous Queene
>   Of *Amazons*, whom *Pyrrhus* did destroy,
> The day that first of *Priame* she was seene,

> Did shewe her selfe in great triumphant joy,
> To succour the weake state of sad afflicted *Troy.*
> (31)

Dilating on the classical allusion in which it personifies and celebrates female power, the simile works to incorporate a reaffirmation
of the male capacity to master that very power: the poet destroys the
subject of his celebration in a parenthetical phrase.

Stephen Greenblatt sees Spenser's self-fashioning as accomplished through symbolic and physical acts of regenerative violence, enacted against those objectified agents of disorder who
threaten a civilization that is centered upon Spenser's sovereign.
According to Greenblatt, "Spenser sees human identity as conferred by loving service to legitimate authority, to the yoked power of
God and the state" (*Renaissance Self-Fashioning,* 222); "*The Faerie
Queene* is . . . wholly wedded to the autocratic ruler of the English
state" (174). It will by now be obvious that in my own view,
Spenser's relationship to royal authority is more equivocal, and the
ideological situation is more complicated, than Greenblatt here suggests. Greenblatt bases his conclusions on an analysis of the episode
of Guyon's destruction of The Bower of Bliss and his binding of its
proprietress, the enchantress Acrasia, in Book 2, canto 12. He states
the interpretive problem of the canto as "why the particular erotic
appeal of the Bower—more intense and sustained than any comparable passage in the poem—excites the hero's destructive violence" (171). But does not the *particularity* of the Bower's intense
erotic appeal itself pose a prior interpretive problem—namely, the
problem of the implicitly gendered position from which most commentators have read the episode? As Teresa de Lauretis writes, in
another context, "the overriding question is: in what ways does
narrative work to engender the subject in the movement of its discourse, as it defines positions of meaning, identification, and desire?"
(*Alice Doesn't,* 10). To write as a male reader, identifying unself-
consciously with Guyon's position, with Guyon's gaze, leads to a
misrecognition of the gender-specific character of the self-fashioning process figured in Guyon's violent repression of his own sexual
arousal. What is being fashioned here is not merely a civilized self
but a male subject, whose self-defining violence is enacted against
an objectified other who is specifically female.[47] This female other is
represented as threatening the male subject with more than sexual
enthrallment: the climactic image of the bare bosomed witch crad-
ling the slumbering youth in her lap makes it evident that she is also
threatening him with maternal engulfment.

The troubling mixtures of attraction and repulsion, desire and fear, aroused in the descriptions of both Belphoebe and Acrasia have their source in the same cultural complex. The curious affinity between these two female figures subverts their ostensible antithesis. This mode of Spenserian allegory has its culture-specific and culturally pervasive grounding in that familiar repertoire of gendered royal images produced and reproduced throughout the reign of Elizabeth: the vestal virgin, consecrated to the service of God; the beautiful mistress, desired by but necessarily forbidden to her courtiers; the thrifty spouse, married to her nation; the loving and selfless mother, dedicated to her subjects' welfare. The social and psychological potency of such images was generated in an interplay between the public and domestic domains. If I say that the *sexual* politics of Elizabethan representation were also a sexual *politics*, I mean to suggest the interpenetration and mutual contamination of sexual and political codes. This culture-specific discourse of power is the cognitive, communicative, and coercive medium in which an Elizabethan subject like Edmund Spenser has been engendered; it is the native language in which he has learned to think, speak, and write of sovereignty and subjection. In a brilliant analysis, Greenblatt assimilates Acrasia, the alien female other, to various forms of ethnic otherness, Amerindian and Irish. At this level, as in the Armada portraits, the queen is clearly the focus of a collective English civilization with which her subjects may readily identify themselves. Within a different configuration of power relations, however, the male/poet/subject may appear to be constituted not in any unequivocal act of self-devotion to the embodiment of the state but instead in the very tension between his impulse to worship and his internal resistance to such an impulse. Within this configuration of relation and identity, the stance of The Faerie Queene toward what Greenblatt calls "the autocratic ruler" of the Elizabethan state becomes necessarily ambivalent—alternately or simultaneously adoring and contestatory—because, for the male subject, the authority and the other are now one and the same.

Writing of Renaissance princes—and, specifically, of the Tudor-Stuart monarchs—Greenblatt argues that "one of the highest achievements of power is to impose its fictions upon the world and one of its supreme pleasures is to enforce the acceptance of fictions that are known to be fictions" (Renaissance Self-Fashioning, 141). This is a compelling formulation but its suggestion of an absolute and totalistic structure of royal power, cynically and successfully recuperating every contestatory gesture, is questionable on both empirical and theoretical grounds. As I have already suggested, the power of the Elizabethan regime to enforce upon Elizabethan subjects the acceptance of its fictions was limited by a severe lack of the necessary material and technological means. In any case, fictions known to be fictions might well be readily acceptable precisely because they served the subjects' interests as well as the sovereign's— interests that may have coincided but were unlikely to have been identical. Greenblatt's formulation makes insufficient allowance for the mediatory individual and collective agency of the prince's subjects in the production of those royal fictions; and for what Raymond Williams calls "the complex interrelations between movements and tendencies both within and beyond a specific and effective dominance": the residual and emergent, oppositional and alternative values, meanings, and practices that counterpoint the voice of "Power" within a polyphonic discursive process.[48]

In the Spenserian text, and elsewhere, we can observe a mode of contestation at work within the Elizabethan subject's very gesture of submission to the official fictions. We might call this mode of contestation *appropriative*, for it does not repudiate the given fictions of power but rather works within and through them, reinscribing them in the culture as the fictions of the speaking or writing subject.[49] Greenblatt characterizes the foregrounding of textuality in Spenser's poetry—its calling of "attention to its own processes"—as a kind of auto-subversion, as the opening up of "an internal distance within art itself by continually referring the reader to a fixed authority beyond the poem" (*Renaissance Self-Fashioning*, 190, 192); "Spenser's art constantly questions its own status in order to protect power from such questioning" (222). What I have been suggesting is that it is precisely when the poet offers to make such referential and deferential gestures explicit—in his encomia of the sovereign—that the text most obstinately refers the reader back into itself. This is not to deny that there exists an authority "beyond the poem," but it is to *un*fix that authority, to put into question its absolute claims upon the subjects who produce the forms in which it authorizes itself. It is precisely by calling attention to its own processes of *re*presentation that Spenser's art calls into question the status of the authority it represents. Perhaps we could say, then, in response to Greenblatt's brilliant provocation, that one of the supreme pleasures available to the subject of power is to impose upon the fictions whose enforced acceptance signifies his subjection, the marks of his own subjectivity. In the process of representing the queen within his discourse, the subject is in some very limited but nevertheless quite real sense also constituting the sovereignty in relation to which his own subjection and subjectivity are constituted. Every representation of power is also an appropriation of power. Thus, Spenser's text may be said to constitute the identity of its Subject/Author in an interplay

between the subject's gestures of subjection and the author's gestures of authority—in those paradoxical celebrations of power that, in
making the poem serve the queen, make the queen serve the poem.

IV

My opening discussion of a new historical orientation in English
Renaissance studies emphasized its relationship to particular intellectual traditions rather than its formation under specific ideological
pressures. Given my subject, it seems requisite to end with a brief
metacriticism of my own place in my text. One way to view the
recent revival of interest in questions of history may be as a compensation for that acceleration in the forgetting of history which seems
to characterize an increasingly technocratic and future-oriented
academy and society. Many of those who profess "the Humanities"
see themselves and their calling as threatened by marginalization
within a system of higher education increasingly geared to the
provision of highly specialized technological and preprofessional
training. In its anti-reflectionism, its shift of emphasis from the formal analysis of verbal *artifacts* to the ideological analysis of discursive *practices*, its refusal to observe strict and fixed boundaries between literary texts and critical texts, the emergent historical orientation in literary studies is pervasively concerned with writing as a
mode of *action*. I do not believe that it compromises the intellectual
seriousness of this concern to see it as impelled by a questioning of
our very capacity for action—by a nagging sense of professional,
institutional, and political impotence.

That Renaissance literary studies should now be alive to such
concerns is not to be explained in terms of any single cause. But one
of the determinations here may be that during the sixteenth and
seventeenth centuries, the separation of "Literature" and "Art"
from explicitly didactic and political discourses or from such disciplines as history or moral and natural philosophy was as yet incipient. Both the pervasiveness of rhetorical models in Renaissance
poetics and the predominance of patronage as a mode of literary
production may have worked to foreground rather than to efface the
status of texts as social and not merely literary productions. Such
texts may more actively invite sociohistorical analysis than do those
later works of our literary canon that have been produced within an
ideology of aesthetic disinterestedness.[50] Because we now seem to
be moving beyond this modern, essentialist orientation to "Literature," we can begin to grasp it as an historical formation that was
only beginning to emerge at the end of the sixteenth century. Inter-

preters of Tudor-Stuart literature thus find themselves now particularly well placed to rearticulate literature as a social practice—and, by so doing, to rearticulate criticism as a social practice. In reflecting upon my own practice in the foregoing essay, I am aware of a strong stake, not in any illusion of individual autonomy but in the possibilities for limited and localized agency within the regime of power and knowledge that at once sustains and constrains us.

NOTES

The present work was completed during my tenure as a Research Fellow of The Stanford Humanities Center, 1984–85. Among the many colleagues and students who have stimulated and criticized portions of this project, Roxanne Klein has a special place; to her this essay is dedicated.

1. See the incisive Marxist critique of structuralism and poststructuralism in Perry Anderson, *In the Tracks of Historical Materialism* (Chicago: University of Chicago Press, 1984), 32–55.
2. Frank Lentricchia, *After the New Criticism* (Chicago: University of Chicago Press, 1980), xiii–xiv.
3. See the brief programmatic statement by Stephen Greenblatt in his introduction to "The Forms of Power and the Power of Forms in the Renaissance," a special issue of *Genre* 15, nos. 1–2 (1982): 1–4. Also see the Introduction to his seminal book, *Renaissance Self-Fashioning: More to Shakespeare* (Chicago: University of Chicago Press, 1980).
4. For a consideration of, and response to, the current theoretical challenge to historical criticism, see "Text and History: Epilogue, 1984," in Robert Weimann, *Structure and Society in Literary History*, expanded ed. (Baltimore: Johns Hopkins University Press, 1984), 267–323.
5. See the forceful critique of traditional historicist Renaissance literary criticism in Michael McCanles, "The Authentic Discourse of the Renaissance," *Diacritics* 10, no. 1 (1980): 77–87. He writes that, "instead of viewing the scholar's enterprise as merely the recovery and explanation of an already constituted Renaissance text, Renaissance studies should recognise that its central task lies in the constitution of that text through an intertextuality whereby two texts are brought together and fused: the constituted discourse of the Renaissance and the constitutive discourse of the scholar himself" (81). For similar arguments regarding the discourse of intellectual history, see " Rethinking Intellectual History and Reading Texts," in Dominick LaCapra, *Rethinking Intellectual History* (Ithaca: Cornell Univeristy Press, 1983), 23–71; and, regarding the discourse of ethnography, Roy Wagner, *The Invention of Culture*, rev. and expanded ed. (Chicago: University of Chicago Press, 1981).
6. On the constitutive discourse of the historian and the genres of history writing, see Hayden White, *Tropics of Discourse* (Baltimore: Johns Hopkins University Press, 1978).

7. For introductions to recent materialist cultural theory, see Raymond Williams, *Marxism and Literature* (New York: Oxford University Press, 1977); Raymond Williams, *Culture* (London: Fontana, 1981); Janet Wolff, *The Social Production of Art* (London: Macmillan, 1981).

8. See Michel Foucault, "The Subject and Power," *Critical Inquiry* 8 (1982): 777–95; and, for a Marxist critique, Peter Dews, "Power and Subjectivity in Foucault," *New Left Review* no. 144 (March–April 1984): 72–95. Of central importance for the sense of "ideology" I am using here is the essay on "Ideology and Ideological State Apparatuses," in Louis Althusser, *Lenin and Philosophy and other essays*, trans. Ben Brewster (New York: Monthly Review Press, 1971), 127–186. For an interesting attempt to synthesize Althusserian Marxist and Lacanian psychoanalytic concepts of the subject and ideology, see Rosalind Coward and John Ellis, *Language and Materialism* (London: Routledge & Kegan Paul, 1977), 61–121; and, for a brief and clear exposition from the perspective of Marxist sociology, see Göran Therborn, *The Ideology of Power and the Power of Ideology* (London: NLB, 1980). For a concise history of the term "ideology," see Williams, *Marxism and Literature*, 55–71.

9. See the cogent formulation of "experience" ("a *process* by which, for all social beings, subjectivity is constructed") in Teresa de Lauretis, *Alice Doesn't: Feminism, Semiotics, Cinema* (Bloomington: Indiana University Press, 1984): "Through that process one places oneself or is placed in social reality, and so perceives and comprehends as subjective (referring to, even originating in, oneself) those relations—material, economic, and interpersonal—which are in fact social and, in a larger perspective, historical. The process is continuous, its achievement unending or daily renewed. For each person, therefore, subjectivity is an ongoing construction, not a fixed point of departure or arrival from which one then interacts with the world. On the contrary, it is an effect of that interaction . . . and thus it is produced not by external ideas, values, or material causes, but by one's personal, subjective, engagement in the practices, discourses, and institutions that lend significance (value, meaning, and affect) to the events of the world" (159).

10. I am indebted to the analysis in Anthony Giddens, *Central Problems in Social Theory* (Berkeley and Los Angeles: University of California Press, 1979), 49–95. For an interesting anthropological perspective on these issues, see the discussion of "Practice" in Sherry B. Ortner, "Theory in Anthropology since the Sixties," *Comparative Studies in Society and History* 26 (1984), 126–66; especially 144–60. The role of human agency in history is at the center of recent debates between "humanist" and "antihumanist" strains in contemporary Marxism: see Perry Anderson, *Arguments Within English Marxism* (London: NLB, 1980), 16–58.

11. "Wordes spoken by the Queene to the Lordes" (Public Record Office: State Papers 12/7), quoted in Marie Axton, *The Queen's Two Bodies* (London: Royal Historical Society, 1977), 38.

12. The quoted words are those of Edmund Plowden, Elizabethan common

lawyer, as quoted in Ernst H. Kantorowicz, *The King's Two Bodies* (Princeton: Princeton University Press, 1957), 13.

13. Quentin Skinner, *The Foundations of Modern Political Thought*, 2 vols. (Cambridge: Cambridge University Press, 1978), 2:353. The central theme of Skinner's study is the origin of this concept in the Renaissance and Reformation periods. Also see the studies by Axton and Kantorowicz cited above in notes 11 and 12.

14. On patriarchal ideology in Tudor-Stuart England, see Gordon J. Schochet, *Patriarchalism in Political Thought* (New York: Basic Books, 1975), 37–98; Lawrence Stone, *The Family, Sex and Marriage in England 1500–1800* (New York: Harper & Row, 1977), 123–218 and *passim*; and, for interesting arguments that practice complicated and modified theory, see Keith Wrightson, *English Society 1580–1680* (London: Hutchinson, 1982), 89–118. On the Elizabethan construction of Woman, see (for example) Audrey Eccles, *Obstetrics and Gynaecology in Tudor and Stuart England* (London: Croom Helm, 1982); Keith Thomas, "The Double Standard," *Journal of the History of Ideas* 20 (1959): 195–216; Linda Woodbridge, *Women and the English Renaissance: Literature and the Nature of Womankind, 1540–1620* (Urbana: University of Illinois Press, 1983). Also see Ian Maclean, *The Renaissance Notion of Woman* (Cambridge: Cambridge University Press, 1980).

15. Reprinted in *Elizabethan Backgrounds*, ed. Arthur F. Kinney (Hamden, Conn.: Archon Books, 1975), 44–70; quotation from 60–61. Originally printed during the reign of Elizabeth's half brother, Edward VI, these homilies were reissued in the first months of Elizabeth's reign and reprinted ten times before it was over.

16. William Camden, *The History and Annalls of Elizabeth, Queen of England*, trans. Richard Norton (London, 1630), Book 1, 28–29.

17. Stafford to Walsingham, November 17, 1583 (Public Record Office: State Papers 78/10, no. 79), quoted in Roy Strong, *Portraits of Queen Elizabeth I* (Oxford: Clarendon Press, 1963), 32, n. 1.

18. See Strong, *Portraits of Queen Elizabeth I*, 40; George Lyman Kittredge, *Witchcraft in Old and New England* (1929; rpt. New York: Atheneum, 1972), 87–88.

19. See "Ben Jonson's Conversations with William Drummond of Hawthornden," in *Ben Jonson*, ed. C. H. Herford and Percy Simpson, 11 vols. (Oxford: Clarendon Press, 1925–52), 1.142, and the editorial note on 166.

20. For Playfere, see F. G. Emmison, *Elizabethan Life: Disorder* (Chelmsford, England: Essex County Council, 1970), 42; for Hawkins, see *Calendar of State Papers: Domestic*, vol. 148, item 34 (Thomas Scot to the earl of Leicester, March 1581). For several other examples, see Emmison, 41–42.

21. For an excellent general discussion of the means by which the ruler secured the compliance of the ruled, see Penry Williams, *The Tudor Regime* (Oxford: Clarendon Press, 1979), 351–405. On the politics of Elizabethan progresses, see my essay, " 'Eliza, Queene of shepheardes,' and the Pastoral of Power," *English Literary Renaissance* 10 (1980): 153–82.

22. See Joel Samaha, "Gleanings from Local Criminal-Court Records: Sedi-

tion Amongst the 'Inarticulate' in Elizabethan Essex," *Journal of Social History* 8, no. 3 (1975): 61–79; and Emmison, *Elizabethan Life*, 38–65.

23. See Roy Strong, *Holbein and Henry VIII* (London: Routledge & Kegan Paul, 1967), 35–54, for analysis and reproductions. For a fascinating study of the mystical politics of the Henrician body, see David Starkey, "Representation Through Intimacy: A Study in the Symbolism of Monarchy and Court Office in Early-Modern England," in *Symbols and Sentiments*, ed. Ioan Lewis (London: Academic Press, 1977), 187–224.

24. The most notable versions are catalogued as paintings nos. 64 (reproduced here) and 65 in Strong, *Portraits of Queen Elizabeth I*.

25. Mary Douglas, *Purity and Danger* (Harmondsworth: Penguin Books, 1966), 115, 121.

26. The extant text is putatively a transcription made on the occasion of the queen's speech by her chaplain, Dr. Lionel Sharp, and first printed in *Cabala: Mysteries of State and Government in Letters of Illustrious Persons* (London, 1654); quoted in Paul Johnson, *Elizabeth I: A Study in Power and Intellect* (London: Weidenfeld & Nicholson, 1974), 320. For other memorials and representations of the queen's appearance at Tilbury in 1588, see Winfried Schleiner, "*Divina Virago*: Queen Elizabeth as an Amazon," *Studies in Philology* 75 (1978): 163–80.

27. See Emmison, *Elizabethan Life*, 57.

28. For a comprehensive and well-annotated survey of court pageantry in early modern Europe, see Roy Strong, *Art and Power: Renaissance Festivals 1450–1650* (Berkeley and Los Angeles: University of California Press, 1984). Also see Frances A. Yates, *Astraea: The Imperial Theme in the Sixteenth Century* (London: Routledge & Kegan Paul, 1975); Roy Strong, *The Cult of Elizabeth: Elizabethan Portraiture and Pageantry* (London: Thames & Hudson, 1977); Stephen Orgel, *The Illusion of Power: Political Theatre in the English Renaissance* (Berkeley and Los Angeles: University of California Press, 1975). Literary idealizations of Queen Elizabeth are collected in E. C. Wilson, *England's Eliza* (1939; rpt. London: Frank Cass, 1966).

29. Michel Foucault, *The History of Sexuality, Volume I: An Introduction*, trans. Robert Hurley (New York: Random House, 1978), 92; italics mine.

30. Michel Foucault, "What is an Author?" in *Textual Strategies*, ed. Josué V. Harari (Ithaca: Cornell University Press, 1979), 159, 141.

31. Robert Weimann, " 'Appropriation' and Modern History in Renaissance Prose Narrative," *New Literary History* 14 (1983): 459–95; quotation from 468–69.

32. See Richard Helgerson, *Self-Crowned Laureates: Spenser, Jonson, Milton and the Literary System* (Berkeley and Los Angeles: University of California Press, 1983). My use of masculine pronouns is intentional: although the Elizabethan "literary system" encompassed a variety of class positions, with very rare exceptions it excluded female writers.

33. "Sir knowing how doubtfully all Allegories may be construed, and this booke of mine . . . being a continued Allegory, or darke conceit, I have thought good aswell for avoyding of gealous opinions and misconstruc-

tions, as also for your better light in reading thereof, (being so by you commanded,) to discover unto you the general intention and meaning, which in the whole course thereof I have fashioned" ("A letter of the Authors . . . To . . . Sir Walter Raleigh"). D. M. Loades, "The Theory and Practice of Censorship in Sixteenth-Century England," *Transactions of the Royal Historical Society*, ser. 5, vol. 24 (1974): 141–57, is a useful introduction to its subject. Also see Annabel Patterson, *Censorship and Interpretation: The Conditions of Writing and Reading in Early Modern England* (Madison: University of Wisconsin Press, 1984).

34. The present discussion incorporates in revised form material originally published in my essay, " 'The perfecte paterne of a Poete': The Poetics of Courtship in *The Shepheardes Calender*," *Texas Studies in Literature and Language* 21 (1979): 34–67. See also Richard Helgerson, "The New Poet Presents Himself: Spenser and the Idea of a Literary Career," *PMLA* 93 (1978): 893–911; and David L. Miller, "Authorship, Anonymity, and *The Shepheardes Calender*," *Modern Language Quarterly* 40 (1979): 219–36. *The Shepheardes Calender* and *The Faerie Queene* are quoted from the often reprinted Oxford Standard Authors edition of Spenser's *Poetical Works*, ed. J. C. Smith and E. de Selincourt (London: Oxford University Press, 1912). I have modified obsolete typographical conventions in quotations from this and other Elizabethan texts.

35. Compare Thomas H. Cain, *Praise in "The Faerie Queene"* (Lincoln: University of Nebraska Press, 1978), 14–24.

36. These lines make orthographically explicit the lay's transformation of Eliza into Elisa: the original printed text consistently distinguishes between Elisa as the subject of the song and Eliza as the subject to whom the song is offered, between the royal image of Colin's own making and the collective royal image embodied in the queen.

37. By the strategy of eschewing a similitude—"But I will not match her with *Latonaes* seede, / Such folie great sorow to *Niobe* did breede" (86–87)—Colin constructs his relationship to Elisa as that of parent to child. The *Calender*'s authorial persona, Immerito, does similarly in the prefatory address "To His Booke": "Goe little booke: thy selfe present / As child whose parent is unkent." Compare Weimann, " 'Appropriation' and Modern History in Renaissance Prose Narrative," 479: "This is the privileged function of the author's activity: to make the means and meanings of the fictional enterprise his own. . . . By the time we come to Sidney and Cervantes, the sense of ownership affects the self-referential quality of the author's language. The ties between product and producer have become so close and so personal that the process of appropriation is sanctioned by metaphors of procreation. . . . The story, the characters, and the multiplication of significance directly result from the author's own invention and labor."

38. In addition to the works by Greenblatt and Helgerson, already cited, the recent Spenser criticism from which I have most benefited includes Jonathan Goldberg, *Endlesse Worke: Spenser and the Structures of Discourse*

(Baltimore: Johns Hopkins University Press, 1981); and Maureen Quilligan, *Milton's Spenser: The Politics of Reading* (Ithaca: Cornell University Press, 1983). Goldberg meditates on the ways in which Spenser's text refigures within it the authoritative texts—both literary and social—by which it has been generated; Quilligan emphasizes the gendered character of Spenser's textual politics, the manifestation in his poetry of the reciprocal pressure exerted between the male writer and his female readership—in particular, that female reader who is also the poet's prince. Also see Michael O'Connell, *Mirror and Veil: The Historical Dimension of Spenser's "Faerie Queene"* (Chapel Hill: University of North Carolina Press, 1977); and Thomas H. Cain, *Praise in "The Faerie Queene."*

39. Fredric Jameson, *The Political Unconscious* (Ithaca: Cornell University Press, 1981), 76.

40. John Harington, *Nugae Antiquae*, 3 vols. (1779: rpt. Hildesheim: Georg Olms, 1968), 2:211.

41. *The Letters and Epigrams of Sir John Harington*, ed. N. E. McClure (Philadelphia: University of Pennsylvania Press, 1930), 125.

42. Nancy Vickers, "Diana Described: Scattered Woman and Scattered Rhyme," *Critical Inquiry* 8 (1981): 265–79. In a paper on "The Comedy of Female Authority," delivered at the 1984 MLA Convention, Maureen Quilligan also brings Vickers's essay to bear upon the description of Belphoebe.

43. Scholars have often pointed to the meeting of Belphoebe with Trompart and Braggadocchio as an imitation/parody of the meeting of Venus with Aeneas and Achates in *Aeneid* 1. The exchange of greeting between Belphoebe and Trompart in *FQ* 2.3.32–33 directly echoes that between Venus, disguised as a nymph of Diana, and her son, Aeneas, in *Aeneid* 1.321–24, 327–28. (Not coincidentally, direct quotations of the latter lines are used as the final emblems of the *Aprill* eclogue, where they are referred to Colin's Elisa.) What is of greatest interest and importance for *FQ* 2.3 is that the conjunction of two classical subtexts—Ovidian and Virgilian—produces a conflation of multiple representations and responses: a loving and punitive monarch, mistress, and mother who is adored, desired, and feared.

44. Thomas Platter recorded a fountain in the park of Nonsuch House that was sculpted with figures of Diana and Actaeon. Paul Hentzner recorded an account of Diana and Actaeon inscribed over the entrance to the park at Whitehall, which he interpreted as a reference to Philip II's courtship of Queen Elizabeth, a presumption punished in the defeat of the Armada. The inscription captures nicely the ambivalence of the goddess/queen: "The chaste virgin naturally pittied / But the powerful goddess revenged the wrong." For these references, as well as that in the following note, I am indebted to a rich essay by Leonard Barkan, "Diana and Actaeon: The Myth as Synthesis," *English Literary Renaissance* 10 (1980): 317–59; see 332–35 on the relevance of the myth to Queen Elizabeth.

45. George Sandys, *Ovid's Metamorphosis Englished, Mythologiz'd and Represented in Figures* (Oxford, 1632), 151–52.

46. Compare Goldberg, *Endlesse Worke*, 159: "There are no other moments like these anywhere in the poem, and they seem to indicate a need to break the text to acknowledge the arrival of the most authoritative figure in the text."

47. For Greenblatt, Renaissance self-fashioning "involves submission to an absolute power or authority situated at least partially outside the self," and "is achieved in relation to something perceived as alien, strange, or hostile"; this "alien is always constructed as a distorted image of the authority," and the identity that is produced in the encounter between them "partakes of both the authority and the alien that is marked for attack" (*Renaissance Self-Fashioning*, 9). It will be obvious that in the fashioning of my own text, Greenblatt's has functioned as both an authority and an other. My disagreements with his admirable book arise within the scope of a shared project; his work has enabled mine.

48. See Williams, *Marxism and Literature*, 108–27; quotation from 121. For another view of the fundamental "heteroglossia" of discourse that undermines the totalization of any ideological dominance, see Mikhail Bakhtin, *The Dialogic Imagination*, trans. Caryl Emerson and Michael Holquist (Austin: University of Texas Press, 1981). Pierre Bourdieu, "Symbolic Power" (trans. Richard Nice), *Critique of Anthropology*, 4 (Summer 1979): 77–85, makes the extremely important point that an ideological dominance is qualified by both the specific professional and/or class interests of cultural producers and by the relative autonomy of the cultural medium being worked: "When we insist that ideologies are always doubly determined, that they owe their most specific characteristics not only to the interests of the classes or class fractions which they express . . . but also to the specific interests of those who produce them and to the specific logic of the field of production (usually transfigured into the ideology of 'creation' and the 'creator'), we obtain the means of escaping crude reduction of ideological products to the interests of the classes they serve . . . without falling into the idealist illusion of treating ideological productions as self-sufficient and self-generating totalities amenable to pure, purely internal analysis" (81–82).

49. Compare Weimann, " 'Appropriation' and Modern History": " 'Appropriation' as an act in literary history will have to be defined as both a text-appropriating as well as a world-appropriating activity. If this activity is proprietary (as constituting juridically definable ownership) on the part of those who sell and buy manuscripts and . . . printed books, it also constitutes a non-juridical mode of making things one's own by which the world in the book and the book in the world are appropriated through an intellectual acquisition on the level of both writing and reading" (465–66).

50. See Williams, *Marxism and Literature*, 11–20, 45–54; Terry Eagleton, *Literary Theory: An Introduction* (Oxford: Basil Blackwell, 1983), 17–53; Terry

Eagleton, *The Function of Criticism* (London: NLB, 1984). I have discussed these issues with particular reference to Puttenham's *Arte of English Poesie*, in "Of Gentlemen and Shepherds: The Politics of Elizabethan Pastoral Form," *ELH* 50 (1983): 415–59; see especially 433–52.

15. TEXTUAL OVERLAPPING
AND DALILAH'S HARLOT-LAP

■

MARY NYQUIST

he said I was a flower of the mountain yes so we are flowers all a
womans body yes that was one true thing he said in his life and the
sun shines for you today yes
—JOYCE, *Ulysses*

Elles n'utilisent pas pour parler de leurs sexes des hyperboles des
métaphores, elles ne procèdent pas par accumulations ou par gra-
dations. Elles ne récitent pas les longues litanies, dont le moteur
est une imprécation sans fin. Elles ne s'efforcent pas de multiplier
les lacunes de façon que dans leur ensemble elles signifient un
lapsus volontaire. Elles disent que toutes ces formes désignent un
langage suranné. Elles disent qu'il faut tout recommencer. Elles
disent qu'un grand vent balaie la terre. Elles disent que le soleil va
se lever.
—WITTIG, *Les Guérillères*

I

IN "Presupposition and Intertextuality," Jonathan Culler discusses
some of the difficulties the notion of intertextuality has come up
against. As initially developed by Julia Kristéva and as elaborated by
Roland Barthes, the rigorously postmodernist concept of intertextuality gestures toward the radically contingent and anonymously
layered character of literary discourse. Yet in practice—even, as
Culler points out, in Kristéva's practice—any analysis of intertextuality that engages individual texts has tended to assimilate itself to
the more limited and conventional study of specifiable sources or
pre-texts. As Culler neatly formulates the dilemma: "[Intertextua-
lity] is a difficult concept to use because of the vast and undefined
discursive space it designates, but when one narrows it so as to

make it more usable one either falls into source study of a traditional and positivistic kind (which is what the concept was designed to transcend) or else ends by naming particular texts as the pre-texts on grounds of interpretive convenience."[1] Culler persuasively shows that in the cases of, for example, Laurent Jenny and Harold Bloom, critical practice is significantly at odds with theoretical doctrine, from which it "falls" away. Yet his own essay seeks to harness the radical potential of intertextuality to the project of determining a text's conditions of intelligibility by investigating its presuppositions. This project involves regarding a text's pre- or co-texts not as sources but rather as constituents of discursive practices which it presupposes. Why, however, a skeptical voice might ask, begin with what the text itself seems to presuppose in the way of conventions and codes? And why focus exclusively on grounds of intelligibility? In what follows, I hope to engage a specific passage from Milton's *Paradise Lost* in ways that open up, rather than delimit, the discursive space it inhabits. If, in the process, the original spirit of intertextuality is not betrayed as Culler almost suggests it must, inevitably, be, I would like to argue that it is because the grounds of this particular text's intelligibility cannot be severed from those of its unintelligibility—an unintelligibility that even if in some sense presupposed by the text, is also, unambiguously, the product of an institutionally dominant masculinist critical tradition.

The starting point for this discussion will be a simile that unfolds in the course of what, both formally and theologically, is supposed to be the central passage of *Paradise Lost*'s Book 9. The passage, which I give in full here, represents the pivotal moments of Eve and Adam's dying and awakening into a fallen consciousness:

> So said he, and forbore not glance or toy
> Of amorous intent, well understood
> Of *Eve*, whose Eye darted contagious Fire.
> Her hand he seiz'd, and to a shady bank,
> Thick overhead with verdant roof imbowr'd
> He led her nothing loath; Flow'rs were the Couch,
> Pansies, and Violets, and Asphodel,
> And Hyacinth, Earth's freshest softest lap.
> There they thir fill of Love and Love's disport
> Took largely, of thir mutual guilt the Seal,
> The solace of thir sin, till dewy sleep
> Oppress'd them, wearied with thir amorous play.
> Soon as the force of that fallacious Fruit,
> That with exhilarating vapor bland
> About thir spirits had play'd, and inmost powers
> Made err, was now exhal'd, and grosser sleep

> Bred of unkindly fumes, with conscious dreams
> Encumber'd, now had left them, up they rose
> As from unrest, and each the other viewing,
> Soon found thir Eyes how op'n'd, and thir minds
> How dark'n'd; innocence, that as a veil
> Had shadow'd them from knowing ill, was gone,
> Just confidence, and native righteousness,
> And honor from about them, naked left
> To guilty shame: hee cover'd, but his Robe
> Uncover'd more. So rose the *Danite* strong
> *Herculean Samson* from the Harlot-lap
> Of *Philistean Dalilah*, and wak'd
> Shorn of his strength, They destitute and bare
> Of all thir virtue: silent, and in face
> Confounded long they sat, as struck'n mute,
> Till *Adam*, though not less than *Eve* abasht,
> At length gave utterance to these words constrain'd.
>   O *Eve*, in evil hour thou didst give ear
> To that false Worm, of whomsoever taught
> To counterfeit Man's voice, true in our Fall,
> False in our promis'd Rising.[2]
>   (9.1034–70)

Playing indirectly, and in familiar Renaissance fashion, with the sexual connotations of dying, this passage suggests what *De Doctrina Christiana* considers the last stage of spiritual death by having Adam and Eve experience a heightened and novel form of sexual dying. It is thereby able to present the epic's central *anagnorisis* dramatically, as an awakening that follows from this dying's "grosser sleep." The *anagnorisis* here is not only what the self-confessedly "tragic" action of Book 9 formally requires, however; it is also a literary enactment of Genesis 3:7, the one verse in Genesis Christian theology has always depended upon in arguing that a guilty consciousness of change is what the Fall both brings and is about: "And the eyes of them both were opened, and they knew that they were naked."[3]

Yet while biblical commentators on this verse have always used the plural pronoun, twentieth-century commentators on *Paradise Lost* have not been similarly capable of respecting the plural "they" in the Samson simile cited above. With only one or two not very clearly developed exceptions, modern critics and editors alike are determined to find in this simile an analogy between Samson's betrayal by Dalilah and Adam's by Eve, in spite of the fact that on the level of syntax alone it is patently obvious that *both* Adam and Eve are being compared with Samson. Even Northrop Frye, by far the

most important and influential of contemporary writers on the relations between the Bible and literature, can claim that the simile
"associates Samson with the fallen Adam."[4] One of the things the
modern misreading assumes is that the Samson simile deploys a
form of proportional analogy, itself presupposing a fixed and hierarchically structured opposition between male and female. This assumption is implicitly at work in annotations on the simile such as
Fowler's, "See *Judges* xvi for the story of Samson's betrayal by Delilah. . . . The comparison between Adam and Samson was traditional"[5]; it is more crudely and explicitly operative when John Knott
asserts that in the simile Milton confirms Eve's guilt by comparing
her with Dalilah and then comments: "And as any reader of *Samson
Agonistes* knows, Milton's insult is worse than calling Eve 'whore,'
since it implies that her treachery is directed against God as well as
Adam."[6] This latter remark is particularly interesting in that it illustrates how in ostensibly speaking for the revered and canonical
author's sternly patriarchal views, a modern critic gives voice to a
misogyny not actually grounded in the text itself. It is Knott who in
his text actually calls Eve "whore," and who complacently assumes
with his reader that in both *Samson Agonistes* and in this simile
Milton is engaged in representing a betrayal.

A brief analysis of the ways in which the historically specific
features of Milton's interpretation of the Genesis story inform this
passage will indicate, however, that the simile actually, as it were,
breaks up its representational ground in order to unfold (from its
laps) a complex of conceptual, semi-allegorical meanings. The Protestant exegetes whose views Milton adopts conceive the Fall as a
linear and progressive process, with the result that what is taken to
be the active and progressive experience of transgression precedes
the moment of conscious discovery. Because the Protestant Fall is a
finely articulated temporal process, *Paradise Lost* cannot conform to
the model implicitly recommended by the *Poetics*, where Aristotle,
using *Oedipus Tyrannus* as his example, states that the best kind of
anagnorisis coincides with the *peripeteia*.[7] In *Paradise Lost* the central
reversal and recognition occur in a sequential rather than simultaneous order, which means that Eve and Adam are represented as
undergoing a change of fortune before they have any consciousness
of having done so. The text dramatizes the dynamic linearity of the
Fall in a number of ways, but perhaps most strikingly when the
intoxicating pleasure got from eating, together, of the forbidden
fruit leads to the much more intense pleasures of sexual desire.
Although as "solace" their love-making is notoriously ineffective, its
ineffectiveness is the very dramatic vehicle of the *anagnorisis*: Eve

and Adam awaken from their troubled sleep to discover their *mutatio in contrarium*. Thus the recognition, though it does not coincide with the reversal, is produced by an ingeniously dramatic mimesis, one that obviously respects Aristotle's suggestion in a later section of the *Poetics* that the discovery should use "probable means," the love-making here being, precisely, the probable means.[8] If this is so, then the simile actually illustrates the intimate and markedly temporal relationship between *Paradise Lost*'s central *peripeteia* and *anagnorisis*. Just as Samson arises from the "harlot-*lap* / Of Philistean Dalilah" to discover that he is "Shorn of his strength," so Eve and Adam arise from "Earth's freshest softest *lap*" (1.1041)—no one in the history of Milton criticism seems to have noticed the carefully plotted paral-lelism here—to discover that they are "destitute and bare / Of all thir virtue." Informing the simile's concern with a retrospective dis-covery of loss is Protestantism's theology of the Word, which is so radically logocentric as to make it possible to align Samson, who has unknowingly been shorn of his strength as a result of breaking his Nazarite vow, with Adam and Eve, who have unknowingly lost their original innocence as a result of denying the Father's Word. Within this logocentric context, the loss of strength or sexual inno-cence is of course not, in itself, of significance; it is the discovery of loss that is supposed to be the ground of meaning, making possible a recognition of the ideal value of that which has unwittingly been lost. This, then, would be why the simile compares Samson in the act of discovering he has lost his strength with Eve and Adam, who in becoming conscious of their loss of sexual innocence experience sensuously and immediately the loss of that most immaterial of theological goods, divine grace.

The absence of this historicized context for interpreting the simile does not alone account for the misconstruing of this simile by mod-ern commentators, however. Though perpetuated institutionally, the misreading of the Samson simile undoubtedly draws on features of an archaic and self-universalizing patriarchal symbolic order, ac-cording to which the representation of lack or loss can only but affirm the hierarchically ordered polarity of the sexes. In the reading I am proposing, the phrases "Shorn of his strength" and "destitute and bare / Of all thir virtue" are complex figures, the former sug-gesting that Samson's unshorn hair functions as a metonymy for his strength, itself a metonymy for his spiritual integrity, while the latter indicates the way Adam and Eve's unself-conscious naked-ness functions as a metaphor for innocence. But read as modern commentators misread the simile, the signifier "Shorn of his strength" would appear unconsciously to efface itself by collapsing

into its presumed signified, Samson's experience of sexual deple-
tion, the detumescence or, symbolically, the castration, Dalilah is
guilty of bringing about. And since Eve cannot be represented as
sharing *that* experience, the entire simile is without more ado taken
to compare its two male subjects. It is of course only (to use Derrida's
coinage) in a phallogocentric discourse, where the phallus as privileged signifier dictates that difference be produced only and always
as difference from the same, that is, from the unitary male subject
who is able always to represent his own oneness, that such a slippage—from a Samson who lacks to a postcoital "they" not capable
of including Eve—can take place. It might at this point be thought
that this critical unconscious is largely a fiction fabricated to fulfill
the needs of a feminist theory of the text's consumption. But the
phallocentric determinants of the Samson simile's misreading are
revealed in a surprisingly literal manner by J. M. Evans in his edition
of Books 9 and 10 of *Paradise Lost* for the *Cambridge Milton for Schools
and Colleges*. In his commentary on Book 9, Evans refers to the *anagnorisis* by saying "Adam's eyes are opened," omitting reference to
either Eve or the Genesis "they."[9] His introduction to the volume
concludes with a chart on which are mapped the differences between "pre-Fall", "Fall", and "post-Fall" states, the final entry of
which opposes "erect penis" on the unfallen side to "flaccid" on the
fallen. Claude Lévi-Strauss is mentioned in the words prefacing the
chart.[10] Later, in the concluding "Topics: Book IX," a specific myth
reported in *The Raw and the Cooked* is cited, a myth linking sexual
intercourse, reproduction, and death. The myth tells the tale of a
first man who, created in a state of perpetual tumescence, was
taught by the first woman how to soften his penis in copulation;
when the demiurge saw the limp penis, he cursed the man, consigning him to the reproductive cycle and therefore to death.[11] While
Evans nowhere explicitly develops a coherent misogynistic misreading of the Samson simile, the textual apparatus he provides
clearly more than enables one. By the time a student of the *Cambridge Milton* gets to Book 11 of *Paradise Lost*, where Michael says to
Adam that "Man's woe" begins from "Man's effeminate slackness"
(11.634), a fairly graphic understanding of that slackness will have
been produced.

   An historicized grasp of Milton's presentation of the Fall would,
in contrast, stress the way in which the simile operates in a typically
Protestant manner to direct attention away from the body *per se* to a
recognition of the inward significance of the bodily signs of a
changed sexuality. Adam and Eve, "each the other viewing," see in
one another the visible signs of an inward change or fall; as Adam

puts it, their eyes are opened to see "in our Faces evident the signs / Of foul concupiscence" (9.1077–78). It is almost as if Milton has constructed an *anagnorisis* that would avoid some of the embarrassments of Augustine's discussion in *The City of God*, where the Genesis opening of the eyes is explicated by the notion that what Adam and Eve's eyes are opened to is the novel disobedience, or involuntary movement of, their bodily members.[12] Since the various contexts in this work, the *De Genesi ad Litteram* and the *Confessions* in which Augustine speaks of unruly motions, disobedient members and so forth make it abundantly clear that his viewpoint is quite literally phallocentric and that he is concerned, not to say obsessed, with the phallus as privileged signifier, the awakening presented in *Paradise Lost* would seem deliberately to transform Augustine's scene of recognition so that what Eve and Adam see is not the involuntary action of the male member but rather the signs of a postorgasmic desire inscribed in each of their faces. If this is the case, then modern misreadings of our simile, with their implicit or explicit primitivizing of the specular gaze, are curiously and significantly anachronistic and ahistorical.

II

So far this misreading has been treated as if it bore no relation whatsoever to the text; as if it projected misogynistic meanings onto a theologically minded passage that would virtuously resist them. I will go on to suggest, however, that the misreading does in a sense belong to the text (at the very least, *Paradise Lost* can be made to own up to permitting it) by discussing some of the masculinist literary and cultural codes that are at work in the Samson simile's immediate context. Since the interaction of these masculinist codes with one another or with those (Aristotelian, theological) codes we have just specified has never been analyzed, a discussion of them will not in any direct or straightforward manner justify or even account for the misreading. Rather, by establishing the complex network of signs into which the simile has inserted itself, what follows seeks to explain why the simile might be incapable of communicating from the grounds of its own intelligibility.

If we turn, first, to the iconographic tradition, we find that several features of the depiction of Samson in subjection to Dalilah are of possible relevance to the context *Paradise Lost* develops for the Samson simile. First of all, the tradition frequently makes use of Josephus's suggestion, at odds with the story as told in Judges, that drunkenness was a condition of Samson's fall. Andrea Mantegna's

Samson and Delilah, for example, portrays Samson reclining, asleep, on Dalilah's lap, while she (rather than her servant, as in Judges) cuts his hair. Entwined around the dead tree that stands beside them is a fertile grapevine, while at Samson's feet is a trough being filled with water issuing from a spout that juts from a rock. As Madlyn Millner Kahr points out, both grapevine and fountain are ambiguous icons. Being associated with the Passion and the Fountain of Life, they remind the spectator that Samson is a type of Christ; but because the vine is connected with Bacchus and running water with concupiscence, they also suggest the vice of Luxury, clearly of direct relevance to the scene being represented.[13] In Book 9 of *Paradise Lost,* the forbidden fruit, once eaten, plays the part of Bacchus's wine: it produces in both Eve and Adam what is explicitly labeled an intoxicated response, and then, "Carnal desire inflaming" (9.1008–13), introduces a new style of love-making. In the lengthy passage cited above, the *anagnorisis* is immediately preceded by lines emphasizing the metaphorical connections between drunkenness and lust as a manifestation of original sin. The iconographic tradition thus could be thought to reinforce the textually and historically "correct" reading of the Samson simile proposed above, since it suggests that *both* Eve and Adam are succumbing, like Samson, to immoderate desire.[14] Spenser's complexly emblematic presentation of the deaths of Mordant and Amavia in Book 2 of *The Fairie Queen* similarly associates the effects of wine (in this case from the cup of Acrasia, who "makes her lovers drunken mad" [2.1.52.2]) with original sin, the taint of which is borne by Rudymane. And it likewise emphasizes the allegorical unity of the couple who in their dying become a *single* "image of mortalitie" (2.1.57.2).[15]

In this context, the two laps in the passage we are examining— "Earth's freshest softest lap" and "Dalilah's Harlot-Lap"—adopt the position of firmly grounding a logocentric hermeneutics, thereby becoming the familiar *terra firma* of an allegorizing Christian literary tradition. But other passages in *The Faerie Queene* employing these icons somewhat complicate the picture. In Book 1, for example, Duessa finds the Redcrosse knight sitting wearily, disarmed, by a fountain that, as the little etiological tale we are told indicates, is an emblematic tributary of the Lake of Idleness. As a result of drinking from it, Redcrosse's "manly forces gan to faile" (1.7.6.4); but, like Samson, Redcrosse perceives his weakness and vulnerability only when, the moment of dalliance over, the enemy—in his case Orgoglio—advances upon him. Although there is no reference to Duessa's lap in this episode, we are provided with a description of their "pleasaunce of the joyous shade" that nevertheless suggests it:

Andrea Mantegna, *Samson and Delilah* (Reproduced by permission of the Trustees of The National Gallery, London.)

"Yet goodly court he made still to his Dame, / Pourd out in loose-
nesse on the grassy grownd, / Both carelesse of his health, and of
his fame" (1.7.7.1–3). The slight syntactical ambiguity here, which
momentarily places "Dame" in apposition with "Pourd out," only
reinforces the figurative association of Duessa with the debilitating
ground.

Redcrosse is of course not the only one of Spenser's knights to lie
in looseness, disarmed, on the grassy ground or a female lap. The
overcoming of masculine purposiveness by feminine wiles is a Renaissance *topos* that has affiliations with numerous classical myths
and texts but whose prototypical actors are generally taken to be
Mars and Venus. Yet as Kahr's study of the iconographic tradition
shows, in certain works, such as those by Lucas van Leyden, Samson himself is depicted as having laid aside his shield and halberd.[16]
If representations of Samson can in this way incorporate details
associated with Mars and Venus, then we should not be surprised to
find that in Spenser the *topos* reaches out to embrace female laps as
dangerously emasculating as Dalilah's. Thus redescribed, the *topos*
informs not only the Redcrosse knight's dalliance with Duessa but
also, and more obviously, the seductions linked with Acrasia. Pha-
edria's unmanning of Cymochles, for instance, is described in a way
that brings several of these motifs together:

> Into a shadie dale she soft him led,
> And laid him downe upon a grassie plain;
> And her sweet selfe without dread, or disdaine,
> She set beside, laying his head disarm'd
> In her loose lap, it softly to sustaine,
> Where soone he slumbred, fearing not be harm'd,
> The whiles with a loud lay she thus him sweetly charm'd.
>
> (2.6.14.3–9)

And in the processional entrance into the Bowre of Blisse which the
reader makes with Guyon, all the icons so far mentioned are gradually, one by one, encountered: Bacchus's vine, the fountain of "infinite streams," the "secret shade," the enchanting lay, the slumbering victim, Acrasia, herself lying on a bed of roses, discovered by
Guyon and the Palmer "with her lover lose, / Whose sleepie head
she in her lap did soft dispose" (2.12.76.8–9), and the useless and
abandoned martial arms and shield.

That Acrasia's breast, together with its dewy drops of perspira-
tion, is "bare to readie spoyle / Of hungry eies" (2.12.78.1–2),
makes strikingly evident the psychoanalytical contours of this *topos*,
which expresses what we would now think of as the male's fear of
being resubmitted to the power of the phallic mother. It is highly

Peter Paul Rubens, *Samson and Delilah* (Reproduced by permission of the Trustees of The National Gallery, London.)

interesting that this same conjunction of images is used by Rubens in his *Samson and Delilah,* which portrays a deeply unconscious Samson asleep in the lap of a Dalilah whose full breasts are exposed to the spectator's view.[17] Read allegorically, the unconsciousness of the victim illustrates the complete subjection of the reason or will to desire or, in the Pauline sense, the flesh. Read psychoanalytically, and in terms that are specifically Lacanian, it represents a desired but feared return to an imaginary unity with the mother, a unity associated with the gaze or the scopic drive. At any rate, having betrayed his code of honor, the victim is in the position of the *infans,* who, not speaking, has no connection with the symbolic order, the linguistic order that Lacan identifies with the father's Law or Word.

Milton's *Samson Agonistes* reminds us again and again that Samson's downfall came about because he verbally relinquished a secret, namely, God's "holy secret," thereby carelessly using language in a way that ruptured his relation with the paternal Word. Garrulity, traditionally held to be a female trait, is the label Samson attaches to his crime, which becomes "shameful garrulity" (491). That Dalilah should have used language as a means of tempting him is no great surprise; but that he, Samson, should have responded verbally shows a contemptible "impotence of mind," which throughout the first part of the drama continues to astonish and enrage. Samson returns repeatedly to his failure to keep his Father's secret, convinced that Dalilah "was not the prime cause, but I myself, / Who vanquisht with a peal of words (O weakness!) / Gave up my fort of silence to a Woman" (234–36). The silence Samson fails to defend is a "fort" because it maintains his relation with the paternal order. Once surrendered, Samson falls into a different order of silence, a silent slumbering on a female lap that is so humiliating *Samson Agonistes* can hardly bear to recall it. When it does, Dalilah's lap becomes, significantly, a harlot-lap, in spite of the drama's unbiblical insistence that she is Samson's wife:

> Then swoll'n with pride into the snare I fell
> Of fair fallacious looks, venereal trains,
> Soft'n'd with pleasure and voluptuous life;
> At length to lay my head and hallow'd pledge
> Of all my strength in the lascivious lap
> Of a deceitful Concubine who shore me
> Like a tame Wether, all my precious fleece,
> Then turn'd me out ridiculous, despoil'd,
> Shav'n, and disarm'd among my enemies.
> (532–40)

Here, once more, are the familiar features of the *topos* I have briefly been examining: female deceit and female seductiveness, their well-to-do half-sister *Luxuria,* the female lap, and its treacherous capacity to unman and disarm its victim.

So far, we have been dealing with laps that are representationally and anatomically grounded by an individual female temptress figure. Like the Latin *gremio,* the Anglo-Saxon "lap" can refer either to the bosom or to the area between the waist and the knees on which, most commonly, a child is held. Yet in Renaissance England, the substantive "lap" may have had a more explicitly sexual connotation than we now suppose, one of the obsolete meanings of "lap" cited by the O.E.D. being the female pudendum.[18] This is, presumably, one reason that Dalilah's lap can be described as "lascivious." The very *topos* we have been discussing, however, turns the lap into what is also metaphorically a lap of pleasure or a lap of luxury—a phrase that is, interestingly, still current. Even when not literalized by a female body, this lap of luxury is always associated with women and thus, from a masculinist perspective, with effeminacy. For example, when Britomart boasts to Guyon about her martial upbringing, she states "Sithence I loathed have my life to lead, / As Ladies wont, in pleasures wanton lap" (3.2.6.6–7). The verbal form of "lap" can similarly invoke this figure, as it does when we learn that Adonis lies with Venus "Lapped in flowres and pretious spycery" (3.6.46.1.5). More obviously sinister is Comus's description of the practice of his mother Circe and the three sirens, "Who as they sung, would take the prison'd soul / And lap it in Elysium" (256/57). Not unrelated, as a final, more ambiguous, example, are the lines "And ever against eating Cares, / Lap me in soft *Lydian* Airs" from Milton's "L'Allegro" (135–36).

Although all laps inviting retreat or associated with rest are undoubtedly enervating female laps, it does not follow that laps can play only this single psychosocial role. For nature, too, has a lap, a fertile lap that in its capacity to bring forth flowers and vegetation would seem to be both innocent and blessed. Even when presented as relatively inactive, as it is when *Paradise Lost* says in describing paradise that "the flow'ry lap / Of some irriguous Valley spread her store" (4.254–55), the innocence of nature's lap is not called into question. And its more actively procreative character seems just as virtuous, as we can see by the way Milton's "May Song" celebrates "The Flow'ry May, who from her green lap throws / The yellow Cowslip, and the pale Primrose" (3–4); or by the way that in Book 4 of *The Fairie Queene* the song that bursts forth in praise of Venus stresses the responsiveness of nature's lap: "Then doth the daedale earth throw forth to thee / Out of her fruitful lap aboundant flowers" (4.10.45.1–2). Passages such as this, which so abound as to not need instancing, would suggest that nature's bounteous lap is in Renaissance texts sharply differentiated from the lap of the temptress or of luxury. But because like Luxuria, nature or the *hortus conclusus* is symbolically female, there is always, inevitably, the possibility of slippage. That Acrasia's victim is named Verdant gives some indication of the direction of this slippage; so does the conjunction, in the examples cited above, of literalized female laps and flowers and grassy grounds. Perhaps the most powerful example of this potential ambiguity appears in Milton's Fifth Elegy, which has the earth call out passionately, and perhaps seductively, to her desired partner, the sun, "Huc ades, et gremio lumina pone meo" (1.95) ["come hither and lay your glories in my lap"]. Is this, or is this not, a lascivious lap?

It should by now be evident that a similar question could legitimately be asked of "Earth's freshest softest lap" in the passage from *Paradise Lost* to which we can now return, having situated it in the context of the iconographic and literary conventions on which it undoubtedly draws. The adjective "fresh" certainly suggests a natural innocence. And one could argue that the superlative forms of "fresh" and "soft" convey the kind of poignancy associated with imminent loss, in part by recalling the language used to describe the initial appearance of "delicious Paradise" in *Paradise Lost* (the "loftiest shade," "statelist view," "goodliest Trees loaden with fairest Fruit" in 4.132–47). But the adjective "soft" is without question implicated in the *topos* of the regressive lap. Viewed retrospectively, from Adam and Eve's awakening as if from a "harlot-lap," both superlatives therefore do more than hint at a potential excess, or even looseness, in this lap's freshness and softness. On the other hand, perhaps a backward glance of this sort is not so useful to an understanding of the operation of this simile as would be an analysis of its dynamic forward movement. If due weight is given to the way a fully dramatized action unfolds between "Earth's freshest softest lap" and "Dalilah's harlot-lap," then it becomes possible to see that the action itself resolves the initially ambiguous or doubtful innocence of nature's lap. Earth's freshest softest lap in effect *becomes* a kind of harlot-lap because while lying on it Eve and Adam experiences a dying into a fallen sexuality. Where Nature initially groaned in response to the forbidden acts of Eve and Adam, it now, more passively, simply lies there, becoming somehow embedded in the final stages of their fall. Its lap—or rather the two laps here becoming one—thus signals by means of this passive participation a general lapse, *lapsus*, a fall, the Fall.

It is of course only the English language that makes possible this particular theological pun, which is interestingly appropriate, even central, to the masculinist biblical and doctrinal story *Paradise Lost* here enacts. If Adam and Eve bring death into the world, it is supposed to be because death becomes inseparably a part of the process of reproduction. But in the Judeo-Christian tradition as well as in *Paradise Lost*, the sign of this inseparability becomes woman. Nature's simple there-ness in "Earth's freshest softest lap" for this reason signals the falling movement into a new and emergent maternity, now associated with death. In his lengthy soliloquy in Book 10, Adam protests the deferring of the death penalty, associated with the Father's thunderous Word, by crying:

> why do I overlive,
> Why am I mockt with death, and length'n'd out
> To deathless pain? How gladly would I meet
> Mortality my sentence, and be Earth
> Insensible, how glad would lay me down
> As in my Mother's lap! There I should rest
> And sleep secure; his dreadful voice no more
> Would Thunder in my ears, no fear of worse
> To mee and to my offspring would torment me
> With cruel expectation.
>   (10.773–82)

We might think we are to take this extraordinary desire for his Mother's lap and its accompanying construction of an oedipal past to be merely a sign of Adam's fallen warpedness of mind. But in Book 11 Michael describes the process of dying naturally in exactly the same symbolic terms: "So may'st thou live, till like ripe Fruit thou drop / Into thy Mother's lap, or be with ease / Gather'd, not harshly pluckt, for death mature" (11.535–37). Together these remarkable passages suggest that in *Paradise Lost*, when Eve and Adam lapse by falling away from the Father's Word and then into "Earth's freshest softest lap," not only death but the (paradigmatically masculine) subject's desire become associated inescapably with nature, mothers, harlots, their laps.

III

Read against this *topos*, the Samson simile's "laps" obviously lose their character as neutral ground, the solid basis of a poetic theology elaborating an unproblematically egalitarian downfall. Yet while symbolically and to some degree threateningly female, "Earth's freshest softest lap" and its counterpart "Dalilah's harlot-lap" do not in themselves call into question the innocence of *Paradise Lost*'s heroine, Eve. If we turn, next, to what eighteenth-century commentators on *Paradise Lost* considered the most noteworthy feature of the entire passage—beginning with line 1029, Adam's "For never did thy beauty," and extending through the opening lines of Adam's "O Eve in evil hour"—this is precisely what we find happening, however. Writing in the *Spectator* in 1712, Addison is the first to draw

attention to the intertextual relation between the scene of Adam and
Eve's love-making and the scene in Book 14 of the *Iliad* in which
Hera, adorned with the enchanting zone of Aphrodite, comes upon
Zeus, who greets her by proposing they make love and by declaring
that he has never before so intensely desired any goddess or woman, including Hera herself. Adam's "converse" with Eve after he has
eaten of the forbidden fruit—in lines immediately preceding the
lengthy passage quoted above—is said by Addison to be an "exact
Copy" of Zeus's passionate declaration to Hera:[19]

> But come, so well refresh't, now let us play,
> As meet is, after such delicious Fare;
> For never did thy Beauty since the day
> I saw thee first and wedded thee, adorn'd
> With all perfections, so inflame my sense
> With ardor to enjoy thee, fairer now
> Than ever, bounty of this virtuous Tree.
>   (9.1027–33)

Although a similar invitation to love-making is uttered by Paris in
Book 3 of the *Iliad*, the scene in Book 14 in which Zeus responds
sexually to Hera's artificially heightened attractiveness is clearly the
principal source of Milton's "copying," which in this instance takes
the form of what we would now call an overt allusion. That the
allusion is unquestionably overt is established by Milton's imitation
of other features of Homer's scene, such as the way the lovers'
verbal exchanges come to an end when Zeus takes Hera in his arms
and they make love on a peak of mount Ida, which, as Addison
notes, produces underneath them a bed of flowers they fall asleep
on when sexually satisfied.

   It is not only Zeus's invitation and the love-making itself that
Milton imitates, however. As Thomas Newton points out in his 1749
edition of *Paradise Lost*, in an annotation modern editors pass on to
their readers, Adam's postdiscovery speech, "O Eve, in evil hour,"
is based on the passage in Book 15 of the *Iliad* in which Zeus lashes
out verbally at Hera upon awakening from a postcoital slumber to
discover that he has, through her, lost control of the battle. Newton
construes the Samson simile correctly: "As Samson wak'd shorn of
his strength, they wak'd destitute and bare of all their virtue."[20] Yet
the awakening he is really interested in is Adam's postcoital verbal
awakening to an outrage that resembles Jupiter's. The intertextual
reading Newton produces tells the story of the progress in the two
patriarchs of an emasculating or effeminate desire: "As this whole
transaction between Adam and Eve is manifestly copied from the
episode of Jupiter and Juno on mount Ida, has many of the same

circumstances, and often the very words translated, so it concludes exactly after the same manner in a quarrel. Adam awakes much in the same humor as Jupiter, and their cases are somewhat parallel; they are both overcome by their fondness for their wives, and are sensible of their error too late, and then their love turns to resentment, and they grow angry with their wives; when they should rather have been angry with themselves for their weakness in hearkening to them."[21] By suggesting an ironic dimension, Newton here modifies Pope's openly misogynistic comments in his edition of this book of the *Iliad*, where he states that both Adam and Zeus, whose "Circumstance is very parallel," awaken "full of that Resentment natural to a Superior, who is imposed upon by one of less Worth and Sense than himself, and imposed upon in the worst manner by Shews of Tenderness and Love."[22] Newton's reading is less stridently masculinist, for he implies that far from being the legitimate expression of patriarchal self-righteousness, the anger verbalized by Zeus and Adam merely indicates, ironically, the defensive self-deception that results when patriarchal superiority becomes unsettled. Where the emphasis of Pope's discussion falls on the evil consequences of female duplicity, Newton's stresses the instability of male superiority. But in spite of this, by concentrating, like Pope, on the similarities or parallels between Adam and Zeus, Newton contributes to a masculinist reading of the passage in *Paradise Lost* we are here considering. Granted, Newton generously remarks that the positions of the two patriarchs are "somewhat" rather than "very" (Pope's choice) parallel. Yet even a qualified parallelism seems the product of a decidedly phallogocentric structure of thought. For it tends to obliterate the difference between the scene of sexual seduction which Hera consciously designs, with an intent to deceive Zeus, and the scene of Adam's transgression against the Father's Word, a scene in which *Paradise Lost* has Eve participate only ambiguously since she is herself deceived. The critics' parallelism also erases the narrative or temporal difference between Book 9's two scenes of temptation against the Word and the scene of the fallen Eve and Adam's love-making on "Earth's freshest softest lap." That even Newton's modest parallelism ends up conflating verbal or intellectual temptation and sexual seduction can be seen in his statement that both Jupiter and Adam "should rather have been angry with themselves for their weakness in harkening to them," a statement that unmistakably, even if unintentionally, echoes the patriarchal Lord's judgment of Adam; the phrase echoed appears both in Genesis 3:17, "Because thou hast hearkened unto the voice of thy wife," and in *Paradise Lost*, 10.198.

But is this difference-denying parallelism generated solely by masculinist commentators or is it implicit in *Paradise Lost's* overt allusion to the *Iliad?* It is of course impossible to imagine on what grounds such a question might be given a definitive answer. One could argue, against the neoclassical commentators cited above, that the allusion functions ironically and that it intends to mark the *difference* between Zeus's anger at his seductress Hera and Adam's, which is "fallen" or inherently and therefore illegitimately self-exculpating. Yet *Paradise Lost* makes any rigorous pursuit of this line of thought rather difficult, since the narrator has already, officially, remarked that Adam was "not deceiv'd, / But fondly overcome with Female charm" (9.998–99). If in referring to the parallel weakness of Zeus and Adam in "hearkening" to their wives Newton echoes both Genesis and Milton's epic, in stating that "they are both overcome by their fondness for their wives" he echoes these very lines from *Paradise Lost.* Newton's echo therefore draws attention to the way the narrator's interpretive intervention itself conflates spiritual fall and sexual seduction, thereby sanctioning a reading of the overt allusion to the *Iliad* which concentrates on the parallels between Zeus and Adam.

If parallelism, thus overcoming difference, can be seen to inform both commentaries and to some degree text, then we must conclude that the allusive context *Paradise Lost* creates for Eve and Adam's postcoital awakening clearly complicates matters considerably, perhaps to the extent of calling into question the notion that the Samson simile has been misogynistically *misread.* To safeguard the reading of the simile I have been proposing, it would seem necessary either to suppress or to make light of this context, for it forcibly reintroduces the very hierarchical polarization of the sexes that that reading has shown to be basically irrelevant. Instead of illustrating, unequivocally, Adam and Eve's mutual recognition of a mutual change, the simile now appears significantly and inescapably expressive of the deeply sexist attitudes that its context, with its exclusively patriarchal spokesmen (Book 9's narrator, Adam, Zeus, and then Addison, Pope, Newton), makes explicit. If Hera is to Zeus what Eve is to Adam, then the Samson simile suggests, in spite of itself, that Eve has the same relation to Adam as her temptress daughter, Dalilah, has to Samson. The sexes become related just as our phallocentric cultural tradition would lead us to expect they would be: the (either "somewhat" or "very") righteously aggrieved Zeus, Adam, and Samson are aligned against the beguiling and deceitful Hera, Eve, and Dalilah.

But what are we to make of the contradictory possibilities for meaning our discussion has so far opened up? The question is tricky precisely because the contradictions have not before been exposed. Dwelling only on Milton's copying of the *Iliad*, eighteenth-century commentators registered no difficulties with the passage. More recently, J. M. Evans simply posits a noncontradictory relationship between allusive context and simile. Referring to Milton's allusive use of the *Iliad*'s scene of immortal love-making in Book 9 of *Paradise Lost* and in its innocent counterpart in Book 4, Evans says: "The point of the allusion is that Hera had deliberately set out to distract Zeus's attention while his rival, Poseidon, assisted the Greeks. The love-making was a political manoeuvre on the wife's part; the husband was the dupe. Hence the balancing allusion to the biblical story of Samson's betrayal by Dalilah, the 'harlot' who sold her body for his secret. . . . The combined effect of these references, internal (to Book 4) and external (to the *Iliad* and Judges), is to make Adam and Eve's erotic siesta seem guilty and to confirm Eve's role as seductress."[23] Evans, author of *Paradise Lost and the Genesis Tradition*, the major scholarly treatment of this subject, here suppresses altogether *Paradise Lost*'s allusion to Genesis, which the Samson simile explicates; and it is obviously suppressed precisely because far from "balancing," the Genesis allusion, with its unequivocal "they," topples the whole structure. Aligning Hera, Dalilah, and Eve, Evans thus mediates a decidedly patriarchal construction of the text, while by minimizing its contradictions he also, simultaneously, produces a stabilizing, or phallogocentric, discourse.

Setting aside previous attempts to master this passage's allusive meanings, however, let us ask again what we are to make of the way the Samson simile's allusive context undermines its ostensible meaning. We could, if we wished to use New Critical terms, talk about the "tension" between the "correct" reading of the Samson simile and its error-inducing context. Invoking the figure of the author, and the psychological determinants the use of this figure sanctions, we could then refer this tension back to Milton's own ambivalence about the relations of the sexes. But we could also, much more appropriately, see in this remarkable instance of intertextuality the signs of an historically, not psychologically, determined ambivalence. In this case, the text would testify to the success with which a dominant patriarchal ideology, here represented by the overt allusion to the *Iliad*, is able to contain and defuse egalitarian sentiments, the limited expression of which might be encouraged, historically, by an emerging bourgeois family structure. To put this another way, the allusive context exposes what will increasingly become the merely formal or juridical status of the equality of the sexes in bourgeois society, an equality here elaborated in the Samson simile. The simile therefore acknowledges that both Adam and Eve are, technically, guilty; it defers to Genesis, signifying, according to the letter of the text, that the eyes of them both have been opened. But it does so in a context that indicates clearly that this does not really matter; that what *really* counts is what has happened to Adam, father of mankind, Man. That in *Paradise Lost* it is a patriarchal figure, Samson, to whom both Adam and Eve are compared is thus of crucial importance, ideologically; the syntactical priority of Samson to the "they" for whom he is a figure suggests that "Samson" functions in the slippery and misleading way the generic masculine still continues to do in our culture. *Paradise Lost* would thus seem to generate the counterpart in poetic discourse of the sexist linguistic practice that codes the word "man" equivocally to mean the generic humankind at the same time that, in context, it most often means exclusively the representative or exemplary male being. If we focus on the context that the allusion to the *Iliad* seems to provide, we find the ostensibly generic "man," as it were, being cancelled by the masculine pronoun "he," which thereby undoes the equality *Paradise Lost* appeared, in the briefly enlightened simile, to endorse.

IV

Up to this point, we have confined our discussion of Book 9's allusive use of the *Iliad*'s scene of immortal love-making to the ways in which *Paradise Lost* re-represents those features of Homer's representation that are basically dramatic, such as Zeus's verbal invitation to make love and his angry awakening, undeceived, into a verbal outburst. But there is another feature of Homer's representation of equal importance to *Paradise Lost* as well as to our discussion of the Samson simile's context: that is the descriptive passage in Book 14 of the *Iliad* in which the earth is presented as responding sympathetically to the sexual embrace of the two gods. The passage follows upon the concluding speech of the dialogue between Zeus and Hera:

> So speaking, the son of Kronos caught his wife in his arms. There
> underneath them the divine earth broke into young, fresh
> grass, and into dewy clover, crocus and hyacinth
> so thick and soft it held the hard ground deep away from them.
> There they lay down together and drew about them a golden
> wonderful cloud, and from it the glimmering dew descended.[24]

This very passage is cited by Comes, who points out that the sexual embrace as presented here by Homer is interpreted by allegorists as transferring generative heat from fire or ether, associated with the superior god, Zeus, to air, the lower but desirous element associated with Hera, thereby producing the fertile rains that can in their turn bring forth spring flowers.[25] In a different but related allegorical equation, not by any means regularly tied to this particular passage, Hera is thought to represent the earth itself. As one mythographer puts it: "and oftentimes also they take Juno for the earth, and in that respect acknowledged as the wife of Jupiter, in that (say they) there falleth from above a certaine powerfull and engendring seed on the earth, by whose strength and vertue it receiveth means and abilitie to bring forth, maintaine, and nourish what we see here produced."[26] The larger masculinist context for this equation is of course the etymological association of *materia* with *mater*, an association that lands us right back in the female lap. Developed philosophically, this equation permits Ficino to state that latent forms "ex materiae eruit gremio" [are brought forth from the lap of matter][27]; reassigned to a mythical figure, it enables Spenser to refer to Love's creative awakening in "Venus lap."[28] In a simpler, more directly mythic form, the lap of the sky-father's spouse appears in lines from Virgil's *Georgics* quoted by Comes and by modern editors of a passage from *Paradise Lost* to which we will now be turning: "tum pater omnipotens fecundis imbribus Aether / coniugis in gremium laetae descendit et omnis / magnus alit magno commixtus corpore fetus" ["Then Heaven, the Father almighty, comes down in fruitful showers into the lap of his joyous spouse, and his might, with her mighty frame commingling, nurtures all growths"].[29]

Although both of Juno's cosmological roles—air to Jupiter's ether or earth to his sky—are potentially present in a simile developed by Book 4 of *Paradise Lost*, it would seem that the former is more directly relevant. The simile self-consciously mythologizes the relation between Adam and Eve, who, having completed the first exchange that has been presented, ceremonially, to the reader, continue their conversation in an erotic embrace:

> hee in delight
> Both of her Beauty and submissive Charms
> Smil'd with superior Love, as *Jupiter*
> On *Juno* smiles, when he impregns the Clouds
> That shed May Flowers; and press'd her Matron lip
> With kisses pure.
> (4.497–501)

As has frequently been remarked, the comparison would seem to want to elevate the already-elevated Adam and Eve, as well as to dignify the aggressively hierarchical nature of their relationship. Yet one of the reasons it can attempt these effects is that it does not function either overtly or covertly as an allusion to the scene of immortal love-making in the *Iliad*. Instead that scene is, as it were, veiled by the allegorical equations only tenuously related to it. It is true that in Book 14 of the *Iliad* and here in *Paradise Lost* the epic couples embrace after concluding a dialogue, and that in both the embrace is associated with the production of flowers. Yet this simile's flowers do not spring forth to provide Eve and Adam with a couch, but are quite clearly figurative flowers. And they are figurative perhaps because they testify to a creative potency that is not in any literal sense here enacted, Adam and Eve's embrace being an erotic not a fully sexual or potentially generative embrace (even though reproductive sexuality is clearly a part of *Paradise Lost*'s prelapsarianism).

As editors since Pope have pointed out, there are, however, two different passages where flowers clearly related to those in the *Iliad*'s scene of immortal love-making do make their appearance in the Edenic landscape of *Paradise Lost*. The more striking occurs in Book 8 where Adam tells the story of his courtship of Eve and of their marriage:

> To the nuptial Bow'r
> I led her blushing like the Morn: all Heav'n,
> And happy Constellations on that hour
> Shed thir selectest influence; the Earth
> Gave sign of gratulation, and each Hill;
> Joyous the Birds; fresh Gales and gentle Airs
> Whisper'd it to the Woods, and from thir wings
> Flung Rose, flung Odors from the spicy Shrub.
> (8.510–17)

Pope relates these lines to the *Iliad* by stating, "The Creation is made to give the same Tokens of Joy at the Performance of the nuptial Rites of our first Parents, as she does here at the Congress of *Jupiter* and *Juno*."[30] Closely associated, though not so vividly linked to the moment of sexual intercourse—which, significantly, does not actually get represented—is the following passage from the narrator's description of the "blissful bower" in Book 4:

> each beauteous flow'r,
> *Iris* all hues, Roses and Jessamin
> Rear'd high their flourisht heads between, and wrought
> Mosaic; underfoot the Violet,

> Crocus, and Hyacinth with rich inlay
> Broider'd the ground.
> (4.697–702)

Of these lines Pope says that they "are manifestly from the same Original"; and that "the very Turn of *Homer's* Verses is observed, and the Cadence, and almost the Words, finely translated."[31]

Though Pope's delight in Milton's praiseworthy translation of Homer's verses is not communicated by modern editors, the relevance of Book 14 of the *Iliad* to these two passages in *Paradise Lost* is generally noted. Yet neither Pope nor subsequent editors ventures to explore the possible relations of these floral passages to the scene of love-making in Book 9 of *Paradise Lost*. Fowler alone mentions that the flowers making up Adam and Eve's "couch" in Book 9 "have *hyacinth* in common with those of the couch prepared by Earth for Zeus and Hera," pointing, besides, to the flowers of the nuptial bower in Book 4. But this is the extent of his commentary.[32] Tillyard actually criticizes the "insertion of the flowery bank" in Book 9's scene of love-making, calling it "strangely inept,"[33] while R. E. C. Houghton, who notes the allusion to the *Iliad* together with the contrast *Paradise Lost* sets up between Book 4 and Book 9, nevertheless can say that "the introduction of flowers here as well as there seems unsuitable, unless it is designed to set the change in the human pair against unchanging nature."[34]

Our earlier discussion of female laps alone suggests the utter inadequacy of these comments. Yet if we are to explore further the filiations of this gathering of epic flowers, we will need to look at some of the competing hermeneutical principles the scene of immortal love-making (not necessarily this Homeric scene alone) has been associated with. Although popular and many-lived, cosmological allegorizations such as those mentioned above have frequently been criticized. Both Plutarch and Origen, for example, mockingly reject such allegorical interpretations, but on grounds that are significantly different. Plutarch, speaking for an ethically based criticism, confidently assumes that the Homeric scene of love-making requires no allegorization because its moral significance is transparent. The lesson that in his view it teaches is very much the one that Addison, Newton, and Pope are interested in, and which is implicit in the reading given the Samson simile by modern commentators, namely, that deceitful wives bring short-lived pleasure.[35] Yet Origen, writing from the more beleaguered position of an early Christian, is not at all sure that pagan texts are so innocent as this, singling out for special scorn a cosmological reading the Stoic Chrysippus gives a pictorial representation of Hera "performing

unmentionable obscenities with Zeus" (presumably fellatio). According to this reading, which Origin clearly finds ludicrously defensive, Hera represents matter that is in the position of receiving
the generative principles of Zeus or God.[36] Although Origen does
not refer to the *Iliad*'s scene of divine love-making, Pope does in a
remark that is not so confident of the innocence or moral purity of
Homer's representation as the comments by him we have so far
mentioned would seem to be. Comparing the scene in the *Iliad* with
its counterpart in *Paradise Lost*, Pope praises Milton's imitation of
Homer in the following manner: "But it is with wonderful Judgment
and Decency he has used that exceptionable Passage of the Dalliance, Ardour, and Enjoyment: That which seems in *Homer* an impious Fiction, becomes a moral Lesson in Milton; since he makes
that lascivious Rage of the Passion the immediate Effect of the Sin of
our first Parents after the Fall."[37] The contrast Pope sets up here
reveals the continuity of the Christian tradition's official disapproval
of pagan scenes such as Homer's. It also suggests without explicitly
saying so that Milton's copying is not mere copying but an appropriation and transformation.

But it is possible that Homer's scene of immoral immortal love-
making has been transformed even more radically than Pope's comfortable moralizing of Milton's moralization of Homer supposes.
Although Pope elsewhere in his annotations refers to Plato, in com-
menting on the story of Hera and Zeus he does not. Nor, for that
matter, does any more recent critic, so far as I know. Yet it would
certainly not be merely fanciful to suggest that the most influential
and moralistic of commentators on Homer has mediated Milton's
own appropriation. In Plato's critique of imitation in Book 3 of the
Republic, Socrates, as is well known, takes Homer to task for representing the gods falsely, in ways unworthy of them and potentially
dangerous to his audience. Among the numerous passages from
Homer that Socrates singles out for censure is the sexual scene in
Book 14 of the *Iliad*, of which he asks, is it really appropriate for
young people to hear "how Zeus lightly forgot all the designs which
he devised, awake while the other gods and men slept, because of
the excitement of his passions, and was so overcome by the sight of
Hera that he is not even willing to go to their chamber, but wants to
lie with her there on the ground and says that he is possessed by a
fiercer desire than when they first consorted with one another"?[38]
What Plato is referring to here is that specific moment in the exchange between Hera and Zeus preceding their love-making in
which Hera pretends to be reluctant to sleep openly on the peaks of
Ida and proposes that they go to the "chamber" Hephaistos has

built. In response, Zeus assures her they will not be seen where they are, for he will gather a "golden cloud" about them. It is at this point that he embraces her and that the earth reacts by breaking forth in floral vegetation. In the passage just quoted from the *Republic*, Plato gives the content of this exchange-as-foreplay (and, on Hera's part, as-cunning) a definite moral significance, yet one that does not save Homer's text, constructing an ethically coded contrast between making love in a "chamber" and casually, "on the ground," in order to stress the shameful shamelessness Homer has here, casually, depicted.

If Plato's moralization indeed structures Milton's allusive use of the *Iliad* in the passage from *Paradise Lost* we are here examining, then its intertextual complexity is even greater than our discussion has so far suggested. Critics have frequently commented on the carefully structured opposition between prelapsarian eroticism and Book 9's postlapsarian lust, and it has also been noted that in Book 9 Adam and Eve do not make it into their "blissful bower." As Fowler has remarked, the indefinite article "a" in "a shady bank" (9.1037) underlines the causal randomness of their choice of place.[39] Further, although this has not ever specifically been remarked, the passages in Books 4 and 8 that can be referred back to their "original" in Homer both have specific reference to the "blissful bower." The passage in Book 8 spiritualizes Homer's scene by having the Earth give "sign of Gratulation" at the nuptial union of Adam and Eve in their "nuptial Bow'r"; the passage in Book 4 describes, specifically, the floor of the bower that the "Sovran Planter" has set apart for his creatures: "underfoot the violet, / Crocus and Hyacinth with rich Inlay / Broider'd the Ground." In Book 9, however, the earth neither ceremonially participates in the love-making nor displays the signs of the artistically arranged naturalness making the ground of the blissful bower a different kind of "Couch." Although nature has participated sympathetically in the falls of both Eve and Adam, it is as if nature here is losing its capacity for response; rather than spontaneously gratulating their sexuality, nature is somehow, seductively, in a potentially ensnaring manner, simply there: "Flow'rs were the Couch, Pansies, and Violets, and Asphodel, / And Hyacinth, Earth's freshest softest lap."

Read in this way through Plato's mediating commentary, the main point of the Homeric allusions in Book 9 of *Paradise Lost* would now seem to be *not* the patriarchally structured polarity of male and female but instead the spiritually structured opposition between the sacred and the profane. The blissful bower, "a place / Chos'n by the sovran Planter" and consecrated for prelapsarian love-making, is the polar opposite of "a shady bank, / Thick overlaid with verdant roof embowr'd."[40] That it is specifically a "shady" bank clearly establishes its affinity with the *topos* of the regressive lap, but this *topos* now seems to have a new context, one that turns Adam and Eve's *al fresco* love-making on "Earth's freshest softest lap" into the polar opposite of the divinely sanctioned activity of making love on the "Broider'd" ground. Indeed, it is tempting to think that the figures of Samson and Dalilah with her "harlot-lap" were initially generated by the profane role played in this structure of oppositions by "Earth's freshest softest lap," the "lap"—rather the two laps—here signifying a lapse.

If this passage shows us Milton reading Homer through Plato's eyes, it probably also suggests a set of oppositions overlapping with that of the sacred and the profane. For Plato the sacred is of course associated with the realm of ideas, with the originals of which the realm of appearance and, *a fortiori*, artistic products are the profane and debased copies. Appropriated by *Paradise Lost*'s Christian platonism, this becomes the opposition between a divinely created or original innocence and its fallen imitation. But the difference between original and copy, which gets translated into the difference between Book 4's prelapsarian sexuality and its fallen counterpart in Book 9, is a difference produced in *Paradise Lost* by Book 9's imitation of Homer's scene of immortal love-making in the *Iliad*. It is also produced by a kind of unveiling of the Homeric scene as the literary site of a sexual act that is simply and unquestionably just that. The allegorizing tradition invoked by the allusion to Jupiter and Juno in Book 4's simile is in Book 9 stripped away to reveal the representational literality of Homer's mimesis. This is a literality that Plato himself associates with drama and that Book 9 would also seem to mark as essentially dramatic, since it presents its generically tragic central *peripeteia* and *anagnorisis* in the context of an overt allusion that relies, for its overtness, on the likeness of dramatic situation and speech in the cases of Adam and Zeus. Yet as we have seen, Milton's imitation of the scene of immortal love-making in the *Iliad* is ultimately mediated by Plato's critique of representation. What Book 9 of *Paradise Lost* would therefore appear to give us is an imitation of a scene in the *Iliad*, which, subjected by Plato to an attack on its shameful debasing of its divine originals, is itself presented by *Paradise Lost* as a debased or fallen version, bringing forth shame in its actors, of its literary "original" in Book 4. To say, as eighteenth-century commentators do, that Milton here imitates or copies Homer, is thus entirely to miss the kind of logocentric critique of imitation that the scene, in this context, seems to constitute. Book

9's profane and self-implicated dramatic mimesis is radically dialectical, in that, by casting a Platonic doubt on the simple there-ness of
its own mimesis, it attempts to preserve its moralizing discursive
distance from the Fall.

It is possible to take this even further, and to argue that the dramatic imitation's two laps, by acknowledging their status as the
fallen mimetic ground of the action represented, could really both
be considered harlot-laps, since in the only two instances in
Milton's poetic works besides this one where the term "harlot" is
used, it is firmly associated, in good antitheatrical fashion, with a
fallen and imitative status. (Obviously relevant here is the derivation of "meretricious" from "meretrix," prostitute or harlot.) In
Book 4, in the hymn to "wedded love" sung when Adam and Eve
enter their blissful bower to make love, the narrator contrasts this
sacred original—an original that, as the narrator's very presence in
phrases such as "I ween" reminds us, is *not* represented—with its
profane and fallen copies:

> Here Love his golden shafts imploys, here lights
> His constant Lamp, and waves his purple wings,
> Reigns here and revels; not in the bought smile
> Of Harlots, loveless, joyless, unindear'd,
> Casual fruition, nor in Court Amours,
> Mixt Dance, or wanton Mask, or Midnight Ball,
> Or Serenate.
>   (4.763–69)

Even more suggestively, in *Paradise Regained* the Son defends himself against Satan's temptation to devote himself to learning the
wisdom of the Greeks by declaring:

> That rather Greece from us these Arts deriv'd;
> Ill imitated, while they loudest sing
> The vices of thir Deities, and thir own
> In Fable, Hymn, or Song, so personating
> Thir Gods ridiculous, and themselves past shame.
> Remove thir swelling Epithets thick laid
> As varnish on a Harlot's cheek, the rest,
> Thin sown with aught of profit or delight,
> Will far be found unworthy to compare
> With *Sion's* songs.
>   (4.338–47)

We are apparently not to notice that the Son articulates this Judaic
version of the opposition between original and copy by drawing on
Plato's critique of Homer, just as *Paradise Lost* does in representing,

against its better knowledge, not deceived, Adam and Eve's lapse into a merely mortal lust.

But what do we do with the Samson simile now? This Platonic turn suggests a way of reading *Paradise Lost*'s allusions to the *Iliad* that leaves intact a nonsexist reading of the simile. If the *Republic* mediates Milton's use of Homer, then it would seem to provide us with a genuine *tertium quid*, one that permits us to acknowledge the presence of the potentially sexist allusive context but does not require that it signify as it has been thought to do. It could even be argued that Genesis and the *Republic*—or rather theology and philosophy—work together to effect a transformation (or *Aufhebung*) of the phallocentric intertext established by the *Iliad*, Judges, and our fallen symbolic order, emptying the allusions of their representational and patriarchal content, and raising from the representational laps(e) a complex of abstract and spiritual significations.

Relying on Milton's Platonic (and therefore logocentric) critique of representation, such a reading would be able to lay claim to stable grounds for the Samson simile's intelligibility. It could do so, however, only by suggesting that theological, philosophical, and poetic discourses join forces in this passage to carve out a space in which abstract meanings appear as if in their original or unfallen transparency. And since the only guarantor of such a neutral, nonsexist transparency would be the textual self-consciousness posited by critical discourse, it is really critical discourse itself that would finally have to be the unacknowledged fourth partner in the work of saving the text. Both textual or authorial self-consciousness and the critical discourse that seeks to posit such consciousness by effacing itself are, of course, ultimately phallogocentric constructs. So while it might be tempting to argue that *Paradise Lost* is not only fully awake to the implications of its masculinist codes but knowingly and subtly transforms them, to do so would be to posit a textual self-consciousness as transhistorically vigilant as the Father's all-seeing eye.

As a quintessentially phallogocentric turn, this reading would also seek to sever the grounds of the simile's intelligibility from its troublesome laps. The misogynistic misreading of the Samson simile obviously needs to be challenged or corrected. But I would like to argue, in conclusion, that the challenge should not dress these laps up in modern, unisex wear. It is not just because they are irreducibly figurative that these laps should be permitted—in good poststructuralist fashion—to disturb the grounds of the text's intelligibility. It is also because, being irreducibly female, they bear the traces of the very same anonymous and nondiscursive forces that have played such a crucial role in the critical discourses mediating *Paradise Lost*'s reception.

That the commentators who have actively misread the Samson simile are near-contemporaries is evidence that we are not in any position to begin pretending we can transcend this reception's history. Further evidence can be found in *Ulysses*, a text that is to contemporary debates about the relations of the sexes and the nature of authorship and authority what for generations *Paradise Lost* has been. Molly Bloom's monologue concludes (in what some modernist and postmodernist theorists are happy to think of as a "feminine" refusal of closure) with recollections of a sexual experience which, like that of Zeus and Hera in the *Iliad*, and that of Adam and Eve in *Paradise Lost*, takes place outside the domestic enclosure, on a mountaintop (here, in a realist mode, the hill of Howth), amidst flowers (not hyacinths but rhododendrons). In a deeply ambiguous gesture, Molly gives Bloom "a bit of seedcake" out of her mouth: she both appropriates a kind of Zeus-like procreative activity and re-enacts Eve's passing of the apple to Adam.[41] *Ulysses* ends here, with Bloom's "mountain flower" (the text's "Gea-Tellus," Joyce's "Ewig-Weibliche") rehearsing the scene of seduction while responding, as if endlessly, in the affirmative. Since *Ulysses*, then, too, in a way overlaps with Book 9's central passage, a feminist critical discourse could just decide that for the time being *Paradise Lost* might as well occupy that discursive space or *lapsus* that is intertextuality itself.

NOTES

1. Jonathan Culler, *The Pursuit of Signs* (Ithaca, 1981), 109.
2. Quotations from Milton's poetry are from John Milton, *Complete Poems and Major Prose*, ed. Merritt Y. Hughes (New York, 1957).
3. Biblical quotations are from the King James version.
4. Northrop Frye, *Fearful Symmetry* (Princeton, 1942), 362. To the best of my knowledge, B. Rajan is the only modern critic to provide anything like a reading that compares both Eve and Adam with Samson; but he does so by stressing a common, newly acquired "blindness to the things of the spirit" (*Paradise Lost" and the Seventeenth Century Reader* [1947; rpt. Ann Arbor, Michigan, 1967], 73). Typically incoherent in its unacknowledged shifts from plural to (androcentric) singular is Henry Blamires' commentary in *Milton's Creation* (London, 1971), 237: "They find their *eyes* indeed *opened* (1053), but not in the way anticipated (cf. 706–8, 985). They are opened to the recognition of their own darkened minds, to the disappearance of that 'veile' (1054) of innocence that has 'shadow'd' them from knowledge of evil. . . . Adam's waking to guilt is like Samson's waking from the lap of Delilah, who, in his sleep, had cut off his hair and thereby

deprived him of his strength. The correspondence underlines the concept
of innocence as positive power, which it is important for the modern
reader to sense. The loss of innocence is a virtual emasculation. 'Shorn of
strength . . . destitute and bare / Of all their vertue' (1062–63); this is
their new condition." E.M.W. Tillyard, in an edition of Books 9 and 10 for
the *Harrap's English Classics* first published in 1960, glosses the simile
correctly, "As Samson of the tribe of Dan woke to find his strength gone,
so Adam and Eve woke to find their innocence gone," 141. But editions
published since that time stubbornly persist in the masculinist reading. In
addition to the texts cited below, R.E.C. Houghton's 1969 edition of Books
9 and 10 for Oxford University Press, for example, annotates ll. 1059–63
with "As Samson lost his physical strength when his hair was cut off
(Judg. 16: 4–20), so Adam lost his original virtue, his moral strength,
through sin and the ensuing sensuality," 172.

5. *The Poems of John Milton*, ed. John Carey and Alastair Fowler (London and
Harlow, 1968), 918. Fowler's phrasing is echoed by Rosemary Syfret,
whose edition of Book 9 (London and Basingstoke, 1972; rpt. 1983) annotates the simile by stating, "The comparison between Adam and Samson
was traditional, as was the comparison with Hercules," 140. As editors
have traditionally pointed out, in Milton's original text there is no stop
after "Shame," which, personified as of masculine gender, has permitted
Fowler to develop a baroque variation on the masculinist reading. Refusing to introduce the stop as other modern editions uniformly do, Fowler
comments, "Adam covers in response to Eve's guilty shame," 917.

6. John R. Knott, Jr., *Milton's Pastoral Vision*, 124.

7. Aristotle, *The Poetics*, trans. G. M. A. Grube, *On Poetry and Style* (Indi-
anapolis, 1958), ch. 11, 22. The dramatic linearity of Book 9's action is
discussed in my "Reading the Fall: Discourse and Drama in 'Paradise
Lost,'" *ELR* (1984), 199–229. The narrative in Judges seems itself to suggest that reversal and discovery are temporally ordered: "And she made
him sleep upon her knees; and she called for a man, and she caused him
to shave off the seven locks of his head; and she began to afflict him, and
his strength went from him. And she said, The Philistines be upon thee,
Samson. And he awoke out of his sleep, and said, I will go out as at other
times before, and shake myself. And he wist not that the Lord was departed from him. But the Philistines took him, and put out his eyes."

8. Aristotle, *Poetics*, ch. 16, 33.

9. J. Martin Evans, ed., *John Milton, "Paradise Lost": Books IX–X* for the
Cambridge Milton for Schools and Colleges, gen. ed. J. B. Broadbent (Cambridge, 1973), 33.

10. Evans, *Cambridge Milton*, 9–10.

11. Ibid., 167–68.

12. See St. Augustine, *The City of God Against the Pagans*, Book 14, chs. 16 and
17, Loeb Classical Library, vol. 4, trans. Philip Levine (London and
Cambridge, 1966), 352–60. See also chs. 3 and 15 of Book 13.

13. Madlyn Millner Kahr, "Delilah," in *Feminism and Art History*, ed. Norma

Broude and Mary D. Garrard (New York, 1982), 125–26. My discussion of the pictorial tradition is completely indebted to this excellent piece.

14. The oneness of Eve and Adam in their Fall is likewise suggested by the allusion in ll. 1042–44 to Proverbs 7:18, where a figure the King James Bible identifies as a "whore" entices a young "wanton" with "Come, let us take our fill of love until the morning: let us solace ourselves with loves." That Adam's "But come . . . let us play" in l. 1027 also echoes this verse indicates, by its gender-crossing, the possible irrelevance of gender to this scene of mutual guilt.

15. Quotations from *The Faerie Queene* are from J. C. Smith's edition (Oxford 1909; rpt. 1964). A thorough study of the allegorical and iconographical contexts for this episode can be found in Alistair Fowler, "The Image of Mortality," *Huntington Library Quarterly* 24 (1961), 91–110. See also Fowler's complementary article, "Emblems of Temperance in *The Faerie Queene*, Book II," *Review of English Studies*, n.s., 11 (1960):143–49.

16. Kahr, "Delilah," 127–30.

17. Ibid., 134–36.

18. Further evidence of the pervasiveness of this *topos* and of the currency of the sexual connotation of "lap" can be found in act 3, scene 2 of *Hamlet*, where the following well-known exchange takes place:

> *Ham.* (lying down at Ophelia's feet)
>   Lady, shall I lie in your lap?
> *Oph.* No, my lord.
> *Ham.* I mean, my head upon your lap.
> *Oph.* Ay, my lord.
> *Ham.* Do you think I meant country matters?
> *Oph.* I think nothing, my lord.
> *Ham.* That's a fair thought to lie between maids' legs.
> *Oph.* What is, my lord?
> *Ham.* Nothing.

The several sexual innuendos here have frequently been remarked. Harold Jenkins, editor of the Arden *Hamlet*, refers the reader to a piece by Marie Collins, who mentions four English morality and interlude plays in which a young hero is portrayed lying or sleeping in a deceitful lady's lap. Collins concludes that Hamlet, knowing this dramatic iconography full well, employs it to cast Ophelia in the role of the dangerous temptress and to suggest that he is, in relation to her, "a vulnerable morality hero" ("Hamlet and the Lady's Lap," *Notes and Queries*, n.s., 28 [1981], 130–32). Yet if we see *Hamlet* alluding here more generally to the *topos* I have been tracking (Spenser's *The Faerie Queene* had of course been published by this time), another reading suggests itself. With reference to this *topos*, the allusion might indicate that there is, possibly, something rather unheroic about Hamlet's substitution of dramatic for revenge action; that, having already, as it were, laid aside his arms, the hero might just as well go all the way and lie in his lady's lap.

19. Joseph Addison, *The Spectator*, no. 351 (April 12, 1712), ed. Gregory Smith (London, 1945; rpt. 1973), 100–1.

20. Thomas Newton, ed., *Paradise Lost* (London, 1749), 2.201.

21. Newton, *Paradise Lost*, 202.

22. Alexander Pope, *The Iliad of Homer*, ed. Maynard Mack, vol. 7 of *The Poems of Alexander Pope*, Gen. Ed., John Butt (London and New Haven, 1967), 193.

23. Evans, *Cambridge Milton*, 173.

24. *Iliad*, trans. Richmond Lattimore (Chicago and London, 1951), 303. All further quotations from the *Iliad* are from this edition.

25. Natalis Comes, *Mythologie*, trans. J. de Moutlyard, rev. and ed. by Jean Baudouin (Paris, 1627; rpt. New York and London, 1976), vol. 1, 97–98. See also vol. 2, 1048–49.

26. Vincenzo Cartari, *The Fountaine of Ancient Fiction* , trans. R. Linche (London, 1599; rpt. Amsterdam and New York, 1973), L–Lii.

27. Cited from *De Immortalitate Animorum*, 15.2, by John Erskine Hankins, *Source and Meaning in Spenser's Allegory* (London, 1971), 257.

28. "Hymne in Honour of Love," ll. 57–63, in *Spenser's Minor Poems*, ed. Ernest De Selincourt (London, 1910; rpt. 1960), 438. Also cited by Hankins, *Source*, 258.

29. Vergil, *Georgics*, 2.325–27; cited, for example, by Fowler in an annotation on *Paradise Lost* 4.499–501, *Milton*, 652.

30. Pope, *Iliad*, 181.

31. Ibid., 182.

32. Fowler, *Milton*, 916.

33. Tillyard, *Milton*, 140.

34. Houghton, *Milton*, 171.

35. Plutarch, "How the Young Man Should Study Poetry," *Moralia*, vol. 1, trans. Frank Cole Babbitt (Cambridge and London, 1927; rpt. 1960), 100–3. I am indebted for these references to Jean Pépin's discussion in *Mythe et Allégorie* (Paris, 1958), 181–84, 349,454.

36. Origen, *Contra Celsum*, trans. Henry Chadwick (Cambridge, 1953), 223.

37. Pope, *Iliad*, 182.

38. Plato, *The Republic*, 3.390, B-C, trans. Paul Shorey, The Loeb Classical Library (Cambridge and London, 1953), 216–17.

39. Fowler, *Milton*, 916.

40. John Hollander discusses the echoing relations of this "shady bank / Thick overlaid with verdant roof embowr'd" with the subsequent "Pillar'd shade / High overarch't" (9.1103–7), both, as he says, "imprinted with the shadowy type of death," and with Book 1's famous "where th' Etrurian shades / High overarch't imbower" (1.302–3), in *The Figure of Echo* (Berkeley and Los Angeles, 1981), 49.

41. Richard Ellmann comments on the possible correspondence between Molly and Eve here in *Ulysses on the Liffey* (New York, 1972), 168–69.

16. HUMANISM AND
THE RESISTANCE TO THEORY

▪

VICTORIA KAHN

I am not bound, said the Count, to teach you how to acquire grace
or anything else, but only to show you what a perfect courtier
ought to be.
—CASTIGLIONE, *Il Cortegiano*

IN A RECENT ARTICLE Paul de Man claimed that the resistance to
theory on the part of conservative literary historians and critics is
simply the "displaced symptom" of a resistance to theory at the
heart of theory itself.[1] Theory in this second sense is defined as
metalanguage that takes as its object the rhetorical or tropological
dimension of language which inevitably interferes with the cognitive or semantic functions of grammar and logic. Whereas we
ordinarily identify theory with a comprehensive system of axioms
and principles of deductive reasoning, or with a Kantian epistemological critique of the conditions of the possibility of knowledge, theory in de Man's sense must be equated with a certain
conception of rhetoric, in which the privileged trope is irony, defined as the indeterminacy or the undecidability of meaning. When
we recall with de Man that the humanities have traditionally been
defined in terms of the trivium of grammar, rhetoric, and logic
(dialectic), the conservative resistance to theory can be seen as a
resistance to the way in which rhetoric puts in question the epistemological stability of language, and with language the trivium
itself.

De Man's definition of theory is by his own admission an historical one (post 1960). But it is also critical of traditional literary history insofar as the latter takes for granted the possibility of understanding, which the conflict between the rhetorical and gramma-

tical/logical modes of language undermines. Thus, the problem of theory and its resistance is not fixed to any one historical period, according to de Man, but relevant to all periods—that is to say, to the problem of periodization itself.

Interestingly, this double meditation on history is reflected in the history of the article itself, which, de Man tells us, grew out of a request from the MLA for an overview of contemporary trends in literary criticism. The commissioned article was never published. "The Resistance to Theory" thus refers both to the MLA's resistance to de Man's article, and to the original article, which, in arguing against the *intelligibility* of theory, proved to be singularly incompatible with the pedagogical aims of the MLA. This publishing nonevent points to contemporary debates about the relation of theory to pedagogy, debates about the desirability—even the possibility—of "doing theory" and of teaching theory in the graduate curriculum. But in problematizing the notion of literary history by reference to the trivium, and specifically to rhetoric, de Man's article also allows us to see its relevance for the study of the literature of earlier periods, in particular the pedagogical imperative of Renaissance humanism. Whether or not we finally accept the deconstructive notion of theory which de Man presents, the tension he identifies at the heart of theory can serve as a useful topic of invention with respect to the humanist conventions of reading and interpretation. For, as we will see, humanism can be defined in the first instance as a rhetorical practice that resists theory conceived of as an epistemological project; but this first resistance is part and parcel of a more complicated, pedagogically motivated resistance to theory conceived of as undecidability. Finally, a survey of some of the humanist texts that exemplify these resistances can help us in turn to see the relevance of sixteenth-century debates on method to the current critical scene.

THEORY AND PRACTICE

To those familiar with the work of Bernard Weinberg and Baxter Hathaway, the identification of Renaissance humanism with a resistance to theory must at first glance seem a dubious one.[2] For if this identification is correct, what are we to make of the many sixteenth-century "trattati di poetica e retorica," the treatises on imitation and commentaries on Aristotle's *Poetics*, the proposed reform of dialectic in the work of Valla and Agricola, the codification of rhetorical and logical forms of argument in English handbooks? Certainly, in all these works there is a discourse of a certain generality that we associate with theory.

On the other hand, Paul Oskar Kristeller, one of the most eminent scholars of the Renaissance, has insisted that while the humanists shared a general interest in moral philosophy, humanism is not properly thought of as a philosophical or theoretical movement. Humanist works, he observes,

> often seem to lack not only originality, but also coherence, method, and substance, and if we try to sum up these arguments and conclusions, leaving aside citations, examples, and commonplaces, literary ornaments and digressions, we are frequently left with nearly empty hands. Thus I have not been convinced by the attempts to interpret these humanistic treatises as contributions to speculative thought.[3]

Are these two perspectives opposed? Or is there something about Weinberg's and Hathaway's "Age of Criticism" that is resistant to theory in Kristeller's sense?

In attempting to answer this question, a first step might be to historicize our first notion of theory as speculative thought, and to ask whether the humanists intended to make a contribution to this realm of inquiry. To the extent that theory is identified with scholasticism, the answer must be no. For again and again, the humanists attack the scholastics for trying to formulate necessary and universal propositions about God's existence and the structure of his creation. Such speculation, according to the humanists, is both illegitimate and useless: illegitimate because human reason cannot know the divine, and useless because even if we were to have contemplative knowledge, such abstractions would not help us direct our earthly civic affairs.[4]

This double complaint is reflected in the humanist critique of scholastic discourse, both for its pretensions to reflect adequately the structure of the cosmos,[5] and for its neglect of the rhetorical, i.e., affective and communicative dimension of language, which is essential to human society and civic life.[6] These complaints, in other words, are directed not simply against the ignorance of the norms and *elegantiae* of classical Latin, but against the important human consequences of such ignorance. The reified ontological vocabulary of scholasticism cannot, by definition, allow for a flexible and pragmatic response to the demands of human society. Yet, as Valla argues forcefully in his *Dialecticae disputationes*, a logic or dialectic that is to be useful must be referred to the social and linguistic criterion of usage or *consuetudo*.[7] Furthermore, to the extent that logic is referred to usage, it becomes identical with those forms of argument which derive from or aim at producing consensus: rhetorical syllogisms, commonplaces, arguments from probability or opinion. Logic, in short, becomes topical and takes as its aim persuasion or conviction rather than apodictic certainty. The humanist resistance to theory is thus in the first instance a resistance to scholastic logic.

But if as a result of the humanist reform of dialectic, rhetoric takes the place of logic as the most important member of the trivium, this does not mean that the humanists would share de Man's conclusion that the trivium has now become epistemologically unstable. For if theory is identified with the epistemological unreliability or un-decidability of rhetorical language, then the humanists want both to acknowledge this potential instability and to resist it. This second resistance takes the form of the claim that if theoretical cognition is unfounded and useless, another kind of knowledge is both possible and desirable: the practical knowledge of human affairs, of social and linguistic praxis. This kind of knowledge the humanists call *phronesis* or prudence, thereby identifying it with the Aristotelian faculty of practical reason or judgment in matters requiring delibera-tion and choice.[8]

Aristotle opposes prudence on the one hand to *theoria* or specula-tion, and on the other to *techne* or productive knowledge. Like *the-oria*, prudence is an intellectual virtue, but whereas theory includes the intelligence of first causes and the necessary and universal knowledge of their consequences (*NE*, 1139a 25; 1139b 15; *An. post.*, 1.71b9–72b4), prudence is concerned with action within the realm of contingent human affairs. These affairs can never be the object of scientific certainty, only of practical deliberation. In this, prudence draws near to *techne*, but while the aim of technical knowledge is to produce an artifact, prudence has no other aim than itself: "In mat-ters of action, the principles or initiating motives are the ends at which our actions are aimed" (*NE*, 1140b 15). Thus, Aristotle con-cludes, prudence "is not a pure science because matters of action admit of being other than they are, and it is not an applied science or art, because action and production are generically different" (*NE*, 1140b). To secure its own realm of action, then, prudence must resist being assimilated to the claims of *theoria* on the one side, and those of *techne* on the other.

While the humanists adopted the Aristotelian definition of pru-dence, they also followed Cicero in arguing that the prudent man is one who knows how to use the rhetorical skills of persuasion to achieve his practical ends. Yet while the orator or prudent man must be able to argue on both sides of a question, he will in any particular case choose one side or another. The further assumption, however, is that by the exchange of opinions, by argument *in utramque partem* between individuals, we can arrive at a socially useful, pragmatic truth. Thus, while Cicero recognized that such argument *in utram-*

que partem could take the form of irony if both sides or points of view were maintained at the same time, for the early humanists the potential undecidability of irony was held in check by social constraints. Pontano, for example, sees Socrates' ironic indirection not as an instance of the rhetoric that puts in question the possibility of meaning and of action, but rather as a rhetorical invitation to his audience to assume an attitude of ethical moderation. But even more significantly, he turns irony into the chief social grace or decorum by identifying it with *urbanitas*.[9] In a move that is characteristic of the humanists as a whole, the epistemological threat of skepticism is contained by the practice of social consensus.

THEORY AND EXAMPLES

Since the realm of practice and choice is also for Cicero and the humanists the realm of rhetoric, the faculty of prudence finds its rhetorical equivalent in the rule of decorum.[10] This rule does not function as a philosophical axiom or as the major premise of a syllogism; it does not subsume particulars or logically entail a necessary and universal conclusion. The rule of decorum cannot be theorized because it is always already the application of the rule. Thus Puttenham writes in the *Arte of Poesie*:

> This decencie is therfore the line and levell for al good makers to do their busines by. But herein resteth the difficultie, to know what this good grace is, and wherein it consisteth. . . . The case then standing that discretion must chiefly guide all those businesse, since there be sundry sortes of discretion all unlike, even as there be men of action or art, I see no way so fit to enable a man truly to estimate of [*decencie*] as example.[11]

Puttenham's recourse to examples in his discussion of decorum is instructive. Just as prudence or decorum cannot be defined once and for all in the form of "scholastical precepts" (271) but must instead be *instanced* in particular examples, so the author wishing to educate the reader's judgment—to make that judgment more prudent or decorous—must also make use of examples. Puttenham's reflection on the resistance of decorum to theorizing, and the consequent necessity of examples, thus leads us to the center of the humanist pedagogical program: the humanist resistance to scholastic theory (which is at the same time a resistance to the epistemological threat that irony may pose to ethics) takes the form of a practice of examples or of an exemplary practice, on the assumption that such examples will involve the reader in a practice of interpretation which is essential for the active life.

The authorial recourse to examples presupposes a faculty of imitation (whether of nature or of prior texts). As Roger Ascham writes in *The Scholemaster*, "Imitation is a faculty to express lively and perfectly that example which ye go about to follow."[12] But such exemplary texts also require an imitative response on the part of the reader. Accordingly, Ascham imagines a "very profitable book" on imitation,

> containing a certain few fit precepts unto the which should be gathered and applied plenty of examples out of the choiceth authors of both the tongues. This work would stand rather in good diligence for gathering and right judgement for the applying of those examples than any great learning or utterance at all. (127)

Contrary to the commonplace books that are assembled by "common porters, carriers, and bringers of matter and stuff together" (128), and which "do not teach you *how it is done*" (129; my italics),[13] Ascham's examples would illustrate an activity of judgment by the fact of their having been selected and presented in a certain order (130). Yet, as an example of such exemplary practice he refers the reader to Erasmus's *Chiliades, Apothegmata,* and *Similiae,* texts that impress us less by their order than by their disorderliness. What, then, is the force of these examples?

That contemporary readers were struck and disturbed by the disorder of Erasmus's works is apparent in sixteenth-century editions of these texts. Conrad Lycosthenes, for example, in his 1557 edition of the *Parabolae sive similiae* classifies Erasmus's similitudes according to theme in order to make the book easier to use. Erasmus himself, however, was careful to insist on the quite different principle of selection that had gone into this work—the "colligendi explicandique laborem" (94, l. 65; cf. 92, ll. 44–51) that distinguished his text from ordinary commonplace books.[14] His aim was not to present all the similitudes he could gather in a logical or thematic order, but to give the reader a taste ("gustus") of these and thus inspire him to seek them in further reading.[15]

Erasmus's *De copia* also deliberately refuses the systematic order Lycosthenes and his readers demanded. But again, this refusal cannot be explained by authorial laziness or carelessness. Rather, it is inseparable from Erasmus's sense that, as Terence Cave has argued, *copia* is less of a repertoire of technical rules for amplification than it is a generative principle or *practice*. Not surprisingly, then, Erasmus introduces a distinction within the notion of *copia* (*copia* of words vs. *copia* of things) only then to deprive it of any *theoretical* significance:

> Although these [*copia* of words and *copia* of things] can be observed anywhere, so closely combined that you cannot tell them apart at all easily, so much does one serve the other, so that they might seem to be distinct only in theory [*praeceptis*], rather than in fact and in use [*re atque usu*], nevertheless, for the purpose of teaching, we shall make the distinction in such a way that we cannot deservedly be condemned for hair splitting in distinguishing, nor, on the other hand, for negligence.[16]

The rest of the work bears out these remarks, for Book 2 on the *copia rerum* concerns examples of linguistic rather than non- or pre-linguistic amplification. Furthermore, there is no evident order to Erasmus's examples. Finally, Erasmus's aim, as in the *Parabolae*, is not to have the reader memorize his examples but to understand the principle or *ratio* informing them. This is particularly obvious in his discussion of the *ratio colligendi exempla*. Taking the example of Socrates' death, and drawing a variety of morals from it, he shows us how this, and all other examples, can be used *in utramque partem* (*LB*, 1. 102 AC). Erasmus's work, then, deliberately eschews logic, not in order to appear more perfectly aesthetic, but to act more effectively upon the reader, to be more conducive to practice. To read these texts, as Ascham argues, is to *use* them (131). Only through use do they give rise to "right and deep judgement in all kinds of learning" (128).[17]

If Erasmus's pedagogical works are eclectic or chaotic in appearance, other exemplary Renaissance texts seem self-contradictory as well. And this is not only true of an obvious paradoxical encomium such as Erasmus's *Encomium Moriae*. As many critics have remarked, the examples ostensibly adduced to illustrate general theoretical claims in, for example, Sidney's *Apology*, Machiavelli's *Il Principe*, or Montaigne's *Essais*, do not simply "fail" to illustrate general precepts, but in failing, succeed in questioning their subordinate status as mere illustrations of theory.[18] Examples in humanist and humanist-influenced texts are resistant to theory because they call for judgment and use rather than naive or slavish imitation. As Karlheinz Stierle has argued, they are problematizing rather than illustrative or problem solving.[19] Like the pragmatic order of Erasmus's texts, they do not invite us to imitate or avoid single examples of virtue or vice, but to imitate the example of the author's discretion as embodied in the rhetorical practice of the text as a whole. But, as the case of Lycosthenes suggests, these self-contradictory texts also pose special problems for their readers. The example of Castiglione's *Il Cortegiano* can serve to illustrate my point.

If the humanists' pragmatic and problematizing examples are responsible for the self-contradictory appearance of many Renaissance texts, they not surprisingly also give rise to the temptation to theorize this (in)coherence. As an editor faced with a compendium of exempla, Lycosthenes could choose to reorganize his text thematically. The problem is somewhat different for the interpreter of an exemplary narrative. Here at least two options are open: one can either reduce the examples to mere ornament and thus ignore them, or one can attempt to bring some kind of order to the examples by privileging one sort over another. An instance of the former is Kristeller's remark, cited at the beginning of this essay. To read *Il Cortegiano* from Kristeller's perspective would be to "leave aside" the text in its entirety. An instance of the latter is Eduardo Saccone's interpretation of *Il Cortegiano*, and since Saccone actually reads Castiglione's examples, it will be instructive to look more closely at his argument.[20] As we will see, Saccone's reading is important both because he points to a significant problem of interpretation in Castiglione's work—the incompatibility of the examples of the courtier's graceful behavior or *sprezzatura*—and because his own interpretation exemplifies a resistance to that incoherence, a resistance, as de Man's article suggests, which a certain conception of theory shares with the pedagogical imperative. (We will return to the problematic pedagogy of these incompatible examples at the end of this essay.)

As Saccone and others have argued, *sprezzatura* is not a quality but an ability; it cannot be simply defined, it must be enacted. Thus Canossa's reply to Gonzaga's request for a definition—"I am not bound to teach you how to acquire grace or anything else, but only to show you what a perfect courtier ought to be"—is itself an example of the *sprezzatura* for which there can be no pedagogical precept or abstract rule. It is appropriate, then, that readers of *Il Cortegiano* should focus on the examples of *sprezzatura* in their attempt to understand this paradoxical disdainful grace, this art that conceals art.

As dissimulation or artfulness, *sprezzatura*, like irony, is inherently ambiguous and equivocal. This ambiguity necessarily introduces the question of the audience, for to be successful the courtier must conceal his artfulness, but to be appreciated as *sprezzatura*, his concealment must be perceived. *Sprezzatura* then seems to presuppose, Saccone argues, a double audience. Yet when we turn to the examples of this ability, we see that they are not easily reconcilable.

In one case we are presented with an orator who conceals his art lest the people should "fear that they could be duped by it" (43–44). In another case, we are shown a courtier who disguises himself as a person of low birth at a country festival, thereby showing

> a certain *sprezzatura* in what does not matter: all of which adds much charm . . . because the bystanders immediately take in what meets the eye at first glance; whereupon, realizing that here there is much more than was promised by the costume, they are delighted and amused. (103)

The example of the orator presupposes a double audience: the naive auditors who perceive only the artlessness of the orator's performance, and those in the know, who admire the artfulness (48). But in the second example, according to Saccone, there is only a single audience and the ambiguity of a single performance is resolved temporally in the gradual realization that the lowly individual is really a courtier. This second example, Saccone goes on to argue, is allegorical, not ironic, and thus not a true illustration of *sprezzatura*. And yet, in Saccone's own reading of the example of the orator he has already reduced irony to univocality, for the division of the audience actually means that neither experiences *sprezzatura* as irony: rather, one perceives it as art and the other as nature. In short, having articulated the principle of the resistance to theory par excellence—that is, the principle of irony (whether humanist or de Manian)—Saccone cannot resist the temptation to theorize that resistance. At the same time, however, he allows us to see that the irreconcilability of Castiglione's examples may itself be the best example of the irony of *sprezzatura*, the best example of a practice of decorum for which there can be no theoretical rule.

Theory and Method

Castiglione's *Il Cortegiano* and Erasmus's pedagogical works were received in England as the arts or handbooks that at least the latter were intended to be. But the precise nature of this reception also points to a shift within the humanist pedagogical tradition: specifically to the efflorescence around mid-century of debates concerning the status of method in humanist discourse. These debates signal one of the ways in which the resistance to the humanist resistance to theory begins to make itself felt.[21]

The humanists' interest in pedagogy, in ever more efficient ways or methods of conveying knowledge to their students, led to an examination of a number of classical texts on method (e.g., Socrates' remarks in the *Phaedrus*, Aristotle's *Posterior Analytics*, and Galen's

Ars parva), which the humanists then interpreted in terms of their own rhetorical preoccupation with invention or the finding of arguments.[22] In the beginning of the sixteenth century, then, while the Greek term *methodus* had no precise philosophical meaning, the humanists tended to identify it with the general pursuit and teaching of knowledge, i.e., with the pragmatic arts of communication as both the means and ends of instruction. Method was technical only in the general sense that it involved the knowledge of the appropriate means to achieve a particular end. Furthermore, contrary to the classical notion of *techne*, humanist method gradually came to suggest orderliness, speed and efficiency.[23] Thus Erasmus writes a *Ratio seu methodus compendio ad veram theologiam perveniendi* (1520), which provides the reader with the essential tenets of his Christian humanism, but could hardly be said to have as its aim the reduction of religion to an art in the classical sense.[24]

Also in the sixteenth century, and partly in opposition to this humanist conception of method, another more scientific conception of method grew up.[25] This notion was modeled on Aristotle's demonstrative or apodictic logic rather than on rhetoric and was concerned with, in Hobbes's words, "the knowledge of [logical] consequences."[26]

In one sense, this scientific conception of method departs even more than the humanist conception from the Aristotelian notion of *techne*. But as a *logic* that permits of, but is not identical with, technical application, it also points up the structural homology between the classical notions of *techne* and theory: the fact that in both cases abstract principles take (epistemological) precedence over practice or the application of such principles.[27] Such a conception of method finds its apotheosis in Descartes, who opposes the apodictic certainty guaranteed by "la vraie méthode" to persuasion "par l'exemple et par la coustume"[28] and who argues that the true model of philosophical method is mathematical reasoning.

This conflict between two notions of method is instructive with regard to the humanist pedagogical program. Clearly, some degree of method appealed to the humanists' desire for educational reform, but the precise nature and aims of that reform necessitated an ambivalence about method as well. For when method is equated with logic or with *techne*, practical deliberation is perforce excluded. The attempt to formalize or systematize the judgment of decorum is thus bound to fail, since it will by definition usurp the function of decorous or prudential judgment. That the humanists were aware of this danger is apparent in Ascham's remarks in *The Scholemaster*:

Indeed, books of commonplaces be very necessary to induce a man into an orderly general knowledge, how to refer orderly all that he readeth *ad certa rerum capita* and not wander in study. And to that end did Petrus Lombardus the Master of Sentences and Philip Melancthon in our days write two notable books of commonplaces.

But to dwell in *epitomes* and books of *commonplaces*, and not to bind himself daily by orderly study to read with all diligence principally the best doctors, and so to learn to make true differences betwixt the authority of the one and the counsel of the other, maketh so many seeming and sunburnt ministers as we have.[29]

Yet, when we turn to the English logic and rhetoric handbooks of Ascham's day, many of them seem concerned precisely with conflating authority and counsel: with providing the student who does not "read" in Ascham's sense with a practical manual of style and argument.

As we see when we compare Puttenham's *Arte of English Poesie* with Cox's *Rhetoric*, or Ramus's and Fraunce's logics, one reason for the great number of such handbooks is the growth of the middle class and the consequent demand for the democratization of learning, in the form of easily accessible techniques. In addressing courtiers, then, Puttenham's *Arte* only seems to be untypical of the late sixteenth-century handbooks, and his own remarks suggest why. The true courtier, he writes, does not need precepts because he is already in the know; that's how he knows he's a courtier (282, 295). Precisely this paradox points up the ambivalent function of the courtesy books. On the one hand, Puttenham's humanistic refusal of theory could be interpreted as an aristocratic gesture, a gesture that, by denying the effort we associate with the *acquisition* of skills, also refuses to make learning accessible to the "common people."[30] Thus Frank Whigham has argued that "the first employment of courtesy literature was the repression of . . . [social] mobility" (18). On the other hand, as Whigham goes on to point out, in codifying and thus making available the rules and signs of courtesy, such literature also "aroused [and, I would add, educated the] ambition" (20) of the nonaristocratic. In the end, Puttenham's aim may not have been so far from that of MacIlmaine, the English translator of Ramus's *Logike*, who complains of "the envious, that thinkethe it not decent to wryte any liberall arte in the vulgar tongue" (8)[31] and who argues that the "ready and easy way" of Ramus's single method will make logical skill available to all. In a similar vein, Abraham Fraunce inquires in the preface to *The Lawiers Logike* (1588), "Coblers bee men, why therefore not Logicians? and Carters have reason, why therefore not Logike? *Bonum, quò communius, eo melius.*"[32] Given the widespread popular interest in method and precepts, it is not surprising that Ramus's reform of logic and rhetoric found a receptive audience in England.

Ramus's concern with method is in one sense the culmination of humanist pedagogy, for, as Walter Ong has shown, theory in Ramus's system is identified with the pedagogical content or usefulness of theory. Pedagogy, in other words, is not simply the means of instruction: it is the subject matter as well.[33] But Ramism also marks the death of humanism, for while the Ramist reform of the arts curriculum seems to derive in part from the humanist interest in method, it actually results in the subordination of invention and disposition to logic, and the reduction of rhetoric to elocution— now conceived of, in the best of all possible worlds, as inessential.

Thomas Sloan has suggested that Ramus's insistence on logic as the only legitimate form of address betrays an anxiety about the power of rhetoric to appeal to the passions. But the elimination of *logos* and *pathos* from rhetoric was not the only consequence of Ramus's reform. For the "one and only method" also does away with judgment, that is, with *reading* in Ascham's sense of the word. If there is only one method, there can be no choice, no practical deliberation. If all realms of inquiry are to be methodized, then it is no longer prudence but *techne* that is the standard and measure of all things. Finally, as Walter Ong has argued, in such a world there can be no dialogue or debate, no sense of decorum as the infinity of possible methods.[34]

Not surprisingly, with this technical model of judgment comes a reevaluation of the status of the example. Illustrative examples are now, as they were later for Kant, superfluous; the use of examples as a form of logical argument is allowed, in which case they no longer, as far as Ramus is concerned, have the status of illustrations. Accordingly, Ramus's textbook on geometry provides the student with theorems but no examples; and Ramus's *Logike* reduces examples (including those from poetry) to instances or forms of logic.[35]

When we return to the English rhetorical handbooks, we can see that, like Ramus's *Logike*, these treatises also betray an anxiety about the use of figurative language—a use that requires practical judgment or discretion, and which may involve an appeal to the passions. Peacham's *The Garden of Eloquence*, for example, associates the control of the potential waywardness of figurative language with the maintenance of the social hierarchy. The—from our point of view—fanatical codification of tropes and figures in this work includes in every discussion of a particular figure a "caution" against the abuse of that figure. It is instructive to compare Castiglione's ironic treatment of *sprezzatura* or Pontano's remarks on *urbanitas* with Peacham's sober advice concerning irony:

> It ought to be forescene, that this figure is not to be used without some urgent cause, or to iest without some fit occasion, nor often used, lest he that useth it be either taken for a common mocker, or else for such a one, as men can not tell how to understand him, or when to beleeve him. Neither is it a meete forme of speech for every sort of people to use, especially of the inferior toward the superior, to whom by some reason he oweth dutie, for it is against the rule of modestie and good manners, either to deride his better, or to iest with him in this forme and maner.[36]

Even Puttenham, whose *Arte of English Poesie* places rhetorical figures within the larger context of a general theory of poetry, shares Peacham's nervousness about the social and political consequences of rhetoric. Though he does not provide us with a caution against the misuse of every figure, he does define figurative language in general as an abuse or trespass of literal language. For this reason, he goes on to tell us,

> the grave iudges *Areopagites* . . . [forbade] all manner of figurative speaches to be used before them in their consistorie of Iustice, as meere illusions to the minde, and wresters of upright iudgement [of the Iudge]. (166)

Furthermore, he remarks that linguistic ambiguity has been known to lead to rebellion, a complaint that will later be taken up by Jonson and Hobbes.[37] But since poets are pleaders rather than judges, their abuses do not deceive; instead they "dispose the hearers to mirth and solace" (167).[38] And yet, even Puttenham feels obliged to give some warning against the vices of speech (256–67), "because we seem to promise an art [in writing this treatise] . . . and to th' end [that] we may not be carped at by these methodicall men" (257). It is significant, in this light, that while Puttenham approves of artifice throughout his work (see 150), in the end he distinguishes between "method" as that which aids nature, and "imitation" as an artifice that is contrary to nature.[39] While he does not develop this notion of method, his brief discussion suggests affinities with Ramus's method as the systematization of *natural* reason.

In terms of the preceding argument for the humanist resistance to theory, then, these English handbooks of rhetoric and logic represent a kind of midway point between the early humanists' emphasis on practice—specifically on a variety of rhetorical practices that

from a logical point of view seem inconsistent or contradictory—
and a subsequent disenchantment with humanism, which takes the
form in the seventeenth century of a return to a logic divorced from
rhetoric, and more importantly to a conception of theory as scientific
demonstration based on the model of mathematical reasoning. To
the extent that these handbooks aim to present the reader with a
technique, they point to an ambivalence at the center of the humanist pedagogical project, an ambivalence caused by the resistance of
prudence or practical reason to the classical notions of *theoria* and of
techne. Such handbooks both answer to and undermine the early
humanists' concern with method.

The Resistance to Humanism's Resistance to Theory

It is one of the ironies of the reception of the humanist resistance to
theory that this resistance was itself perceived as too theoretical.
Machiavelli's remarks in chapter 15 of *Il Principe* are probably the
most famous example of this complaint:

> since I intend to write something useful to an understanding reader, it
> seemed better to go after the real truth [*verità effettuale*] of the matter
> than to repeat what people have imagined. A great many men have
> imagined states and princedoms such as nobody ever saw or knew in
> the real world, for there's such a difference between the way we really
> live and the way we ought to live that the man who neglects the real to
> study the ideal will learn how to accomplish his ruin, not his
> salvation.[40]

But if Machiavelli perceives his humanist predecessors as too ide-
alistic and prescriptive, other critics of humanism objected that humanism was not theoretical, by which they meant logical, enough.
Such a view finds its first powerful exponent in Bacon, by whom
even method—whether rhetorically or Ramistically conceived—is
found wanting.

Bacon's critical revision of the humanists' rhetorical conception of
method is apparent in his use of humanist terminology against
itself. He divides his program for the advancement of learning according to the traditional rhetorical categories, but in doing so, he
extends the meanings of these terms far beyond the realm of
rhetoric:

> The *Arts intellectual* are four in number; divided according to the ends
> whereunto they are referred: for man's labour is to *invent* that which is
> sought or propounded; or to *judge* that which is invented; or to *retain*

that which is judged; or to *deliver over* that which is retained. So as the arts must be four: *Art* of *Inquiry* or *Invention: Art* of *Examination* or *Judgment: Art* of *Custody* or *Memory:* and *Art* of *Elocution* or *Tradition*.[41]

Thus, for example, invention retains its rhetorical definition as the finding of arguments, but it acquires the new and more important meaning of the finding of arts (127): "Neither is the method or the nature of the traditional material only to the *use* of knowledge, but likewise to the progression of knowledge" (140; cited in Howell, 370). Elocution, on the other hand, is no longer identified with figurative language, but rather with method as the communication of one's knowledge.

Yet, while Bacon retains the Ramist emphasis on logic as the "sole custodian of method in communication" (Howell, 374), he objects to the *premature* methodizing of Ramus's single way (32). In addition to a magisterial method of communication, which hands down the conclusions of one's research, it is necessary to devise a "probative" method (140), i.e., one that conveys knowledge in the order in which it was discovered and thereby incites to further learning.

Bacon's attempt to formulate a method that is more pedagogically effective than that of Ramus depends on the reintroduction of a division between knowledge and pedagogy which Ramus had done much to close. Similarly, Bacon's refusal of the traditional sixteenth-century distinction between theoretical and practical knowledge appears at first glance to be part of the humanist insistence on the unity of the active and contemplative lives (35).[42] But whereas prudence or praxis is the model of cognition for early humanists, Bacon subordinates action to theoretical speculation and thus reduces practical reason to technology, i.e., to the productive knowledge of *techne*. As Bacon writes in the *Novum Organum* (Aphorisms, 3)

> Human knowledge and human power meet in one; for where the cause is not known the effect cannot be produced. Nature to be commanded must be obeyed; and that which in contemplation is as the cause is in operation as the rule.[43]

That later readers perceived Bacon's return to theory—his resistance to practice in the humanist sense—is apparent in Kant's acknowledgment of Bacon and his followers in the epigraph and in the Second Preface to the *Critique of Pure Reason*:

> They learned that reason has insight only into that which it produces after a plan of its own, and that it must not allow itself to be kept, as it were, in nature's leading strings, but must itself strew the way with principles of judgement based upon fixed laws, constraining nature to give answer to questions of reason's own determining. (B xiii)

Clearly, this monological constraint of nature is incompatible with the early humanists' resistance to theory, their insistence on inter-subjective dialogue or rhetoric *in utramque partem* as the model of human cognition and action.

THEORY AND PEDAGOGY

With the current revival of interest in rhetoric, the questions of method and of the relation of theory to practice, specifically the practice of interpretation, are once again at the center of literary studies. If we now return to *Il Cortegiano*, we can see how the in-terpretive problem posed by *sprezzatura* provides us with an alle-gory of contemporary critical debate. Take *sprezzatura* as a figure for the resistance to theory in de Man's double sense. On the one hand Gonzaga's refusal to give precepts represents the conservative and aristocratic disdain for theory: the refusal, say, of the academic es-tablishment to examine its own critical presuppositions. (*Sprezza-tura*, as Castiglione tells us, is never disinterested.) On the other hand, *sprezzatura* can be a figure for the irony of a de Man, who refuses the pedagogical imperative because of its incompatibility with the resistance—or irony—at the heart of theory itself. The first position might be described as a theory that hides a theory (the orator's New Criticism); the second as a theory that undoes theory (the disguised courtier's deconstruction). While the representatives of these two positions seem to be opposed, their shared identity as courtiers points to a fundamental similarity: a concern with a for-malist analysis that obscures or refuses to name its political and ideological interests. Finally, in both cases, though for different rea-sons, literature is "untainted by history."[44]

But there are other positions in the court of criticism as well. While de Man equates one kind of theory with method, Jonathan Culler opposes them, claiming that theory offers a general account of liter-ature ("its forms, its components, their relations"), whereas method aims to resolve local problems of interpretation.[45] This distinction derives from Culler's desire to shift the focus of literary studies from specific acts of interpretation to the study of the rules and conven-tions governing all interpretation. Not surprisingly, such a view of theory, unlike de Man's, is presented as being compatible with the pedagogical imperative, and thus apparently with method in the humanist sense. Culler, then, is like Ottaviano who, in Book 4 of *Il Cortegiano*, provides *sprezzatura* with a humanistic defense against the charges of self-interested deceit on the one hand, and mere aesthetic formalism on the other, by casting the prince as a governor, and the courtier as a pedagogue. Thus Cesare Gonzaga complains,

Truly, signor Ottaviano, one cannot say that your precepts are not good and useful; nevertheless, I should think that if you were to fashion your prince accordingly, you would rather deserve the name of a good schoolmaster than of a good Courtier. (319)

Teaching theory on the graduate level, Culler argues, will allow the student to engage in interdisciplinary studies and thus provide a very practical defense of the continuing relevance of the trivium within the university curriculum as a whole.

Culler's portrayal of the role of theory in responding to the economic pressures of the job market, and to the declining status of the humanities, reflects both our humanist desire to make the liberal arts useful and relevant, and our posthumanist ambivalence about practice, our turn toward a technical conception of pedagogy. Departments of literature no longer train their students in philology because there is no demand for such learning. Universal education has led to a catholic, generalizing approach to the liberal arts, one that in turn gives rise to the demand for easily accessible techniques of reading and interpretation. One form this Ramist technology of the liberal arts may take is the "ready and easy way" (or version) of theory, even of a theory of undecidability or indeterminacy. In an article on the history of practical criticism, Geoffrey Hartman offers the humanist response to the scientific or technological model of literary theory: "To methodize indeterminacy would be to forget the reason for the concept."[46] The problem, for both Hartman and Culler, and it is the humanist dilemma, is how theory can resist its assimilation to method and still be useful or practical.

Finally, there is a more moderate position to be taken with regard to the separation between theory and practice implied by some of Culler's pronouncements. A number of respondents to a recent article against theory remind us that if theory and method are different, theory and practice can and should be articulated dialectically.[47] Theory has for too long been associated with (even as it reacts against) the Kantian search for the epistemological grounds of interpretation, i.e., with the subordination of practice to a speculative model of the truth.[48] This Kantianism finds its courtier representative in the figure of the neoplatonist Bembo, for whom "knowledge must always precede desire" (336), and whose goal is "contemplation of the universal intellect" (354). The aim of the dialectical critic, however, is to formulate theory as a "metapractice," or "practice about practice," one that is necessarily bound up with desires, interests, intentions to persuade.[49]

This dialectical articulation of theory and practice should be distinguished from de Man's conception of the irreducible moment of practice at the center of theory, or the interference of the rhetorical and cognitive dimensions of the text. For while many "dialectical" critics would applaud de Man's equation of rhetoric with the impossibility of reading a text in terms of phenomenological categories (cognition as vision), they would not identify this impossibility with the undecidability of meaning. In fact, one could argue that such an identification is the consequence of a frustrated desire for contemplation of the "universal intellect." Terry Eagleton suggests as much when he writes, "Meaning may well be ultimately undecidable if we view language contemplatively, as a chain of signifiers on a page; it becomes 'decidable' . . . when we think of language as something that we *do*, as indissociably interwoven with our practical forms of life."[50] Accordingly, the dialectical articulation draws near to the humanist pragmatic resistance to theory, and thus to the humanist conception of the pedagogical imperative. At the same time it points up the tie between this imperative and the recent (re)turn to literary history on the part of many literary theorists. If the goal of humanist pedagogy is to educate the judgment, the faculty of decorum, it necessarily involves the determination of what is appropriate at a given moment and in a given historical context. Accordingly, Federico Gonzaga advises the courtier to "consider well what he does or says, the place where he does it, in whose presence, its timeliness" (98), and earlier Ludovico remarks on the sense of historical difference that will inform every correct imitation of antiquity:

> Cicero in many places reprehends many of his predecessors, and in censuring Sergius Galba declares that his orations have an antique cast to them; . . . so that, if we attempt to imitate the ancients servilely, we shall not be imitating them. And Virgil, who (as you say) imitated Homer, did not imitate him in language. (53–54)[51]

If we now return to de Man's remarks about literary history cited at the beginning of this essay, we may be able to see the humanists' rhetorical sense of history, and their dialogical or dialectical sense of the relation of theory to practice as a *via media* between the reified periodization of conservative literary historians on the one hand, and de Man's skepticism on the other. Like Emilia's gentle reminder to Bembo in *Il Cortegiano*—"Take care, messer Bembo, that with these thoughts your soul, too, does not forget your body" (357)— the revival of interest in humanist rhetorical theory, and in the humanists' rhetorical conception of history, can serve to remind us that *theoria* is not our only "theoretical" option. Roland Barthes was writing as a Renaissance humanist and a contemporary theorist of literature when he claimed that "the theory of the text can coincide only with a practice of writing."[52]

NOTES

The epigraph is taken from *The Book of the Courtier*, trans. Charles Singleton (New York, 1959), 41; Count Ludovico Canossa is speaking to Federico Gonzaga.

1. De Man's article, "The Resistance to Theory," was published in *The Pedagogical Imperative*, ed. Barbara Johnson, *Yale French Studies* 63 (1982): 3–20. I owe the germ of this essay to a conversation with Debra Fried of Cornell University. Thanks are due as well to The Society for the Humanities at Cornell, under whose auspices this essay was written.
2. See Bernard Weinberg, ed., *A History of Literary Criticism in the Italian Renaissance*, 2 vols. (New York, 1961); idem., ed., *Trattati di poetica e retorica del Cinquecento*, 4 vols. (Bari, 1974); Baxter Hathaway, *The Age of Criticism* (Ithaca, 1962).
3. Paul Oskar Kristeller, "The Humanist Movement," in *Renaissance Thought, The Classic, Scholastic and Humanistic Strains* (New York, 1961), 17–18.
4. On the first point, see the *Epistolario di Coluccio Salutati*, ed. Francesco Novati, *Fonti per la storia d'Italia*, 4 vols. (Rome, 1891–1911), 3. 447; 4. 176. On the second, see Salutati, *De nobilitate legum et medecine*, ed. Eugenio Garin (Florence, 1947), 32, 136, and *passim*. See also Valla's criticism of Aristotle in the general preface to his *Dialecticae disputationes* for not engaging in civic affairs (in *Opera omnia*, ed. Eugenio Garin, 2 vols. [Basel, 1540; Turin, 1962], 1.644).
5. I am thinking here of the medieval scholastic definition of truth as *adequatio intellectus et rei*.
6. See Salutati, *Epistolario*, 1.179–80; 3.606–10; 4.142; and Leonardo Bruni, *Ad Petrum Paulum Histrum Dialogus*, in *Prosatori latini del Quattrocento*, ed. Eugenio Garin (Milan-Naples, 1952), 60.
7. See Valla, *Dialecticae disputationes*, Preface 3, *Opera omnia*, 1.731. See also Valla's *In eundem Pogium libellus secundus, Opera omnia*, 1.385. On this appeal to *consuetudo*, see Salvatore I. Camporeale, *Lorenzo Valla: Umanesimo e teologia* (Florence, 1972), especially 149–71; Nancy Struever, "Lorenza Valla: Humanist Rhetoric and the Critique of the Classical Languages of Morality," and Charles Trinkaus, "The Question of Truth in Renaissance Rhetoric and Anthropology," both in *Renaissance Eloquence*, ed. James J. Murphy (Berkeley and Los Angeles, and London, 1983), 191–206, 207–20.
8. The following quotations from the *Nicomachean Ethics* (hereafter abbreviated *NE*) are taken from the translation by Martin Ostwald (New York, 1962).
9. See Cicero, *De oratore*, 2.47.269ff.; and Giovanni Pontano, *De sermone*, ed. S. Lupi and A. Risicato (Lugano, 1954), Book 2, ch. 7, 65: "Those who use

irony moderately, in those things which are public and manifest to all [i.e., without the intention to deceive], are seen to be urbane [*urbanos*] and to win a certain favor or esteem [*gratiam*] among their fellow citizens." See also Book 6, 197 on Socrates.

10. See Cicero, *De officiis*, 1.43.153 and *Orator* 21.71–72.

11. George Puttenham, *The Arte of English Poesie* (Kent, Ohio, 1970), 268–70. *U*'s and *v*'s have been regularized. All further quotations will be from this edition and pagination will be indicated in the text. For similar reflections on the difficulty of providing a rule of imitation, see the passages cited by Thomas M. Greene in his chapter "Sixteenth-Century Quarrels: Classicism and the Scandal of History," in *The Light in Troy: Imitation and Discovery in Renaissance Poetry* (New Haven and London, 1983), especially 171.

12. Ascham, *The Scholemaster* (1570), ed. Lawrence V. Ryan (Ithaca, 1967), 114. Further references will be given in the text.

13. See Sidney's remarks in *An Apology for Poetry*, ed. Geoffrey Shepherd (Manchester, England, 1973), 101: The poet "so far substantially . . . worketh, not only to make a Cyrus which had been a particular excellency as Nature might have done, but to bestow a Cyrus upon the world to make many Cyruses if they will learn aright, why, and how that maker made him."

14. See Erasmus, *Parabolae sive similia*, in *Opera omnia*, ordo 1, tome 5, ed. Jean-Claude Margolin (Amsterdam-Oxford, 1975), 94, l. 65; cf. 92, ll. 44–51. On Lycosthenes, see Margolin's Introduction, 34–75; on the difference between the *Parabolae* and ordinary commonplace books, see 8.

15. See *Parabolae*, 94, ll. 66–70. See also Erasmus's remarks on the purpose of his *Adagia*, in *Opera omnia*, ed. J. Leclerc (Leiden, 1703–6; rpt. Hildesheim, 1962), vol. 2, 711 CD; 712E–713D. Henceforth this edition will be referred to as *LB*.

16. *On Copia of Words and Ideas*, trans. Donald B. King and H. David Rix (Milwaukee, Wis., 1963), ch. 7, 16; *LB*, vol. 1, 6 AB. On the *De copia*, see Terence Cave, *The Cornucopian Text: Problems of Writing in the French Renaissance* (Oxford, 1979), 3–34. On the example of Socrates' death, referred to below, see Marion Trousdale, "A Possible Renaissance View of Form," *ELH* 40 (1973):179–204.

17. See Ben Jonson, *Timber or Discoveries*, in *Ben Jonson*, 11 vols., ed. C. H. Herford, Percy Simpson, and Evelyn Simpson (Oxford, 1925–52), 8.628: "*Now*, that I have informed you in the knowing these things [respecting reading]; let mee leade you by the hand a little farther, in the direction of the use; and make you an able Writer by practice" and ff.

18. See Margaret Ferguson's chapter on Sidney in *Trials of Desire: Renaissance Defenses of Poetry* (New Haven and London, 1982); Eugene Garver, "Machiavelli's *The Prince*: A Neglected Rhetorical Classic," *Philosophy and Rhetoric* 13 (1980):99–120. I am grateful to Nancy Struever for sharing with me her unpublished "Machiavelli and the Critique of the Available Languages of Morality in the Sixteenth Century." On Montaigne, see Karl-

heinz Stierle, "L'Histoire comme exemple, l'exemple comme histoire," *Poétique* 10 (1972):176–98.

19. Stierle, "L'Histoire," especially 186–87, 193.

20. Eduardo Saccone, "*Grazia, Sprezzatura* and *Affettazione* in Castiglione's *Book of the Courtier,*" *Glyph* 5 (1979):34–54.

21. In *Light in Troy,* Thomas Greene charts an analogous development in sixteenth-century debates about imitation, specifically the imitation of Cicero. Greene shows how, in a number of treatises in the second half of the century, the flexible standard of judgment which is required for successful imitation gives way to a concern with method and with inflexible rules. See especially 176 ff.

22. This paragraph relies on the discussions of method by Walter Ong, *Ramus, Method, and the Decay of Dialogue* (Harvard, 1958); and Neal W. Gilbert, *Renaissance Concepts of Method* (New York, 1960). See also Cesare Vasoli, *La Dialettica e la retorica dell'Umanesimo: 'Invenzione' e 'Metodo' nella cultura del XV e XVI secolo* (Milan, 1968); as well as his "La Retorica e la dialettica umanistiche e le origini delle concezione moderne del 'metodo,'" *Il Verri* ser. 4, vol. 35 (1970):250–306. Ong writes that Hermogenes is one source of the humanists' rhetorical conception of method (231). He cautions us against the fluidity of such terms as *methodus, ars,* and *doctrina* in the sixteenth century (156 ff.); see also Gilbert (60).

23. Gilbert, *Concepts of Method,* 66.

24. The *Ratio* was originally published in 1519; the term *methodus* was added to the title in 1520.

25. Gilbert, *Concepts of Method,* xxiv, 13, and passim.

26. Thomas Hobbes, *Leviathan,* ed. C. B. Macpherson (Harmondsworth, England, 1975), pt. 1, ch. 5, 115.

27. See *Nicomachean Ethics,* 1141a 10 ff., where Aristotle discusses the use of the term *sophia* to describe the technical knowledge involved in art or craftsmanship, as well as the knowledge of theoretical wisdom (which includes the intelligence of first principles and the scientific knowledge of *theoria*). See also Ostwald's note 24 in same text. On this similarity between *theoria* and *techne,* see Hannah Arendt, *The Human Condition* (Chicago and London, 1958), 301–4, especially 301–2: "The decisive point of similarity, at least in Greek philosophy, was that contemplation [*theoria*], the beholding of something, was considered to be an inherent element in fabrication [*techne*] as well, inasmuch as the work of the craftsman was guided by the 'idea'. . . ."

28. Descartes, *Discours de la méthode,* ed. Etienne Gilson (Paris, 1930), 19.

29. Ascham, *Scholemaster,* 107. See Francis Bacon, *The Advancement of Learning,* ed. G. W. Kitchen (London, Melbourne, and Toronto, 1973), 135, for a similar warning against the dangers of commonplace books; as well as Erasmus's *De copia,* Book 1, ch. 9, on the necessity of forming a storehouse of *copia* through the reading of primary texts.

30. The phrase is taken from the prefatory letter to *The Logike of The Moste Excellent Philosopher P. Ramus Martyr,* trans. Roland MacIlmaine (1574), ed.

Catherine M. Dunn (Northridge, California, 1969), 9. Further references will be given in the text. There has been much recent discussion of the audience of Puttenham's work, in particular of the way in which his discussion of rhetorical figures codifies modes of social interaction in the Elizabethan period. See Daniel Javitch, *Poetry and Courtliness in Renaissance England* (Princeton, 1978); Louis Adrian Montrose, "Of Gentlemen and Shepherds: The Politics of Elizabethan Pastoral Form," *ELH* 50(1983): 415–59; and Frank Whigham, *Ambition and Privilege: The Social Tropes of Elizabethan Courtesy Theory* (Berkeley and Los Angeles and London, 1984).

31. MacIlmaine continues: "Thou seest (good Reader) what a grounde they have to defend their opinion, and howe they labour only to roote out all good knowledge & vertue, and plante mere ignorance amongest the common people" (9). See also Leonard Cox, *The Arte or Crafte of Rhetoryke* (ca. 1530), ed. Frederic Ives Carpenter (Chicago, 1899), who writes that his work will be useful for students, lawyers, ambassadors, and preachers (41).

32. Abraham Fraunce, *The Lawyer's Logic*, ed. R. C. Alston (Menston, England, 1969), Preface.

33. See Ong, *Ramus*, 156–67, especially 161, on Ramus's identification of *methodus* and *theoria*. See also Lisa Jardine, *Francis Bacon and the Art of Discovery* (Cambridge, England, 1974), 29, for a similar remark about Agricola. See also the definition of dialectic at the beginning of Ramus's *Logike*: "Dialecticke otherwise called Logicke, is an arte which teachethe to dispute well"; and Melancthon (quoted in Ong, 159): "Dialectic is the art or way of teaching correctly, in order, and lucidly" (*Erotema dialectices*, Lib. 1).

34. Thomas O. Sloan, "The Crossing of Rhetoric and Poetry in the Renaissance," in *The Rhetoric of Renaissance Poetry from Wyatt to Milton*, ed. Thomas Sloan and Raymond B. Waddington (Berkeley and Los Angeles, and London, 1974), 212–42. Paradoxically, while Ramus ideally excludes pru-' dential judgment from his single method, he recognizes the need for a kind of prudence in addressing a recalcitrant audience—an audience for whom the light of reason has been obscured. The "prudential method" thus allows for all those rhetorical devices of indirection, whether in figurative language, invention, or disposition, which are antithetical to logic strictly conceived. The significant difference between the Ramist and humanist conceptions of prudence is that what was for the humanists a necessity—the practical faculty of deliberation and choice in contingent affairs—has with Ramus itself become an object of contingency and choice. Prudence is no longer essential but rather, like figurative language, ornamental.

35. See Kant's remarks on the superfluousness of examples in the first Preface to the *Critique of Pure Reason*, A viii–ix. The quotation below is taken from the translation by Norman Kemp Smith (London, 1950). On Ramus's geometry textbook, see Gilbert, *Concepts of Method*, 85. On the

example as a form of logical argument, see Ramus's *Logike*, Book 2, ch. 16, 56–58.

36. Henry Peacham, *The Garden of Eloquence (1593), A Facsimile Reproduction* (Gainesville, Florida, 1954), 36.
37. Puttenham, *English Poesie*, 267. See also Jonson, *Timber or Discoveries*, 593, and Hobbes, *De cive*, in *English Works*, 11 vols. ed. Sir Thomas Molesworth (London, 1839–45), 2.xiii; as well as *Leviathan*, ch. 17, 226.
38. This defensive move is analogous to the one Sidney makes in his *Apology* (123–24), when he claims at one moment that poetry is mere play. See Margaret Ferguson's discussion of this strategic move in *Trials of Desire*, especially 151.
39. This is not to say that Puttenham always uses the term imitation in a pejorative sense; see, for example, *English Poesie*, 20.
40. Niccolò Machiavelli, *The Prince*, trans. Robert M. Adams (New York, 1977), 44.
41. Bacon, *Advancement of Learning*, 122. On Bacon's use of rhetorical terminology, see Jardine, *Francis Bacon*, and Wilbur Samuel Howell, *Logic and Rhetoric in England, 1500–1700* (New York, 1969), 364–76.
42. See Jardine, *Francis Bacon*, 97–98.
43. Francis Bacon, *Works*, ed. J. Spedding, R. L. Ellis, and D. D. Heath, 15 vols. (Cambridge, Mass., 1857–61), vol. 8, 67–68.
44. Terry Eagleton, *Literary Theory: An Introduction* (Minneapolis, 1983), 92; see also 146 on the similarities between New Criticism and deconstruction.
45. Jonathan Culler, "Literary Theory in the Graduate Program," in *The Pursuit of Signs: Semiotics, Literature, Deconstruction* (Ithaca, 1981), 210–26, especially 218.
46. Geoffrey H. Hartman, "A Short History of Practical Criticism," in *Criticism in the Wilderness: The Study of Literature Today* (New Haven and London, 1980), 269. The whole essay is relevant to the dilemma of the humanities discussed by Culler.
47. Steven Knapp and Walter Michaels's "Against Theory" appeared in *Critical Inquiry* 8 (1982):723–42. The responses to it appeared in *Critical Inquiry* 9 (1983):727–800.
48. See in particular the articles by Jonathan Crewe, "Toward Uncritical Practice," 748–59, especially 750 on the necessity of a dialectical conception of the relation of theory to practice; and Adena Rosmarin, "On the Theory of 'Against Theory,' " 775–83, especially 776 ff. on the Kantian epistemological conception of theory.
49. Steven Mailloux, "Truth or Consequences: On Being Against Theory," *Critical Inquiry* 9 (1983), 766. The notion of dialectic here and in the following paragraph is not Hegelian, but dialogical, mutually determining. I am not claiming that all the respondents to Knapp and Michaels agree, but rather that some of the respondents point to a nonexclusive, nonhierarchical conception of the relation of theory to practice.
50. Eagleton, *Literary Theory*, 146–47.

51. Erasmus's remarks in the *Ciceronianus* on the correct imitation of Cicero are representative of this dialectical or dialogical conception of history: "What effrontery would he have then who required us always to speak in a Ciceronian style? Let him first restore to us the Rome which existed at that time; let him restore the senate and the senate house, the conscript fathers, the knights, the people in tribes and centuries. . . . Since then the entire arena of human affairs has been altered, who today can speak well unless he greatly diverges from Cicero? . . . Wherever I turn, I see everything changed." Cited by Greene, *Light in Troy,* 182.

52. Roland Barthes, "From Work to Text," in *Image, Music, Text,* trans. Stephen Heath (New York, 1977), 164.

NOTES ON CONTRIBUTORS

DEREK ATTRIDGE holds a Chair in English Studies at the University of Strathclyde, Glasgow. He is the author of *Well-weighed Syllables: Elizabethan Verse in Classical Metres* (1974) and *The Rhythms of English Poetry* (1982), and is completing a book on questions of literary language as they arise in the works of James Joyce and some earlier writers.

TERENCE CAVE is Fellow and Tutor in French at St. John's College, Oxford. He is the author of *Devotional Poetry in France 1570–1613* (1969) and *The Cornucopian Text: Problems of Writing in the French Renaissance* (1979), and has edited several anthologies and collective volumes, including *Ronsard the Poet* (1973). He is currently writing a book on 'recognition' (Aristotelian *anagnorisis*) in theory and practice.

EUGENIO DONATO was Professor of French and Comparative Literature at the University of California at Irvine at the time of his death in 1983. He was co-editor of the influential collective volume, *The Languages of Criticism and the Sciences of Man* (1970), republished in 1972 as *The Structuralist Controversy*, and was the author of important articles ranging in subject matter from Poliziano to Lévi-Strauss.

JOHN FRECCERO is Rosina Pierotti Professor of Italian at Stanford University. He has written essays on Donne, Svevo, and Antonioni, and numerous studies on Dante. He has recently published *The Poetics of Conversion* (1986), a volume of his writings on the *Divine Comedy*.

RENÉ GIRARD is the Andrew B. Hammond Professor of French Language, Literature, and Civilization at Stanford University. Among his publications are *Mensonge romantique et verité romanesque* (translated as *Deceit, Desire, and the Novel*, 1966); *La Violence et le sacré* (*Violence and the Sacred*, 1977); *Des Choses cachées depuis la fondation du monde* (1978); *"To Double Business Bound": Essays on Literature, Mimesis, and Anthropology* (1978). Girard recently published *La Route antique des hommes pervers: essais sur Job* (1985). Forthcoming from the

Johns Hopkins University Press is *The Scapegoat*, a translation of *Le Bouc émissaire* (1982). He is currently at work on a book on Shakespeare.

STEPHEN GREENBLATT is Professor of English at the University of California at Berkeley. He is the author of *Renaissance Self-fashioning* (1980) and co-chair of the journal *Representations*. He is currently at work on a study of Shakespeare.

THOMAS M. GREENE is Frederick Clifford Ford Professor of English and Comparative Literature at Yale University. His most recent book is *The Light in Troy: Imitation and Discovery in Renaissance Poetry* (1982).

RICHARD HALPERN is Assistant Professor of English at Yale University. He is writing a book on English literature in the transition from feudalism to capitalism.

VICTORIA KAHN is Assistant Professor of English at Princeton University. She has most recently published *Rhetoric and Skepticism in the Renaissance* (1985). She is currently at work on a study which deals with the reception of Italian humanism in England and France.

ULLRICH LANGER is Assistant Professor of French at the University of Wisconsin at Madison. He is the author of *Rhétorique et intersubjectivité: "Les Tragiques" d'Agrippa d'Aubigné* (1983) and of the forthcoming *Invention, Death, and Self-Definition in the Poetry of Pierre de Ronsard* (1986). He is currently at work on a study of the relationship between theological reasoning and narrative strategies in the literature of early sixteenth-century Italy and France.

LOUIS ADRIAN MONTROSE is Professor of English Literature in the Literature Department of the University of California at San Diego. He has published widely on Elizabethan drama and poetry, pastoral forms, and courtly performances. He is currently completing a book on the representation/appropriation of Queen Elizabeth in Elizabethan culture.

MARY NYQUIST is a Fellow of New College at the University of Toronto, where she coordinates and teaches in the Women's Studies Programme; she is cross-appointed to the Literary Studies Programme at Victoria College. She is the author of *Joyning Causes: Discourse, Gender, and Milton*, a forthcoming study.

PATRICIA PARKER is Professor of English and Comparative Literature at the University of Toronto. She is the author of *Inescapable*

Romance: Studies in the Poetics of a Mode (1979), co-editor of *Centre and Labyrinth: Essays in Honour of Northrop Frye* (1983), *Lyric Poetry: Beyond New Criticism* (1985), *Shakespeare and the Question of Theory* (1985), and is currently completing two books, *The Metaphorical Plot* and *Dilation and Delay: A Study on Shakespeare and the Renaissance.*

DAVID QUINT is Associate Professor of Comparative Literature at Princeton University. He is the author of *Origin and Originality in Renaissance Literature* (1983) and translator of *The "Stanze" of Angelo Poliziano* (1979). He is currently at work on a study of epic poetry.

TIMOTHY J. REISS is Professor of French and Comparative Literature and Associated Professor of Philosophy at Emory University. He is the author of *Toward Dramatic Illusion* (1971), *Tragedy and Truth* (1980), *The Discourse of Modernism* (1982), and is currently working on both a discursive theory of the development of modern political philosophy and a comprehensive theory of the history of societies definable as totalities. Within this latter theory, he analyzes various specific cultural discourses: his *The Meaning of Literature* will shortly be in press.

DIANA DE ARMAS WILSON is Adjunct Assistant Professor of English at the University of Denver. She has published essays on Cervantes and is currently working on a book entitled *The Dulcinea Projection.* She was recently guest editor of a special issue, "The Rhetoric of Feminist Writing," of the *Denver Quarterly.*

The Johns Hopkins University Press

LITERARY THEORY/RENAISSANCE TEXTS

This book was composed in Palatino
by the Composing Room of Michigan
from a design by Laury A. Egan. It was printed
on 50-lb. Sebago Eggshell Cream Offset paper
and bound by the Maple Press Company.